The Films of Mike Leigh

The Films of Mike Leigh is the first critical study of one of the
most important and iconoclastic directors of British independent
filmmaking. Although active since 1971, Leigh has come to the
attention of an international audience only in the 1990s through
films such as *Secrets and Lies*, *Career Girls*, and *Topsy Turvy*.
Like Robert Altman, John Cassavetes, and Tom Noonan, Leigh
works with a small group of actors, building his films during
months of private rehearsal. The script is written during this
process. In this volume, Ray Carney examines Leigh's working
method and films in the intellectual and social contexts in which
they were created. He also argues that Leigh cannot be considered
simply within the British realist tradition of Osborne and Loach.
All of Leigh's major works, from *Bleak Moments* and *Abigail's
Party* to *Meantime*, *High Hopes*, *Life Is Sweet*, and *Naked* are
treated, and shown to be among the greatest and most original
works in all of cinema.

Ray Carney is Professor of Film and American Studies and Director of Film Studies at Boston University. He is the author of ten
books, including *The Films of John Cassavetes: Pragmatism,
Modernism, and the Movies*; *The Films of John Cassavetes: The
Adventure of Insecurity*; *American Vision: The Films of Frank
Capra*; *Speaking the Language of Desire: The Films of Carl
Dreyer*; the BFI monograph on *Shadows*; and *Cassavetes on Cas-
savetes: A Life in Art*. General editor of Cambridge Film Classics,
he is regarded as one of the world's experts on independent film.
He has a Web site at: <http://people.bu.edu/rcarney>.

Leonard Quart is Professor of Cinema Studies at the College of
Staten Island and the CUNY Graduate Center. He is an editor of
Cineaste, author of the revised and expanded edition of *American
Film and Society Since 1945*, and coauthor of *How the War Was
Remembered: Hollywood and Vietnam*.

CAMBRIDGE FILM CLASSICS

General Editor: Ray Carney, Boston University

The Cambridge Film Classics series provides a forum for revisionist studies of the classic works of the cinematic canon from the perspective of the "new auteurism," which recognizes that film emerges from a complex interaction of bureaucratic, technological, intellectual, cultural, and personal forces. The series consists of concise, cutting-edge reassessments of the canonical works of film study, written by innovative scholars and critics. Each volume provides a general introduction to the life and work of a particular director, followed by critical essays on several of that director's most important films.

Other Books in the Series:

Mike Leigh working on *High Hopes*

The Films of Mike Leigh

Embracing the World

Ray Carney

Boston University

with contributions by

Leonard Quart

College of Staten Island

CAMBRIDGE
UNIVERSITY PRESS

PUBLISHED BY THE PRESS SYNDICATE OF THE UNIVERSITY OF CAMBRIDGE
The Pitt Building, Trumpington Street, Cambridge, United Kingdom

CAMBRIDGE UNIVERSITY PRESS
The Edinburgh Building, Cambridge CB2 2RU, UK   http: //www.cup.cam.ac.uk
40 West 20th Street, New York, NY 10011-4211, USA   http: //www.cup.org
10 Stamford Road, Oakleigh, Melbourne 3166, Australia
Ruiz de Alarcón 13, 28014 Madrid, Spain

First published 2000

Printed in the United States of America

Typeface Sabon 10/13 pt.   *System* DeskTopPro/UX [BV]

A catalog record for this book is available from the British Library.

Library of Congress Cataloging in Publication Data
Carney, Raymond.
The films of Mike Leigh : embracing the world / Ray Carney.
Leonard Quart.
p.   cm. – (Cambridge film classics)
Filmography: p.
Includes bibliographical references.
ISBN 0-521-48043-4 (hc.). – ISBN 0-521-48518-5 (pbk.)
1. Leigh, Mike, 1943–   – Criticism and interpretation.
I. Carney, Ray.   II. Title.   III. Series.
PN1998.3.L445C37   2000
791.43'0233'092 – dc21   99-30993
CIP

ISBN 0 521 48043 4 hardback
ISBN 0 521 48518 5 paperback

The trouble is on screen everyone is perfect. They're a perfect heavy. They're a perfect good guy. That's boring. I encourage the actors not to be better than they are.

                          – John Cassavetes

Truth is what is. Not what should be. Truth is what is.

                          – Lenny Bruce

Contents

Editorial Note

Leonard Quart contributed the "Biographical and Cultural Introduction" and Chapter 13, "Desperate Lives: *Naked.*" Ray Carney wrote the rest of the text, chose the photographs, and wrote the captions.

Acknowledgments

Grateful acknowledgment is made to Mike Leigh for providing viewing copies of several unreleased or otherwise unavailable films and plays, including his *Five-Minute Films*, *The Short and Curlies*, *A Sense of History*, and *The Permissive Society*.

Simon Channing-Williams of Thin Man Films helped in locating some of the illustrative material and gave permission for its use. Gratitude is expressed to The Ronald Grant Archive and the Kobal Collection for photographic material. Irv Stimler at Water Bearer Films in New York, who has released Leigh's important early work on video, kindly provided additional photographic material. Mary Corliss and Terry Gheskin of the Museum of Modern Art Film Stills Archive, as usual, provided information helpful in tracking down otherwise elusive material.

Closer to home, I would like to thank Jon Westling, President of Boston University, for personally taking an interest in and encouraging my work. It is unprecedented in my experience for a major American university to be led by someone of such intellectual depth and seriousness.

Boston University is a teaching institution in which a faculty member's highest responsibility, correctly in my judgment, is to his classes and students. At a crucial juncture, Provost Dennis Berkey and Dean Brent Baker helped me to arrange my teaching and advising obligations in a way that made completion of this and other projects possible.

I owe a debt of intellectual gratitude to my graduate and undergraduate students, to whom many of these ideas were presented in earlier forms. I would single out Eumni Lee for special mention. My distinguished colleague George Bluestone read an early draft of this manuscript and made many helpful suggestions. Preliminary versions of some of the chapters were presented in panel discussions, lectures, and other events sponsored by the Olympia Film Festival (where I conducted a Master class on Leigh's short films), the University of Virginia Film Festival, the Sydney Film Festival, the Australian Film Institute, the Harvard Film Archive, and the Columbia Seminars at the Museum of Modern Art. I thank them all.

Debbie Northall, Ken Holmes, and Nancy Maguire in the College of Communication at Boston University provided invaluable assistance with various logistical and research arrangements. John Gianvito translated several French interviews for me. My student, Michael Price, helped with proofing the text.

My personal assistant, close friend, and roller-blading buddy, Diane Cherkerzian, helped me in too many ways to list. I couldn't have written this book without her. I dedicate it to her with love and appreciation.

Ray Carney
Boston, Massachusetts

Biographical and Cultural Introduction

Mike Leigh was born in 1943, the son of a Jewish doctor whose father had come to London from Russia. All of Leigh's grandparents were Yiddish-speaking immigrants (he even had a great-grandfather who was editor of a Zionist newspaper before World War I), and Leigh is both proud and critical of his Jewish background.[1] However, it has only been in recent years that he has begun to talk openly about his ethnic past and been a member of a socialist Zionist youth group, Habonim.[2] However, after visiting Israel under Habonim's auspices in the summer of 1960, he became disillusioned with Israel's policies toward the Arabs and dropped out of the movement. It wasn't until 1991 that he was willing to go back to Israel, accepting an invitation to attend the Jerusalem Film Festival, which was showing *Life Is Sweet*.[3]

Leigh's family kept a kosher home and were active Zionists, but neither has he been traditionally religious nor, as an adult, shown any interest in or formal identification with Jewish communal and cultural organizations. Despite these feelings, his Jewish roots are an undeniable part of who Leigh is, though they are a private rather than public aspect of his life. Those roots are also a factor that, he admits, have contributed to his being an outsider and rebel. Jewishness, however, has never been the subject of his art (excepting the unpleasant, middle-class Jewish characters in *Hard Labour*, who live in a house only two doors from where he grew up), though he has talked vaguely of making a film about the world of his parents and grandparents. Still, the shouting and general tumult of a certain type of Jewish family life has affected how he depicts family interaction in his work. Further, Leigh holds that there cannot be anything more Jewish than the tendency of his films both to posit

I

questions rather than provide answers and to take pleasure in both lamenting and laughing at the human predicament.

Leigh grew up middle-class in a grimy, industrial working-class area of Salford, Lancashire, a city near Manchester that he sees as looking just like a Lowery painting.[4] He went to predominantly working-class primary and grammar schools, and by choice has lived in working-class areas most of his life. Even in those early years, Leigh felt ambivalent about his own class background – he was the doctor's son in a working-class neighborhood – and conscious of the effects class has on people's lives. He was, in his words, "an insider and outsider, all at once"[5] who was culturally bilingual, a boy living in a middle-class family whose deepest sympathies rested with working-class people. But those sympathies never meant that Leigh affected a working-class persona (as a number of middle-class young people do in present-day England). He never aimed, as an adolescent, to become or pretend to be a worker; it was the artistic and bohemian life that attracted him then and he still identifies with now.

Leigh was not much of a student and left grammar school at seventeen with only three O-levels (passing O-level exams is an ordinary academic achievement, whereas passing A-levels is a mark of academic excellence and necessary for entry into the best universities), though he did act in school plays. He then entered the Royal Academy of the Dramatic Arts (RADA) on scholarship. It was a school that prepared "its students to become actors who would get on with the job, working competently with discipline and with the minimum of fuss."[6] Though at this point in his life Leigh had not yet defined his notion of theater, he found most of RADA's much respected course of study sterile and unsatisfying, and he peripatetically went on to study at the London Film School, the Central School of Art and Design, and the Camberwell College of Art. It was Camberwell that provided Leigh with what he considers his one profound experience as a student: "I was in a life drawing class at Camberwell one day when I suddenly had this clairvoyant flash. I realized that what I was experiencing as an art student was that working from source and looking at something that actually existed and excited you was the key to making a piece of art."[7] What that gave Leigh as a filmmaker, playwright, storyteller, and an artist generally was a sense of freedom. "Everything is up for grabs if you see it three-dimensionally, and from all possible perspectives, and are motivated by some kind of feeling about it."[8]

The experience at Camberwell provided Leigh with a powerful epiphany about the direction his art should take, but his singular, idiosyncratic approach also was nourished by the cultural and social currents of the early to mid-1960s. There was no one influence that Leigh looked to as his artistic or intellectual model, but the era was one in which the rebellion of the young against the materialism and political exhaustion of an older generation had become a commonplace. During this period in England, jazz clubs, "happenings," and beat poetry flourished, the theater saw Beckett's and Pinter's plays produced, the massive CND marches took place, the Beatles emerged, and of course the British New Wave cinema of directors such as Lindsay Anderson, Tony Richardson, and Karel Reisz appeared (they made Leigh aware that the everyday world he knew could be put on film). Nevertheless, as a passionate filmgoer, Leigh was less influenced by the relative directness of the English realists than by watching the more complex, lyrical, and textured films of the French Nouvelle Vague and the work of directors like Jean Renoir, Satyajit Ray, Ermanno Olmi, and especially Yasujiro Ozu.

Leigh's first creative efforts, however, were not in film but in the experimental theater of the late sixties. There were stints at the Royal Shakespeare Company in Stratford under Peter Hall, the East-15 Acting School, the Royal Court Upstairs, and the Manchester Youth Theatre. From his very first play, *The Box Play* in 1965, however, he was primarily motivated to work in the theater as a means of acquiring sufficient skills to make films. For Leigh, "theatre is secondary,"[9] and despite the fact that he wrote twenty-two plays, his prime passions were always involved in looking at and shooting films. There is no question, however, that working in the theater gave him a true understanding of what actors go through in the creation of character. In addition, throughout his film career he has remained a theatrical presence, devising plays that the Royal Court and the Hampstead Theatre Club produced (*Abigail's Party, Ecstasy*).

Leigh's film career began with his first theatrical release, *Bleak Moments*, in 1971, and took off when he began to make films for the BBC in 1973. By 1988 he had directed eight low-budget features and a number of short films for television. So before Leigh achieved widespread critical recognition for full-fledged theatrical releases such as *Life Is Sweet, Naked*, and *Secrets and Lies*, he spent years making original, sometimes brilliant, films for television. Because these films were small in scale and most often dealt with daily life and relationships, they did not garner the same critical considerations as his theatrical releases. Leigh, though aware of how budgetary limitations constricted what he could do stylistically with these films, never saw them as any less important than his theatrical releases.[10]

The whole category of television film is problematic, as much of Britain's film output is either made directly for television or subsidized by Channel Four and the BBC for theatrical release and then television presentation. As a result, some of Britain's best directors, Stephen Frears, Ken Loach, Peter Greenaway, Alan Parker, Richard Eyre, and Alan Clarke among them, have made a significant portion of their films for television. These works were strikingly different from the formulaic made-for-television films in the United States. A number were personal works dealing with British themes. Almost none of the films adhered to the American disease-of-the-week genre (breast cancer, AIDS) or that other staple, tabloid cinematic re-creations of true stories of child and wife abuse, drug addiction, homelessness, and murder.

Many of the films get right to the heart of English class power, envy, resentment, and entrapment. Leigh is clearly political, a man of the left and a Thatcher hater who views the "reactionary" Tory governments as helping to destroy the fabric of English society. His films of the eighties, in particular, were shaped by the same political and social environment that spawned other contemporaneous British films critical of Thatcherism: Richard Eyre's skewering of the triumph of the ersatz and the inauthentic in public and private life in *The Ploughman's Lunch*; Chris Bernard's romantic fable about the Liverpudlian working class's attempt to escape their entrapment in *Letter to Brezhnev*; and Frears and Kureishi's condemnation of greed and affirmation of the spontaneous and the anarchic in *Sammy and Rosie Get Laid*.

The period between *Home Sweet Home* and *High Hopes* saw Thatcher securely established, and the British political left and center too fragmented and impotent to challenge her. Even if a schism had not occurred between the Labor Party's social democratic, center, and hard-left wings, Thatcher had already successfully poached on the loyalty of the party's prime constituencies: the skilled working class and manual laborers. She garnered their support by leading the nation to a flag-waving, putative victory against Argentina in the Falklands war, and by promoting the expansion of share ownership and the sale of council flats to tenants (turning one million families into homeowners). In novelist Julian Barnes' sardonic analysis:

> Mrs. Thatcher's achievements were, in political terms, remarkable. . . .
> You could survive while allowing unemployment to rise to levels pre-

viously thought politically untenable. You could politicize hitherto unpolitical public bodies and force the principles of the market into areas of society presumed sacrosanct. You could sharply diminish union power and increase employer power. You could weaken the independence of local government by limiting its ability to raise money. . . . You could make the rich richer and the poor poorer until you had restored the gap that existed at the end of the last century. You could do all this and in the process traumatize the Opposition.[11]

The result was a Thatcher ethos shaped out of her sense of political certitude and moral rectitude, and characterized, in the main, by a hunger for status, gross materialism, unembarrassed consumption, and contempt for the poor. The pursuit of self-interest became the dominant force in British culture.

Britain, dominated by Thatcher and New Right thought, which emphasized increased income and consumer choice over governmental social protection and regulation, had become a country where acquisitive individualism and aggressive self-interest thrived. The South of England and London had become richer and more yuppified, while the industrial North's steel towns and mining villages had begun to wither away. Despite the high tech and financial industries flourishing in the South, and the proliferating boutiques, bistros, building cranes, and glass office buildings, the number of homeless rose nationwide to a million and 20 percent of the people lived under the poverty line. Also, burglary, car thievery, and vandalism greatly increased, and Britain held the dubious distinction of having the highest per capita prison population in the European community.

Thatcher reversed a forty-year line of economic development where incomes had gradually grown more equal in Britain. By 1988 she had succeeded in turning around the whole process. The best-off tenth of the population now enjoyed nearly nine times more income than the worst-off tenth. In London, well-heeled computer executives, stockbrokers, and tourists hurried past adolescent runaways begging dolefully outside Central London tube stations and warily perched on the steps leading down from the National Theater.

Film turned into a political weapon against the Thatcherite tide. Of course, it is not as if the political and social criticism in Leigh's and Frears-Kureishi's work made a significant dent in the Thatcher ethos. Their films, however, did offer an alternative to the image of a prosperous, entrepreneurial, and triumphant Britain that Thatcher's favorite ad agency, Saatchi and Saatchi, and much of the daily press promoted.

Heritage films like *Chariots of Fire*, *A Passage to India*, and *A Room with a View* also advanced, in a more complicated and ambivalent manner, the portrait of a sanguine, victorious Britain. The heritage films, despite criticizing some aspects of the culture and society of the past, and implicitly contemporary life, still turned their gaze away from the turbulent present. They did this by invoking in a pictorial, decorative style enveloped in nostalgia, a more serene, pastoral Britain. The Britain depicted in these films offered a portrait of a relatively balanced, hieratic world that, despite its inequities and imperfections, soothed rather than disturbed educated, middle-class audiences.[12]

In contrast, a number of the films dealing with 1980s Britain portrayed it as an urban society – heterogeneous, socially divided and fractured, and permeated with large pockets of unemployment and poverty. These films, however, made no claim to provide answers to Thatcherism, eschewing promoting or even intellectually exploring an alternative political perspective. Thatcher's Britain had produced an ever-changing social landscape where the power of social institutions that had once carried moral and political weight, like unions, left-wing political groups, and even the class system, had eroded. In the words of director Michael Radford (*Nineteen Eighty-Four*), eighties Britain had become too complex a phenomenon for any single ideology to explain, and "all things we were taught to believe had crumbled away."[13]

The one political certitude that many of the directors, including Radford, and the films shared (without ever turning to poster art or agitprop) was that an arrogant, vindictive Margaret Thatcher was the one unambiguous political villain in Britain. It was as if directors of American politically oriented works like *Country* and *Do the Right Thing* had begun to punctuate their films with barbed and contemptuous remarks aimed explicitly at Ronald Reagan and had turned him into the prime source of all that had gone socially and politically wrong during the 1980s. If most of the British directors of the Thatcher years (excepting Ken Loach, whose explicitly socialist appeals to an increasingly beleaguered working class remained unchanged) did not have an antidote to Thatcherism, they at least shared a belief that Margaret Thatcher was at the heart of what they felt was going wrong in Britain.

Leigh's work was shaped by this political perspective; yet despite his antipathy his films carry no political agendas, nor do they offer political alternatives or solutions in the Ken Loach mode. Leigh does not share Loach's Marxist vision that the world is divided roughly between those who hold power and those who are its victims, and that the possibility for radical social change still lies with the working class. Undiscerning critics often lump Leigh and Loach together, because they are independent, noncommercial directors who spent much of their careers working on television and share a penchant for making realistic films about working-class characters. Their ways of dealing with politics and their formal strategies, however, differ radically. According to Leigh, Loach would regard him politically "as, at best, a lily-livered liberal."[14] Leigh's films rarely provide answers – his world is too ambiguous, too bound by contradiction, to be given a schematic reading – while Loach permeates his work with a class-conscious, radical social agenda.

In most of his films Leigh successfully captures the emotional drives and inwardness as well as the speech patterns and tastes of his characters, usually satirizing them a bit while simultaneously respecting their feelings and selfhood. It is a delicate line that Leigh draws and more often than not balances with great agility. But not always. Sometimes the films get so bogged down in caricature and over-the-top behavior[15] (Leigh was a skilled enough cartoonist to make a living at it) that he reduces his characters to their class stereotypes. Their class and culture become the prime definitions of their identity, and they begin to lose their individuality and layering as characters. They become outsized figures, sometimes interesting but operating like characters who belong in some other, less nuanced, comic-routine based film. It's something Leigh tries hard to avoid – being antipathetic to constructing character in a facile and reductive manner, and always trying hard to achieve an ensemble effect – though he succumbs to it at points.

The depictions of Rupert and Laetitia Booth-Braines and Aubrey in *High Hopes* and *Life Is Sweet*, respectively, illustrate the problem. Leigh's parody of the Booth-Braineses is a bit broad. It is plausible that couples like Laetitia and Rupert engage in coy baby talk before sex, use cucumber slices as eye patches to shut out the light before going to bed, and generally sound, in their empty chatter, like extras from *Brideshead Revisited*. Still, their almost unrelieved offensiveness seems excessive even for the smug upholders of the success-obsessed Thatcherite culture: narcissistic Laetitia thanking God that she's been blessed with such beautiful skin; stuffy Rupert harshly telling Cyril and Shirley to take Mrs. Bender away, as if she were a dog. Leigh etches his targets sharply, but a touch less anger toward them on his part would have given these characters more emotional resonance, and the social satire would have greater effect and depth.

In some of Aubrey's scenes in *Life Is Sweet*, Leigh's penchant for cartooning goes over the top. The restaurant scenes are too excessive to connect in tone with the central family sequences, and Aubrey's character doesn't quite achieve the mixture of poignancy and drollery that was Leigh's aim. When the restaurant's opening night proves to be a predictable fiasco, Aubrey's drunken, rolling-around-the-floor rage, self-loathing, and lust for a concerned Wendy (who is doing him a favor by working as a waitress for the night), make him tediously ridiculous rather than granting him genuine pathos.

When Leigh's characters are convincing, it is because he knows just when to prevent their idiosyncrasies and tics from becoming as excessive as Aubrey's are in his big scene. At such times, in his construction of character and narrative Leigh eschews the formulaic and conventional for the ambiguous and open-ended.

Starting with *Bleak Moments*, Leigh's films have been in the general tradition of English realism, which has been one of the dominant strains in British cinema. Realism's beginnings in British film can be found in the social documentary cinema of the thirties, whose founder, publicist, distributor, and leading figure was John Grierson (the only movie he directed was the Eisenstein-influenced *Drifters*), and in the work of the more formally adventurous and poetic Humphrey Jennings (*Fires Were Started*), who found in Britain's feelings of national unity and community during World War II the perfect moment to convey his sense of the grandeur and tragedy of men at war.

The social documentary movement sought to create a public sphere of responsible and engaged film that would be distinct from a class-bound, escapist commercial cinema. The films produced under the Grierson rubric (*Night Mail, Housing Problems, Coal-Face*) were committed to telling stories that would explain and improve reality for the mass of people, the moral taking primacy over the aesthetic. Still, a film like *Night Mail*, which depicted workers processing mail on the postal express train as it moved overnight from London to Glasgow, carried a strong aesthetic consciousness. *Night Mail* evoked the rhythm and beat of the train, and a strikingly composed look of the landscape it traversed, by integrating image, Benjamin Britten's musical score, and a verse narration by W. H. Auden to capture the poetry of men at work. Grierson's prime concern, however, was to create a socially useful cinema – not an aesthetic one – that depicted the workings of the society at large rather than the lives and feelings of individuals. The Grierson documentaries contained no specific political line or social critique, just a generalized commitment to a rational society, a democratic culture, and the dignity of work.

The heirs to the Grierson tradition in English cinema were the liberal humanist Free Cinema films of the 1950s (Lindsay Anderson's *Every Day except Christmas*), and the New Wave features (ranging from Jack Clayton's conventionally directed *Room at the Top*, which appeared in 1959, to Anderson's passionate and emotionally primal *This Sporting Life* in 1963). The key figures in the Free Cinema movement, Anderson, Karel Reisz, and Tony Richardson, moved from documentaries that were personal expressions which aimed to evoke the poetry of the everyday world to narratives that attempted to focus without condescension on working-class characters, locales, and concerns (though all the directors were upper-middle-class and Oxbridge-educated, making films about lives they saw from the outside that had little or nothing to do with their own). They used a new group of non–West End actors with strong regional accents (e.g., Albert Finney, Tom Courtenay) who were able to convey working-class authenticity through vernacular speech and raw, volatile behavior in a manner that less full-blooded British movie stars of the time, like Dirk Bogarde or John Mills, were incapable of projecting.

The films were not in the Grierson mode but, like Karel Reisz's *Saturday Night and Sunday Morning*, committed themselves more to psychological than documentary realism. They explored the desires and hopes of their working-class protagonists and their heroes' ambivalent relationship to working-class culture rather than getting to the heart of the structure and texture of the communities in which they lived and worked. The New Wave films tended to use their locations – the streets, canals, factories, row houses of provincial industrial cities – to sometimes striking, sometimes clichéd pictorial effect. In a number of the films, many of the locations did not serve as an integral part of the narrative or organically relate to the characters. For example, the shots of back-to-back houses and industrial sites rarely worked as a window into the structure and ethos of working-class life. Still, the New Wave films captured the way working-class homes, streets, pubs, dance halls, beach resorts, and factories looked – the appearance if not the essence of working-class life. They also projected a social vision – more a moral and cultural critique than an overtly political one. The films centered on protagonists who, in varied ways, affirmed the autonomy and integrity of the individual. These were men and women who felt their soul and spirit threatened by a set of social and cultural forces. Their credo was best summed up in *Saturday Night*'s Arthur Seaton's terse line, "Don't let the bastards grind you down." There was no alternative political or social vision inherent in Seaton's response, just one man asserting his own sense of individuality amid all the conformist pressures he felt were destroying it.

Leigh's films look very different from the films of the British New Wave. No single film of his, except for *Naked*, is dominated by a single figure – a heroic/antiheroic protagonist. (Even in *Naked*, despite Johnny's charismatic presence, all the other characters are much more than mere plot devices.) He builds all the films on an ensemble of actors, with five or six characters often playing central roles. His characters are so individuated and true that, like people in the real world, their emotions aren't predictable or fixed. If the trajectory of the lives depicted will never change, he doesn't neatly prescribe or homogenize his characters' behavior. In each film some fresh and unique detail, bit of business, personal quirk, emotion, or idiosyncrasy is conjured up. Leigh captures the variety of human behavior, connecting equally to both the emotionally lost and destructive and the relatively balanced and life-affirming of his characters.

The emphasis in Leigh's films is rarely on the landscape or cityscape bounding his characters' lives. He has no interest in providing a documentary realist vision of the way the world looks in his films. It's not his wont to emulate the New Wave pattern of shooting scenes depicting characters walking along canals, visiting fairs and beach resorts, and interacting in pubs. When Leigh uses the public world, he doesn't make it aesthetically or sociologically vivid enough to provide release or escape for his characters or the film audience. He almost never has his characters interact with the public settings that surround them. It's the people who are central, not the buildings, streets, and neighborhoods they inhabit or pass through or the cafés and pubs they eat and drink in.

Leigh mainly stays with interiors, the behavior of his characters, and the small-scale incidents that are his films' dramatic spine. There is no Chayevsky-style emotional underlining or editorializing. In Leigh's work his characters can be pathetic but never bathetic. He is usually too satiric, clear-eyed, and tough-minded an observer to allow a sense of pity or mawkishness to creep into his films.

The New Wave films' depiction of urban and working class life depicted worlds closer to Mike Leigh's own experience than David Lean or Carol Reed ever cared to treat. His notion of realistic cinema, however, differed radically from Richardson and Anderson's. For Leigh their films seemed artificial and contrived, they just weren't the kind of vital, improvisatory cinema to which he was committed.[16]

Leigh's films owe more to the work of independent American directors like John Cassavetes and Robert Altman and, curiously enough, to the Ealing comedies of the 1950s that he grew up watching than to the New Wave.[17] He took pleasure in films like *Man in the White Suit* and *Kind Hearts and Coronets* because they were funny, character-driven, and provided the action with a social context.[18] Cassavetes' *Shadows* inspired Leigh when he first saw it.[19] The film shared with his own work a minimal narrative, low-budget, ensemble cast, and a behaviorally oriented, improvisatory quality. However, Leigh never saw Cassavetes as an influence, for he found some of his work "tedious – limited to the actors, really – spewing it out – which is the antithesis of what I've been concerned with – getting the essence of the real world."[20] With Altman, Leigh shares a gift for seamlessly mixing the poignant, the farcical, and the satiric (though with greater psychological depth), and linking it to a critique of the workings of society and culture. Altman, being a director critically rooted in American culture, a society that barely recognizes the existence of class, has demonstrated little or no interest in dealing with the nature of class culture and power. Altman's work also differs from Leigh's in being both self-reflexive and reactive to Hollywood genres, and indulges in the type of virtuosic camera movement and editing that Leigh has never shown much interest in.

Leigh's directorial method demands from him a capacity to work arduously and obsessively – day and night, six days a week – once the process has begun. He begins with a group of actors (not stars) who themselves must exhibit a single-minded, rigorous devotion to the work. (Some actors are unable to adjust and fall by the wayside during the process.) They arrive with lists of people they know, and Leigh then has them discuss these people with him. Leigh picks the character he is interested in, bearing in mind the other characters he is assembling and the general area the film is going to explore (e.g., the catering business in *Life Is Sweet*). He then sends the actor off to do research and build up the personality by creating an entire history (a backstory) and giving him or her emotional depth and a psychological and social structure. It is crucial that the actors maintain some critical distance and not become overidentified with the characters they are playing. Leigh wants his actors to demonstrate objectivity and refer to the character in the third person.[21] He also makes it clear to the actors that these are not acting exercises where actors must be inventive, but an exploration to capture both the surface and the heart of the person they are playing. They build some of the character on personal observation, the rest on invention and improvisation. Leigh works closely with each actor alone, developing a past as well as behavior, values, and psychological makeup in the present.[22] Leigh says when his working relationship with the actor succeeds, "it is a kind of love affair,"[23] where mutual rapport and understanding take place.

Once he sets the characters, Leigh introduces his actors to each other and has their characters interact and improvise together in situations that he has devised. The actor, however, only knows what the character knows about the people he acts with. Leigh demands secrecy from the actors, so none of them knows more about the other characters than what they would share on the general level of experience. The actor discusses the character's behavior and inner self with Leigh alone and nobody else. Meanwhile, Leigh is building dramatic conflict between the characters and constructing a plot, forcefully moving it all toward a final rehearsal period when he gives the improvisations final shape. It is then that he expands, contracts, and refines the characters and dialogue. (Scenes are never created during the earlier improvisations, just the premises for them.) That's where the three-to-five months of improvisation and often fourteen-hour days are distilled into final language. Leigh manipulates and works closely and empathetically with the actors to get the right word and gesture before he begins shooting, attention to detail being everything. Short scenes are often the result of hours of improvisation and refinement. Leigh pulls together not only the dialogue but the selection and structure of scenes and the camera placement, reflecting during rehearsals about the distance he wants to shoot a scene from.

When the film goes before the camera the improvisations are over. There is a final script, and Leigh adheres to it. There is nothing anarchic or free-form about his directorial methods. He allows no one to just take off and emote. He is in total control of the set, collaborating on a shot's setup with his cinematographer, gauging the amount of light that is necessary, attentive even to the color of a folder a character is carrying, and with great precision taking care that the music and sound are just right.

What makes Leigh unique is his ability to construct a humorously bleak and desperate world[24] filled with characters whose comic behavior springs from their essence as human beings. The comedy connects to their genuine agony and joy, and there are no scenes geared to just getting easy laughs. In a recent film, *Career Girls*, Hannah (Katrin Cart-lidge), one of Leigh's female protagonists, is over the top and comically manic as a college student. Nonetheless, one always senses the insecurity and profound pathos that lie just beneath Hannah's aggression. That is Leigh's trademark – an almost preternatural gift for capturing, with emotional honesty, complex behavior.

I

Stylistic Introduction:
Living beyond Consciousness

On the whole, life for most people is – get born and survive as best you can for as long as you can, till it's all up. The norm for most people in the world is that life is hard work; it's tough. It's not about being winners or losers. It's about coping. The minute anything extraordinary or exotic happens [in a film], I get bored. Most movies are about extraordinary or charmed lifestyles. For me what's exciting is finding heightened drama, the extraordinary in the ordinary – what happens to ordinary people . . . the entirely disorganized and irrational business of living.

– Mike Leigh

The best way to define the distinctive qualities of Leigh's work (and the implicit challenge it presents for viewers) is to notice its difference from mainstream American film. Hollywood movies are basically devoted to achievement. Characters are defined in terms of their ability to do things (anything from freeing the hostages to getting the girl) – frequently by being pitted against each other in tests of wit or prowess. Hollywood understands life as essentially a matter of competition, achievement, and reward.

A narrative organized around a series of problems for characters to solve or goals to achieve appeals to American viewers for at least two reasons. First, it makes the story easy to follow. Characters' progress (or failure to progress) can be measured in an almost step-by-step way. Second, it ties in with one of the basic myths of American culture: the faith in the virtues of doing. For someone who subscribes to the ideology of capitalism, this narrative form is fundamentally encouraging. It's a "can-do" vision. Willpower, diligence, pluck, and resourcefulness can solve any problem.

Mike Leigh's films are organized along different lines. In the first place, he rejects struggle and competition as sources of value. He is more interested in his characters' ability to interact sensitively than in pitting them against each other. When *Abigail's Party* and *Who's Who* depict characters competing for attention or jockeying for power, they are clearly offering nightmare visions of life.

The problems Leigh dramatizes are not the kind that have solutions – particularly practical ones. *Bleak Moments* explores the situation of flawed characters interacting in imperfect ways but never in the least suggests that there is a way out of their situation. *Hard Labour* presents another group of figures who are trapped in various ways but doesn't suggest that there is anything in particular they can do to break free. Leigh's work suggests that there are situations that can never be escaped from, and aspects of our personalities that can never be repaired.

Leigh's movies are not about performing a task or achieving a goal. The drama is generated out of states of being more than acts of doing. The interest of *Nuts in May* is not anything Keith does at one moment, but what he is throughout. In *Life Is Sweet*, what Aubrey and Nicola do in a given scene is far less important than what they are in every scene.

Since what you are is not something that can be altered by an action, the films are not really about events. Rather than competing in the realm of action, Leigh's figures are placed in situations in which their ways of feeling and thinking are compared. It's not how your words and deeds conflict with mine, but how your way of knowing differs from (or overlaps with) mine. You see, feel, and understand life in one way; I see, feel, and understand it in another.

The most obvious illustration of how this comparison and contrast of points of view creates drama is the films in which characters with more or less opposite points of view are thrown together. Many of Leigh's films pair figures who are, in effect, each other's antitypes. In *Meantime*, a middle-class do-gooder is paired with a lower-class layabout who resists being "helped." In *Grown-Ups*, a lost-in-space teacher is forced to deal with his most uncontrollable former students when they move in next door as adults. In *Nuts in May*, a yuppie camper who has reduced all of life to a routine is plunked down next to lower-class campers whose rowdiness resists his systems of organization and understanding.

More often, the contrasts are not so blatant. Many of Leigh's groupings involve characters whose perspectives and attitudes differ quite subtly. The drama of *The Kiss of Death*, for example, is generated by differences in the sexual attitudes of figures whose points of view are similar in some respects and different in others: the sexual cluelessness of two boys is compared with the sexual knowingness of two girls; the chaste, marriage-mindedness of one of the girls is compared with the moral "looseness" of the other girl; the romantic earnestness of one of the boys is compared with the erotic sniggering of the other. Even minor characters briefly factor into the comparison and contrast process: in the same film, for example, the "dirty-minded" attitudes toward sexual relations of one boy's boss, and the painfully unromantic relationship of a man and woman the boy visits in the course of his job contrast with the young people's attitudes.

The "plot" is less a matter of external events than the interplay of alternative points of view.[1] This can confuse audiences. Differences in feelings and points of view are harder to follow than events. That is why many American viewers are left scratching their heads at what is "going on" in a Leigh scene or what they are supposed to be "getting" from it.[2] As Cassavetes once said about his own work: "The lights go down and the audience says 'Let's get going,' but the film is *already* going – someplace they don't realize." The drama doesn't depend on external conflicts and struggles. The opening scenes of *Nuts in May* show a married couple on vacation in the country, checking into a campground. The drama begins long before they have any actual disagreements. It is already unfolding in how they sing together as they drive, how they interact with each other and the camp manager as they check in and set up camp. In *High Hopes*, when one of the married couples has a conversation prior to going to sleep, the drama is taking place at the speed of light, even with the characters flat on their backs.

As the repeated bedtime conversations in *High Hopes* suggest, Leigh's fundamental organizational device is the paralleled scene. The films are virtual echo chambers of compared imaginative positions. The viewer becomes a connoisseur of the contrasts, even when the characters are completely oblivious to them. In *The Kiss of Death*, for example, it isn't that the various young people notice the differences between each other's ways of feeling and thinking, but that a perceptive member of the audience does. In fact, it is an essential aspect of Leigh's vision of life that most of his characters are so locked inside themselves that they don't even realize there is a difference between their point of view and that of another character.[3]

As the preceding suggests, contrary to the situation prevailing in most mainstream films, in Leigh's work the consciousness of the main character or characters is not the organizing center. That is to say, the drama is played out, not in the character's mind, but the viewer's. This decentering of the drama away from the main characters' consciousnesses is, in fact, one of the defining aspects of Leigh's work (which resembles some of Alan Clarke's in this respect) and is something about which I shall have much more to say in the pages that follow.

Because Leigh's films are narratives, there are some "doings" in them, "events" that superficially resemble those in a Hollywood movie – arguments, power struggles, schemes in which one figure attempts to get the better of another – but these "actions" function, not in the conventional Hollywood way to generate counteractions that eventually allow a winner or loser to be determined, but as dramatic externalizations of characters' points of view. Leigh's "plots," such as they are, are less something that happens *to* the characters than expressions of what the characters are. Gloria disrupts the Butchers' household in *Grown-Ups*, Keith clashes with Honkey and Finger in *Nuts in May*, Barbara tries to give Colin a job in *Meantime*, and Andy purchases the caravan in *Life Is Sweet*, not to create actions or counterevents, but to open windows into the souls of the figures involved. Events reveal the characters' strengths or shortcomings – as when Alison Steadman's character responds to a medical emergency in one way in *Abigail's Party* and in an entirely different way in *Life Is Sweet*. Behavior is event and character is narrative. What someone is, is what happens to him.

When the problem is not outside but within a character, there is no need to give him or her an external problem. What the character is, is more than enough for him or her to deal with. The "plot" of most of Leigh's works is not something inflicted on you by someone or something else, but what it is to be a certain kind of person, to have a particular way of thinking and feeling. What you are is what you have to deal with.

That is a further reason why there are almost never any particular actions Leigh's characters are asked to take in the course of his films. Action can never be a solution to an internal problem. There is nothing to do when the problem is how you feel and think. You can adjust your actions in response to someone else, but how can you adjust your identity? How can you change what you *are*? As in classic drama, the only possible "solution" is an act of insight. Leigh's subject is the possibility of personal transformation. In this respect, his work is essentially as spiritual as that of Dreyer or Tarkovsky.

The Hollywood film's emphasis on a character's ability to do things is related to its definition of identity in terms of volition. The characters played by Michael Douglas, Jody Foster, Meryl Streep, and Harrison Ford *are* the choices they make. They are their intentions, plans, and acts of will. If they decide to do something daring, they are daring; if they decide to be careful, they are careful; if they decide to do something mean, they are mean; if they decide to be loving, they are loving. The drama in Hollywood films is generated almost entirely by characters' moment-by-moment thoughts, feelings, wishes, and plans – and the conflicts between them. What Michael Douglas wants and intends (and how it conflicts with what Glenn Close or Demi Moore wants and intends) is the motor that drives *Fatal Attraction* or *Disclosure*. Characters are their surging, shifting states of consciousness. Identity is awareness.

On the face of it, this may seem a natural or even inevitable definition of selfhood, but Leigh shows how much it leaves out. His work demonstrates that reducing selfhood to consciousness represents a stunningly superficial definition of who we are. The realm of choice, volition, and will only skims the surface of what his characters are. Identity does not emanate from consciousness but from structures of character that antedate and underpin our superficial, momentary thoughts, feelings, and volitions. Sylvia, Peter, Keith, Beverly, Aubrey, and Nicola will still be who they are, no matter what they think or intend or attempt to do at any particular moment. When what one is is constituted by an entire body of lived experience, the relative importance of passing states of consciousness pales.[4]

Leigh lowers the center of gravity of identity. He moves what we are from our heads and hearts to a deeper place. Identity is not the reflection of thoughts and desires, but something beneath them that might be said to be the source of them. The drama in Leigh's work is not created by what a figure *decides* to do, but what he *is* independent of his decisions. Sylvia's failure to connect with Peter in *Bleak Moments*, Keith's conflict with his neighbors in *Nuts in May*, Gloria's clashes with Dick and Mandy in *Grown-Ups*, and Beverly's painful interactions with Susan in *Abigail's Party* are not traceable to these figures' intentions and desires.[5]

Thus the drama in Leigh's work is not the result of choices and decisions. He sees life in other terms: You have your personality and I have mine. How do our ways of knowing interact? Our relationship is based, not on our wishes or wills (a superficial and evanescent connection), but on deep, abiding structures of feeling. Whereas American film understands life ethically, Leigh is preethical. A better way to put it would be to say that Leigh defines ethics not as a series of choices but as a pattern of behavior. Morality is not located at the level of the will. It is not traceable to our intentions, feelings, or decisions. It is what we are, even when we aren't aware of it, even when we don't intend it.

The result is not moral nihilism: Leigh wants us to judge, and to judge firmly, but to judge on the basis of a person's whole character and the details of his or her actual expressive performance, not on the basis of an intention, idea, or desire. We are not saved or damned on the basis of what we want and believe (a very simple thing) but on the basis of what we are (a far more complex and more interesting matter).

In mainstream film, a character's understanding of himself is unassailable. You can know what you are; you are what you feel you are. In *Fatal Attraction* or *Disclosure*, when Michael Douglas acts in a certain way (nasty, cunning, clever, trusting, innocent), he knows it. He understands his own goals and intentions as well as a viewer does. First-person truth is trusted in the way many people innocently trust first-person truth in their own lives. (I *want* to be so-and-so; I *intend* to be so-and-so; I *believe* myself to be so-and-so; therefore I *am* so-and-so.) The intentional self and the actual self are the same. There is only one self and we can know it.

Leigh pulls the realms of thinking and being apart. Good intentions are not good enough. Your behavior can reveal you to be something entirely different from what you think you are or intend to be. Wishing, wanting, and trying only skim the surface of being. Character is deeper than consciousness (indeed, is usually opposed to it). What we are goes beyond our capacity to know it. The structures of personality that Leigh is exploring are almost never knowable by the person defined by them. Whereas American films are implicit celebrations of knowing, Leigh's films are depictions of the life that flows beneath awareness.

In fact, one of the main sources of drama in Leigh's work is the fallacy of self-knowledge. Peter sincerely *believes* he is taking an interest in Hilda in *Bleak Moments*, even as he patronizes her. Beverly honestly *thinks* she is the soul of kindness and consideration in *Abigail's Party*, even as she bullies and harasses her cocktail party guests. Melody sincerely *feels* she is "bonding" with Stan in *Home Sweet Home*, even as she repeatedly insults him and misunderstands virtually everything he says. Aubrey truly *imagines* himself to be sexy, cool, and hip, and Nicola is genuinely *convinced* that she is the only member of the family who cares about others, even as scene after scene of *Life Is Sweet* demonstrates that they are very nearly the opposite of their ideas of themselves.

These characters are not hypocritical. They are not trying to deceive anyone. (If that were the case, we would be back in the mainstream view of personality where a character knows what he or she is doing.) They are sincere. The problem is that feeling is not being, and to feel, think, or believe something, however sincerely, is not enough. Feelings of love may be expressed in hurtful ways. Attempts to help someone may be misguided; we can drop the lifeboat on the heads of the people we sincerely intend to rescue.

It's not like that in mainstream films. One might say that Hollywood movies let us indulge in the luxury of seeing everyone *the way we see ourselves* – as insides viewed from the inside – while Leigh's films force us to see characters *the way others see us* (and the way we see others) – as outsides viewed from the outside. It is the difference between judging from intentions (the way we normally see ourselves) and judging from actions (the way we customarily see others). For ourselves, our ideals, motives, and emotions *are* us; for others, what we are can be completely unrelated to or in contradiction to our own understanding of ourselves. Our behavior and expressions can admit of interpretations other than our own. (The real threat of Leigh's work, if we can accept it, is always against our own complacent belief in the infallibility of our knowledge of ourselves.)

Is it any surprise that most viewers prefer the Hollywood vision? Its equation of identity with consciousness not only simplifies life and art but reinforces our fantasy of self-knowledge. Hollywood characters *are* their own views of themselves. There really is only the character's own view of himself; no other view is reasonable.[6] The self is one thing through and through. In contrast, Leigh's characters always have at least two selves – what they are to themselves and what they are to others, and the two almost never coincide.

The more general way to understand this situation is to see that while most American film idealizes experience, in both the vernacular and philosophical senses of the term, Leigh deidealizes it. American film understands experience as mental events (depicted in the characters and evoked in the viewers); Leigh understands it as expressive events (which require complex acts of interpretation on the part of both characters and viewers). The ideal view dives beneath phenomenal reality to anchor understanding in intentional depths; the other navigates turbulent expressive surfaces. Inner states count for so much in American movies (and are so reliable and trustworthy as sources of information) because they are, in effect, all there is. Leigh's films imagine a wholly other world, external to our desires, beyond our hearts and minds, and not necessarily accessible to them.

From classic Hollywood melodramas like *Citizen Kane, Now, Voyager, Casablanca,* and *Psycho,* to more recent works like *Mr. Holland's Opus, Forrest Gump, My Best Friend's Wedding, Face/Off, Titanic,* and

The Truman Show, mainstream American film is fundamentally a depiction of *inner* worlds. It focuses on states of vision, feeling, and thought. The importance of social interactions is played down and that of imaginative reactions played up – which is why moments of looking, being looked at, thinking, and feeling are the most important events in these works. For both their viewers and their characters, these films are about *seeing and feeling things* – participating in states of insight and emotion – not about socially, verbally, or physically interacting in a practical way with someone else.

The whole stylistic enterprise of these films is devoted to providing windows into characters' souls. Musical orchestrations and expressionistic lighting cue us into characters' emotions; close-ups let us look deep into their eyes and savor the expressions on their faces; blocking and framing techniques and editing rhythms and juxtapositions let viewers vicariously participate in characters' emotional and intellectual states; most of the dialogue involves expressing opinions, beliefs, fears, doubts, hopes, plans. It would be only a slight exaggeration to say that every effect is directed toward the end of making consciousness visible and audible – to keeping both the viewer and other characters focused on internal states. When characters meet, mind meets mind. Your emotions meet mine; your intentions are pitted against mine: your ideas, goals, and plans are compared with mine.

These films implicitly suggest that life is less a matter of behavior than of feeling; less about expressions than intentions. The presentation of inner states is not only more important than, but usually takes the place of practical interaction. If a character tells us how he is feeling or thinking (by saying it in a line of dialogue), or if the style of the film shows it (with a close-up, lighting effect, or musical orchestration), the character usually need not do anything at all to express it in the world. "Interaction" is almost entirely imaginative. In all of the important or memorable scenes in Alfred Hitchcock's work (the most extreme example of this idealizing tendency in mainstream film), the characters might as well be brains in vats communicating through mental telepathy. But Hitchcock is only the most obvious example. In shot after shot in virtually every mainstream movie, what is presented are states of feeling and thinking. Identity is mental. We are our internal states. Experience is equivalent to states of subjectivity. The most intense, important, and meaningful moments in life consist of thoughts and feelings (which need not be spoken or otherwise expressed). Life is visionary – in both the optical and the imaginative senses of the term.[7]

The subjectivization of experience in mainstream films is one of the reasons why viewers are so easily able to identify with the characters in these films, becoming the victims in *Schindler's List*, the unsung heroes in *Saving Private Ryan*, the romantic lovers in *Titanic*, the nebbish with a heart of gold in *Manhattan*, the tough guy in *Terminator*, or the hipper-than-hip swingers in *Boogie Nights*. The outer lives of the characters in these films do not remotely resemble those of the viewers, but the inner states are the same. As long as what we are is equivalent to our basic thoughts and feelings, there *is* no difference between us and the characters played by Kate Winslett or Arnold Schwarzenegger. The viewer can frictionlessly slip inside the character's skin. The character is always comprehensible in terms of the viewer's *own* ways of thinking and feeling. Their motives are *our* motives. Their ideas are *our* ideas. Their generic thoughts and emotions give us versions of our own understandings of ourselves. Leigh, on the other hand, asks us to go out of ourselves, to leave our own ways of understanding behind and inhabit genuine otherness – in a far deeper sense than is dreamt of by the multiculturalists.

The imaginative transformation simplifies experience (not to mention making it intelligible in foreign markets – you don't need subtitles or familiarity with cultural customs to understand emotions). While practical performance involves complexities of timing, tone, timbre, and the mastery of local expressive conventions, emotional states are more or less universal. We all have the same glands. The nonspecificity of idealist presentation contributes to the genericness of its effects. When an experience is made equivalent to its imaginative and emotional value, its uniqueness is diminished, its outlines simplified, its complexity attenuated. In being taken up into the mind, reality is softened. Differences between figures that would be gray and fuzzy in expression become black-and-white when translated into ideas and feelings. Even the most imperceptive viewer notices how in Hollywood movies characters are simpler and their conflicts more clear-cut than outside the movies.

Most American viewers are so accustomed to this idealization of experience that they fail to see how it skews their understanding of life. If something is everywhere, it is invisible.[8] Leigh shows what it looks like for a film to proceed differently. His work rejects ideal relations to experience – for both characters and viewers. It deidealizes experience and expression. Insides are replaced by outsides. Leigh's characters' consciousnesses must always be translated into practical forms of social interaction. Their insides are never directly visible – neither through their words and actions, nor through the visual and acoustic styles of the works they are in. The viewer is held in the realm of expression and behavior, not empathizing with feelings and thoughts deep within a character, not identifying with the character, dropping into the character and "becoming" him or her, but – as in documentary film – standing outside of it, off to one side of it, scrutinizing opaque, impenetrable surfaces. Leigh holds us on the surface and, more than that, implicitly says that surfaces are all that matter.

Contrary to everything our culture tells us (and everything we may want to believe), Leigh argues that experience is not reducible to subjectivity. Consciousness never stands free of its warped, partial, imperfect, shifting expressions. Leigh's characters cannot simply "think" or "feel" their goals, purposes, and relationships, but must express them in a thousand practical details. Feelings must be converted into actions. Emotion must be exteriorized by being shared. Leigh's characters are not their thoughts and feelings, but their social interactions, movements, gestures, tones of voice, and facial expressions. They must *perform* their thoughts and feelings in front of, in concert with, and in response to other characters. They must *enact* their impulses in the world. (In Leigh's favorite phrase, they must move from abstractly thinking about something to "getting on with it.") That is why to think back on most of the great scenes in Leigh's work is to remember particular vocal tones and facial expressions, bodily shapes and movements, and practical verbal and social interactions: Sylvia's joking, playful, embarrassing, clumsy conversations with Norman and Peter; Mark's razzing of Colin and verbal sparring with Barbara; the dramatic skits Cyril and Shirley improvise together; Wendy's subtly different tones and styles of conversational interaction with everyone she meets. Characters have voices and bodies. They are not merely (or chiefly) their thoughts and feelings.

For a shorthand formulation of the difference between the two understandings of identity, compare Tom Hanks' Forrest Gump with David Threlfall's Trevor in *The Kiss of Death*. Both figures are well-meaning, physically clumsy, and fairly inarticulate. Yet in the case of Forrest Gump, we are never allowed to forget that beautiful intentions underpin his homely expressions. Fine sentiments and pure ideals lurk beneath the homespun surface, instructing us to disregard the surface. As far as the audience's view of Gump goes, he might as well be made of glass. He is transparent. We look past his humble exterior and admire his tender soul (a move into the interior assisted by the film's voice-over narration). He is all inside. Leigh's Trevor, in contrast, might be said to be all outside. He *is* his expression of himself – however halting and imperfect. He is opaque. His inside is inaccessible. What you see is what you get. There is no release from the visible.

The difference between the two expressive traditions is reflected in the different kinds of acting in the two bodies of work. Most American acting plays down surface expressions and plays up indications of "deep" thoughts and feelings. In the most extreme illustrations of this kind of acting – seen in Hitchcock's work with Jimmy Stewart and Cary Grant or Capra's with Gary Cooper – surface expression is diminished almost to the vanishing point while cinematic style picks up the expressive burden. Acting becomes a kind of pantomime: The actor stands still with a neutral expression on his face while musical orchestrations, lighting effects, plot events, scripted remarks, or intercut close-ups of looks, glances, and stares suggest thoughts or feelings surging just beneath the surface. Even much more complex and nuanced forms of American acting, like the performances of Marlon Brando, James Dean, and Montgomery Clift, are significantly still built up from the inside out. All Method acting is based on the belief that what is in the depths is more important than what is on the surface. Feeling is primary; expression secondary. American acting is almost always based on depths rather than surface expressions precisely because it has internalized the set of understandings I have described: namely, that there is a realm of subjectivity that anchors and is ultimately more important than the relatively "superficial" details of social or verbal expression.

The acting in Leigh's work reverses these priorities. It puts a premium on surfaces (nuances of voice tones, facial expressions, gestures, body language), more or less letting the depths take care of themselves. It is more about outsides than insides, less about states of thought and feeling than about the enactment of those states. Selfhood is not (as in the Method) something hidden deep within us, anchored in secret dreams and unspoken desires, but is a concept that summarizes the overall effect of the intricate network of expressions we employ. Leigh would undoubtedly agree with Oscar Wilde's witticism that it is only superficial people who do not judge by surfaces. That is also why Leigh is not interested in discussing a character's internal states – his motivation, thoughts, emotions – with the actor during rehearsal. The issue is not what the character would think or feel in a certain situation, but what he would say or do. Manners are morals. Even the casual viewer picks up on the difference when he notices the importance of generalized stylistic effects in American film (lighting, editing, and sound effects that suggest subjective states) and their relative unimportance in Leigh's work.

The difference between an idealized and unidealized presentation of experience is what an American viewer registers as the "rawness" of Leigh's characters or the "roughness" of their interactions.[9] Leigh's characters feel lumpy, their expressions muddy, and their interactions bumpy in comparison with those in Hollywood films because it is almost impossible for practical social expressions and interactions to achieve the purity and clarity of abstract statements of subjectivity and stylistic indications of consciousness. Characters in idealist films can "speak" their thoughts and feelings (in both the verbal and stylistic senses of the term) more clearly and powerfully than Leigh's can, because their "speech" is freed from the compromises, fallibility, and imperfection of speech as it is encountered outside of the movies. In *Psycho* Hitchcock can lay in a little spooky-dooky music on the sound track, throw a spot on an actor's face, or use expressionistic camera angles to create states of feeling that have an unworldly purity, clarity, and intensity. In *Citizen Kane* Welles can use short lenses, outsized sets, and shadows to express the title character's megalomania and loneliness with a directness and purity that the compromised, mediated personal expressions in Leigh's work never attain. The smoothness and completeness of idealist presentation is replaced in Leigh's work by the halting, rough particularity and imperfection of actual physical and verbal expression.

Just as the characters in a mainstream film commune visionarily with each other and their surroundings (effortlessly taking in meanings simply by glancing at someone or something), so do the viewers of mainstream films take in the characters and their situations in a visionary way. That is to say, idealist film not only allows characters to read each other's minds, it makes the viewer a mind reader. The conflation of visionary forms of interaction is, in fact, the central narrative project of Hollywood film, which not only allows characters to relate to each other in terms of states of thought and feeling but encourages the viewer to relate to the characters in the same way. The viewer encounters the on-screen experience in the same idealized, visionary way the characters do, expanding imaginatively within the character and situation – "identifying" with the character, "becoming" him or her, feeling what the character feels. The viewer leaves his real identity behind and sympathetically lives through a group of figures for a period of time. He effortlessly shares those figures' states of thought and feeling – seeing what they see, knowing what they know. He frictionlessly inhabits other consciousnesses. (The conflation is facilitated by the use of subjectivity editing conventions and mood-music orchestrations.) In the final scene of *Casablanca*, Bergman and Bogart read each other's minds, imaginatively expanding and visionarily merging, and the viewer switches into the same resonantly empathetic, imaginatively expansive appreciation of them.

Leigh's work requires an entirely different and more demanding mode of viewing. Viewers cannot commune visionarily with his visuals. They cannot expand imaginatively within his scenes. They cannot live vicariously through ("become") his characters. His figures repel identification. His camera placements don't encourage the viewer to see things through their eyes. His music and visuals don't allow the viewer to participate in unmediated states of feeling and thought.

The viewer has to work much harder to come to grips with Leigh's work also because things are much less clear than in the other kind of movie. Visionary stylistic effects, the staple of American film, are fairly simple and static in their significance. The import of a spooky orchestration on the sound track, a beautiful female face, a key-lighted shot can be taken in almost effortlessly. Meanings mapped on the body are invariably cryptic, multivalent, and changeable. In *Bleak Moments*, is Peter's ungainliness charming or dismaying? Are Sylvia's jokes a way of reaching out to others or holding them at a distance? Are Norman's stammerings and hesitations soulful or shallow? Even once we do bring their significance into focus, the problem is that performed meanings won't stand still. Created in time and extended in space, they continuously melt and transmute, shimmering with changing resonances.

Based as they are on a screenwriter's moral and thematic abstractions, and interacting with other characters in terms of their own abstract intellectual states and emotions, American characters have the experiential thinness of figures in an allegory or a dream. They and the interactions between them are as smooth and featureless as the ideas in which they originated. There is, as John Cassavetes once put it, no behavior. Everything is somewhat generalized. They represent ideas about ourselves, rather than the complex perceptual events we really are. They are generic and abstract. They lack details (which is why you can almost always take them in at a glance). Nothing could be less like Leigh's presentations. Details are everything in his work. There is nothing but specific, local expressions. There is no avoiding particulars – for the viewer or the characters.[10]

Given his nonvolitional understanding of experience, it is not surprising that Leigh once told an interviewer that in order to understand someone it would not be sufficient to hear the person talk about his or her ideas and feelings. He said that he would need to know what the person did for a living, where he or she was born, and what his or her family was like. It would be a mistake to attribute Leigh's comments simply to British class awareness. Leigh was making a statement about the nature of identity. He was telling the interviewer that our dreams and desires are not the most important things about us. Identity is not mental. It is not disembodied. It is not optative.

The famous colloquy between Madame Merle and Isabel Archer in Chapter 19 of Henry James' *The Portrait of a Lady* can provide one final additional perspective on the difference between the two understandings of selfhood.[11] In the quotation that follows, Merle's conception of selfhood comes first, as a response to Isabel's declaration that it won't matter how her lover dresses or what kind of house he lives in:

"When you've lived as long as I you'll see that every human being has his shell and that you must take the shell into account. By the shell I mean the whole envelope of circumstances. There's no such thing as an isolated man or woman; we're each made up of some cluster of appurtenances. What shall we call our self? Where does it begin? Where does it end? It overflows into everything that belongs to us – and then it flows back again. I know a large part of myself is in the clothes I choose to wear. I've got a great respect for things! One's self – for other people – is one's expression of one's self; and one's house, one's furniture, one's garments, the books one reads, the company one keeps – these things are all expressive."

This was very metaphysical; not more so, however, than several observations Madame Merle had already made. Isabel was fond of metaphysics, but was unable to accompany her friend into this bold analysis of human personality. "I don't agree with you. I think it is just the other way. I don't know whether I succeed in expressing myself, but I know that nothing else expresses me. Nothing that belongs to me is any measure of me; everything's on the contrary a limit, a barrier, and a perfectly arbitrary one. Certainly the clothes which, as you say, I choose to wear, don't express me; and heaven forbid they should!"

For the purposes of the present argument, I would suggest that the Hollywood understanding of identity is close to Isabel's, while Leigh's is closer to that of Madame Merle. Translated into the terms of the preceding discussion, Isabel defines selfhood in terms of consciousness, while

Madame Merle defines it in terms of expression. Isabel's identity (or at least the identity she aspires to have), like the identities of characters in Hollywood movies, is a more or less direct reflection of her wishes, dreams, and desires. (In fact, there is really very little else to her.) Madame Merle, in contrast, like Leigh, says that subjectivity only matters insofar as it is externalized in forms of practical performance.

The point of invoking Isabel Archer is to suggest the seductiveness of the idealist position. The equation of the self with its volitions, intentions, thoughts, and desires is a vision of virtually unlimited possibility. It imagines the individual to be fundamentally unbounded and undefined. The self is open-ended and free. The motto of these films is no different from the get-rich-quick maxim: Anything you can see you can be: anything you can conceive and believe, you can achieve.[12] Where identity is so thoroughly mental, there are virtually no constraints on it. Characters in American film are capable of being or doing almost anything. They truly are American Adams, freed from the limits of history, memory, and social contingency. Hollywood and Isabel imagine our identities to be responsive to our consciousnesses, and consciousness itself to be fundamentally open-ended, unbounded, and free.

Unlimited possibility doesn't come without a price, however. Insofar as a character can be anyone, he or she must to some extent forfeit being someone. The idealist position manifests itself as a characteristic blankness or vacancy in the acting and the verbal and physical expressions of the characters in Hollywood films. Leigh himself has commented that the figures in American film strike him as "ciphers."[13] George Bailey, Mary Hatch, Jefferson Smith, Rick, Ilsa Lunt, Charles Foster Kane, Marion Crane, "Top Gun," Forrest Gump, "The Terminator," and Truman Burbank are as unindividualized as comic-strip figures. They are Everyman (or Everywoman), not someone but anyone: generic placeholders performing generic functions in generic narratives – the archetypal father, mother, crusader, cynic, romantic, megalomaniac, and so on. The psychological indefiniteness and sociological vagueness of these characters and their situations is dictated by the refusal to place fundamental limits on personal expression and achievement (and is what makes it so easy for a viewer to become them).

Leigh has a different vision of what we are. His characters are not general but particular, not anyone but someone, not Rorschach inkblots for viewers imaginatively to fill in, but particular individuals with specific traits and attributes who resist imaginative appropriation – by other characters and by the viewer. Characters' acts of resistance to other characters' imaginative appropriations of them constitute the plots of most of the films. And their resistance to viewers' imaginative appropriations is the reason Leigh's work challenges audiences.

Leigh devotes weeks of his rehearsal process to working with his actors to arrive at definite forms of movement, speech, and expression precisely because he believes so strongly in each figure's specificity. He understands that although people's intentions are more or less the same – who doesn't want to be successful, happy, or good? – their ways of expressing them are different. In *Life Is Sweet*, Andy and Aubrey are more or less identical in terms of their desires (they both aspire to work for themselves). But their expressions of their desires are as different as night and day.

In Leigh's world, precisely because we cannot escape our personalities, we are not open-ended, free, and able to live our dreams. We cannot be or do anything we imagine. We are not infinite in possibility, but fundamentally limited and constrained. Leigh's characters have particular identities that stand between them and their visions of themselves. They are tangled up in their pasts (social background, upbringing, personality, and memories), their futures (obligations and responsibilities), and everything around them (jobs, families, and personal forms of expression). The specificity of the characterizations and performances is critical to the meaning of Leigh's work. His characters are particular individuals, grounded in specific sets of circumstances, mannerisms, ways of talking (including the specific local accents that drive many American viewers up the wall in *Four Days in July*, for example), and ways of knowing that they can never escape. Each has distinctive pacings, rhythms, memories, and physical attributes. There is no realm of thoughts, feelings, and intentions free of these contingencies – no realm of ideas, feelings, or intentions not inflected by what we are. Contrary to Isabel Archer's dream, there is no realm of consciousness that is free of social contingency and psychological particularity. We and all of our expressions are fundamentally mediated and compromised. That acknowledgment of our limitations is what American viewers often find depressing about Leigh's work. His characters' expressive possibilities are radically constrained. They can never be anything other than what they are.

Leigh, like Madame Merle, tells us that although we may dream in the subjunctive we must live in the indicative. Ideals can be expressed only in compromised, imperfect, unideal forms. But that is not a situation to be regretted, according to either of them. It is a stimulation to creative performance *within* the limits that contain us. Trevor can never be other than Trevor in all of his goofy, clumsy imperfection, but he can be the most sensitive, responsible, interesting Trevor possible. Colin will never be able to leap outside his own imaginative limitations (or even to imagine the possibility, as Isabel does), but he can work within them. Shirley and Wendy cannot escape the families of relationships that hedge them round. They must work with what they have – just as Leigh does as a director – working *within* the limits of the personalities and expressive possibilities of the particular actors available to him.

These characters cannot be anything because they are so clearly something. Character sets an absolute limit on what each can be and do. Sylvia, Peter, Gloria, Keith, Beverly, Shirley, and Wendy can never be fundamentally different from what they are, even if they wanted to be (which they don't).[14] Leigh's characters have "character" in the root sense of the word. Their figures are more or less permanently etched in a hard surface. Characters in American movies might, in contrast, be said to have "personality," in the sense of the word that is applied to the host of a television game show: a superficial, ephemeral congeries of attributes. In the latter case, identity is malleable; in the former, it is virtually unchangeable. Leigh's figures are locked in emotional and intellectual boxes from which they can never escape. They must be themselves – which would be a terrible limitation if they did not have extremely complex and creative selves to be.

Leigh's work dramatizes the individual's capacities for creative performance within inescapable limitations. His characters can never melt and swoon into a cloud of possibility the way Isabel Archer can; they cannot transcend the social forms of expression that define them. There is no unconditioned realm of consciousness into which they can withdraw. Like ballerinas, they cannot leap outside the music that both energizes and constrains their performances. They must find a way to express themselves, uniquely and creatively, within social and psychological forms and structures that inexorably limit who they are and what they can say and do.

2

Fictitious Selves: *Bleak Moments*

The things which engage my interest are all those areas of life in which people are trapped. Trapped by mores, habit, and received behavior patterns. . . . In Paris, they made a lot of comparisons between *Family Life* and *Bleak Moments* because of the psychiatric side of both films. It's a red herring. . . . [The mentally retarded problem] is a device by which to discuss people who are trapped. You could say that Hilda is the least trapped of all those five central characters.

– Mike Leigh

Social science understandings have triumphed in so many fields that it should not be surprising that film criticism has also been affected. Films are treated as being more or less direct emanations of the social and ideological understandings of the culture that produced them, and their content is translated into a set of sociological generalizations about race, class, power, and gender. Such an approach may work with the products of the Hollywood assembly line, but it simply doesn't suffice for Leigh's work. In fact, one of the things that stands in the way of the appreciation of Leigh's films is the way they frustrate ideological interpretation. They don't offer the kind of portable truths many critics want.

The problem is larger than the fact that Leigh's depictions do not conform to liberal pieties about the working class; his films offer ways of understanding that are fundamentally opposed to those of sociology.[1] Sociological criticism is premised on the notion of shared characteristics. It treats persons as being members of groups and situations as being representative. It downplays differences. In contrast, Leigh's vision is radically individualistic. Leigh does not trace identity to the things we share with a group (racially, sexually, economically, or ideologically), but locates it in the things that make us distinctively ourselves (our feelings, thoughts, and sense of who we are). He is utterly committed to personal uniqueness. Like Dickens, he parades such bundles of quirks and eccentricities before a viewer's eyes that it is impossible to treat his characters as representatives of anything. To generalize about their social "situation" or psychological "problem" would be to overlook most of what makes them interesting. The very fascination of the characters in *Bleak Moments* resides in their unpredictable, unsystematic, expressive idiosyncrasy.[2]

Whereas the ideological critic can fly ten thousand feet above the experience of a scene or a character (treating it as a type, a symbol, a metaphor, an abstract representation of a general situation), the interpreter of Leigh's work must dive into and become intimate with specifics, synchronizing his rhythms and sensitivities with their shifts and changes. Whereas sociological analysis reduces scenes and characters to their outlines, Leigh's characters and situations live in their details. They are nothing in general and everything in particular; nothing out of time and everything in it. They *are* their second-by-second expressive fluctuations – a hesitation in a line delivery, a fleeting facial expression, an idiosyncratic gesture, a tonal nuance, an unexpected bodily movement. Not to attend to these details is to miss the experience Leigh offers.[3]

The difference between the two kinds of criticism is the difference between emphasizing systems or individuals, structures or structure-breaking impulses. It ultimately comes down to whether you focus on systematic aspects of experience that are larger than the individual and that constrain individual performance or on individual movements of feeling and imagination that figure possibilities of free performance within the system. Unfortunately, nonsystematic expression is simply written out of most academic criticism. The scholar invariably chooses to devote attention to abstractions rather than particulars, to structures and systems rather than individuals and eccentricities. The repetitive aspects of a work of art and the generic expressions within it are treated as being of far more importance than the nonsystematic aspects, personal expressions, and singular moments.

The structuralist vision is basically an attempt to inflate the importance of what would otherwise be felt to be merely "aesthetic" or "emotional" inquiries. Artists' and characters' expressions are treated as being sociologically or ideologically representative (or as failing to be), in an attempt to make the inquiry matter more. Personal, unique, individual emotional states are viewed as not being important enough to merit study in themselves. Needless to say, such a critical bias has serious ramifications. It radically skews the definition of experience. The inside drops out of life. When experience is understood in terms of its external qualities (its sexual, social, and ideological dynamics), it becomes its outsides. Characters are reduced to external relations of power, dominance, control, and their position in a system. Their individuality disappears. Their merely private concerns, feelings, dreams, and aspirations – everything that makes them unique and not representative – cease to be accounted for. (In fact, if the private, internal realm is acknowledged at all, it is treated as being a reflection of yet one more general, abstract system of power relations.) In a word, identities are skin-deep for the ideological critic.

Leigh's focus is on the inside – though, as I have mentioned at several points, the inside is only visible in his work insofar as it is expressed in visible expressions. He is less interested in superpersonal structures of knowledge (the bureaucracies and cultural systems that surround us) than in individual forms of knowing. For Leigh, all of the traps that snare us are internal ones, and all of the important battles are fought within the individual heart and soul.

This observation should suggest the chasm that separates Leigh's understanding of experience from that of an ideologically based critic or artist. Though the social and economic situations of Leigh's characters are invariably specified, they are not determinative. In his view, institutions don't cause our problems and institutions cannot solve them. Nothing beyond the structure of our own thoughts and emotions can be blamed for our predicament and nothing outside of ourselves can remedy it. The poorest of Leigh's characters could win the lottery, or the richest be forced out onto the streets, without their basic dramatic problems changing.

One only has to compare Ken Loach's *Ladybird, Ladybird* with Leigh's *Home Sweet Home* or his short, *Probation*, for the difference between the two viewpoints to be clear. Whereas Loach mounts an institutional critique, the social systems and bureaucracies in Leigh's work are only individuals writ large. *Home Sweet Home* dramatizes the relationship of two social workers, Dave and Melody, to a client, Stan, and his daughter, Tina, but for Leigh the social workers are ultimately just messed-up people.[4] One might say that while Loach looks at the effect, Leigh studies the cause. Loach studies bureaucracies; Leigh examines the individual qualities that make bureaucracies the way they are. The main characters in *Ladybird, Ladybird* are victims of a social agency's depersonalizing understandings. Leigh refuses to make Stan and Tina victims of anybody or anything. *Home Sweet Home* makes clear that, even if all social workers were to disappear from the universe, Stan and Tina's relationship would not improve one whit (and in fact would very likely get worse, since in the absence of a pushy, intrusive, boorish Melody, Tina would get *no* visits or trips home at all).

There is an ultimate fairness in Leigh's view of life. We get what we are. Nothing is inflicted on us (just as nothing outside of ourselves can save us). We create our own problems and we ourselves must solve them. It would be hard to imagine a view of experience more at odds with the blame-games played by most cultural studies critics. Leigh's characters can never blame anything or anyone – least of all "the system." External forces (figured by concepts like "power," "gender," and "class") have no ultimate authority over what we are. We are *responsible* for our own fates. The enemy, if there is an enemy, is inside. Odd as it may sound to say it, the writers on cultural studies and neo-Marxist filmmakers like Loach are actually more optimistic than Leigh, for while the social-work bureaucracy (Loach's target) may conceivably be re-formed, the human heart and mind (Leigh's subjects) are all too deplorably what they are for all eternity. I would argue that the institutional critique is in fact the simpler, more superficial, and more naive way of understanding these situations. The labyrinths of the human heart are far more tortuous and Byzantine than the corridors of power that constitute the welfare system. The bureaucracies of the individual imagination are far subtler and more insidious than those of any man-made institution. And if you say you don't see that or don't understand how that could possibly be, why that is precisely what Leigh's work exists to show you.

Given the fact that Leigh's characters and situations have an unusual degree of geographical, economic, and social specificity, sociological approaches to his work have been difficult for him to shake. In the earliest interview I have been able to locate, he was, in fact, already defending his work against the sort of generalized ideological interpretation that later commentators would apply to *Naked* and *Secrets and Lies*. His interviewer characterized *Bleak Moments* as a "naturalistic" study of a "lonely alcoholic spinster," and, with the bluntness he would become famous for, Leigh shot back that Beckett would be a better reference point than Osborne, and that his film was "about other things": "[*Bleak Moments*] uses naturalistic metaphors, but is in fact anti-naturalistic. My work is like Beckett in this respect. . . . I did not want to treat the problems of an alcoholic, of a shut-in, etc. My film is about other things."[5]

34

I would like to devote the rest of the chapter to exploring what those unspecified "other things" might be. Insofar as *Bleak Moments* is an anthology of defective identities, one of the things Leigh is clearly interested in is the imaginative box called character in which characters trap themselves in their attempts to be someone. The simplest (and most simply comic) illustrations of what this means involve Pat and Sylvia's boss and a waiter in a Chinese restaurant who serves Peter and Sylvia on their date.

The boss spends most of the workday uttering lame witticisms and spouting pseudoprofound philosophy ("I wonder where all the people are going . . ."). It would be easy to write him off as a well-meaning dimwit and be done with him; however, I would suggest that Leigh is using him to depict a more general predicament. The boss's problem is not simply that his jokes are not as funny or his thoughts as profound as he thinks they are; his problem is that he is not who he thinks he is. He fancies himself a witty, entertaining raconteur with a personal relationship to his employees, when in fact he is actually regarded by them as a kook and a weirdo. He thinks his humor opens doors to intimacy and brings him emotionally close to them, when it actually erects walls. The boss is imprisoned in a fiction. He imagines he is one thing, justifies his whole life in terms of his achievement of it, and works to maintain and live up to it, but it is in fact something entirely different. His whole identity is based on a lie he tells himself.[6]

In the case of the waiter, Leigh choreographs a hilariously understated sequence in which virtually everything Peter and Sylvia say and do disconcerts him. Leigh's presentation illustrates the difference between focusing on the institution or the individuals within it. The scene might have been used to poke fun at abstract codes of behavior – in this case, those involving dining in a Chinese restaurant (where, for example, customers use numbers rather than names when they order). But Leigh instead focuses on the waiter's tones and mannerisms, with the effect that the scene is more about the waiter than the restaurant. Its subject is not the rules, but the person who believes in them. The waiter, not unlike the boss, has trapped himself in a role – the role of waiter in a Chinese restaurant.

As I mentioned in the Stylistic Introduction, parallelism is one of the basic organizational devices in Leigh's work. The reason one can be sure that the subject of the scenes with the boss and the waiter represents a problem of self-definition is because they are positioned in a narrative that depicts related problems in many other figures. For example, Leigh cuts between the Chinese restaurant scene and one involving Hilda, Pat, and her mother in which Pat baby-sits Hilda while Sylvia and Peter are out on their date. She takes her to her elderly mother's and gets into an argument with the mother about her false teeth (which are out on the table) before serving tea. The argument starts off fairly lightly and comically (more or less in the same tonal register as the restaurant scene) but turns dark and shockingly painful, plunging from Marx Brothers farce (with Pat and her mother squabbling over the placement of the denture box, which Pat attempts to hide) to Bette Davis weepie (with mutual recrimination, bitterness, and tears) in a matter of seconds.

The shocking and unexpected tonal reversal (one of Leigh's most common and brilliant artistic effects) completely blindsides us, catching us off balance emotionally, forcing the pain home all the more powerfully because our guard has been let down. We suddenly realize that the scene is not about false teeth, manners, or hospitality. The triviality of the provocation and the passionateness of Pat's treatment of her mother tell us that what is at stake is nothing less than Pat's definition of herself. The scene is about Pat's frustration at living with her mother, her desire to assert herself as being independent of her control, and above all, her conviction that she is more sophisticated and worldly than her mother. The scene is about Pat's conception of who she is. However bizarre it may seem – and Leigh deliberately makes it as bizarre as possible – Pat imagines herself to be Martha Stewart. (The fact that the retarded Hilda is incapable of noticing, let alone caring about, the false teeth in the first place only heightens the touching absurdity of Pat's role playing.)

The scene a few minutes later, in which Pat tucks Hilda in bed, deepens our view of the fallaciousness of Pat's definition of herself. She plays a game of "this little piggy" on Hilda's fingers just prior to saying good night; but Leigh makes clear that the real game being played is an inner game – one Pat is playing with herself. It is the baby-sitter's fantasy. The spinster Pat is imagining herself to be Hilda's mother. She feels how easy it all is, how satisfying, how natural, how completely suited to motherhood she is! She tells herself that she is emotionally closer to Hilda than even Sylvia is. She tells herself that *this* is what it is to be a mother. In Pat's mind, for a moment, she *is* Hilda's mother.

Needless to say, however enticing, however passionately believed, it is a lie. Leigh is nothing if not a truth teller, and he is dedicated to revealing the fallacies in the stories we tell ourselves about ourselves to cheer ourselves up. He has Hilda get just a little too frisky and unintentionally bump Pat. The daydream evaporates. Pat precipitously aborts

Pat and Hilda – trapped in who they are (Photo courtesy the Kobal Collection: BFI/Memorial)

the game, icily reasserts control, and upbraids Hilda. The moment not only reveals how rigid Pat's conception of game playing (and motherhood) is; it reveals the utter falsehood of her sense of herself. Her fictional Mommy role clearly depends on Hilda's obediently playing the fictional role of appreciative daughter. The first moment Hilda diverges from it (by acting the way a real child does), Pat is unable to function. In a sense, Hilda is reprimanded because she dares to come out of "character" (in a limiting, fictional sense of the concept) and actually be an unpredictable, uncontrollable person.

Leigh's use of parallelism again helps the viewer interpret the scene by comparing Pat's relationship with Hilda with Sylvia's, who interacts with Hilda in a different way. Sylvia is kind, but also firm. She is playful at moments, but serious at others. While Pat's performance of Mommy, like all impersonations, is mechanical and monotonic, Sylvia's is fluid, inventive, and genuinely responsive. While Pat's role playing depends on feeling superior to and in control of Hilda, Sylvia treats her as an equal. Pat casts Hilda as a supporting actress in a drama in which she stars;

Sylvia allows Hilda to be a free and independent person. In short, real love is entirely different from the fantasy.

Peter embodies the final and most important example of the problematics of personal identity. Just as it would underestimate Leigh's intention merely to consider the boss a loquacious jerk, the waiter a humorless functionary, or Pat a clumsy baby-sitter, so it would be a mistake to see Peter merely as a pedant or a snob. The things Peter does to others (the ways he patronizes or attempts to impress them) are trivial; the things he does to himself are fatal. The scenes in which he quizzes Norman about his background, interacts with Hilda, takes Sylvia on a date, launches into a disquisition on McLuhan, and interacts with a colleague are more than illustrations of pseudointellectualism; they reveal basic fallacies in his conception of himself. Like the others, he has a mistaken idea of who he is.

The deep drama in Leigh's work is always inward (even though our only access to it is by studying characters' outsides). He is less interested in the lies we tell others than in those we tell ourselves – in this case, all the ways in which we delude ourselves about who we are and what our lives mean. Leigh's work demonstrates that, although our minds can trick us, our emotions and the events we live through ultimately speak true. Life trips up our lies. Narrative events uncover painful truths that we may have devoted our entire lives to denying. Everything that happens to a character reveals what he or she really is. The boss's intended jokes and witticisms fall flat, drawing blank stares and creating embarrassed silences. The waiter gets flustered and impatient when customers don't buy into his idea of himself. Pat's tearful argument with her mother, her fight with Hilda, and, in a scene near the end of the film, her breakdown in front of Sylvia are indications that the fictions she attempts to pass on herself are ultimately unsustainable.[7]

The fallacy of Peter's role playing is revealed most vividly in his interactions with Sylvia on their date. He is unable to free himself from the rigidity of his definition of himself to be able to respond freely to anything – from the absurdity of the meal in the Chinese restaurant and the stupidity of her lame jokes to her sexual invitation. Using Sylvia as an artistic alter ego, Leigh presents a series of scenes that are designed to encourage Peter to unbutton his sense of himself (literally and figuratively). But he defends himself against the threat.

It is fitting that Peter and Pat, as male and female doppelgängers, face off halfway through the film. One of the great moments in the film is their semicomic Mexican standoff following Sylvia and Peter's return

Sylvia and Peter at the Chinese restaurant – open and closed identities; play and seriousness; holding experience loosely and tightly (Photo courtesy the Kobal Collection: BFI/Memorial)

from their date. Pat, who has been upstairs with Hilda, comes down to retrieve her purse and discovers that Peter is blocking access to it. (Unknown to him, the purse is on the floor almost between his legs.) Since she doesn't want to embarrass him by asking him to move, and he doesn't have a clue as to what she is reaching for, for a long moment they stand face to face paralyzed by confusion. What makes the moment so bizarrely hilarious is the gratuitousness of their mutual embarrassment. If either character simply said what he or she was thinking, the entire misunderstanding would evaporate. But what Leigh wants us to see is that both are too committed to *appearing* "considerate" to *be* genuinely considerate: Pat is too "genteel" and "deferential" and Peter too "polite" and "gentlemanly" to realize what a difficult position they are putting each other in. They are both too busy *playing* "responsive" to *be* responsive, too intent on *acting* "sensitive" to *be* sensitive.

Leigh is one of the great masters of comic tone, and his control of tone is crucial to the complexity of the effects he achieves. All the scenes

I have mentioned are comic, yet we feel sympathy for the figures in them. We laugh at Peter and Pat during the purse scene but also feel *with* and *for* them, empathizing with their genuine confusion about what they are trying to do and be. Leigh never ridicules Pat and Peter. The comedy is not dismissive or jeering in the Robert Altman way, but gentle and sweet. It would be easier if we could merely dislike the characters; instead, we feel their awkwardness and discomfort.

John Cassavetes once responded to an interviewer who asked him how hard it was to get his point of view into his films by saying that his goal was not to get his *own* but his *characters'* points of view in. The question was not how *he* felt about them, but how *they* felt about themselves. In a similar vein, Leigh's characters are never mere exteriors to be judged from the outside; each has an inside – a consciousness, however flawed, that is respected. As in Jean Renoir, everyone has his reasons. Even in the cases of the boss and the waiter, two of the least important speaking parts in the film, Leigh makes sure that we feel *their* points of view – their neediness, insecurity, and unhappiness. Even they aren't turned into cartoons or treated merely as fools.

What makes Pat's "this little piggy" game, Pat and Peter's purse scene, the scenes in the restaurant and at the office, or the scenes involving Peter and Sylvia so powerful is that, because we feel we are encountering the characters' side of things and the characters are felt to be acting from their own centers of being (which are perfectly meaningful and coherent to them), we don't feel that *Leigh* is doing something to them, but that *they* are doing it to themselves. It is not he who makes them look foolish, but they themselves.

Equally important to the effect is the slowness of our discovery process. One of the subtlest aspects of Leigh's work is how it delays judgment. Understanding is incremental. Mainstream movies employ quicker ways of knowing. They generally provide a hook on which to hang the interpretation of a character or scene as early as possible. If it is done stylistically – by means of a lighting effect, a mood-music orchestration, a tendentious framing, a "black hat" bit of action – the meaning can be indicated almost instantaneously. See this? Hear that? Get it? Got it.

Leigh replaces what might be called knowledge as insight with knowledge as acquaintance. Rather than seeing (or being told) something about an experience up front, the viewer is required *to live through* a complex, unglossed experience, piecing an interpretation together step by step. One might say that while Hollywood attempts to create a feeling of godlike omniscience in the viewer, Leigh makes us realize the all-too-human partiality and incompleteness of each of our continuously revised understandings.[8] We understand Leigh's characters and situations, not with the instantaneous insight that movies usually provide, but the way we understand things in life outside of the movies – gradually, hesitantly, provisionally. Understanding out of time is replaced by understanding in time; shorthand knowing gives way to longhand. The gradualness and tentativeness of the knowing process affect the final status of the knowledge attained. Leigh's truths stay localized, his forms of knowing gradual and evolutionary, no matter how many times we see the movies. The experiences in Leigh's work must be undergone for a long time before they can be understood (if they can be understood at all).

Leigh provides shifting, partial views of characters and situations that allow for multiple (and sometimes even conflicting) understandings. This is what is potentially misleading about my own preceding observations about Pat, Peter, the boss, and the waiter. My account necessarily involved looking back on them and their scenes from a certain imaginative distance, but they are actually encountered by a viewer of the film far less clearly and summarily. I vividly remember my own experience of viewing *Bleak Moments* for the first time with a friend. I was mystified to the point of bewilderment. After the first scene with the boss, I whispered in her ear, "What's his problem?" Following a scene with Peter, "Is this guy as weird as I think he is?" After a scene with Norman, "What a bizarre movie. What's going on?" The questions weren't rhetorical. I didn't know what to think about what I was seeing. I was lost. Even after the movie was over, I still couldn't have described what I had seen or say what the film was "about." I remember my best guess was "something to do with failures of communication and linguistic problems," since there was so much stammering, inarticulateness, and misunderstanding – and so much blathering on about language by Peter. When it came to how I felt about the characters, I couldn't make up my mind about any of them. Was I supposed to like any of them? Was I supposed to hate any of them? Was I supposed to blame Peter for the disastrousness of the date? Or was I supposed to blame Sylvia? How was I supposed to feel about Norman – was he hopeless or promising as boyfriend material? Was Sylvia actually propositioning him in one of the final scenes, or was I just imagining that? If so, did he realize it and deliberately reject her overture, or was he oblivious to the whole thing? The characters and situations resisted all of the standard psychological and moral can openers in my interpretive Swiss Army knife. They defeated being narratively sorted into any of the customary categories – good or bad, right or wrong, victim or villain.

You are not really responding to *Bleak Moments* if you haven't changed your mind about Hilda, Peter, Pat, and everything else at least a few times in the course of watching it. Leigh's narratives are structured to stay just a little ahead of us, to prevent us from figuring out characters and interactions prematurely, to force us to stay open. As he put it to an interviewer: "Whatever film you watch, assuming you've seen a film before, you immediately go into one program or another, or plug into an expectation system. If the film is any good, these expectations are constantly confounded."[9]

Throughout his career, Leigh has spoken to interviewers about his process of shifting the view and adjusting the viewer's relationship with his characters and situations. As early as 1975, he was arguing: "When people tell me that I'm just producing slices of life . . . they don't realize that it's all based on a very particular kind of story-telling. What I do is to invite the audience to go through a process of identifying, reacting to, reacting against, sympathizing with, caring for, getting cheezed off with, a complex set of interactions between people."[10]

How we come to know Pat can stand for all. Leigh keeps slightly changing the view in order to prevent a viewer from pinning her down with a simple judgment. In the early scenes (when she talks to Sylvia about the medium, for example), she seems peculiar, but her obvious sincerity, good intentions, upbeat energy, and the cheery tone with which Joolia Cappleman delivers even her nuttiest lines prevents us from judging Pat negatively. The unintentionally comic effect of many of her remarks and gestures is actually fairly endearing. Pat seems odd, but likable. As always in Leigh, the humor disarms harsh moral judgment. It teases us into amused sympathy. Pat seems not objectionable but touchingly clumsy.

The first scene that even suggests she is a problem (or has a problem) is the one in which she interrupts Norman's guitar lesson by rudely passing around a birthday card and tossing Hilda candy. But even in this scene, the triviality of what she does and her clear obliviousness to the effect she is having prevents us from being too hard on her. (To make sure we aren't overly critical of her, a minute later Leigh even has her apologize for interrupting.) She still seems merely eccentric and comically oblivious of the impression she makes on others.

Leigh deliberately does not reveal Pat's more negative qualities until we have gotten to know her too well simply to condemn her. By the time the scenes involving Pat's shouting match with her mother and her unkind treatment of Hilda occur, it is impossible to be too hard on her, because we have been put in a position to appreciate both her loneliness and her frustrated maternal desires. We see her behavior less in terms of inflicting pain on others than as an expression of her own unhappiness.

One final adjustment remains. As if to make absolutely sure that we don't close our hearts to Pat, near the end of the film Leigh inserts the scene in which she momentarily breaks down in tears.[11] A viewer would have to be made of stone not to be moved by her wail of despair. If nothing else has, the breakdown forces us to reassess all of Pat's preceding cheeriness and to realize that it has been covering up deep unhappiness throughout the film. We have come full circle by this point, with a completely different understanding of Pat than we had at the beginning, not only seeing her flaws more clearly, but (and this is the genius of Leigh's delay of final judgment) seeing them more sympathetically. The proof is that when, in a final scene at work that parallels the initial one, Pat proposes taking Hilda to a faith healer, we interpret her wacky remarks entirely differently than we did when she made similar ones about a spiritualist in a scene near the beginning of the film. Rather than being amused (as we were in the initial scene), we are touched.

Our understanding of Peter is equally incremental. In effect, Leigh presents several slightly different Peters – all of whom are true. In a few early scenes, he seems merely comical and clumsy. As he fumbles with Sylvia's front gate, he might be M. Hulot. We smile and feel sorry that even simple things challenge him so much. Awkwardly interacting with the childlike Hilda (asking her at one point "How are *we*?" in his most inappropriate Oxbridge drawl), he might be a young Professor Rath, a comical pedagogue who forgets that life is not a schoolroom. But at this point Peter's stuffiness seems innocuous since, no matter how stilted his manner, he genuinely seems to care about Hilda (and, given her state of retardation, is in any case not really hurting her feelings). But just as we are growing comfortable with the Hulot/Rath reading, Leigh pulls the rug out from under us. He inserts a scene in which (while Sylvia primps upstairs prior to going out with him) Peter interacts with Norman and his superciliousness no longer seems amusing: It feels a little cruel. We wonder whether we have been too easy on him, even as we can't quite make up our minds about whether we are making too much of the moment.

The magic has been worked. Leigh has made judgment difficult (and dismissive judgment impossible). As with the comparable scenes involving Pat, by withholding Peter's cross-examination of Norman until we know so much about Peter and his way of interacting with the world, Leigh has made it difficult to decide how we feel. Given everything we know about Peter by the time we see him grilling Norman, we judge that, *from his own point of view*, he is completely unaware of the impression he is making and is probably simply trying to be "friendly" – even if the result is a textbook example of how *not* to be friendly.[12] To further complicate judgment, when Sylvia finally comes downstairs, Leigh scripts Peter's exchange with her to be really quite considerate and thoughtful. We can't pigeonhole him as cruel or insensitive.

I have mentioned the comic tone of many of *Bleak Moments'* scenes. Not only is all of Leigh's work informed by a fundamentally comic sensibility, but one of the most important signs of a healthy imagination in a Leigh character is a sense of playfulness. Play is not only evidence of desirable exuberance and energy but a demonstration of imaginative freedom.

That is to say, it is absolutely critical to Leigh's definition of Sylvia that she teases, jokes, and plays games with virtually everyone she meets, even if she does it so subtly and undemonstratively that more often than not the joke is lost on them (and on many viewers). Her playfulness ranges from the silly (affectionately sticking her tongue out at Hilda – which, given Hilda's IQ, is probably as complex a joke as the girl can understand) to the sly (the goofy, serious, clumsy, flirtatious mind games she plays with Norman and Peter in parallel scenes). She is an off-balance acrobat of semantic somersaults and tonal backflips. Sylvia's humor is awkward and unpolished, but it demonstrates her ability to remain unoppressed by every situation in which she finds herself.

Playfulness is Sylvia's defining difference from both Peter and Pat, neither of whom seems even to have a sense of humor. Pat's game of "this little piggy" is proof of the absence of playfulness in her play, and Peter's dour conversation about *Peanuts* with a colleague at school makes the same point about him. It is revealing that, while Peter is irritated and upset by the waiter in the Chinese restaurant, Sylvia is amused. Sylvia shows us that to be able to laugh at a situation (not just the waiter but the general awkwardness of the whole date) is to redeem it. She understands what her creator does: that even embarrassment and discomfort can be sources of entertainment if you can look at them in the right way.

If play is the ability to take an imaginative step off to one side of experience, seeing it as it were from another perspective, it is clear why Pat and Peter are humorless. They are incapable of getting outside themselves even for a second. They are unable to entertain any perspective on experience other than those they are already up to their eyebrows in. The reason the purse scene is so screamingly funny to a viewer (even as it is so excruciatingly painful to its participants) has less to do with Pat and Peter's physical inability to get out of each other's way than with their inability to get out of their own mental ruts. They are unable to see themselves the way the other character or the viewer sees them. They take themselves too seriously to see how funny life can be. They lack self-awareness.

Humor is a way of holding more than one thought in mind, of feeling more than one thing at a time. Even the retarded Hilda does better than Pat or Peter in this respect. Pat brings Norman's guitar playing to a screeching halt with her single-minded comments, unable to set aside her own point of view even for a moment, while Hilda at least shows that she can simultaneously clutch candy and listen to music. Peter, similarly, has only one way of taking everything and one way of interacting with everyone. He is always the schoolteacher ponderously holding forth. He can't forget who he is. In the metaphor of the scene in which he is stacked up with cups and plates, he lacks the ability to balance multiple feelings without losing his grip. Norman, faced with an identical predicament in a parallel scene, sees the humor, awkwardness, stupidity, and silliness of the situation; Peter is merely flustered.

To play is also to leave behind formulas for expression and interaction (whether they take the form of the "by the numbers" rules for ordering the waiter believes in, the recipes for conversation Peter relies on, the rules of game playing Pat employs with Hilda, or the canned witticisms the boss inflicts on his employees). Play requires that you genuinely open yourself to the emotional challenges of an uncontrolled sequence of events.

The ultimate difference between Pat and Peter and Sylvia that their different capacities of play reflect involves their respective degrees of flexibility, nimbleness, openness, and responsiveness. Pat's "because-I'm-the-mommy-that's-why" interactions with Hilda and Peter's canned speeches about communication represent states of fatal emotional closure, rigidity, and unresponsiveness. As Peter's lecture-room style of disquisition and Pat's conversational non sequiturs and self-referential tangents tell us, while the feelings and relationships around them flow and shift, they stand still. Play requires responsiveness, but Peter and Pat are incapable of responding to anything but their own needs and ideas. Like Sylvia's boss (who, despite his incessant "jokes," also lacks any sense of "play" in the interactional sense of the word), Pat and Peter are both fundamentally monologists. Talk for them is a one-way street. Leigh is always in favor of characters (and actors) who genuinely listen and respond to one another, who allow for a little "play" – a little looseness, freedom, surprise, and possibility – in the course of their interactions.

In the dramatic metaphor that runs throughout Leigh's work, offered the opportunity to improvise, to work with another character in a genuinely open-ended process of emotional and intellectual exploration, Pat and Peter not only refuse to depart from their predetermined "scripts" but attempt to impose them on others. It is telling that when Sylvia teasingly attempts to short-circuit Peter's lecture on McLuhan by saying she prefers to "watch the radio," he is completely unable to respond to the joke and take a new tack. He merely rephrases his original remark and continues where he left off. The aesthetic and the ethical are always intertwined in Leigh's thought and work, and he understands that a performance that refuses to go "off the book" not only makes for aesthetically bad art but for ethically bad living. The lesson of all his work is that we must learn to improvise, to hold ourselves subtly open and responsive, in both life and art.

At the same time, Leigh realizes that genuine openness and responsiveness never play as smoothly as a "scripted" relationship. The interactions between Sylvia and Norman or Sylvia and Hilda are far more halting and less polished than Peter's speechifying – so rough, in fact, that early reviewers of the play upon which the film was based thought Sylvia, Norman, and some of the other actors had become rattled and forgotten their lines. What they failed to understand is that what they thought was dramatic roughness was only the splinters that always accompany the breaking up of overly smooth forms. We are so accustomed to the depiction of characters who live scripted lives that when a work finds a way to represent more complex realities and relationships, we assume something must have gone wrong. We are so used to the idealizations of mainstream film that we assume these deliberate deidealizations (the conversational stammerings, pauses, longueurs, and non sequiturs, in this instance) are mistakes – as if Leigh didn't know how to make a scene play more smoothly, rapidly, and wittily, when those are the very things he works to defend his scenes against. In short, we prefer the neatness of Hollywood's lies to the messiness of Leigh's truths.

The beauties in Leigh's work are invigoratingly rough ones. Even his most admirable characters and most amicable relationships (like the relation between Hilda and Sylvia or Norman and Hilda in this film) are marbled with imperfections. Most movies implicitly flatter their viewers by encouraging them to identify with characters who are more articulate and organized than life ever allows us actually to be. It's flattering to imagine that life has such grandiose possibilities. But it's false. Leigh's characters are not glamorous, witty, and romantic in this ideal way. They cannot speak their hearts or minds with eloquent phrases. Every expression and intention, even the best and most loving, is ineluctably compromised, flawed, and mediated.

If the value Leigh places on a semicomic stance is not clear from the contrasts between scenes involving how Norman and Peter respond to Sylvia's jokes or the differences between how Sylvia and Pat play with Hilda, it should be from the way Sylvia's tone overlaps with Leigh's. To a large degree, Sylvia *is* Leigh. She has almost the exact same amused (and occasionally cracked) perspective on experience that he displays as a filmmaker. In her irreverence and unpredictability (always as expressed in her halting and imperfect way), Sylvia is a portrait of the artist – realizing Emerson's vision of the poet who "is free and makes free." Sylvia's sense of humor is her creator's.[13] She pokes fun at pomposity. She makes entertainment out of awkwardness. She puckishly "decon-structs" (long before Derrida's followers had taken the fun out of the concept) confining social rituals. She plays with who she is. In short, she enlarges life's possibilities.

Just as Sylvia's playfulness is a way of loosening up tense situations and allowing a little wiggle into stiff relationships, so Leigh's comic perspective is a way of holding experience loosely and leaving room for a little "play" in the viewer's relation to it. The point is to prevent pinning down experience with an overly tight interpretation. Just as Sylvia does in her interactions with others, so Leigh's humor is a way of denying the viewer mechanical, prefabricated forms of response. Any one of the scenes I have mentioned – the one in the Chinese restaurant, Pat's fight with her mother about the false teeth, Peter and Pat's face-off over the purse, the guitar party scene, and the conclusion of Peter and Sylvia's date – illustrates the effect. Leigh's weird mix of moods, tones, and perspectives suspends us in an emotionally unresolved position. We are left feeling contradictory and even mutually exclusive emotions at the same time: Is what we are seeing a laugh-riot or shocking? Hilarious or painful? Funny or touching? Sad or entertaining? Silly or serious? It is impossible to decide. The mismatch of mixed-up tones frustrates canned interpretations. The moments will not be emotionally pigeon-holed. They defeat easy readings. It's a wonderful place to get a scene – or a human interaction – to.[14]

Leigh's comedy (like Dickinson's, Welty's, or Cassavetes', for that matter) is a way of seeing things at an angle to received understandings. Leigh's relish of comical idiosyncrasy and eccentricity – whether it takes the form of presenting oddball characters (like the entire cast of *Bleak Moments*) or nutty situations (like the false teeth and purse scenes) – is a rejection of "conventional" roles (like Pat's conception of being a mother), "received" identities (like Peter's conception of being a teacher), and "canned" views of experience (like Peter's view of communication). To be able to play with expressive conventions in the way both Leigh and Sylvia do is to free yourself from their tyranny.

The chief form of reductiveness that all of Leigh's films fight against is moral judgment (or at least the various forms of humorless closed-mindedness that generally pass for moral judgment in our culture). One of the most important functions of Leigh's humor is to resist moralisms of all stripes (just as the eccentricity of a Marx Brothers or Ealing picture does). Leigh knows that, at least as they are normally employed, con-cepts like "right" and "wrong," "good" and "bad," are too rigid, pinched, and narrow to do justice to most of life. Pat understands life in moral terms (judging everyone in her path, from her mother to Hilda to Sylvia). Peter understands life in moral terms (judging Hilda for her retardation and Sylvia for her sexual forwardness). Many characters in subsequent Leigh films – from Mr. Thornley and Mrs. Stone in *Hard Labour* to Linda and Sandra in *The Kiss of Death* to Keith and Barbara in later works – will follow in this straight, narrow, and very judgmental path. But Leigh knows that judging is a much weaker and far more limited way of relating to experience than enjoying, no matter how "shocking" or "dismaying" the experience may be. He knows that an essential step in understanding anything truly is to allow yourself to be entertained by it. That is the relationship his films want viewers to open themselves to. The point is to substitute the richness of experiencing in place of the poverty of evaluating. Leigh's lightly comic tone – like Sylvia's – is his way of doing that: of appreciating experiences rather than making judgments about them; of allowing oneself to become emo-tionally involved with and amused by things rather than sternly holding oneself outside of and above them.[15]

For both Sylvia and her creator, comedy is also a way of imaginatively

Functioning in a step-by-step universe – "The long love scene in *Bleak Moments* was the result of fourteen improvisations, one of which ran for four hours. The scene in the film was a distillation of all that." – Mike Leigh

levering yourself a little outside of experience and freeing yourself slightly from its excruciations. To be able to laugh at a situation or your own performance within it is to keep it in perspective. To joke about something is to avoid being lost in it. You allow yourself to wonder about it, to explore it. For a character like Sylvia (or for the viewer) to be able to see the wacky humor in a situation (rather than being offended, wounded, or morally outraged by it, as Peter invariably is) is to inhabit the same imaginative position that Leigh does as an artist – half-inside and half-outside the experience, slightly above it yet still in touch with it, emotionally exposed and vulnerable to it but not overwhelmed by it.

Vulnerability and exposure are things Sylvia repeatedly risks (never more bravely than when she asks Peter to kiss her or take off his trousers, or when she approaches Norman after Peter leaves), and things Peter is terrified of. As his conversations with Hilda, Norman, Sylvia, and the fellow schoolteacher demonstrate, Peter must always be in control.[16] Like the boss, he emotionally walls himself off from everyone he meets. It is significant that, notwithstanding all of his talk, talk, talk,

Peter reveals virtually nothing about himself or his feelings to anyone at any time. There is no exposure, no risk, and no possibility of real intimacy in any of his scenes. Peter always plays the role of teacher – superior and unequal in every interaction. It is fair to surmise that the ultimate reason he rejects Sylvia's sexual offer in the kissing scene is that it would require him to sacrifice both his self-control and his control over their relationship. He would have to relinquish his "conversational gambits" and intellectual stances. He would have to follow her lead and abandon himself to the uncertainty of emotion and the challenges of an open-ended relationship.

As subsequent films will demonstrate, one's insecurity about who one is, is the ultimate enemy of discovery. Peter's insecure attempts to "be" something are the source of his rigidity; his rigidity is the cause of his fear of being wrong; and his fear of being wrong is what makes him need to judge Sylvia in the way he does. Moral judgments are caused by one's own uncertainty and insecurity. As Mr. Thornley, Mrs. Stone, Ralph Butcher, Keith, Barbara, and other Leigh characters show us, one's own fears not only screen out authentic contact with but end up hurting others. Fear is cruelty. Fear kills life.

Although we sometimes talk as if later works were axiomatically more mature than earlier ones, "artistic development" is a questionable concept. In many respects, Leigh's first film is as sophisticated as anything he will ever do, and in any case almost all of the preoccupations of his later work are already fully present in it.

One of the explorations that will run throughout Leigh's oeuvre is the predicament of characters trapped in self-protective roles and routines who are forced to deal with experiences that defeat their designs for living. The boss's fake chattiness, Peter's pseudointellectualism, Pat's forced chipperness, and even Norman's twitchy meekness are all ways of avoiding life. Sylvia (and to a lesser extent, Hilda) embody principles of disruption that attempt to break through and break down their routines (though, in their different ways, Pat, Peter, and Norman successfully defend themselves against the attacks). Though Leigh could not have realized it when he made the film, the drama enacted in *Bleak Moments* would be the master narrative for all of his subsequent work.

3

Personal Freezing and Stylistic Melting: *Hard Labour*

If anything could stand still, it would be crushed and dissipated by the torrent it resisted, and if it were a mind, would be crazed; as insane persons are who hold fast to one thought, and do not flow with the course of nature.

– Ralph Waldo Emerson

In his *Biographia Literaria*, Coleridge argued that the primary exercise of the imagination is not high-level cognitive events like thoughts, dreams, and fantasies, but basic perceptual activity – how we see, hear, and feel the world. The functioning of our senses, what we notice and care about (or don't) from one second to the next is the supreme embodiment of our imaginations. Leigh's early works – particularly *Bleak Moments, Hard Labour, The Kiss of Death, Grown-Ups*, and *Meantime* – confirm Coleridge's observation. They don't just tell interesting stories about unusual figures; they give us new eyes and ears, new powers of perception. They open a new world to view. One might say that only a weak artist thinks the function of art is to leave the ordinary world behind to fly off into a realm of dreams or fantasies. Leigh offers new ways of feeling and seeing the world we live in.[1]

Of course, seeing and feeling freshly are easier said than done. We are born into patterns of feeling and thinking that are hard to get beyond. We encounter experience through such a haze of intellectual clichés and hand-me-down emotions that our perceptions are as conventional as our television shows. The vision of most artists is blurred by an additional set of conventions about what can be shown, felt, and thought in works of art. That is why most films, even more than most lives, screen out reality at the very moment they proclaim they are showing it to us.

The effect of these conventions of thought and feeling, on both life and art, is the subject of Leigh's work. His films are about breaking free from limiting habits of thought and feeling on the part of the director and actors as much as the characters. Leigh engages in the same struggle for originality as an artist that his most interesting characters are asked to enact in their lives.

One of the conventions Leigh reacts against most forcefully is cinematic idealization in its various forms. He systematically deidealizes the cinematic experience, not only in the emotional sense of exposing a viewer to experiences and expressions less "pretty" or "elegant" than those in Hollywood films, but in the perceptual sense of replacing mental expressions and relationships with sensory and bodily ones.[2] He pushes cinematic expression downward from the eyes, mouth, and face of his characters (the realm of abstract thoughts, feelings, and intentions to which close-ups, lighting effects, and mood-music orchestrations in mainstream films direct our attention) into the realms of sensory experience and physically embodied social interaction.

In line with the rest of American culture, Hollywood film systematically dephysicalizes experience, imagining it to be something that happens inside us. Leigh emphasizes the outsides of experience. Life does not take place chiefly in our heads and hearts (in the Hitchcockian vein) but in our hands, bodies, and interactions (in the Renoirian mode). Experience is not a matter of thoughts and feelings but of bodies and social expressions. The truths in Leigh's work are not set in a realm of disembodied, denatured vision; they are enacted in the realm of the senses. Our supreme expressions of ourselves, in both life and art, do not take place somewhere above and beyond the necessary confusions of perceptual life and the imperfections of actual social interactions (as two millennia of Platonic thought would have it), but in the world. There is no world beyond the world. There is no emotion except in a body, no thought without a thinker, no expression without a particular personal accent or twist. There is no view from nowhere, no depersonalized understanding, no general expression. While Hollywood is devoted to derealization, Leigh's entire project might be labeled one of realization.

Bleak Moments illustrates how Leigh shifts the drama from mind to body, grounding expression in the realm of gestures and movements. Mere words are too generic, too abstract, too impersonal to convey the kind of meanings Leigh is after, which is why, in scene after scene, truth is a product of characters' body language, vocal tones, pacings, and timbres. The way Norman hunches his shoulders, avoids eye contact, and nervously tugs at his mustache, and how Sylvia arches her neck, tilts her head, and raises her eyebrows "speak" more eloquently about their emotional states than any of their words do. The way Hilda slouches and holds her legs "unfemininely" apart with her skirt hitched up, or the way Pat clutches her handbag in her lap, sitting with her knees primly pressed together and her skirt snugged down, tell us more about them and their states of emotional openness and closedness than any of their dialogue does. Words, being mental expressions, are forms of evasion; the body tells true.

Pat, Peter, and the boss's verbal facility clearly counts *against* speech as a conveyor of meaning. Silence is more expressive than their speech. The boss's pseudointellectual banter, Peter's "conversational gambits," and Pat's nattering on represent even more extreme linguistic failures than Norman's stammering or Hilda's inarticulateness. For Hilda to slap Sylvia, to throw herself on the floor, or to toss away a gift from Pat may be rude and disobedient, but at least it is not to mince words in Peter's or the boss's way. Hilda "speaks" her feelings more truly through the language of gesture, and Norman by playing his guitar, than Peter ever does verbally. It is surely not coincidence that the film's two most inarticulate characters, Hilda and Norman, develop the most intimate relationship. It is as if to say that intimacy not only does not require words but only becomes possible when they are left behind.

Sylvia makes the same point in her plea to Peter that they should stop talking and simply "touch" each other. (And she is right. If Peter would only let her touch him, there might actually be hope for them.) One way we can tell that Leigh endorses Sylvia's statement is that his style itself does something similar to what she advocates. Leigh's cinematic style always functions as a guide to how a viewer is supposed to understand a scene. Its ways of knowing and feeling are meant to be compared with the character's, to help a viewer understand the figure's strengths and weaknesses. Where Leigh's cinematic style and a character's personal style overlap, Leigh is implicitly endorsing the character's ways of knowing and interacting; where they differ, he is implicitly critiquing them. In this instance, Leigh's stylistics endorses Sylvia's belief in the truth-value of physical expression by presenting the scene in which Sylvia alludes to the value of touch almost entirely nonverbally, as a silent pantomime of uncomfortably mismatched bodily positions, gestures, and movements.

Leigh's presentation in all of his work is radically *embodied*. That is why to remember any of his characters is less to remember *what* they say, think, or feel than *how* they express it: in *The Kiss of Death*,

Trevor's clumsily unbalanced gait and mistimed giggle; in *Grown-Ups*, Dick's snaggle-toothed smirk and snarl, lizardlike supineness, and retarded speech rhythms, and Mandy's round-shouldered stance, facial slackness, and tonal flatness; in *Meantime*, Mark and Colin's contrasting facial expressions, timings, and postures. Leigh's goal is to bring us to our senses.

Hard Labour rubs our noses in sensory experiences: auditory realities like the noise of silverware scraping on plates and lips smacking during a meal (and the burps, belches, groans, and grunts of the diners after it is over); corporeal realities like Mr. Thornley's distended belly, hairy back, and greasy, uncombed hair; visual realities like the disarray of a kitchen littered with dirty pots and pans, a supper table with half-eaten food and skims of congealed grease on the plates, and a messy bedroom with an unmade bed.

We feel the claims of the sensory world all the more insofar as Leigh declines to inflect his scenes metaphorically. To watch films like *Psycho*, *Citizen Kane*, *2001*, or *Pulp Fiction* is to move through worlds in which nothing is simply itself; everything is a symbol, a metaphor, a bearer of imaginative meaning. Objects and events are systematically shifted one notch to the side to mean something slightly more general or abstract than their bare phenomenal reality. We are so used to this process that we hardly notice it. No one looks at the actual physical details of the house in *Psycho*; rooms and objects are treated as repositories of sexual secrets, figurations of middle-class fears and taboos. The sled in *Citizen Kane* is not one you could get splinters from; it and all of the other objects and spaces in the film are figurations of emotional states. The space stations in *2001* are not feats of mechanical engineering but imaginative constructs, statements about the displacement of nature by culture. The pop, schlock allusions in *Pulp Fiction* represent a series of inside jokes about the artificiality of the world the characters inhabit. What these films do virtuosically virtually every American movie does to some degree. Objects, characters, and events are rendered in a kind of shorthand or code. This remark means this; that action means that; that place is significant for this reason. The world is allegorized. Reality is derealized.

Leigh refuses to make the abstracting move. His scenes, objects, and characters resist being translated into generalized meanings. They maintain their sensory particularity and physicality. In this respect, Leigh's works resist most film critics' customary forms of understanding as much as they resist those of most Hollywood-trained viewers. Most film criticism is unreflectively committed to an agenda in which sensory events are translated into abstractions (at this particular moment in critical history, frequently involving race, gender, and ideology). The value of the work is regarded as being the extent to which this can be done to it. A work like *Thelma and Louise* or *Blade Runner* that is highly generalizable is treated as being, by definition, more "important" or "significant" than a work like *A Woman Under the Influence* or *The Killing of a Chinese Bookie* that does not generalize its argument. Leigh's work not only denies the critic the opportunity for such acts of expansion; it argues that to do this is to do an injustice to both the work and the world. In abstracting experience, we take it up into the mind and denature it; we rob it of its sensory heft and bodily tangibility. We distance ourselves from it and lose contact with it. A large part of his narrative project is devoted to bringing viewers back to sensory consciousness, and weaning critics away from generalized metaphoric and symbolic forms of understanding. The point is to force them to come to grips with perceptual and temporal truths about characters and scenes that critical abstractions flatten or erase.

Many of the films, in fact, build the conflict between the lure of abstractions and the claims of the body and sensory experience into their narratives. They dramatize the fallaciousness of abstract stances and intellectual relationships. In Leigh's view (as the problems that figures like Peter, Keith, Barbara, and Nicola get into demonstrate), perceptual life is more complex and interesting than ideas about it. The translation from perceptions to conceptions is always a simplification. When an inchoate sprawl of perceptions is reduced to a unified field of conceptions, its perceptual thickness is thinned; its prickly sensory edges are smoothed and slightly simplified.

Perhaps even more important, insofar as experience is taken up into the mind, it is encountered less pressingly and urgently. There is a difference in the viewer's comfort level. Abstractions allow him to control the experience and hold it at a slight emotional distance. A metaphoric or symbolic understanding is a slightly cool one. The raw, less intellectually digested sensory experiences of Leigh's work ask more of the viewer. His nonabstracted presentation provides the feel of experience *before* it is converted to knowledge. Watching his films is less like learning *about* something (the mainstream viewing experience) than living *through* it. His work takes away the customary cinematic "aboutness." Knowing is replaced by experiencing. Understanding is replaced by undergoing.[3]

55

If there is any doubt about how Leigh's sensorily embodied forms of presentation deny the viewer customary forms of intellectual distance and control, one has only to watch *Hard Labour*'s hairy-back scene with a college class. Students who sit impassively through a slasher movie cringe, squirm, and squeal in disbelief at Leigh's scene. The physicality of the moment disconcerts them precisely because it refuses to be intellectualized. It would be so much easier if it functioned metaphorically or abstractly. It would be "about" something. It would be thinkable. It would be safe.

Ideas, abstractions, and understandings not only remove us from the intimate intensity of sensory experience; they remove us from its movement, because they stand still. One of the ways Leigh tests the viewer is by asking him to move from the stasis of conceptions to the flowingness of perceptions. The viewer must surf a shifting wave of present-tense perceptual events without dropping out of the experience to anchor himself in an abstract, static interpretation.

As is always the case in Leigh's work, the challenges a viewer is presented with are mirrored by the challenges a character is presented with. For a character, as much as for a viewer, to cling to any abstract position, identity, or relationship – no matter how admirable in the abstract – is to be doomed. Formulated stances of any sort are the enemy. Virtue is never the result of a fixed state of mind (however "virtuous" it may seem to be). It is responsiveness. *Any* state of mind, rested in, is a trap, a dead end for development. Characters and viewers alike must flow with the flow of experience.[4]

The drama within the drama in most of Leigh's films is how character after character shows himself incapable of flowing in this way. Even as the experiences around them surge and shift, they lock themselves into one position. It is metaphorically resonant that there are references to muscle spasms in both *Hard Labour* and *Abigail's Party*, since so many of the characters are seized up in states of emotional and intellectual cramp. In *Hard Labour* the cramps take many different forms, from Mrs. Stone's flustered inflexibility to Mr. Thornley's abusive iterations. (Leigh is clearly having fun with names. It is as though the cramping is so pervasive that it has comically entered into the names of the characters themselves.)

Leigh employs two kinds of contrasts that help the viewer understand characters' emotional problems. The most obvious one is the contrast he establishes by pairing a less flexible with a more flexible character. A subtler one is the contrast he establishes between his own and his characters' respective styles. Two scenes involving Mr. Thornley illustrate both kinds of contrast: the first, an interaction with a tallyman (door-to-door salesman); the second, an interaction with his boss.

In the first, Mr. Thornley complains to a character named Mr. Philips about a pair of shoes he bought from him. Leigh plays against the cliché of the door-to-door salesman only interested in making the sale (as well as cutting against the grain of the rest of the film, where virtually every other character behaves brutishly) by having Mr. Philips *not* brush off Mr. Thornley's complaints but listen to him sensitively and kindly respond with an offer of a new pair of shoes. However, even as the salesman attempts to allay his anxieties, Thornley continues to rant and rail at him. A viewer is initially baffled by Thornley's querulousness – until it dawns on him that Thornley is so locked into an emotional pattern of uncertainty, insecurity, and mistrust that he can't break out of it. Even when offered the possibility to, he can't free himself. He is shackled by the ball and chain of his memories and the weight of his past understandings.[5]

Much of the scene's pathos is traceable to the contrast between Mr. Philips' and Mr. Thornley's personal styles. While Mr. Philips is emotionally open and giving, Mr. Thornley is suspicious, guarded, and closed. While Mr. Philips is subtly and fluidly responsive, Mr. Thornley is rigid and mechanical. But the deeper and more revealing contrast is between the imaginative styles of Mr. Thornley and his creator. Mr. Thornley's canned, repetitive style contrasts with Leigh's attentive and exploratory camera work. Mr. Thornley's emotional monotone contrasts with Leigh's registration of second-by-second shifts of emotion in characters' faces. Above all, Mr. Thornley's state of being mired in the past contrasts with the stunning present-mindedness of Leigh's presentation. Since the two figures' relative positions have not been summarized or otherwise indicated in advance, in order to understand the scene a viewer is forced to follow it in an absolutely step-by-step way (listening to what Mr. Thornley says, then listening to Mr. Philips' response, then listening to Mr. Thornley's response to that, and so on, deciding how to interpret each moment one step at a time), unable to anticipate the next moment or predict in advance where the scene is going. This process-oriented presentation forces the viewer into a mode of understanding by reference to which Mr. Thornley's argumentative circlings, stallings, and backtrackings seem all the more pathetic. That is to say, Leigh induces a kind of stylistic triple vision, in which the flowingness of his cinematic style implicitly endorses Mr. Philips' ability to leave patterns behind even as it places and critiques Mr. Thornley's entrapment in inherited mental routines.

A subsequent scene involving Mr. Thornley and his boss sets up even subtler contrasts between the fluid responsiveness of Leigh's cinematic style and the mechanical, iterative rigidity of his characters' personal styles. Thornley is at his job as a night-watchman when his supervisor, Mr. Shore, makes a brief visit to check up on things and deliver his paycheck. Leigh presents a shifting sequence of unglossed events that deliberately keep the viewer in the dark about what is going on. Even more mysteriously, enticingly, and unpredictably than in the scene with the tallyman, the viewer is put on the qui vive, following the beat-by-beat progress of an utterly unpredictable interaction, making sense of each comment from Mr. Shore and each reply from Mr. Thornley as it happens, without the benefit of a supervening theory. The present-tense mode of presentation forces the viewer simply to stay absolutely in the moment – watching, wondering, surmising, and revising his conclusions as he goes along.

As the scene begins, the viewer has no information about the supervisor's personality, his relationship to or opinion of Mr. Thornley, or Mr. Thornley's relationship to and opinion of him. Are they friends or rivals, uncomfortable with each other, jocular coworkers – or what? Leigh not only withholds background information but scripts much of the scene so as to have the supervisor make a series of deliberately cryptic remarks that can be interpreted in opposite ways. For example, when the boss asks Thornley for a password, it's impossible to tell whether he is ribbing him or being serious. When he makes a comment about Thornley's signature on the pay stub, one doesn't know whether it's meant as a joke or a put-down. Keith Washington delivers his lines so as to make it impossible to tell whether the supervisor is dead serious or hilariously deadpan, whether he is trying to put Thornley at ease or offering digs, whether he is joking or holding Thornley at arm's length. (This ambiguity is not a mere trick played on the viewer but an observation about the way many men actually do interact; a great deal of male interaction is pitched at this precise in-between place where a joke may be both a joke and a way of avoiding intimacy – a point where the distinction breaks down.)

What makes the scene even more mysterious and unpredictable than the one with the tallyman is the fact that, rather than standing still, the relationship of the two men goes through a number of shifts in tone and mood. Though it is hard to characterize the unresolved and shifting subtleties of specific moments in a few words, it is fair to say that Mr. Shore seems fairly guarded and distant at the start (when he asks for the password and briefly glances around the warehouse); then somewhat snide and condescending (as he rifles through the pay envelopes); then almost playful; then seems to open up emotionally (as he and Thornley get into a brief conversation about the hanky-panky that can take place on a business trip when a man's wife is not with him); then suddenly stiffens and turns hard and critical, reasserting his distance from Thornley (by criticizing the way he is dressed); then, finally, lightens up a bit (softening his tone and addressing Thornley by his first name as he eases himself out).[6]

If we are determined to translate the shifts in beats into a psychological "narrative," it might involve something about how characters like Mr. Shore and Mr. Thornley can start off being guarded and standoffish (due to the formalities of their professional relationship); then the senior figure can loosen up, allowing the junior to loosen up in response; then, as if in fear of having become too familiar and personal, the senior figure can suddenly reestablish his distance, taking the other along in response; then slightly regret the stiffening and soften up a bit. But, the important point is that however we fill in the characters' specific motivations, the subject of the scene is surging, changing states of emotional thawing and freezing.

Even more than being about the psychological relation of two characters, the scene is about the difference between the flowingness of Leigh's cinematic style and the frozenness of both Shore's and Thornley's personal styles. The stylistic stereo effect is one of the most important aspects of Leigh's work. In film after film, his cinematic style establishes a standard of fluidity and responsiveness by reference to which the characters can be judged. In this instance, his willingness to stay in the moment, his openness to a range of different viewpoints, his attentiveness to shifts in emotions makes us feel that anything is possible and there is no predicting what will happen in the next second, even as Thornley and Shore show themselves unable to realize the imaginative possibilities Leigh's style represents. That is to say, even as Leigh gives the viewer an experience of supreme present-mindedness, they figure past-mindedness. Even as his style revels in tonal and emotional pattern breaking, they show themselves locked in mechanical patterns of behavior and relationship. Even as he tells us that every moment is new, they plug every experience into prefabricated, preexisting emotional subtexts.

Leigh's stylistic flowingness almost always exceeds his characters' personal ability to flow with it. In *Bleak Moments*, Peter and Pat are emphatically *not* able to give themselves over to the emotional mercuriality of the scenes in which they find themselves. While Leigh's tones move, they stand still. While his camera work and editing figure present-tense alertness and supple responsiveness, they imprison themselves in their limiting senses of who they are. While the cinematic experience flows and surges, their identities are frozen in place. As in the work of Henry James, Hawthorne, or Shakespeare, the style opens up imaginative possibilities that the characters are unable to live up to.

Leigh's work is comic but never merely comic. There is almost always something painful to the laughter. And the pain is important to the meaning of these scenes. Leigh's narratives are designed to point out genuine problems in his characters' relationships to experience – and to ask viewers to think as much as laugh. The indignities Peter and Pat suffer in the course of *Bleak Moments* and those Mr. Thornley undergoes in *Hard Labour* point up the fallaciousness of their stances. The conflicts that arise between them and other characters and the resistance they meet with at every turn are lessons, if they could only receive them (which of course, given who they are, they can't). The shock they experience is a wrecking ball designed to break down their emotional walls and shatter their patterns. Unfortunately, rather than learning from their struggles, Mr. Thornley, Pat, Peter, and most of Leigh's other trapped figures resist learning as much as most people in life do.

The scene between Thornley and Shore reveals another aspect of Leigh's style: how, just when an audience may feel it has figured out a character or event, Leigh will reveal something new. Mr. Thornley is one of the most limited and predictable characters in Leigh's oeuvre, yet even he has unexpected sides to his personality. His meekness in front of his boss, his playful banter (however clumsy), and his responsiveness to Mr. Shore's emotional overtures are utterly unexpected. In sum, even Mr. Thornley, entombed as he may be in emotional concrete in every preceding scene, apparently can briefly melt and flow under certain circumstances.

This process of keeping just slightly ahead of the viewer (and frustrating his attempt to predict where a scene or character will go) is one of the most important aspects of Leigh's work. In the terms of the metaphor I have been employing, one might say that Leigh thaws his own films' incipient freezings. He breaks up his works' own emerging patterns. That is to say, Leigh's enemy is not only the emotional patterns characters fall into, but the emotional patterns works of art fall into – the patterns we call "character," "plot," "psychology," and "motivation."

As characters and situations start to compose themselves around a feeling or interpretation ("Thornley is this. . . . Mr. Philips is that. . . . The boss is this other kind of person. . . . This interaction will probably go thus and so . . ."), Leigh decomposes them. As characters and relationships start to resolve, Leigh will throw them out of kilter by revealing a new fact or changing the view. If things start to get too neat, he will mess them up. If interactions are about to seem too predictable, he will reveal something at odds with what preceded. Leigh's work is pitched against its own continuously emerging systems of intelligibility and coherence.[7] The experiences he presents resist reductive interpretation. The goal is to prevent figures or events from congealing – even the already more than partially congealed figures here. The point is to keep things moving, even things as stuck in their own ruts as these scenes and figures. Even in this film of dead ends, characters and interactions are a little unpredictable.

This continuous thawing of ever-impending freezings, this destabilization of stabilities, this endless movement away from successively attained positions is one of the most exhilarating aspects of Leigh's work. His style represents a vision of experience as resisting comprehension in terms of any static system of understanding. Life, in this view of it, bubbles out of every intellectual or emotional container in which a character or viewer may attempt to confine it. Experiences slip through each successive interpretive net in which we attempt to capture them.

I would emphasize that it is not a question of knowing more or responding more sensitively. These experiences keep moving away from the generalizations arrived at by even the most sensitive and alert viewer because they don't have a final, complete, absolute existence beyond the particular, shifting times and circumstances that bring them to us. Their existence is *only* contingent. The exhilarating impression is of life inexorably on the move. If a character or relationship is interesting to Leigh (like Sylvia's relationship with Peter in *Bleak Moments*, Trevor's with Linda in *The Kiss of Death*, Mark's with Colin in *Meantime*, Cyril's with Shirley in *High Hopes*, or Wendy's with her husband and children in *Life is Sweet*), it is impossible to pin down.

Leigh's pattern breaking in *Hard Labour* is not confined to the scene between Mr. Thornley and Mr. Shore, or limited to those two figures. Several other scenes involving Mr. Thornley (including those in which he chats with his son and a fellow barfly in a pub) move him in other, unexpected directions. In the case of Mrs. Stone, at several points, just as we are about to conclude that she is as hard-hearted as her name, Leigh has her briefly act chatty, thoughtful, or kind. She makes a vaguely personal remark to Mrs. Thornley, employs a sweeter tone when giving her directions (in the scene involving the mirror), or gives her a small gratuity (in the silver-polishing scene). There is a little latitude for characters to be slightly different from themselves at moments. (Though not completely different: The tip Mrs. Stone gives Mrs. Thornley is the most minuscule possible. Character may melt and flow, but it doesn't simply evaporate into thin air.)

As far as Mrs. Thornley goes, just when we might be about to decide that she has sold her soul to servitude and has no independent identity, Leigh unexpectedly reveals that there is more to her. In an early scene, we see her walking to work and chatting with a friend. A bit later, we see her helping a Skih woman who is having trouble with the coin slot of a machine in a laundromat. (This scene is a brilliant illustration of how much Leigh can accomplish in a short time. In something like a minute, the incident completely alters our view of Mrs. Thornley, who goes from being a servant to servants to helping out someone worse off than herself.) In a subsequent scene, Leigh shows Mrs. Thornley wearing a poppy, watching television, and smiling to herself while she is ironing. Mrs. Thornley is *not* completely defined by her housework. Though it may be on the horizon of visibility, she clearly has an independent imaginative life, thoughts and feelings separate from her work, unknown to her family. That is also the reason Leigh includes both her chat with Ann about pregnancy and the scene in the confessional. Both (though the latter is quite clumsy about it) demonstrate how Mrs. Thornley's consciousness eludes the viewer's previous systems of understanding. She is, to some small extent, free.[8]

Hard Labour poses the question asked by all of Leigh's films – namely, to what extent can a character actually *live* the ideal of emotional openness and responsiveness that Leigh's style imagines? As I suggested in the Stylistic Introduction with the Isabel–Madame Merle contrast, Leigh's films are committed to the social expression of consciousness. Imagination alone is never enough; it must be performed. It is not enough for him or one of his characters simply to *see* something. There must be an I for the eye. All of Leigh's works raise a series of interrelated questions concerning whether the freedom of consciousness that his style embodies is something to be found only in works of art or can be realized in the actual world of human interaction. To put it more simply, can a lived relationship between people actually flow with the same delicacy, sensitivity, and responsiveness as his verbal, photographic, and editorial flowings? At first glance, *Hard Labour* would seem to answer these questions negatively. There would appear to be no character or relationship that even comes close to living up to the sensitive responsiveness of Leigh's scripting, photography, and editing. But I would argue that there is a positive example in the film – one that anticipates the most complex and hopeful interactions in later works like *Meantime, High Hopes*, and *Life Is Sweet*.

It is typical of Leigh to find possibility at the very bottom of the social pecking order, so it should not be surprising that the most fluid and sensitive interaction in *Hard Labour* involves the Thornleys' daughter, Ann, and her Pakistani cabdriver boyfriend, Naseem (brilliantly played by a young Ben Kingsley), and takes place in a dilapidated cab dispatcher's office. In Naseem and Ann's brief interaction, Leigh beautifully captures a state of genuine emotional openness that no other conversation in all of *Hard Labour* attains. Ann and Naseem partner each other with a quickness and litheness that Mr. Thornley and the tallyman, Mr. Thornley and his boss, Mr. Thornley and his wife, Mr. and Mrs. Stone, and even Ann and her mother never approximate.

The narrative event behind the scene is that Ann's friend, Julie, has become pregnant by her married boyfriend and Ann has asked Naseem to make arrangements for her to have an abortion. While the abortion is taking place, Naseem and Ann wait together at the cab stand for Julie's call to be picked up following the procedure. As the scene begins, Ann is jittery and anxious, understandably concerned about Julie's welfare. Did she make the right decision? Did Naseem make the right arrangements? Is Julie all right? When will she call? Initially, Ann is almost as closed off as her father, as trapped in a self-created mental cage; but Naseem delicately calms her down and gradually allays her fears. Then, in the subtlest and kindest possible way, Naseem reassures Ann about his own love for her and his determination that she herself will never be put through a similar experience. Touched by Naseem's care and concern, Ann allows herself to be comforted. (In one of Leigh's typically economical bits of structural ingenuity, in order to establish Naseem's special capacities of caring, Leigh shows him calming down a distraught cab customer just prior to turning to the task of comforting Ann.)

Ann and Naseem's brief interaction is one of the most delicately responsive relationships depicted in all of Leigh's work. What makes it most extraordinary and memorable is that this subtly shifting, hesitant dance of courtship is not "indicated" or "summarized" in the Hollywood way. It is not merely outlined or suggested – created with mood-music orchestration, soulful key-lighting, or shot-reverse-shot sequences of eyes looking at eyes. In short, it is not just a mental or imaginative achievement. It is embodied. It is not abstract or general. It is particularized. It is performed in space and time, in one specific gesture, tone, and statement after another. Ann and Naseem's respective states of emotional closure or openness are registered in a hundred tiny details. It is *enacted* in their supply responsive tones of voice as they share energy and emotion, in Naseem's refined hand gestures and reassuring body language, in delicate glances and flickers of feeling that pass between them.

The scene stands as one of the greatest examples of subtle give-and-take in Leigh's oeuvre. Just as he did in the scenes involving Mr. Thornley and the salesman or his boss, Leigh puts us in a present-tense state of awareness; a viewer feels his way through the scene the same way the two lovers feel their way into intimacy – step by step, second by second, one event after another. What sets the scene utterly apart from any of the other scenes in the film is that, rather than staking out and defending fixed positions, Naseem and Ann *live* the possibilities of sensitivity and responsiveness that Leigh's style exists to honor. They show that such possibilities are not confined to art.

But of course Ann and Naseem are on the very edge of the narrative, not centrally important to it; and, in any case, as my entire argument has been suggesting, they are not the most supremely sensitive ones in *Hard Labour*; their creator is. The sensitivity of Leigh's presentation informs every scene of the film. In the nimbleness of his scripting, directing, and editing, Leigh earns the right to indict the rigidity and insensitivity of the other characters. His subsequent films will explore the question of whether such imaginative possibilities can be lived for more than a short scene on the fringes of the narrative. A viewer will have to wait fifteen years, for the characters of Cyril and Shirley in *High Hopes*, to see Leigh dare to construct an entire film around a relationship this subtly responsive.

4

Existence without Essences: *The Kiss of Death*

I don't put in all kinds of semaphores to make sure that unintelligent members of the audience get it. I just put it in there like it is.

– Mike Leigh

It is sometimes said of a painting that it is two paintings: the one you see at a distance and the one you see up close. In a similar vein, there are at least two different experiences in each of Mike Leigh's movies: the one you have while the film is running and the one you have thinking back on it later. The difference is that a viewer of a painting generally takes in the big picture first and moves in to study the details later, while in a Leigh movie the close-up view – the rough, unassimilated, raw experience you have while you are watching it – may be the only thing visible for a long time. The big picture may not emerge for a while, if ever.

Hollywood attempts to minimize the difference between the two views. In an effort to keep the viewer continuously informed about the big picture, details are continuously linked to a larger pattern of significance. A problem-solving or goal-oriented narrative is one way of doing that. A viewer knows what to pay attention to, and what it means, by referring it to the general goal being pursued. If something assists the characters in solving their problems or answering their questions, it matters; if it doesn't, it doesn't. If it helps the viewer to decipher the meaning of Rosebud, the Monolith, or the house on the hill, it's important; if it doesn't, it isn't. Another way of keeping the viewer from getting lost in the details is to define the main characters in terms of a set of narrative functions. You can give them tasks to accomplish, questions to answer, or problems to solve that will endow them with instant, ready-to-wear identities. Or you can make the characters representatives of basic psychological or moral qualities (a character is turned into a Michael Douglas or an Al Pacino "good-hearted tough guy," given a "big hurt" in the *Kane* or *Nixon* vein, or set loose on a trail of revenge, like Eastwood or Schwarzenegger). However it is accomplished, the result is the same: conceptions replace perceptions; the viewer doesn't really have to deal with the details.

Now, though all artistic presentation involves some degree of simplification (after all, you can't show everything or leave the meanings of experiences completely undetermined), Leigh's work minimizes it. His narratives are not task-oriented. His characters are not reducible to essential traits, nor is the meaning of their interactions narrowed by being given specific purposes or goals.[1] In terms of my painting metaphor, Leigh minimizes the presence of an overarching system of signification that holds the details in place and that releases the viewer from paying attention to more or less everything. The perceptual diversity and multivalence is not unified by being given a reductive conceptual framework.

The mainstream movie encourages the viewer to take shortcuts through the experiences presented. Because experience is treated somewhat abstractly, as a series of problems to be solved and goals to be achieved, the viewer follows it as a series of points to be attained in which the details and nuances of intervening moments may be skipped. Viewers and characters move from one essential point or goal to the next in discrete steps. The muddled middles of life are leaped over.

Leigh provides experiences that will not be boiled down in such ways, life that resists being reduced to abstract points. He creates a world in which more or less every moment is potentially as interesting and important as every other. The details *are* the experience. Intellectual and emotional shortcuts are minimized. You can't leap from point to point; there is nothing to do but live with Leigh's figures and interactions moment by moment, beat by beat. His films suggest that the close-up view may not only be the only available one but the only true one.

The result is a viewing experience that causes problems for many viewers. They walk into *Bleak Moments* or *The Kiss of Death* looking for a dramatic "issue" to focus the story, narrative "goals" to organize their viewing experience, a psychological "handle" to pick up the characters, "questions" to answer or "problems" to solve, can't find any, and decide that the work is "poorly organized," "maddeningly slow," or "a series of conversations that get nowhere" (as three of my students put it). The interactions of Leigh's figures are so open-ended and nontendentious that they seem pointless or random to some viewers. The films frustrate their customary intellectual and emotional designs.

The oxymoronic effect is that Leigh's scenes can seem both easy and hard, both straightforward and maddeningly oblique and elusive, at the same time. To revert to the painting metaphor one last time, the viewer may be able to see many perfectly clear details but find that the "big picture" somehow eludes him, even after the film has ended. Although scenes may not be particularly difficult to follow as *experiences*, they resist being translated into what would normally count as *knowledge*. The films look simple: There are no poststructuralist mystifications or narrative dislocations, yet it may be difficult to say exactly what has transpired emotionally or psychologically in the course of a scene, how you are supposed to feel about a particular character or interaction, what "point" is being made by a sequence, or whether the characters have "gotten anywhere" or "achieved anything" by the end of the movie.

As I have pointed out, the experiences in mainstream films feel fundamentally different from those we have outside of the movie theater; they are focused and clear in a way life is not. Leigh provides something closer to the feeling of life as it is actually lived. We move through *The Kiss of Death*[2] not unlike the way we move through experiences in our lives, encountering Trevor, Ronnie, and the girls the way we encounter real people – awash in details, immersed in particulars, grappling with surfaces without access to resolving depths. When we do attach meanings to characters or interactions, they are tethered more loosely than a meaning in a Welles or Hitchcock film. There is tentativeness that cannot be gotten beyond.

As the simplest possible illustration, consider how Trevor's book reading differs from a cinematic event like Charles Foster Kane's purchasing of statues or Norman Bates' neatness. The Welles and Hitchcock events hardly exist as raw data; they are all *meaning*. Trevor's reading, in contrast, has the opacity of fact; there is no determinate meaning attached to it. Is it an act of withdrawal from the unpleasant realities of his job as an undertaker's assistant? Is it evidence of professional inattentiveness and irresponsibility? Is it a way of avoiding social interactions (which clearly make him uncomfortable)? Is it a sign of a rich and fertile imagination? Is it positive evidence that he has an imaginative life apart from his job? Or negative evidence of his oddness (since he apparently reads only horror stories)? Leigh never weakly specifies which of these quite different (and contradictory) meanings we should attach. Trevor's reading suggests depths but doesn't provide access to them. It deepens his character but does not explain it.[3]

To turn to a somewhat more important example, Trevor often giggles in response to something another character says. It is probably his most frequent conversational response; yet if we ask what his laugh means, we are in the same position as when we ask what his reading means. We entertain various hypotheses without being able to settle on any definite interpretation. Is the giggling a sign of simplemindedness, nervousness, amusement, shyness, clumsiness, or what? It is really impossible to pin it down in this way; its meaning is slightly underdetermined.

It is difficult to know with any degree of certainty *anything* that Trevor and Ronnie are feeling and thinking in *The Kiss of Death*. Most of their behavior and expressions do not illustrate definite states of thought or feeling (and certainly not the states of focused purposefulness that motivate characters in the other sort of film). Expression becomes slightly mysterious – as much for the characters in the film as for the viewers of it.

Mystery in this sense is an entirely different thing from the mystifications of Hitchcock or the Coen brothers. The questions their work raises are ultimately answerable (and invariably *are* answered in their films' final scenes). The questions Leigh's work raises are not puzzles to be solved but indications of a density of experience that must be lived into. There is no hidden depth, no unexpressed desire, no secret identity or relationship to be ferreted out. Leigh is not concealing Trevor's and Ronnie's thoughts and feelings but doing something much more radical: he is liberating their characters from being organized around (and understood in terms of) fundamental thoughts and feelings. It is not that intentional depths are veiled (in the Charles Foster Kane or Norman Bates way), but that they don't exist. There is no secret intention or thought to be discovered. Trevor and Ronnie's lives are not organized around central, controlling motivational states. Even they couldn't tell us what they are doing most of the time.

Consciousness is dislodged as a unifying organizational center. Characters played by Meryl Streep and Jack Nicholson are almost always able to tell us what they are thinking or feeling or why they are saying or doing something at any moment. It is not only that Leigh's characters misunderstand their own motives and goals (though they repeatedly do); in most scenes they don't *have* any particular motives, plans, goals, or ideas behind what they are doing. They are not *trying* to be what they are or to do what they do. Their identities are not only beyond their abilities to control or change them, they are beyond their ability to be *aware* of them. Leigh rejects stylistic or verbal presentations of underpinning thoughts and feelings, not to make things hard on a viewer, but because he doesn't believe in the *existence* of underpinning thoughts and feelings as explanatory essences.

While stylistic effects or verbal statements of a character's goals and intentions offer resolving "deep" views, the forms of acting and performance Leigh presents leave the viewer studying fluxional behavioral surfaces without access to static intentional depths. The viewer cannot escape from the confusions of expression into the clarities of intention. There is no release from the turbulent, turbid, mixed messages of the actual, which is why we can never know figures like Sylvia, Pat, Mrs. Thornley, Trevor, or Ronnie the way we can know Norman Bates, Charles Foster Kane, or the Hal 9000 computer.

The emphasis on intentional states in Hollywood film reflects a unitary conception of personal identity – as if people were one thing through and through. Apparent vagaries of behavior and expression are harmonized by being traced back to an underpinning, resolving thought, emotion, or purpose. Leigh simply does not believe that our identities are unified in this way. In his view, a central unity does not necessarily underlie the heterogeneity of our experiences and expressions. Leigh's most interesting characters do not have fundamental, overarching "motives" or "goals." They do not have "plans." They do not have "visions" of what they "want" or "need." There is no realm of deep "feelings" or unexpressed "intentions" to discover. There is no substructure of essential "thoughts," "purposes," and "desires" that can clarify the genuine vagueness, open-endedness, and unformulatedness of their interactions. Leigh denies that life is organized (and comprehensible) in terms of essential states of consciousness.

The very point of Leigh's narratives is to create situations where game plans do not apply. They suspend the characters in an unresolved middle ground of feelings and relationships that maximize the possibilities of unpredictable, unbalanced, unprogrammatic interaction. Characters don't have purposes and goals; as in life, they discover what they are doing only after they have done it – if they ever understand their experiences at all. They just can't see very far – an ontological myopia which can be sad in a serious scene or tender, touching, and endearing in a comic one.

The Kiss of Death is organized around the interactions of fairly confused and unreflective young people who do little more than "hang out" together. Trevor and Ronnie, as friends, and Trevor and Linda and

Ronnie and Sandra, as potential lovers, feel their way toward or away from each other in an awkward, hesitant emotional dance in which there are frequent missteps, lots of stepping on toes, and no way of seeing beyond the present position. Given who they are and what they are doing, they really can't know what they want from each other (or whether they want anything at all). If Trevor and Ronnie knew what they were doing, what they wanted, where they were heading, or how to get there – if they had clear purposes and definite goals – they wouldn't be nearly as interesting as they are. They would become the kind of characters played by Charlie Sheen or John Travolta. *The Kiss of Death* would become *Saturday Night Fever.*[4]

In the sequence that culminates in Trevor and Linda's "kiss-of-death" scene, for example, it is impossible to know exactly what Trevor wants from the encounter or what his intentions are, not because his feelings and intentions are concealed from a viewer, but because they are concealed from him. To put it more accurately, Trevor doesn't have definite feelings and intentions. He doesn't know what he wants from the encounter. His entire life is lived as a state of not-knowing.

In fact, there are few surer signs of limitation in Leigh's work than for characters to think they *do* know who they are, what they want, where they are headed, or what they are doing. To assign a destination to desire is to stunt life and limit possibility. If you think you know what you are doing, you are almost always wrong. Pat and Peter have clear goals and purposes; Norman, Sylvia, and Hilda don't. Mr. Thornley knows what he wants; Naseem and Ann feel their way step by step. Keith lives by a game plan; Ray, Honkey, and Finger don't even know what they are doing while they are doing it. Barbara is on a mission; Colin isn't. It is evidence of Linda and Sandra's limitations in *The Kiss of Death* that they *do* have clear-cut purposes and goals (attempting to use sex to manipulate and control Trevor and Ronnie). All of *The Kiss of Death* is devoted to pointing out the limitations of their designs for living.

The dramatic structure of *The Kiss of Death* is indebted to Jean Renoir's *Boudu Saved from Drowning.*[5] In the Renoir film, Boudu, the natural man, invades the petit bourgeois family of Madame and Monsieur Lestingois and creatively disrupts its routines. He reveals emotional and psychological problems that were there all along but of which the bookseller and his wife were unaware. The most interesting aspect of Renoir's conception of Boudu is that he is both positive in some ways and negative in others. By violating rules and breaking up established routines, he salutarily forces characters (and viewers) to question cultural conventions and understandings even as his anarchic destructiveness in other respects affirms their value.

The superficial connection between Trevor and Boudu is that David Threlfall's shuffling gait, slouched posture, and tattered appearance more than slightly resemble those of Renoir's Michel Simon. The deeper connection is that Trevor is less a conventional protagonist who performs actions than someone who provokes reactions and forces other characters to reexamine their situations. He is a catalyst who destabilizes every situation he is injected into – forcing adjustments, reassessments, and reevaluations everywhere he goes. He is a rock other characters' ships crash into – specifically those of Linda and Sandra.

Although they are fairly different from each other, both girls have equally closed conceptions of their lives and experiences. They are know-it-alls: They think they know who they are and what the meaning of their lives is. They have formulaic notions of how they and their sexual partners should behave, and use sex as a form of power to force their understandings on others. At the point *The Kiss of Death* begins, Sandra has already succeeded with the meek Ronnie. Linda begins to go to work on Trevor, but he is a wild card whose responses neither girl can predict or control – which is, of course, why he threatens them.[6]

But *The Kiss of Death* is not merely about how Trevor forces others out of their routines and understandings but also about how he is also forced out of his own. A character's voyage of self-discovery via crisis and breakdown is one of the master plots of Leigh's work. His narrative goal is to undermine and destabilize *all* fixed positions – in this case, not just those of the girls but those of the boys as well. Everything is put in motion.

That defines the major difference between *Boudu Saved from Drowning* and *The Kiss of Death* and explains why Leigh's film is ultimately more complex than Renoir's. Trevor's destabilizations, unlike Boudu's, destabilize the destabilizer as well. Renoir's Boudu is not fully and complexly human. He is almost entirely a narrative device or contrivance. He exists to mess up others' lives and disrupt their illusions. Though he changes them, since he is not a full-fledged character he himself remains unchanged and unaffected by everything that happens. Leigh's "Boudu," on the other hand, is affected by others as complexly as they are affected by him. Sandra's nagging, Ronnie's feelings of romantic entrapment, Linda's sexual knowingness, and events connected with his job transform Trevor in the course of the film (though so subtly that many viewers miss it). At the start, he is a goofy teenaged boy not that different from a big puppy dog. By the end, he has become caring, self-reflective, capable of being hurt. He has reassessed who he is. He is growing up, though, as always in Leigh's work, it is done without moving him even an inch beyond the inherent limitations of his character.

One of the turning points in Trevor's transformation is his attendance at the death of a baby. Leigh makes it clear that he is accustomed to dealing with old people on his job. In parallel scenes he is shown to be quite relaxed – to the point of being tenderly facetious – in dealing with an old man and an elderly woman; but a newborn infant clearly reaches him in a deeper place. The boy with a baseball cap encounters something he can't clown around about. Yet at the same time, it is crucial to the effect that Leigh refuses to exaggerate or melodramatize the change. After tending to the baby's body, Trevor never says a word about what he is feeling or thinking – to Ronnie, Linda, his mother, or his boss. All the most attentive viewer notices is that, after returning home, he is slightly more subdued than usual, and that he goes up to his room and, for the first time, rather than reading, stares at the ceiling. The subtle, really quite understated contrasts with other scenes are the only things that indicate anything has changed. Viewers accustomed to Hollywood's more emphatic inflections will certainly not notice that anything at all has happened.

The subtlety of the effect is of the essence. Trevor himself doesn't understand what has happened to him or know what he is feeling. Since consciousness is never decoupled from character in Leigh's work – since understandings and recognitions don't come "pure" but are always entangled, constrained, and limited by preexisting forms of understanding and expression – there can be no visionary breakthroughs or epiphanies. There are no unmediated insights or visions (in the Isabel Archer in Rome mode) in Leigh's work. Unlike American film, visions are never merely visionary. Emotion is always mediated by personality. Insights are never absolute or unconditioned. Consciousness is never sprung free from character. Trevor doesn't leave his imperfect personality or flawed capacities of understanding behind just because he has an experience that profoundly affects him. Even after his experience with the baby, he still is the same slightly goofy, more than slightly irresponsible Trevor he was before. Consciousness is always socially contained.

If Trevor's behavior had changed more markedly in response to the death of the baby, if Leigh had allowed the transformation to be purer, more emphatic, or more absolute (inserting emotionally charged mood music or a kick-lighted close-up of Trevor's face, for example), or if David Threlfall had played the moment or its aftermath more broadly and emphatically, we would be in a Hollywood movie. Trevor would be Forrest Gump, *Rain Man's* Charlie Babbit, or *Shine's* David Helfgott. There would be a realm of unsullied feeling lurking just beneath the impure expressive surfaces of life, waiting to be liberated. In a word, Trevor wouldn't *really* be as flawed and inarticulate and confused – that is to say, as profoundly complex and moving as he is.

As we already saw in *Hard Labour's* shoe salesman scene, and as the clash between Trevor and the girls illustrates, one of Leigh's favorite dramatic devices is to pair figures with "fixed" forms of expression with others who are to some extent "free" and "unpredictable." Static identities are pitted against dynamic ones: Peter meets Sylvia; Mr. Thornley meets Mr. Philips; and, here, Linda meets Trevor.[7]

Many of the meetings between characters in Leigh's work compare the extent of ontological openness or closure in his characters. Trevor's confusion, disorganization, or irresponsibility disrupts Linda's rules for how the dating game is supposed to be played. Leigh's narrative project throughout this film is to assault Linda's systems of knowing, to break up her formulas for feeling, so that ultimately both she and Trevor can move through experience together in the same open-ended, unformulated way that Leigh wants the viewer to move through the film itself. (Though, like so many other figures in Leigh's work, Linda fights the process and never completely opens herself up.)

Leigh's ideal viewer follows the interactions between Trevor, Ronnie, Sandra, and Linda in the same way that Leigh's ideal characters are asked to participate in them – for the pleasure of following the twists and turns of a journey that has not been limited to a fixed emotional itinerary or foreseeable intellectual goal – for the excitement of going on a trip that has not been mapped out in advance. That is why watching these scenes is less like watching a race along a preestablished course with a predetermined destination (the American model) than a chess game in which the relationship of the figures shifts more or less with every move. The path through a scene is slightly unpredictable and mysterious. The viewer is left at least a little in the dark about the direction a relationship will take, what a character will say or do next, and, above all, what precisely a character "intends" or "means" by what he or she says or does at a particular moment.

Since Leigh's most interesting characters are not limited to pursuing a fixed goal or expressing a monotonic motive, they can break their own patterns and swerve away from their own past tones and styles. They can change their minds, their relative positions, their attitudes toward each other. That, in fact, is one of the most exhilarating aspects of Leigh's scenes. They not only keep the viewer unusually alert but suggest that experience is forever unfinished. The relationship of characters seems exceptionally fluid, free, and alive. Leigh's world is an open-ended one in which nothing is predetermined. It is one in which new and surprising possibilities continuously emerge. In this respect, and contra the appreciators of his "bleakness" and "despair," Leigh's vision is stunningly optimistic, no matter how hard the economic and social conditions of the characters or how unidealized the presentation may be.[8]

Most mainstream films (especially "artistic" ones) rely on visionary stylistics of one sort or another to communicate meaning. Framing, camera positioning, lighting, sound, and editing effects summarize abstract, imaginative meanings about characters and their situations. Leigh (at least up until the time of Naked) simply never employs such effects. The result is a different kind of meaning in his work. The meanings in works employing visionary stylistics are abstract and imaginative; those in Leigh's films are practical and worldly. Those in visionary works are mental and disembodied; Leigh's are social and physical.

Beyond that, as I discussed in the Stylistic Introduction, a Leigh character is not defined in terms of disembodied, unexpressed mental states and purposes. Experience is not anchored in subjectivity. It is not something that takes place inside you. It involves the outsides of life. Leigh's figures don't abstractly think or feel or intend something, but express themselves through practical, worldly forms of social, verbal, and bodily interaction.

The result for both a character in a Leigh film and a viewer of it is an entirely different relation to the world than the other kind of film elicits. The generalized intentions and purposes of the mainstream character endure over time. A volitional self is more or less unchanging. A mental identity is fairly stable and constant. States of subjectivity are relatively static. The performed self of Leigh's figures is the opposite. It is shifting and fluxional in the extreme. It keeps changing. The world of ideas, goals, and intentions stands still; the world of specific, temporally shifting interactions is dynamic and volatile. Leigh's truths are spatially and temporally on the move. Beyond that, they are physically grounded and sensorily embodied. Insofar as they are not abstract but embedded in practical expressions, they require the viewer to maintain contact with the shifting perceptual surfaces of life. These expressions are in motion and can only be understood by a viewer willing to put himself in motion to keep up with them. The viewer must be much more alert and energetic as he picks his way, beat by beat, though the experiential density of a shifting, perceptually embedded experience.

To understand these experiences, as to understand a great jazz performance, is not to leave the perceptual events behind in order to arrive at a final understanding outside of them, but to plunge *into* the sensory flow, immersing ourselves in its details, synchronizing our rhythms with it. Though every tendency of the Platonic intellectual tradition goes against it, Leigh's work argues that we must learn to think and know *in* space and time, not outside them.

Many sequences in *The Kiss of Death* illustrate the point, but I shall mention only two. The scene early in the film in which Sandra, Ronnie, and Trevor go to a pub and Trevor meets Linda takes the viewer on a roller-coaster ride of shifting moods, positions, and relationships that resists summary precisely because the meanings won't stand still. An even more virtuosic example is the sequence later on that culminates with Linda and Trevor's "kiss-of-death" scene. Leigh keeps the moods and meanings in motion throughout the entire five- or six-minute interaction. The sequence begins with Trevor showing up at Linda's front door after a romantic spat. Linda is still mad and doesn't want to let him in, but it is typical of Leigh's desire to keep things up in the air that a series of tonal flutters and hesitations in her voice indicate that, even though the physical door is blocking his progress, the emotional door to her heart is at least a little open. Linda and Trevor verbally joust with each other until, only a minute or two later, the tone and feeling of the scene changes completely when a hysterical neighbor requires their aid. Her mother has fainted going up the steps. The scene that follows upstairs in the other apartment (in which Trevor interacts with the elderly woman) shimmers with new tones and feelings. Trevor displays aspects of his personality neither Linda nor we have seen before: gentleness, tenderness, concern for the elderly woman's welfare, and a shy playfulness and wit that puts her at ease. (Linda is both resentful and admiring of his aplomb.) Only four or five minutes after the standoff on Linda's front stoop, Leigh has brought us almost full circle tonally – from gravity and chilliness to comedy and warmth. The scene has created a narrative caesura making the tonal shift of Linda's invitation of Trevor into her house possible.

Michael Coveney has summarized the "kiss-of-death" scene that ensues in Linda's living room as follows: "The more predatory Linda becomes, the more laughable Trevor finds the situation;"[9] but it is precisely such formulaic positions (and formulas for understanding) that both Leigh and his characters avoid. Linda may seem sexually "predatory" at moments, but she is also emotionally needy and touchingly vulnerable at others, and tender and solicitous at still others. Trevor may be amused by Linda's forwardness in some respects, but his laughter may just as plausibly be evidence of confusion, embarrassment, shyness, and discomfort. The subjunctive is necessary not only because a viewer doesn't know exactly how Trevor feels but because Trevor himself does not know. Even to say that Trevor or Linda is ambivalent or uncertain would be verbally to resolve a state of affairs that is far more complex and more fluxional than words like *uncertainty* or *ambivalence* normally connote.[10]

The fluxionality is everything. Almost all of Leigh's major scenes have the same step-by-step quality as the "kiss-of-death" scene. To remember any of the great moments in Leigh's work is not to recall a static effect (a striking frame composition, lighting effect, or musical orchestration, as in *2001*, *Citizen Kane*, *Psycho*, or *Manhattan*) but a sequence of temporal events. Over and over again in his work, Leigh presents two or more figures feeling their way toward, away from, and back toward each other in time. Even confining oneself to the scenes I have already discussed in the two previous films, one has only to remember the guitar party scene, the purse scene, or Peter and Sylvia's "kissing" scene in *Bleak Moments*, or the interactions between Mr. Thornley and the salesman and his boss, and between Ann and Naseem in *Hard Labour* to appreciate the process-orientation of Leigh's vision of life. Time cannot be factored out of the experience. The time these scenes take *is* the experience of them. They exist only *in time*, and are nothing out of it.[11]

The deeper point about time and further difference between Leigh's work and mainstream film is that his temporality is not teleological. It is not about getting anywhere. It's the difference between the way time functions in *Casablanca* and the way it functions in *Tokyo Story* – the difference between time as a deadline, and time as duration. *Casablanca*, *Psycho*, *Citizen Kane*, and *2001* set deadlines for accomplishing things or conduct races in which the characters compete to get to the finish line first. Leigh's characters and viewers, like Ozu's, do not move through their experiences to get out of them, to arrive at a point of clarification and resolution beyond them. There are no visionary insights, no flashes of awareness, no position attainable outside of these movements (or subsequent to them). One simply lives through a series of temporal events. As in Ozu's work, which imagines a sequence of generational adjustments, an unending chain of substitutions in which one character's problems are replaced by another's without any particular end point, one event simply follows another in Leigh. There is nowhere to get, no end to the process, no release from time.[12]

Leigh's scenes are not reducible to their end points. A viewer doesn't watch them to find out what will finally happen or where the characters will end up, but to participate in a course of events. (As is illustrated by the "kiss-of-death" scene, the actual endings of most of Leigh's scenes are generally pretty anticlimactic. Nothing much really "happens" in the plot sense of the concept. Characters don't get anywhere.) As Pat and Peter maneuver around each other in the "kissing" scene, Mr. Thornley interacts with the salesman or his boss, or Ann and Naseem dance their little dance of courtship in the cab stand, none of these moments is about its outcome. Sylvia and Peter's "kissing" scene in particular – like Trevor and Linda's "kissing" scene – is less about whether the kiss does or does not occur than the parries and thrusts, moves and countermoves, emotional openings and closings, approaches and withdrawals that take place during the course of it. Both scenes are among the most thrilling sequences in all of cinema, but the thrill is not related to where events end up, but to the excitement of the journey. We don't watch to see where someone gets, but how things go.

Temporal experience is employed in mainstream film to suggest the possibility of a release from temporality. Hitchcock is only the most obvious illustration of a filmmaker whose temporal meanings always hold out the promise of a final atemporal perspective. The viewer is spoon-fed bits and pieces of information about Norman Bates, the neighbor across the courtyard, or Madeline/Judy, in order ultimately to attain a final view that leaves the partial views behind. Little by little becomes all; provisional is replaced by final; temporal knowing gives way to atemporal truth. One might, in fact, argue that the only reason viewers are willing to suffer through the excruciations of Hitchcock's deliberately tantalizing and calculatedly torturous temporal presentations is because of their confidence that they will ultimately be released from the frustrating limitations of temporal understanding. Leigh goes in the other direction. His temporal presentation denies release from temporality. Viewers of the films are asked to do the same thing as the characters: endlessly to renegotiate understandings, pursue new possibilities, and adjust their responses without end.

The ways of knowing employed in Leigh's work are inherently slower and more provisional than those in the other kind of film. It is in the nature of performed meanings that they emerge more gradually than stylistically indicated ones. A lighting effect, musical orchestration, or tendentious camera angle can tell us what a character is feeling clearly and definitively, once and for all, whereas the way he walks or talks does not necessarily declare such a clear or final meaning. Social and physical expressions unfold slowly and tentatively. Leigh's viewer is asked to stay in the flow of shifting social interactions; there is no position outside it.

The focus on abstract, absolute, unperformed states of consciousness in the mainstream film contributes to the detemporalizing of the experience. In allowing the viewer to make the move from the fluxionality and uncertainty of expressive surfaces to the clarity and stability of intentional depths, the mainstream film allows him to enter into a slightly relaxed relationship with phenomenal reality – the temporal and spatial flow of what he sees and hears on screen. He is slightly released from having to pay attention to the shifting perceptual surfaces of life. Once he has figured out how a character feels or thinks in a particular scene, he doesn't have to watch the scene all that carefully. He can more or less coast until there is an indication of a new internal state. The subjectivization of experience encourages the viewer to rise above the perceptual mutability and clutter of phenomenal experience and to take an abstract, atemporal view of events.

Leigh, in contrast, asks the viewer to learn to live *in* time. He must become present-minded, negotiating second-by-second courses of events. Viewers must be willing to be put on the edge of their seats, noticing, listening, pondering, wondering, speculating, and responding – watching for flickers of emotions in faces and the ebbs and flows of interaction, listening to vocal flutters, following the beat-by-beat evolution of shifting relationships – *without* the prospect of a final release. His work renews the claims of the actual. It asks us to embrace the world in all of its mess and mutability.

Both viewers and characters are required to accept this vision of life. There is no goal to attain, no problem to solve, no riddle to answer. There is only living to be done, experience to be undergone. Leigh tells us that there can be no final perspective – no view that is not piecemeal, imperfect, and incomplete. There is no final *Kane*-like visionary clarification to be attained by the viewer, no resolving *Casablanca*-like epiphany or insight for the characters at the end of *The Kiss of Death*. Trevor, Ronnie, Linda, and Sandra merely affect each other a little – and then go on.[13] Our inveterate cultural quest for product must give way to an appreciation of process. Knowledge (substantive) gives way to knowing (participle). Or, to put it more precisely, a static state of "knowing" is replaced by a dynamic process of "experiencing." The truths in these films do not stand still like the classic concept of knowledge but flow like experience. The quest for the essences of epistemology must give way to a willingness to function within the flowing movements of history.

5

Defeating Systems of Knowing:
Nuts in May

> There is a struggle, an anxiety within me, between the anarchist – the public exploder or piss-taker – and the slob.
>
> – Mike Leigh

The customary comparison of Mike Leigh with Robert Altman on the ground of their common satiric intent represents a fundamental misunderstanding of Leigh's work. *Nuts in May* is not really a send-up of Birkenstock vegetarians, and if it were it would be a much less important and disturbing film than it is. The characters' problems would be so far from the experience of the average viewer that the movie would be trivial. Most of us are not tree-huggers or folksingers. *We* don't drink raw milk or chew our food seventy-three times. If that's what the film were about, Keith and Candice-Marie could be written off as kooks, and *Nuts in May* would be little more than a derisive jeer at the weirdness of a few "nuts" (as the title somewhat misleadingly puts it).

Leigh is not interested in mocking someone else but in showing us things about ourselves. As he has often insisted, there is no "them" in his work. Everywhere we look, we are meant to see ourselves. His hell is never reserved for other people. That is what makes his films so unsettling. We are supposed to take them personally. If we don't, we're not really paying attention.[1]

Keith and Candice-Marie's dietary and behavioral eccentricities are symptoms of a state of imaginative derangement that, in Leigh's view, runs throughout society. They have become cut off from their own experience by culturally received ideas and emotions. For this relisher of sensory, physical, and behavioral particularities, there could be no greater heresy than basing your identity and emotions on abstractions.

80

To do so is to lose touch with reality and, in effect, make yourself unreal. Characters like Keith and Candice-Marie have gone insane in a far more insidious and dangerous way than any of Hitchcock's or John Carpenter's protagonists. The form of insanity they represent is something he dramatizes in film after film.

I have already mentioned the importance of Jean Renoir's *Boudu Saved from Drowning* to Leigh, and, like Lestingois and Anne-Marie, Keith and Candice-Marie have allowed reality to be so thoroughly transformed by thought (literary, in the case of Lestingois; scientific, in the case of Keith; sentimental, in the case of the two Maries) that actual contact with experience has become unthinkable. When the world is taken up into the mind to this extent, reality is derealized beyond recognition. Lestingois imagines nature to be a realm of pastoral beauty, and Keith and Candice-Marie, respectively, transform country life into a Mr. Science experiment and a child's fairy story. For Keith, eating is not a sensory experience but a series of calculations involving nutrition, calories, and chews; exercise not a spontaneous expression of energy but a page from the *Royal Canadian Handbook*; a storm or a body of water not a lived experience but a stream of statistics; and a hike a pedometer reading and a series of "views" in a guidebook. In Candice-Marie's conception of them, gypsies, farmers, and cottages are romanticized beyond any recognizable connection with the way things actually are. The past is romanticized as much as the present: The lords and ladies she conjures up in the Corf Castle scenes never existed outside of the pages of a novel. In this universe, no matter where you pitch your tent, you can't get outside of your own head. Nature has been replaced by culture. Thinking not only distorts but displaces experiencing.

Leigh drives home the fraudulence of Keith and Candice-Marie's relationship to each other and the world through a series of ironic juxtapositions (some obvious, others more subtle) in which their idealized understandings come smashing up against radically unidealized views. The final five minutes of the film illustrate the stereo effect. While Keith and Candice-Marie treat the farmer whose land they are camping on and his female helper as a romantic rustic and milkmaid, Leigh allows the viewer to eavesdrop on a salacious conversation between them. Just after Keith and Candice-Marie have enthused about the wonder of natural sights, sounds, and occupations, Leigh cuts to the thoroughly unbucolic sights and sounds of the farm's filthy cooped chickens and mechanical milking machine.

The concluding sequence tops everything. While Candice-Marie unfurls a scarf in the wind, plays her guitar, and sings about the splendors of nature, Keith obeys the call of nature in another sense – with great difficulty picking his way though a barbed-wire fence, up a stony hillside, through a dense undergrowth of brambles and thistles, and past a threatening sow, searching for a place to relieve himself. The strand of toilet paper he leaves streaming in the wind after gingerly negotiating the barbed-wire fence brilliantly and corrosively contrasts with a previous shot of Candice-Marie's streaming silk banner.

Renoir uses Boudu, and Leigh uses Honkey, Finger, and Ray to attempt to force Keith and Candice-Marie to open their eyes to the most unruly, unromantic part of nature of all – human nature; but Leigh understands as well as Renoir did that humankind cannot take very much reality, and that, for someone in love with fictions, fictions will never ultimately be displaced, no matter how much they clash with truth.

The ultimate fictions that enthrall Keith and Candice-Marie are ideas not about the world but about themselves. Their intellectualized relationship to nature is evidence of an even more disturbing intellectualized relationship to their own lives and experiences (a subject Leigh will explore further in *Abigail's Party* and *Who's Who*). In their resistance to processed food, Keith and Candice-Marie have unconsciously swallowed all manner of processed thinking, canned feeling, and shrink-wrapped selfhood. In this orgy of intellectual recycling, everything has been precooked and predigested. Their identities are as received, their emotions as dictated by fashion, and their "views" (in both the perceptual and intellectual senses) as secondhand as the opinions in the travel guides they slavishly follow. In their quest for culturally certified "naturalness," they have become completely artificial. Leigh wants us to see that, if there is even a shade of "naturalness" in his movie, it resides in figures like Honkey and Finger, not Keith and Candice-Marie or the well-trodden paths they hike.

All of Leigh's work explores problems of selfhood and identity, and the major problem with taking your feelings and opinions from outside yourself, in his view, is that you lose track of who you really are. Keith thinks he is a paragon of reasonableness, when actually he is an imaginative terrorist. Candice-Marie thinks she is a flower child devotee of peace and love even as she unceasingly nags and bullies Keith about not being loving enough.

The way we can detect the hollowness of Keith and Candice-Marie's role playing is not only through the contradictions between what they say and do, and the ironic discrepancy between what they say they see and what Leigh shows us (as on the pig farm), but through the unimaginativeness, inflexibility, and unresponsiveness of their performances. In Leigh's view, when you play a part that is emotionally and intellectually inauthentic, the result will always be a rigid or mechanical performance. A false role can never be truly spontaneous, free, or responsive.

In the implicit dramatic metaphor that informs most of Leigh's work, Keith is a bad actor or director who mechanically adheres to a preestablished script and is terrified of any departure from it. This is the significance of his reliance on texts of various sorts (instructions on putting up his tent, notebooks, maps, tour itineraries and schedules, a numbered guidebook, and the campground regulations he quotes) for virtually everything he says and does. Keith is unable to go "off-book," to improvise creatively on the margins of a text, or to allow the least bit of departure from the "script." He tyrannizes over everyone around him, insisting on adherence to (and punishing departures from) his predetermined "scripts" for experience. That is the point of a climactic scene late in the film, when Keith and Candice-Marie invite Ray to their campsite to have tea. Keith functions like a bad movie director, who dictates the most minute details of Ray's and Candice-Marie's blocking (where they should stand for the photograph), line readings (in the song), and feelings about and interpretation of their roles (in the talk about nutrition).

For a filmmaker so clearly committed to the value of expressive individuality and spontaneity, the result of attempting to pre-script and overdirect human interaction is not only expressive boredom but the erasure of fundamental individual differences. While Leigh's cinematic style respects individual structures of feeling and points of view, Keith's personal style denies the existence of any point of view other than his own. He cuts everyone and every interaction to fit the Procrustean bed of his own interests, stage-managing all conversations and directing all interactions to conform to his own interests. He is Leigh's anti-matter, negative body double – the paradigmatic Hitchcockian artist who makes life too purposeful, too meaningful, too orderly – and in doing so takes the spontaneity, surprise, and fun out of experience – the play out of play.[2]

The point is made editorially by Leigh's alternations between the relentless seriousness and purposefulness of Keith and Candice-Marie's interactions and the zany, purposeless interactions that Ray, Honkey, and Finger engage in. Whatever we may think about the latter group's lapses in taste and judgment, in the scenes in the campground, the tavern, and the tent, Ray, Honkey, and Finger interact in genuinely independent, idiosyncratic, and creative ways. While Keith and Candice-Marie's activities and conversations are as predictable as their bedtime ceremony of "kissing Prudence goodnight" or their hikes and drives "by the numbers," there is no predefined path (or point) to any of Honkey's, Finger's, and Ray's crazy, unpredictable interactions. While Keith and Candice-Marie enslave themselves to systems and routines, Honkey and Finger embody energies that emphatically defy systematization. They are Boudus, and the Boudu in Leigh is attracted to their unregimented, madcap expressions. (It is typical of Leigh to locate vitality in the silliness and scatology of figures at the very bottom of the social hierarchy.)

Although Leigh's work is Renoirian in its love of eccentricity and respect for individual differences, it differs from Renoir's in its strongly ethical take on the individual's social responsibilities and the moral judgments it makes on this basis. While the Frenchman (true to his culture) almost completely suspends moral judgment and allows his characters to "have their reasons," the Brit (true to the culture of Jane Austen, Charles Dickens, and George Eliot) judges his figures in terms of their ability (or inability) to interact sensitively and responsively. If Peter, Mr. Thornley, Mrs. Stone, Keith, and Candice-Marie were characters in *The Rules of the Game*, they would be treated as harmless eccentrics; in *Bleak Moments, Hard Labour*, and *Nuts in May*, they are meant to be judged for their ethical failures – firmly and negatively.

Nuts in May introduces a new element into this process of judging the characters that distinguishes Leigh's later work from his earlier. The films from *Nuts in May* on all have what might be called a "justice structure." Characters who are socially inadequate or insensitive are made to pay a narrative price for their shortcomings. They are punished for their deficiencies – generally near the ends of their films.

To avoid misunderstanding, however, one must immediately add that Leigh's sense of "justice" and "punishment" differs from the children's-book apportionment of prizes and penalties in which Hollywood films specialize. While movies like *Wall Street* and *Fatal Attraction* mete out justice in material ways (by granting or denying characters power, financial success, worldly accomplishment, or a sexual partner), the consequences of being good or bad in Leigh's work are almost entirely internal, spiritual, and emotional. Characters are punished by undergoing a breakdown or simply by suffering due to an inherently contradictory or deluded position.[3] As Henry James said of the Prince in *The Golden Bowl*, to be in a false position is its own punishment. No external, added retribution or worldly retaliation is necessary. The universe trips up our plans; society resists our designs; our souls punish us. Selfish or inconsiderate relationships with others contain the seeds of the character's own undoing. Stupidity and callowness create their own emotional penalties. We burn in hells of our own making.

The organization of Leigh's narratives from this point on in his career clearly reflects this justice structure. What you are and how you deal with others *is* your punishment (or reward). Keith's punishment is simply having to deal with the problems he himself creates. If he is obsessed with campsite silence, he will have to deal with noise. If he is convinced that nature is pure and beautiful, he will have to deal with its ugliness. If he is devoted to the enforcement of "laws," he himself will suffer under the enforcement of them (as the enjambment of the "laws of the country code" scene with the scene with the policeman demonstrates).

The plate tectonics of Leigh's method are to take a character with faults and stress him along his fault lines. Leigh will bring a flawed character into contact with precisely those figures who most reveal his weaknesses. Keith the planner, organizer, and manager is confronted with Ray, Honkey, and Finger, whose expressions and behavior defy being organized along any of the lines he has in mind. In *Who's Who* and *Abigail's Party*, Nigel and Beverly, a host and hostess whose fondest dream is to preside effortlessly over the ideal party, undergo a Walpurgisnacht in which everything that can go wrong does.

Being stressed in this way is not necessarily a bad thing; for it is to be put in a position to see life truly at last. The misunderstandings, arguments, explosions, and implosions near the ends of *The Kiss of Death, Nuts in May, Abigail's Party, Who's Who, Grown-ups, Home Sweet Home, Meantime, High Hopes, Life Is Sweet, Naked,* and *Secrets and Lies* represent opportunities for characters to face up to their own internal contradictions and denials. To be broken down is, at least potentially, to be forced to break free from limiting systems of understanding. For Pat, Trevor, Keith, Nigel, Gloria, Christine, June, Hazel, Barbara, Valerie, and Nicola to break down is at least to recognize that they have a problem. The characters in Leigh's work who show themselves incapable of breaking down, who maintain their routines against all odds, clinging to their old understandings with a death grip – figures like Peter, Mr. Thornley, Mrs. Stone, Beverly, Ralph, Stan, Christine, Rupert, Laetitia, Johnny, the twenty-third earl of Lete (in *A Sense of History*), and almost everyone in *Who's Who* – are the truly lost souls. As in Greek tragedy, the ends of many of Leigh's films offer potentially transformative moments of *anagnorisis* – moments of potentially revisionary insight in which a character is given the opportunity to reevaluate everything he or she knows and believes up to that point.

But the possibility almost always remains only a possibility. Keith's breakdown does not lead to a breakthrough. As the remainder of *Nuts in May* demonstrates, he reverts to pattern almost immediately. That, I take it, is the point of the final scene on the pig farm, in which we see that, even after all the indignities Keith and Candice-Marie have been forced to suffer, they have apparently learned nothing.

In this respect, they are not that different from most of Leigh's other principals. In *Bleak Moments*, Peter not only never repents of any of what he lives through, he apparently never realizes there is anything to repent. In *Hard Labour*, Mr. Thornley and Mrs. Stone learn nothing during the entire film. In *Abigail's Party*, Beverly apparently doesn't learn anything even when her husband drops down dead at her feet.

Although it can seem depressing to a viewer accustomed to Hollywood's relentlessly upbeat endings, the failure of these figures to learn or grow does not represent despair about human nature on Leigh's part, the cynicism of which he is sometimes accused. It simply reflects a different understanding of the relationship of consciousness and character from that in American film. The reason the characters played by Bruce Willis, John Travolta, or Harrison Ford can be so malleable is that their consciousnesses are separate from their personalities. Their hearts, souls, and minds are free and unconstrained. The result is figures who can spiritually turn on a dime, who can change simply by deciding to or by having a new experience.

The deeper way to explain the difference between Leigh's work and mainstream American film in this regard would be to say that Leigh does not believe in the existence of consciousness (at least as American films define it). Americans (à la Isabel Archer) are committed in advance to the existence of a realm of freedom beyond psychological contingency and social constraint, and consciousness (by whatever name we call it: thought, emotion, imagination, vision, conscience, awareness, insight) is the concept they have invented to justify their belief. "Consciousness" is simply the name they give to the fundamental freedom they imagine to underpin life. It signifies a fluid, free-floating, unconditioned place free from social control or historical limitations.

Leigh doesn't accept that such a free and unconditioned place can exist. In his work, nothing can ever float free of social, personal, or historical contingencies in this way. Consciousness is not and cannot be decoupled from character – which is to say we might as well stop talking about it as if it were separable from what a character is, or (which is the same thing) as if it were able to change what the character is. What you are is what you are; there is nothing else, no part of you outside of what you are. There is no free place within you; no external fulcrum on which to place a mental lever that can be used to affect what you are separate from what you already are. Everything about you is equally contingent. There is and can be no absolute, unconditioned realm of free thought, emotion, or awareness. Leigh's leopards cannot change their spots by realizing, seeing, feeling something, because a character's thoughts, feelings, insights, and visions are as constrained as the rest of his identity. Your consciousness is anchored in the same enduring structures of personality as your manners, your tone of voice, or your behavior – and is as resistant to change.

In Leigh's view, then, to have characters like Keith and Candice-Marie reform or even come to understand their problems would be to tell a fundamental lie about what they are. It would be to suggest that characters can, in effect, at some point leave their characters behind; that they can get outside of their own personal points of view to embrace an impersonal, objective, "correct" one. In his work, they can't and don't. That is why, even when the falsity of a character's position is revealed to a viewer, it is still almost never revealed to the character himself. To be as imperceptive and trapped in one's own way of understanding as Peter, Mrs. Stone, Mr. Thornley, Keith, or Beverly show themselves to be is by definition to be incapable of learning something completely at odds with that way of understanding.

The denial of catharsis in Leigh's work is related to his displacement of his drama outside the consciousness of his main characters. As different as they are from one another, American movies like *Psycho, Casablanca, A Place in the Sun,* and *On the Waterfront* all put individual consciousness at the center of the work. America is still living out the legacy of Romanticism, and these works are fundamentally Wordsworthian in their method. They dramatize the suffering, growth, and maturation of an individual's consciousness. But Leigh organizes his narratives around doing rather than knowing and, in fact, argues that life's doings can be entirely separate from acts of knowing. We desperately *want* Peter, Keith, Beverly, the twenty-third earl of Lete, and many other Leigh characters to *know* what they are *doing*, but that linkage is exactly what Leigh (gleefully and diabolically) denies us.

The withholding of insight dovetails with a larger narrative project in which Leigh is engaged. If characters were transformed (or, conversely, if they were more decisively or materially punished) at the ends of the films – in this case, if Keith either came to see the error of his ways or were thrown off the campsite or arrested by the policeman he meets – the viewer would be let off the hook. If figures like Peter, Mr. Thornley, Mrs. Stone, Keith, Candice-Marie, or Beverly were either redeemed or punished, the viewer could sit back, relax, feel good about the outcome (if it were insight), or feel superior or laugh at the character (if punishment were the result). Justice would have been done. The viewer's sense of propriety would be satisfied. The package would be tied up with a bow on top. That is exactly what Leigh doesn't want to happen. The point is to prevent a movie-of-the-week emotional release, resolution, or clarification. If Keith were granted a final insight, realized what was wrong with himself, repented his ways, or were decisively punished, the tension the entire preceding film worked to create would be dissipated. The threat would go out of the work.[4]

Leigh's denial of catharsis or emotional resolution is designed to leave the viewer in an unresolved, uneasy emotional state – a place of discomfort and irresolution. The point is to force him into a personal, active relationship with the material, necessitated because there is unfinished emotional work to perform. He must work through it, even after the film is over, grappling with it emotionally. The point is to put the viewer in the most emotionally and intellectually challenging position possible.

A related aspect of Leigh's method is his denial of the opportunity to expand emotionally within a scene. Whereas most mainstream filmmakers strive for an emotional enlargement at climactic moments, Leigh works against it. For example, in Keith's fight with Finger, Leigh deliberately prevents the viewer from becoming too swept up in the tortured intensity of the scene by making it comic at points. The tone won't build in any one direction. In fact, it is frequently difficult for a viewer to know what he should feel (in this case whether he should laugh or wince) at a particular moment.

Beyond the tonal multivalence (which runs throughout his work), Leigh also refuses to let any one character's emotions dominate. Such focusing in on a figure's (or group of related figures') emotional states is a standard part of the emotional intensifications of scenes in mainstream film. One or another character would be allowed to be the "star" of the scene, and his or her feelings would be focused on. But Leigh deliberately keeps changing the view, forcing a viewer to recognize that there are other characters with entirely different points of view that must be taken into account. There is almost always more than one thing going on and more than one way to feel about it.[5]

Another way Leigh challenges the viewer is by creating scenes, characters, and events that resist easy interpretation. American movies generally allow a clear moral mapping of characters and situations. Characters are divided into opposing camps or teams, and the actions of figures in the two groups are able to be glossed as good or bad. Leigh will not simplify things by organizing his narratives in such ways. The viewer cannot simply take one character's side or strap himself into one character's "correct" interpretive perspective and go with it. There is almost never a clear-cut right or wrong, a hero or a villain, in his work. Everyone is doing his or her best yet is also a little compromised or imperfect. Events similarly frustrate simple judgments. Actions are neither black nor white. Everything and everyone is somewhere in the middle, gray and in-between. Personalities and situations are pitched at a point where opposite things can *both* be true. In *Meantime*, Barbara is both kind *and* patronizing, and Mark is both caring *and* selfish. In *Naked*, Johnny is both charming *and* obnoxious, smart *and* daft, kind *and* cruel. In *Abigail's Party*, Beverly is both well-meaning *and* insensitive.

Unlike Altman, Leigh won't make his characters *entirely* foolish, and even if a viewer may eventually judge them to be so, it is impossible to arrive at this conclusion as early in the narrative as Altman would allow it. Though we may eventually arrive at a negative judgment of Keith and Candice-Marie, it is easy to misremember how gradually and tentatively we come to it. In the scenes at the start of the film in which Keith records his expenses in a ledger book, expresses objections to paying for the campsite in advance, or insists on scrupulously following the steps for pitching the tent, he may seem eccentric, but Leigh takes care not to make him look completely ridiculous.[6] In the scenes that follow, many of Keith and Candice-Marie's ideas about healthy living are just plausible enough to make us a little uncertain how to feel about them.

That is what is misleading even about my own previous characterization of Keith. The actual viewing experience of *Nuts in May* is not nearly as clear as a retrospective understanding of it. Though we may have a fairly negative impression of Keith by the end of the film, for most of the first hour Leigh pitches scenes at an in-between point that makes it hard to judge him harshly.

In the scene in which Keith and Candice-Marie have their first squabble with Ray about his radio, for example, Leigh prevents us from locking into a simple reading of Keith as being wrong and Ray right. He prevents us from writing off Keith as a crank or spoilsport by setting up the situation so as to make Keith's request not entirely unreasonable: Ray *is* playing his radio extremely loud; he *is* sitting far away from it in a tree (making Ray seem somewhat nutty); he admits he is not really listening to it; the radio *is* tuned to the most inane AM station imaginable; and Ray doesn't turn it down even a little as a token gesture of conciliation when he goes back to his tent. Though we may not have a lot of affection for Keith and Candice-Marie, given the circumstances, we cannot dismiss them as kooks either. (If there is a crank in the film, at this point it looks like Ray, not Keith.)

But Leigh makes it just as hard to lock into a reading that Keith is right and Ray is wrong by orchestrating subsequent events to change our view. A few minutes after he has Keith politely ask Ray to turn his radio down, Leigh has him be gratuitously rude to Ray (after Keith sees Candice-Marie talking with him in his tent). But lest we then reverse our conclusion and write Keith off as a boor, our judgment of him is adjusted upward a few minutes later when he apologizes to Ray. And so it goes. At every moment we are about to pigeonhole Keith (or Candice-Marie) the view is slightly adjusted. The film proceeds by continuous course corrections that keep forcing viewers to change their minds. Our emotions constantly shift. The point is to prevent easy readings and to delay final readings. Understanding is gradual and evolutionary. It is impossible for the viewer to relax into any one formulaic response and coast with it. There is nothing to do but stay open and engaged.[7]

Another way in which Leigh makes things hard on a viewer is by providing neither a viewer-surrogate "reactive" character nor an "authoritative" directorial point of view to guide interpretation. In a Hollywood movie, when in doubt a viewer can get his bearings by consulting either the feelings and attitudes of one of the principal characters or the style of the film (the use of music, lighting, framing, etc.). The perspectives of the viewer, the director, and the important characters (to the extent that they are intelligent and virtuous) almost always agree about the "correct" view or reading of a scene. In *Psycho*, Hitchcock's and the viewer's understanding of Norman Bates is more or less identical to Arbogast's, Ralph's, and Lila's. As the advertising slogan goes: When they talk, we listen. The fact that Norman's understanding of himself differs from the understandings of the viewer, the director, and the other important characters is, in fact, proof of his insanity. The fact that Marion Crane does not understand Norman in the "right" way is the reason she is at a disadvantage in dealing with him.

There is no comparable authoritative, "right" way to understand

Candice-Marie, Keith, and Ray in their sing-along – the need to get others to validate who you are

things in Leigh's work. He uses neither cinematic styles nor the views of other characters to provide dependable glosses on characters and situations; other characters' views have no more authority than our own independent conclusions. While the Hollywood film continuously guides the viewer and reassures him that his judgments are correct, Leigh lets him draw his own conclusions with very little help or reassurance. He is on his own. There is no god (or godlike view) to turn to in moments of doubt.

To put it in other terms, Leigh's work does not conflate viewpoints; the understandings of various characters are not the same and do not cumulate in a single inclusive view. In fact, there are likely to be as many different understandings of a figure or a situation in a Leigh scene as there are characters in it. In the campfire scene in *Nuts in May*, for example, Keith thinks he is enforcing the "country code"; Finger and Honkey think he is crazy; Candice-Marie is afraid for his welfare; and the viewer has a view slightly different from any of theirs (at the start of the argument, certainly a more comic view). Minds do not blend. Perspectives do not merge. On the contrary, as this scene raucously demonstrates, they clash. Characters embody a variety of unique, unassimilated perspectives. They do not see things in the same way, and the viewer cannot see things through their eyes, let alone attain a perspective that includes or subsumes the various individual views. In contrast to a thriller or mystery film, there is no single interpretative truth that everyone, character and viewer, can agree on; there are only truths – unassimilable, unmerged, individual perspectives.

Keith's argument with Honkey and Finger illustrates how Leigh makes it difficult for a viewer to take sides. Even if we may tend to agree with Honkey and Finger in feeling that Keith is out of line in giving them orders, Leigh makes siding with them difficult by presenting them negatively. If they had more class or style, if they were really innocent of wrongdoing, if they were sensitive and intelligent, it would be easy to take their side. But Leigh makes them genuinely hard to like. They *do* disturb other campers with their noise; they *aren't* very smart (or even very funny); they *are* boorish; their choice of camping food and attire (note Leigh's repeated tight-shots of Honkey's shoes) *is* ridiculous; and Finger's decision to light an open fire *is* dangerous. Do we really want to find ourselves agreeing with *them*, taking *their* side in the argument? The point is that Leigh does everything in his power to prevent the face-off between the two couples from being turned into the "innocent" lower-class campers versus the Yuppie "meanies."[8]

Control of tone is a large part of the process of complicating judgment. Leigh's scenes are pitched at an in-between tonal place that denies the viewer the luxury of settling into a simple reading of a character or event. Most of the scenes in *Nuts in May* in particular are neither clearly one mood nor another; they blend humor and sadness, comedy and seriousness, absurdity and plausibility. The viewer feels sorry for Keith, dislikes him, fears him, and laughs at him – by turns and often at the same time. The mix of feelings is one more method Leigh uses to complicate judgment and delay final understandings for as long as possible.

The brilliance of Leigh's use of humor is worth special mention. Particularly in the first hour of *Nuts in May*, Keith's behavior is just funny enough that it is hard to get too morally indignant about it. The humor disarms judgment. Because he is presented in such a wacky way, we can't simply condemn Keith. We judge him to be more "mad" (for example, in his chewing lecture or quest for raw milk) than dangerous, more zany than threatening. Many of Leigh's other works use comedy similarly to forestall or delay simpler, more categorical, and less sympathetic interpretations. I have already pointed out how our amusement at

Peter's clumsiness (along with our feelings of pity and sympathy) prevent us from being overly (or prematurely) judgmental in *Bleak Moments*.

The tonal shifts are as important as the tonal suspensions and irresolutions in complicating our relation to the material. Consider how many different moods there are leading up to and during the campfire scene. The night before the blowup, Leigh shows Honkey, Finger, and Ray playing a game of darts at a local pub. The mood is easy, relaxed, and lightly humorous. The next scene, back in Honkey and Finger's tent later the same night, is low farce – with farts, sex jokes, "Irish intelligence tests," squeals, and peals of laughter. The silliness is then interrupted by and intercut with the emotional intensity and seriousness of Keith's protests over the noise the group is making. The sequence that immediately follows the next morning starts off with the comical rant of Keith's "citizen's arrest"; turns into the half-nutty, half-serious argument between Keith and Finger; is followed by a crazed melee; and suddenly and unexpectedly gives way to Keith's tears and Finger's muttering to himself. We are laughing at Finger and Keith one minute, frightened by them (and for them) the next, and at least somewhat sympathetic the next. Keith goes from being ridiculously bombastic ("You are breaking the law of the campsite and the laws of the country code"), to being both comical and serious (in the combination Keystone Cops/*Deliverance* face-off with Finger), to seeming frighteningly dangerous and out of control (as the fight escalates), to genuinely moving us to sympathy and pity with his pain and grief (when he starts crying and runs into the woods). Which is the real Keith? To ask which interpretation, which personal point of view, or which tone is the "right" one is to realize how Leigh takes us beyond the notion that there is any one correct view of such a complex event.[9]

The overall narrative of *Nuts in May* employs similar tonal swerves. The film starts out so comically and innocuously and escalates in seriousness so gradually that the pain and gravity of the situation sneaks up on a viewer and genuinely shocks him when it finally becomes clear. In the particular case of the campfire scene, for example, the fight between Keith and Finger seems much more horrific and frightening than if the entire film had been pitched in the same tonal register.

All of Leigh's work is really quite slyly subversive in this respect. It frequently tricks a viewer into laughing at something that is gradually revealed to be not really funny. Precisely because the viewer cannot see the awfulness coming, he is in an incredibly open and vulnerable emotional state. He eventually squirms all the more because he has been emotionally unprepared for the direction the narrative takes. He has been tricked into letting down his guard. The first acts of most of Leigh's works, both on stage and in film, seduce a viewer into liking (or at least laughing at) characters he will eventually come to fear, hate, or pity. The result is to make the viewer a kind of accomplice to the horror. He is teased into at least slightly sympathizing with (and frequently seeing parts of himself in) characters who are later revealed to be horrors. The effect is to spring a kind of trap on the viewer. He is *implicated* – emotionally invested – in a situation that he will subsequently be forced to condemn. He goes along with something he will subsequently regret assenting to.

Nuts in May puts us in the most untenable position imaginable: We are forced to admit both that Keith and Candice-Marie share some of our own qualities *and* that they are profoundly flawed and inadequate. For the first half-hour or so, we laugh at and slightly empathize with Keith. Leigh presents him just engagingly enough to earn our amused sympathy. Though we see that he is fallible and has shortcomings, we recognize aspects of ourselves in him: feelings of intellectual superiority to and of being better than the lower-class rabble he is forced to deal with. Then it slowly dawns on us that he is in *real* trouble. But the full extent of his deficiencies becomes clear only *after* we have partially identified with him. When the untenability of our position is revealed, we experience a genuine shock of recognition. When the contradiction in our own position is exposed, we are precipitated into an emotional and intellectual state of crisis not entirely different from the one undergone by Keith in the campfire scene.

Leigh's work does what the greatest art always does: maneuvers viewers into a place where formulaic responses won't suffice, where emotions are conflicted and hearts are torn, where they must take things personally. It is a wonderful place to get a work of art to – a place of growth. While Hollywood flatters its viewers, Leigh chastens his. *Schindler's List* lets its viewers feel good about feeling bad, since they can congratulate themselves on their ability to tell the good guys from the bad guys. *Pulp Fiction* curries favor by allowing its viewers to feel they are clever enough to get the in-jokes and pop-schlock allusions. *Nuts in May* goes in the opposite direction. It deliberately tries to rock, upset, and confuse the viewer. It tries to break down the categories he came in with.[10]

If we are not at least a little chastened, surprised, or made to feel stupid or imperceptive at least several times in the course of each of

Leigh's films, if we are not a little lost, afraid, or upset about what we are being put through, they haven't done what they were intended to. This is what it means to say that the ultimate threat of Leigh's work is directed less against his characters than his viewers. The videos should come with warning labels: "May be dangerous to your mental health" (translation: "May force you to discard your clichéd understandings"). The point is to rattle our complacencies, to force us to let go of preconceived notions and actually start thinking freshly, opening ourselves to the actual flow and complexity of experience.

So important is this process to Leigh that it should not be surprising that it is built into the narrative of many of the works. Keith here (like many other characters in other works) undergoes precisely the same breakdown that a viewer may undergo. To attempt to tailor your experience to fit an abstract scheme of understanding is always to invite trouble in his work. Letting go of preconceived categories and habitual patterns of response is what both viewers and characters are asked to do (and resist doing). It is not too much to argue that Leigh's goal is to move both his viewers and his characters (to the extent they will allow themselves to be moved) to a place beyond knowing.

6

Losing Track of Who You Are:
Abigail's Party

Many people are frustrated. . . . the greatest frustration comes from being unable to
be yourself, from being forced to play the roles that society imposes on us.

– Mike Leigh

There have been two basic responses to *Abigail's Party*. The negative
one is epitomized in Dennis Potter's comments in his London *Sunday
Times* review of the original television broadcast. Potter argued that
Leigh

> diminished the characters . . . to a brilliant puppetry of surface obser-
> vation. The thin wires of prejudice and superficial mimicry can nearly
> always be seen, tangled up with the words. What one gets is a portrait
> – and a very revealing one – of the social assumptions and insecurities
> of that peculiar group of people who earn their bread by acting. This
> play was based on nothing more edifying than rancid disdain, for it
> was a prolonged jeer, twitching with genuine hatred, about the dread-
> ful suburban tastes of the dreadful lower middle classes. . . . A long
> tradition asserts that it is enjoyable to get on the other side of the ding-
> dong doorbell in a new suburban villa and trample mud into the wall-
> to-wall carpets. *Abigail's Party* was horribly funny at times, stunningly
> acted and perfectly designed, but it sank under its own immense con-
> descension. The force of the yelping derision became a single note of
> contempt, amplified into a relentless screech. As so often in the mine-
> fields of English class-consciousness, more was revealed of the snob-
> bery of the observers rather than of the observed.[1]

In sum, in Potter's view, *Abigail's Party* reveals Leigh to be one of
those snotty, university-educated artiste-intellectuals who thinks that
anyone who lives in the suburbs, works for a salary, and can't quote

Marcuse from memory is less than human. It is a view of Leigh's work that resurfaces throughout his career in statements to the effect that Leigh hates the middle and upper classes even more than he hates the lower classes and reserves his rare sympathies for Marx-reading hippies like *High Hopes'* Cyril or anarchists like *Naked's* Johnny.

The positive interpretation (sometimes in response to the negative) praises Leigh's psychological perspicacity in dissecting the sexual hypocrisy and social insecurity of the petite bourgeoisie. In this reading, the "gorgonic Beverly" (Michael Coveney's term) is a sexually frustrated, man-eating monster who, in effect, succeeds in murdering her husband in the final scene because she can't dominate him. As Michael Coveney puts it: "The whole point about Beverly is that she is childless . . . [and her] grotesque exterior carapace is a mask of inner desolation."[2] Ian Buruma offers a similar psychological reading of Laurence. According to Buruma, Laurence is "an anxious estate agent, with high cultural aspirations (Beethoven's Ninth on the stereo), [who] is being slowly destroyed by the endless humiliation meted out by his wife."[3] Coveney also calls attention to Laurence's "suppressed racism" and his "short fuse and anxiety to please and impress."[4] The only character about whom Coveney has anything good to say is Angela, who, he maintains, has an "inner warmth and well-meaning center." Even though "she is indeed embarrassingly grotesque and painfully gushing and anxious to please, . . . she is also patently a very good nurse."[5]

I would argue that one interpretation misses the point of *Abigail's Party* as much as the other. Potter trivializes the film by literalizing it. His whole charge of snobbery is based on the belief that Leigh is criticizing the class-defined externals of Laurence and Beverly's lives (their furniture, clothing, and music), when in fact he is only using their outsides to indicate problems with their insides (the ways they think and feel). Leigh's objection to Beverly and Laurence is not the snobbish one that their car and condominium are mass-produced, but the spiritual one that their ideas and emotions are. Their stereotypical externals are only dramatic externalizations of their stereotypical internals. Their off-the-peg clothing only matters as evidence of their off-the-peg souls.[6]

Unfortunately, in an attempt to rescue Leigh from the charge of snobbery, the opposite approach trivializes *Abigail's Party* just as much by reducing it to a series of psychological platitudes. If the film were really about Beverly's frustration over being "childless," Laurence's "suppressed racism" and need to "impress," or Angela's "inner warmth," it would not even be worth discussing; it would be a Spielberg or Stone film. There is no news in these clichés, no insights or discoveries about human nature, nothing to challenge or teach a viewer anything. They are a hash of recycled, received understandings that weren't true the first time – about the need of women to have children, of men to be strong, and of everybody to be warm.

This is the trouble with virtually all common-sense psychological analysis (and why I forbid my students to employ it). It tames what is dangerous and normalizes what is subversive by turning a work of art into a conventional expression of bourgeois values. Of course, that dumbing-down is the very reason for the popularity of such approaches: They make plays, films, and novels understandable to Mom and Pop: "The heartbreak of Beverly's childlessness, the sadness of Laurence's humiliation and insecurity, the cruelty of his compensating racism, and the inner warmth of the well-meaning Angie. Ah, yes, I see. It's all so clear."

So clear and so worthless. A work of art is turned into a needlepoint bromide. What was painful and shocking is made palatable. What was perceptive is made trite. What was challenging is made uncontroversial. The Norman Rockwell truisms threaten no one, because they apply to no one. They are emotionally neutered. We might as well talk about the "gorgonic" Cleopatra's "desolation at her state of childlessness," Antony's being "slowly destroyed by the humiliation she metes out," and Charmian's "warmth and well-meaning." *Antony and Cleopatra* becomes indistinguishable from a Judy Blume novel. Chekhov becomes James Herriott.

What is lost in the translation is the art. All the complexities (created by the language, the pacing, the shaping, the tone, the acting) that make a work of art different from and infinitely more interesting than an article in *Psychology Today* disappear. *King Lear* becomes the story of a proud old man abused by ungrateful daughters; *Othello* becomes the tale of a devoted wife mistrusted by an insecure husband. Is that really why people have read Shakespeare for four centuries? It is the Philistine's view of art. One can almost hear Laurence talking about one of the books in his collection this way.

Psychological analysis treats personality, behavior, and expression in a fundamentally simpler way than Leigh (or Shakespeare) does. It understands personality as consisting of separable attributes and localized "problems" with distinguishable causes and effects. In this instance, Beverly's "problem" is her childlessness; it affects her in certain ways; to cure it she should clearly either have a child or get over it. Life becomes an Ann Landers column. The situations Leigh depicts are more general and less tractable. They aren't caused by anything in particular, like childlessness, racism, or being humiliated. They don't have solutions, like having a baby or standing up for yourself. And they can't be separated from everything else the person is. Beverly's problem is what she *is* – everything she feels, knows, and believes – not something that does or does not happen to her. Laurence's problem is his understanding of the meaning of his life, not some separable set of beliefs about how foreigners have affected real-estate values.

In focusing on emotional or intellectual "problems," psychological analysis (and mainstream filmmaking) overlooks character as a problem in itself. Being someone, having a character, is not something that can simply be taken for granted. There are many ways of *having* a character, many different ways of *being* someone. The study of those ways is one of the subjects of Leigh's work. His films are explorations of ways of being – emotional territory far less tractable and more complex than what Dear Abby deals with.[7]

The emotional and imaginative aberrations Leigh is interested in are larger in scope, more disturbing, and more resistant to solution than the psychological and moral "problems" bourgeois drama takes as its subject. That they are childless and in an unhappy marriage is not what interests Leigh about Beverly and Laurence. He is more subversive and less sentimental than Coveney and Buruma dream. Beverly and Laurence's problem is less that they are troubled individuals than that they are not individuals at all. They portray crises of identity in which the existence of personal identity itself is brought into question. (*Who's Who* and *Home Sweet Home* will go even further in this direction.) One might say that their problem is less psychological than ontological, less a matter of needing something about themselves to be changed than a question of there being someone to be changed. Beverly and Laurence have become expressions of abstract cultural styles. While conventional drama never questions the reality of personal experience and expression (or their seminal importance), *Abigail's Party* imagines a world in which personal identity, personal experience, and personal expression have ceased to exist. Beverly and Laurence have become semiotic functions of their environment.

Sets and props are usually not of decisive importance in Leigh's actor-centered work (which imagines the individual, not the costume or setting, as the fundamental source of meaning and value); but it is no accident that Leigh specifies the set and props in great detail in the stage directions of *Abigail's Party* – from Beverly and Laurence's chrome furniture, "ornamental fibre-lamp," and "room divider shelf unit," to

Laurence's "executive case" and the *Cosmopolitan* magazine on Beverly's coffee table. The point is not snobbishly to mock their bad taste (as Potter would have it), but to indicate the extent to which even their living room has been usurped by cultural styles. Their furnishings, the way they dress, and the way they talk and interact are equally emanations of the world of fashion. These figures are not only seen in a landscape but are in many respects indistinguishable from it.

Abigail's Party is a house of mirrors in which reflected images have completely replaced the originals – Beverly, for example, being less a hostess than something much more unsettling: someone *playing at* being a hostess. In a sense, there is no Beverly. When we look for her we find only an actress playing a part, a ventriloquist's dummy mouthing someone else's words, an impersonation of a person. She has given up her identity, such as it is, to play a *role*, which she acts out not only in public but, more disturbingly, even in private. That is the importance of the opening minute or so in which she is alone on camera. We watch her "acting" even when no one else is present. She is performing not for an audience – her husband or her guests – but doing something much spookier: performing for herself, validating herself *to herself*. In this night of the living dead, there is no Beverly separable from the part she plays. Her identity is completely synthetic – a shaky structure of prefab "attitudes," poses, self-regarding routines, and shopworn hostess-with-the-mostest affectations. Like some brilliant, performing circus animal, Beverly provides a dazzling "display" of canned phrases, gestures, and tones that simulate states of thinking, feeling, and caring without ever getting within three martinis of the reality.

And not just Beverly. Everyone and everything is part of a dramatic production, another reason the props and setting have a different status from those in Leigh's other works: As with parts of two of the films that follow this one, *Who's Who* and *Home Sweet Home*, Leigh has created a drama in which, in effect, the characters already act as if they are in a drama. Beverly and Laurence treat their living room as a set, their clothing as costumes, and their entire lives as a dramatic production. As a hostess and real-estate agent, they are never not "acting," never not working for an "effect."

We can recognize the theatricality of Beverly's performance not only through Alison Steadman's tonal archness in her line delivery, which inserts brackets around each of Beverly's gestures and quotation marks around each of her utterances, but even in the script. There is something artificial, imitated, derivative, or inauthentic about virtually every line of dialogue Beverly utters. It all feels "scripted" – and it is, not by Leigh, of course, but by Beverly.

Beverly inhabits a realm – call it hostess-speak – in which verbal expressions bear no relationship to real feelings (or an inverse relationship, as in the case of the syrupy "please" she intermittently coos in Laurence's direction, which is not in the least a polite request but a snarled imperative and threat). Like the Hollywood air kissing Beverly's speech resembles, social interaction in this world becomes a kind of bad acting in which you "indicate" your emotions instead of actually feeling them. (Real emotion would only get in the way, impeding the smoothness of the performance and embarrassing the intended recipient.) Since each of the participants in the drama knows it is all theater, the fraudulence, the archness, is not concealed but cultivated and proclaimed, as a way of expanding their identities and intensifying their presence.

As that way of putting it is meant to suggest, the problem Leigh is examining is much deeper than what is normally connoted by insincerity. Beverly (like all of the other characters in *Abigail's Party*) is not covering up "hidden" feelings and thoughts. That would be an entirely more conventional dramatic situation. It would suggest that she knows what she is doing. It would imply that she was simply trying to fool people (a fairly simple situation in life and art), when the real problem is that she is fooling herself (a much more interesting state of affairs). Beverly is completely and utterly sincere; she means what she says; she is not being deceitful. Which is the true problem. There is no reality lurking in the depths; *everything* is fake. Beverly's ideas and emotions are no different from her jewelry: Both are equally cheap knockoffs. Her most private, inner experiences are as clichéd as her expressions.

Most films, particularly American ones, cultivate what might be called a "surface-depth" understanding of the relation between falsity and truth. Surfaces, appearances, expressions are potentially delusive or misleading; truth lies in the depths. It is hidden somewhere underneath visible expressions. In this view of life, if you cross-examined Laurence and Beverly in private, and dug for the truth, you could get them to confess to their lies. This simply is not the situation Leigh imagines. He holds us on the surface and, in fact, tells us that the surfaces are all there are. There is no realm of "truth" underneath or distinguishable from the realm of "falsehood." There are no secrets to exhume. There are no psychological depths to mine – or at least none that matter – in *Abigail's Party*. No one is being deceitful. No one is covering up anything. That would simplify understanding. We could dive down and discover the truth as we do in films like *Citizen Kane* or *Casablanca*. The situation Leigh imagines – here and in all of his work – is far more complex. There is nothing but slippery, shifting, multivalent surfaces. There is no realm of unsullied, uninflected "reality" underneath. *Everything is compromised*, contingent, mixed. There is no place of purity and truth.[8]

Life in Beverly's world is conducted entirely on emotional autopilot, as when Sue shows up with a bottle of wine and Beverly goes into a "surprised and pleased" routine (that Alison Steadman's acting brilliantly identifies as a "routine"). One empty sentiment succeeds another in a cascade of vacuity – from Beverly's token puzzlement and token surprise, to her token squeal of delight that it is Beaujolais, to Sue's token apology that it isn't more "special," to Angela's token nod of agreement. Nor have I revealed something the characters themselves don't realize. The reason everyone involved in the conversation can carry it off so smoothly is that they all *know* it's all feigned, formulas, a kind of social tennis game that guests and hosts play. You would have to be a fool (or never to have attended a cocktail party) actually to think a single syllable was a genuine, spontaneous expression of personal emotion.[9]

BEVERLY: Did you bring that, Sue?
SUSAN: Yes.
BEVERLY: Is it for us?
SUSAN: Yes.
BEVERLY: Oh, thank you, Sue!
SUSAN: It's nothing very special, I'm afraid.
BEVERLY: Ah. Isn't that kind, Ang?
ANGELA: Yes.
SUSAN: Not at all.
BEVERLY [*Unwrapping the bottle*]: Oh, lovely! 'Cos Laurence likes a drop of wine, actually. Oh, it's Beaujolais. Fantastic!

As Beverly's final ejaculation reminds us, since her expressions and feelings are disconnected from reality, her most casual comments can be screwed up to an emotional pitch that actual life seldom merits. For Beverly, everything but everything is "fabulous," "fantastic," or "great"– uttered with a tone as *faux* peppy as that of a cheerleader (when it isn't *faux* tragic, as when she is pronouncing something "terrible" or "awful").[10]

Even her deep, dark confidences and stage-whispered asides are fake. They are not genuine instances of searing honesty or daring self-revelation (which would be dangerous to herself and shocking to her listener), but dime-store knockoffs of real insights and confidences – which is why she can serve up a new personal disclosure every two or three minutes, can assume the automatic agreement of her listener in advance, and can couch each of her putative "revelations" in more or less the same prefab verbal form, beginning with one of four or five identical canned phrases ("Let's face it . . . ," "Mind you . . . ," "Don't get me wrong, but . . . ," or "Let me put it to you this way . . .").

Leigh's hostess-with-the-leastest lives in a world of soap-opera understandings and bumper-sticker substitutes for thinking. Consider the cascade of clichés Beverly utters as José Feliciano's "Light My Fire" plays on the stereo. (Angela, as usual, plays yes-woman to Beverly's deep thinker.)

> BEVERLY: . . . [*Turning the record up.*] Fantastic, isn't he?
> ANGELA: Yeah. I know this one.
> BEVERLY: Yeah? Don't you think he's sexy, Ang?
> ANGELA: Yes. But it's a pity he's blind.
> BEVERLY: Yeah. Mind you, I reckon that makes him more sensitive. D'you know what I mean?
> ANGELA: Mmm. Yes.

It should not be surprising that most of Beverly's comments and observations take the *n'est-ce pas* form (expressed in phrases like "Right?" "You know what I mean?" or "Don't you think?"). She is so hermetically sealed inside her own private world of self-validating references and self-referential allusions that there is no room for any other point of view. Her talk is punctuated with implicit insistences on agreement, even as her response to others' observations takes the perfunctory form of an iterated "Yeah, yeah" or "I know" – as if she doesn't need to listen because she already knows anything they might tell her. It is as impossible for Beverly ever to be really surprised at anything (except in a pretend way) as it is for her to learn anything. Even more than Keith in *Nuts in May*, she rules over a kingdom of knowing in which there is no imaginative space for anything but her own preestablished forms of understanding, to which she brooks no contradiction. Even the baby-talk coo of Beverly's tone (especially when directed at her husband), far from expressing tenderness, is a form of emotional and imaginative bullying. The motto of this childless woman might be "Because I'm the Mommy, that's why," and her condescending, know-it-all tone makes it clear that none of her charges should ever dare argue with Mom.

Sue, Laurence, Beverly, Angela, and Tony at Beverly's party – "One of the prevailing themes or issues in all the films is the hopelessness of being truthfully what we are, as opposed to what other people expect – what our received roles are. And that does manifest itself all the way from the central character in *Hard Labour*, whose problem is she's confused about what other people expect of her, right through to *Life Is Sweet*, which contains characters like Nicola and Aubrey, who are receptacles of received notions of how they should be." – Mike Leigh (Photo courtesy the Kobal Collection: BBC)

In the dramatic metaphor that runs throughout most of Leigh's work, Beverly is an actress who contradicts her creator's understanding of every aspect of good acting. While Leigh asks his actors genuinely to listen to and interact with others, and shape their performances in subtle relation to theirs, Beverly can only solo. She is not really responsive to anyone or anything. While Leigh's conception of identity is radically relational and open, Beverly's is closed and canned.[11] She plays a part in which every gesture, inflection, and tone of voice has been worked out in advance, and in which there can be no real learning or discovery. Like Keith, Beverly has shut up shop on what she might be, because she thinks she knows who she is.

While Leigh's work rejects the Hollywood star system (in which one actor more or less controls everything and everyone around him), Beverly insists on being the star of every scene in which she appears (and on treating everyone else as a supporting player). Flattening everyone in her path with her steamroller verbal style, Beverly leaves no room for imaginative perspectives different from her own. There could hardly be more serious shortcomings for a dramatist devoted to the virtues of ensemble interaction and circulation among different points of view. While Leigh honors personal differences, Beverly is invulnerable to and unreachable by the emotional claims of others. While he is a paragon of multiple-mindedness, she is a nightmare of single-mindedness. For her, there can be only one way of understanding everything – hers. Her conspiracy of knowing erases all sense of otherness – not only with her plain-vanilla guests but even with certifiable "others" like José Feliciano. Her taste in music is intended to show that, like a bad film critic, she doesn't ask the work to teach her something new, to take her out of herself, but to conform to her own clichéd formulas and predetermined modes of understanding.

The passages I have cited are generally humorous in effect, but Leigh characteristically mixes humor and seriousness in a way that keeps the viewer from laughing them off or simply laughing at the characters. Even though Beverly and Laurence may seem ridiculous in some ways, they are so earnest that we can never merely write off their performances as absurd. As he does in all of his work, Leigh walks the tightrope between seriousness and funniness so perfectly that much of the time the viewer doesn't know whether to howl with laughter or crawl under his seat with embarrassment at what Beverly or Laurence is saying or doing. Or else the tone will shift. If we are laughing one minute, we are squirming or cringing the next. The mix of tones, and changes of tone, keep us off-balance. We can't emotionally pigeon-hole the experience. Leigh keeps us from climbing into a tonal La-Z-Boy; we can't recline into an easy feeling. The mixture of humor and pain (which resembles Chekhov, the supreme master of this tonal effect) forces the viewer beyond automatic responses. He must grapple with mixed-up, unsorted feelings.

The scene in which Beverly boorishly cross-examines Sue about her divorce and relationship with her former husband illustrates the trademark Leigh blend of real pain with screamingly funny comedy. Sue is deeply upset and embarrassed by Beverly's questions, even as Beverly is hilariously oblivious to Sue's feelings – blithely turning everything Sue says into movie-of-the-week clichés.

With respect to my earlier observation about Beverly's inability to understand any point of view other than her own, it is telling that even at the moments when Sue attempts to rebut Beverly's clichéd misunder-standings, as in her negative response to Angela's question about whether she had "a lot of rows" with her husband, Beverly remains unflappable: "Well, there you go. You see, it *doesn't* always follow." Once more, there is no escaping from Beverly's smothering knowingness, no opening out of her life-denying circle of smugness. When one one-size-fits-all formula for understanding has to be jettisoned (that divorcees "have rows"), it is replaced by another ("Well, there you go.") In her own mind, Beverly is right even when she is wrong.

Laurence is as trapped in canned routines and received notions as Beverly. Leigh summarizes the formulaic quality of his expressions only a few minutes into *Abigail's Party*, when we overhear his side of a telephone conversation with a real-estate client. It is a regular Potemkin village of Sales Talk disconnected from emotional truth or reality:

> Hullo, Mrs. Cushing? Laurence Moss here. . . . Wibley Webb! . . . Yes, Mrs. Cushing, we have run him to ground, and you'll be happy to know that I'm now in the throes of retrieving the key! . . . Not at all, not at all – all part of the service! . . . Ah, yes . . . now, when would be best for you? . . . No, no, I'll fall in with you, Mrs. Cushing. . . . How about tomorrow morning? . . . My pleasure, Mrs. Cushing, my plea-sure. . . . Now, what time would suit you best? . . . No, I'm at *your* service, Mrs. Cushing. "He who pays the piper calls the tune!" You name the hour and I shall appear! . . . No, really, I insist. . . . Early? Not at all, Mrs. Cushing – up with the lark, you know. . . . Don't mention it, Mrs. Cushing, it's my privilege. . . .

In his fake enthusiasm, chitchatty sycophancy, stilted obsequiousness, and all-round groveling, Laurence takes being the Organization Man further than William Allen White ever dreamed. There is no man; there is only the organization. When, a few minutes later, Laurence tells An-gela about his fondness for Minis ("I find the Mini economical, efficient, and reliable, and the most suited to my purposes"), his impersonal tone and generic diction communicate the extent to which he has internalized the ad campaign. Leigh is focusing less on a verbal problem than a crisis of identity. Laurence has given up his personal identity to become a walking, talking advertisement. Where we look for an individual or listen for the sound of a personal voice, we hear only the echo of television jingles and radio slogans. When he tells us that he changes his car every year, at the very moment he is priding himself on being an independent thinker and discerning consumer, he reveals that he is actually a consumption zombie.[12]

Laurence's third extended sequence is the exchange that Coveney relies on as the basis for his "suppressed racism" charge, but Leigh is dramatizing something more complex than Coveney perceives. Laurence cross-examines Sue about the changes she has noticed in the racial composition of the neighborhood since she moved in. The following excerpt captures Laurence's style:

> I expect you've seen a few changes since you've been here, eh, Sue? . . . Oh, come on, Sue – surely you must have seen some changes? . . . Ah, yes, the houses! But what about the people? The class of people, now don't you think that's changed? . . . The tone of the area – don't you feel it's altered? . . . You don't think it's gone down?

Coveney's mistake is thinking that the meaning of Laurence's remarks is expressed by their content when what really matters is their form. It is similar to what we already saw with Beverly. Her responses to the music or gift of wine are not really about José Feliciano or a bottle of Beaujolais; they are about playing the role of sensitive, gracious hostess. Laurence's remarks are less about race relations than about professing to care about such issues at such a moment in such a way. He is making a show of his intellectual seriousness and historical awareness for Sue. (Tim Stern's tones beautifully communicate how Laurence almost pleads to be taken seriously by Sue.) He is playing Professor, delivering a lecture to a captive audience, giving his party "class" and demonstrating how different he is from his wife (sparring with her by changing the subject and seizing control of the conversation).

Laurence thinks he is displaying his intellectual depth and seriousness, but his sociological observations are as second-hand as his opinions about real estate or cars. For this twentieth-century Polonius, "thinking" apparently consists of uttering a series of hackneyed phrases in a sententious tone. Rather than displaying real thought, the sequence is merely a staged recitation of a clichéd set of middle-class anxieties and journalistic formulas.

Laurence's notion of conversation is just as bullying, just as much a one-way street, with him as traffic cop, as Beverly's. He is not seeking to learn new things, to understand different points of view, but to elicit answers he has already decided upon. He is less interested in having a conversation than in being a monologist, which emerges not only in the way he browbeats Sue until she coughs up the "correct" answer to his questions about the decline of the neighborhood, but in his smug, patronizing tone (which is brilliantly captured by Tim Stern's delivery). Like *Bleak Moments'* Peter, Laurence's concept of conversation is a little like giving someone an oral exam.

The fact that Peter and Laurence both came from the same part of Leigh's brain is even more obvious when Laurence works in pretentious references to his book and art collection. With his framed Van Gogh (affectedly pronounced with a hard "gh") poster, thumbnail critical pronunciamentos ("They called him a Post-Impressionist, but to my mind he was more of a Symbolist"), fondness for Beethoven, and leather-bound editions of Dickens and Shakespeare ("our heritage, but you can't really read it, of course"), Laurence fancies himself a suave, sophisticated connoisseur even as his paint-by-numbers opinions reveal him to be the rankest of Philistines.

Like Ozu's work, each of Leigh's films and plays is better understood less as a slice of life than as a tightly integrated artistic universe in which a related set of imaginative problems and issues are presented and explored with an almost scientific thoroughness. Variations and permutations on a central set of problems are laid out, compared, and contrasted. That is why it is trivial to approach Beverly and Laurence as a squabbling, suburban couple; as I have been trying to demonstrate, they are male and female versions of a common imaginative predicament Leigh wants to study. They represent a particular kind of identity crisis, seen from different perspectives, which takes different forms in different situations.

There is a passage in Jean-Paul Sartre's *Being and Nothingness* that made a big impression on Leigh as a young man, which can throw light on the imaginative situation he is exploring. One reason it appealed so powerfully to the young actor (beyond the fact that his intellectual coming-of-age coincided with the height of Sartre's influence) is that it is couched in explicitly dramatic metaphors. It occurs in the discussion of "bad faith," and is worth quoting at length:

> Let us consider the waiter in the café. His movement is quick and forward, a little too precise, a little too rapid. . . . All his behavior seems to us a game . . . he is playing at being a waiter in a café. . . . This obligation is not different from that which is imposed on all tradesmen. Their condition is wholly one of ceremony. The public

demands of them that they realize it as ceremony; there is the dance of the grocer, of the tailor, of the auctioneer, by which they endeavor to persuade their clientele that they are nothing but a grocer, an auctioneer, a tailor. A grocer who dreams is offensive to the buyer, because such a grocer is not wholly a grocer. Society demands that he limit himself. . . . There are indeed many precautions to imprison a man in what he is, as if we lived in perpetual fear that he might escape from it, that he might break away and suddenly elude his condition.

In a parallel situation, from within, the waiter in the café can not be immediately a café waiter in the sense that this inkwell is an inkwell, or the glass is a glass. . . . [If I am the waiter in question, the problem is that] there is no common measure between [the waiter's] being and mine. It is a "representation" for others and myself, which means that I can be he only in representation. But if I represent myself as him, I am not he; I am separated from him as the object from the subject. . . . I can only play at being him; that is, imagine to myself that I am he. And thereby I affect him with nothingness. In vain do I fulfill the functions of a café waiter. I can be he only in the neutralized mode, as the actor in Hamlet, by mechanically making the typical gestures of my state and by aiming at myself as an imaginary café waiter through those gestures taken as an "analogue." . . . I am a waiter in the mode of being what I am not. . . .

But bad faith is not restricted to denying the qualities which I possess, to not seeing the being which I am. It attempts also to constitute myself as being what I am not.[13]

Sartre's concepts of "representation" and "playing" run throughout Leigh's work. (In fact, the waiter walks out of the above passage and into *Bleak Moments'* Chinese restaurant more or less unchanged.) It is hardly an exaggeration to say that one of the central themes of Leigh's work is what Sartre here calls "bad faith" (or what we might call issues of authenticity and inauthenticity). In film after film, Leigh explores the situation of figures who, in Sartre's sense of the concept, "play at" being what they are and deceive themselves in the process. He is interested in characters who (like many of Shakespeare's and Chekhov's) pass fictions on themselves.[14]

It is one thing to lie to others, to pretend to be something you are not. Beverly and Laurence are guilty of that, of course. But it is even worse to lie to *yourself*, to fool *yourself* about who you are. That is the core imaginative situation Sartre imagines, and *Abigail's Party* (and most of Leigh's other works) explore. Beverly and Laurence have mistaken ideas of who they are and what their lives mean. They have surrendered their identities to inherited cultural styles and mechanical emotional routines – and don't even know it. They have been brainwashed by their own press releases and in the process lost track of who they really are. Beverly sincerely and honestly believes that she is sexy, thoughtful, considerate, and caring; Laurence, that he is cultured, refined, and intellectual. Needless to say, neither could be further from the truth. They are living lies – which wouldn't be such a serious problem if they knew they were doing it. To have a problem that you don't even know is a problem, to be trapped in a trap you don't even realize is a trap, is to have a real problem – far beyond the fake Hollywood kind. The situation Leigh and Sartre are describing is not created by consciousness and is not accessible to consciousness, which is why in the title of his play Sartre calls it one with "no exit."

Beverly and Laurence are trapped in emotional routines they don't even realize are routines. In their different ways, over many years, each has constructed a fictional world of beliefs and habits, of notions of how to act and how to feel about particular things, of what views to hold and what matters in life. They have learned what to think, whom to love and whom to hate, whom to admire and whom to fear. They carry it all around with them everywhere they go. It's an enormous burden of emotions, ideas, and conceptions of themselves to have to bear (and a great challenge to live up to). It consumes their lives. But the point of *Abigail's Party* is to show us that it's all an unreal game of blindman's bluff.

That should suggest why moral condemnations of the characters – at least as such moral judgments are customarily couched – miss the point of *Abigail's Party*. Moral understandings of a character's behavior generally presume that the character is aware of what he or she is doing, has a knowledge of the differences among various courses of action, and the ability to choose freely among them. Leigh is sketching a situation far more frightening and insidious. Beverly and Laurence have neither awareness, nor knowledge, nor freedom in those senses. Not only do they not *intend* to be what they are, they don't even *know* they are being what they are. They don't realize that they have enslaved themselves to arbitrary ideas. They aren't choosing to browbeat or manhandle their guests. They genuinely are trying to be kind. They mean well. And yet, needless to say, they *are* absolute moral horrors.

This view of morality can confuse American viewers, first, because most American mass art and culture are based on a volitional view of morality that puts a premium on the importance of acts of will; and second, because the American conception of motivation is heavily indebted to the Romantic movement (and its melodramatic descendants), which views actions and expressions as epiphenomena of states of subjectivity. In either conception, we understand people's behavior by reference to their inner states. We judge them, just as we judge ourselves, by their intentions. If you mean well, you can't really be bad.[15] There are characters with good desires, souls, and hearts – and characters with bad. It comes down to internal states. Leigh's characters are incomprehensible in such terms. Everyone, no matter how awful, has good intentions. What matters is what comes out, how one's intentions are expressed. Hollywood subjectivity gives way to documentary objectivity.

One might say that the ultimate difficulty of these other films is the difficulty of ferreting out buried secrets, of discovering hidden psychological clues that will explain the surfaces; while the ultimate difficulty of Leigh's work is not in the depths but on the surface. His work is an appreciation of the mystery not of the invisible, but of the visible.

Beverly and Laurence's shortcomings (and those of every other character in *Abigail's Party*) are less failures of morals than of selfhood. Deceiving others is an ethical problem; deceiving yourself runs deeper than that. The issue is not the lies Beverly and Laurence tell, but the lies they live. *Abigail's Party* is less about an ethical than an existential failure of character.

Leigh's conception of Beverly and Laurence is of a piece with the rest of his work. His characters never really know themselves or are in conscious control of their identities. To be conscious of your own identity or have reliable knowledge about your own character, you would have to break consciousness free from character. Even beyond that, identity is far too deeply rooted and too complex to be something you simply decide upon or will into existence.

Indeed, as Sartre suggests, to *attempt* to be anything, to *choose* to play any role whatsoever, is to place oneself in a fatally false position – as if you could pick out a self and wear it the way you do a suit of clothes. Leigh's work is littered with the disintegrated remains of characters who *try* to be something – from Pat's attempts to be a mother, Keith's attempts to set himself up as defender of the ecosystem, and the attempts of Samantha, Nigel, and most of the other young people in *Who's Who* to be "adult," to Barbara's attempts to play Good Samaritan, Valerie's attempts to be fashionable, and Aubrey and Nicola's attempts at playing "chef-patron" and "resident feminist," respectively. It is decisive proof of the fraudulence of Beverly and Laurence's identities that they are so clearly *mental*. They represent *ideas* about themselves – states of consciousness, played out in acts of will.

The preceding should suggest that Beverly and Laurence's verbal "bullying" is evidence of a more disturbing problem than a mere desire to dominate or control others. It is an attempt to get others to buy into their own definitions of themselves. Since their identities are so precariously cobbled together, they need others to keep them up. The more fundamentally false their ideas about themselves are, the more they attempt to be something they are not, the more they need to have them validated by others in order to prove who they are. If they simply *were* what they are (rather than *trying* to be it), they wouldn't be so desperate for confirmation. They need to convince others in order to convince themselves.[16]

One can feel the unnaturalness of these identities in the energy that is consumed in maintaining them. We feel the pressure in everything Peter, Pat, Keith, Beverly, Laurence, Gloria, and Christine do. They are in a state of constant tension. While Leigh himself is clearly in favor of relaxed, "shaggy and baggy" identities, expressions, and relationships (as films like *High Hopes* and *Life Is Sweet* illustrate), the expressions, relationships, and identities of these characters are forced, hard, serious, tense, and "tight." Because their identities are not "natural" but "willed," these characters hold themselves together with the emotional equivalent of gritted teeth and nerves of steel, such enormous energy does it take to maintain fundamentally false relations to their own experience.[17]

In denial of their true emotional needs, alienated from what they really are by their ideas about what they are, it is not surprising that each of these figures eventually goes to pieces. The internal contradictions are ultimately unsustainable. The tension is unbearable.[18] The masquerade can only be continued for so long before the mask slips. The will breaks down under the strain of holding everything together. The papered-over fissures tear apart. If you attempt to build a skyscraper out of toothpicks, it is bound to collapse sooner or later.

Sometimes the collapse comes quietly and can be a positive event. Near the endings of *The Kiss of Death, Meantime, High Hopes,* and *Life Is Sweet,* characters' old ways of knowing give way and they come to new understandings of themselves and their relationships with others. In other films – like this one, *Nuts in May, Grown-Ups,* and *Home Sweet Home* – the ground bewilderingly drops out from under a character, as if his or her world were coming to an end, without the promise of renewal or redemption. The collapse is violent, wrenching, and unenlightening. Keith, Beverly, Gloria, Hazel, June, Barbara, and Valerie have their lives turned upside down as their fundamentally false relationships to their own experience are revealed, yet apparently learn nothing at all in the process.

Leigh's focus, as always, is not on transforming his characters but his viewers. From Molière to Altman, the danger which satiric work courts is that the audience may end up feeling superior to the characters and emotionally untouched by their situations. If that were the case with *Abigail's Party*, it *would* be the film Dennis Potter described. The greatness of Leigh's achievement (here and in all of his best work) is that he denies viewers the luxury of holding at emotional arm's length the experiences he provides. As awful as Beverly and Laurence are, Leigh keeps us from hardening our hearts to them. They aren't totally caricatures or cartoons. The issues they embody remain "live." They retain their power to trouble us. We cannot simply dismiss but must work through them.

It is worth touching briefly on some of the ways Leigh does this in *Abigail's Party*, not only because he employs similar techniques in other films, but because it is a clue to the power of his work. I have already mentioned how the tonal mixture of comedy and seriousness, farce and pain, keeps us from simply laughing off scenes. We are forced to sympathize with characters, almost against our wills, even as we are unable to treat them entirely as jokes. In addition, as I pointed out in *Nuts in May*, Leigh arranges his narrative to make sure that the seriousness of the overall situation sneaks up on a viewer, catching him off-guard or by surprise. The temporal unfolding of the disclosures in his narratives is one of the secrets of their power.[19]

For much of the first hour of *Abigail's Party*, there is no hint of the depth of the emotional hot water we are about to be plunged into. Like earlier figures such as Peter, Gloria, and Keith, Beverly and the whole cocktail party gathering seems quite comical initially. We think we are in an entirely lighter film than ultimately develops, smiling at Beverly and her weirdly mismatched collection of guests. The humor puts us at ease, disarms moral judgment, and gives us no inkling of what is to come.

Leigh presents Beverly in particular in a way that prevents us from being too hard on her. She doesn't seem like an ogre at first. She is fairly attractive and nicely dressed. She may seem a bit eccentric and wrapped up in herself but is not clearly reprehensible. She stays just this side of objectionable. Furthermore, she is quite witty. She is too funny and too outrageously outspoken simply to dislike. Though Beverly seems a bit testy and naggy at points, we probably attribute her agitation to preparation weariness and party excitement. At points early on, we may even take her side, sympathizing with her criticisms of Laurence. He *does* seem to be an absent-minded workaholic. Perhaps she is right to be impatient and exasperated with him. We may find ourselves agreeing, at least a little.

The result is that when the true horror of Beverly's relationship with Laurence starts to become clear, it hits us all the more powerfully, because we have been emotionally lulled into going along with it. We suddenly realize that what we were laughing at wasn't really all that funny. We have to play catch-up, reassessing everything we have seen thus far. As in *Nuts in May*, the trick Leigh has played has, in effect, made us accomplices to the situation. We are implicated in Beverly's treatment of Laurence; we feel a little guilty and embarrassed by our previous amusement. Leigh has laid a kind of trap for us. By the time the awfulness of the evening (and the hostess) is revealed, we are up to our eyes and ears in some degree of emotional involvement with Beverly. Our preceding laughter makes what follows feel even more horrific than it would have otherwise.[20]

Leigh will also prevent us from dismissing flawed characters, or from maintaining a coolly judgmental stance above, beyond, and completely untouched by a figure, by providing slightly more positive views of a character just when we might be ready to dismiss (or jeer at) them. At the very point in *Abigail's Party* at which we might be about to write off Laurence, Angela, or Beverly as hopeless, shallow, or cruel, Leigh inserts speeches that force us to regard them just a little more sympathetically. I have in mind the moments in which he gives each of them a speech in which he or she shares his or her feelings about art or music. Laurence unexpectedly confesses his feeling of desperation and emptiness by talking about how he envies "musicians and artists," because they are "born with one great advantage in life . . . *their talent.*" Immediately following that, Angela tells a story from her childhood about how she embarrassed herself playing the piano in front of a group of strangers. And following that is the moment I have already quoted in which Beverly turns up the recording of "Light My Fire" and enthuses about José Feliciano's "sensitivity."

We are suddenly and unexpectedly forced to look at the characters in a slightly more sympathetic light. While we have probably been judging them on the basis of their outsides up until this point, these meditative moments open windows that remind us that they have insides. The speeches are in character, so it isn't that what they say suddenly redeems them or reveals them to be entirely different people. (Laurence's view of artists is callow, Angie's story is quite fatuous, and, as I already noted,

Beverly's is shallow, clichéd, and patronizing.) But notwithstanding all that, we are forced to see all three in a new way – to recognize that they aren't just bundles of tics and mannerisms. They have feelings and private perceptions. They have doubts, dreams, fears, and aspirations. We are fleetingly no longer in a satire or comedy of manners; we are no longer looking at exteriors; we are in a drama of consciousness. Leigh's use of a musical soundtrack (which runs throughout the sequence) is particularly effective in this respect. As first Laurence, then Angela, and finally Beverly talk, the music subtly shifts its emotional resonance. Though it starts out fairly tritely, it ends up being quite moving and evocative, subliminally drawing us into a sensitive state of feeling.

As I already noted, another way in which Leigh complicates judgment is by making it clear that (as is the case in all of his work) none of these characters *intends* any wrong. Beverly is *trying* to be kind and thoughtful even when she grills Sue. Laurence is *trying* to be sophisticated and hospitable even when he browbeats Sue into agreeing with him about the decline of the neighborhood.

Furthermore, Leigh shows us that (though they cannot understand it in the way we do) both Beverly and Laurence are *suffering* (just as Keith's crying ultimately revealed him to be in *Nuts in May*). Rather than hating them, we feel sorry for them, as we would for anyone who is trapped in a painful situation (even if it is of their own making). We can't really condemn them insofar as we feel the pain they are in. (To communicate that pain is one of the functions of allowing them to talk about their feelings in the moment with the music.) We can't stand in judgment on Beverly or Laurence or close our hearts to them because we are forced into such awkward intimacy with them, forced to feel what they feel, forced to feel how unhappy, how needy, how desperate for approval they are. The pain Beverly in particular is inflicting on herself is at least as great as the pain she inflicts on others. She tortures herself as much as she tortures anyone else.

It is this aspect of Leigh's work that makes it supremely great. Though he presents characters who are profoundly flawed, we feel that their own unique feelings are honored and their points of view respected. They are not viewed from the outside but from within. Rather than being *mocked* and *jeered at* (as Potter mistakenly accuses Leigh of doing), these characters are *understood*. Their frustrations are acknowledged. The full complexity of their self-inflicted doom is appreciated. Characters imagined this deeply and sympathetically, from the inside, reach into our hearts and make claims on us precisely because they are *not* demonized, even if their cries are the screams of the eternally damned.

7

We Are the Hollow Men:
Who's Who

"I'll also sort of spend time doodling on a page, where you sort of go – and this is very private. I don't show this to anybody. . . ." Leigh now removes a cocktail napkin from his coat pocket and begins to draw something resembling a family tree. He writes down the names of all of the major characters from the film, connecting them with various lines and symbols, taking time out to remind me that this may seem somewhat simplistic only because he is basing it on a finished film and not one in development: "You see, people say to me, 'Do you know the story [when you begin]? Do you know the end? Do you know the narrative?' The answers to those questions are no, no, and no. But those of us who know about filmmaking and conception know that there's a difference between a view of the linear construction of the narrative and the dynamics of the play – which is what that drawing is. This is a way of visualizing the potential film, and by thinking that through, you give yourself a structure in which you then start thinking of what it means thematically, what you're trying to say here."

– Scott Foundras

Leigh's work is seldom appreciated as being as artistically advanced as it actually is. Perhaps that is because his narratives pass for simple "realism," or because most critics tend to identify cinematic sophistication with particular formal mannerisms – virtuosic camera movements, visual and acoustic sublimities, spatial dislocations, abrogations of chronological presentation – to which Leigh is averse.[1] Whatever the reason, he has seldom been given credit for the complexity of his vision.

Far from being "slices of life," each of Leigh's films is organized around a series of emotional comparisons and contrasts, with a thematic tightness that is really quite striking. *Bleak Moments* explores forms of awkwardness, distance, fears of intimacy, and failures of communication; *Nuts in May* compares forms of willfulness and unresponsiveness; *Home Sweet Home* investigates forms of romantic self-deception and imaginative escapism; *High Hopes* and *Life Is Sweet* examine the relation of abstract ideals and goals to practical human expressions of intimacy and affection. As in Ozu's work (which is to my knowledge the most extended cinematic illustration of this structural house-of-mirrors effect), virtually all of the characters in each film are versions of each other. They figure alternative destinies or represent variations of each other's pasts and futures (as Ozu's older- and younger-generation figures almost always do). The parallelism allows us to compare different responses to, different ways of coping with, the same imaginative situation. In fact, this aspect of Leigh's work is so central to its meaning that recognizing and registering the imaginative comparisons and contrasts is far more important to understanding the film than following the plot is.

Although it might appear to be a fairly straightforward satire of the British class system, *Who's Who* is an echo chamber of comparisons and contrasts of various forms of imitation, posing, and inauthenticity. The film (which thematically concludes the "hollow man" trilogy begun with *Nuts in May* and *Abigail's Party*) presents a nightmare vision of individuals on the brink of erasure as searching and radical as anything by Chantal Akerman or Peter Greenaway. Leigh goes even further than he did in his previous works in terms of employing parallel constructions to compare and contrast scenes, characters, and events.[2] *Who's Who* is an intricate mesh of visual, verbal, psychological, and narrative rhymes and half-rhymes. One form this takes is the paralleling of the words, actions, and mannerisms of "low" and "high" characters – as when Alan wears an ascot and drinks sherry in two scenes, and Nigel, Giles, Francis, and Lord Crouchurst do the same or similar things in others.

Alan looks even more ridiculous than he otherwise might insofar as his mimicry of upper-class manners is intercut with the performances of authentic uppers; the viewer sees how different the real highbrows are from his fantasies of them. But the first sign of *Who's Who* being more than a conventional satire is the fact that the comparison goes beyond the usual one of mocking the "low" characters' pretensions. Leigh's irony functions in *both* directions. Insofar as the uppers are narratively associated with Alan's and April's imitations of them, their bloodlines come off looking not that different from April's cat genealogies. Even more interestingly, at certain points the comparison is not ironic. Alan and April are not being satirized. There seem to be more true heart and soul in Alan and April's mock-ceremonies – however comically inappropriate, absurd, and stilted they may be – than in the real ceremonies of the upper-class figures. The disturbing implication is that the imitation may be more real (in feeling and meaning) than the original. Rather than mocking Alan and April, we actually start to care about them, in a weird, comical way.

The repetitions and linkages in *Who's Who* also involve words and phrases (sometimes spoken by the same character, at others by different characters). For example, early in the film, while waiting for the elevator, Alan runs into his boss, Francis, and asks how his wife is. Francis says she is "flourishing as ever." After they get into the elevator, the boss reciprocates by asking Alan how *his* wife is doing. When Alan replies that April is "flourishing as ever," neither cracks a smile.

There are many other examples of the verbal echo-chamber effect. In another scene, we hear Francis, who works in an investment house, consoling someone about his financial problems by uttering "Bad luck!" with a jaunty tone of voice. Then, a few minutes later, in the scene after the one between Francis and Alan, Lord Crouchurst uses the exact same phrase with the exact same intonation to console Francis for not having time to take a vacation. On his part, Alan employs a series of "rhyming" phrases in various conversations – for example, two or three times telling different characters that he and his wife keep "open house."

The verbal repetitions partly function in a conventionally satirical way. The vacuity of Francis', Lord Crouchurst's, and Alan's rhetoric is being satirized. Alan's and Francis' "flourishing as ever" and Francis' and Lord Crouchurst's "Bad luck!" come off as the pronouncements of characters mechanically cycling through canned verbal anodynes. All three are being mocked for their vapidity, and Alan is also being satirized for aping his superiors. But, just as in the doubling of "high" and "low" gestures, costumes, and ceremonies, there is something more than irony going on here. Concepts of satire and mockery do not do justice to the effect of Leigh's linkages. The repetitions do more than mock the characters; they fundamentally alter the cinematic experience. The viewer processes information differently from the way he does in a mere "realistic" narrative. To see or hear something twice is to see or hear it differently than when one encounters it once. When scenes are rhymed and events cross-referenced, they are subtly drained of a degree of emotional impact and immediacy. When phrases are echoed, not only does a little of the meaning leak out of them, but their "phraseness" is revealed. The viewer no longer sees and hears meanings and actions but poses, formulas, stances. The systematization of the system becomes salient.[3]

Our understanding of character also shifts. Since the characters not only speak in a kind of code ("breast man," "leg man," "Bad luck!"

"flourishing as ever") but pass the phrases from person to person, a viewer doesn't experience any of the speakers – even the first one – as an originator of his own expression; each is only a reflector of preexisting phrases and tones. Where everyone and everything echoes someone or something else, the notion of an originating, controlling, first "voice" becomes meaningless. To borrow Emerson's term, there are *only* "referred existences."

The clear impression is that the language speaks the speakers, rather than the other way around. The characters become, in deconstructionist terms, "semiotic functions" of an "episteme." Even more than *Abigail's Party* did, *Who's Who* leaves behind the personalism of traditional drama. The film experiments with drama not generated by or anchored in individual consciousness. It is less about individuals than the systems that define them, which is why to discuss any of the characters as individuals with personal psychological or emotional problems would be to miss the point, as my chapter on *Abigail's Party* already argued. The figures in *Who's Who* take the phrase "style makes the man" to another level, where the man disappears and only the style remains. Individuals no longer exist; everyone is a type, a generic bundle of received forms. Alan, Anthony, Francis, Nigel, Giles, Samantha, and the others are less individuals than tuning forks vibrating to preexisting cultural frequencies.[4]

Nuts in May and *Abigail's Party* make clear Leigh's attitude toward all forms of group thinking, group feeling, group identity, and group expression. There are few artists who are more vehemently opposed to homogenization of values and standardization of emotions. The individualism of Leigh's own style – its focus on quirks, crotchets, and eccentricities of all sorts, its relishing of verbal and physical idiosyncrasy – is his implicit reply to the expressive world he imagines here.

The insistent parallels, repetitions, and linkages in *Who's Who* change the nature of the artistic experience by placing words, gestures, and actions, as it were, in quotation marks. Leigh takes what was merely a tendency in *Abigail's Party* and *Nuts in May* and elevates it to the status of a law of nature. Roger Sloman in *Nuts in May* and Alison Steadman and Tim Stern in *Abigail's Party* were able, by employing a slight hesitation in their speech rhythms, an archness in their tone, or a somewhat mechanical cadence in their line deliveries, to "bracket" particular words and phrases and suggest that they were received expressive formulas. In those films, it was an intermittent effect; here, virtually *every* line delivery and interaction has this bizarre quotational quality. Beyond that, when

Beverly called José Feliciano "fantastic," "sexy," and "sensitive" or Keith lauded the virtues of vegetarianism, we felt that their expressions – however shallow and received – carried some personal conviction or feeling. But when it comes to Nigel's, Anthony's, or Samantha's words, more often than not, they are *only* phrases. It is *all* what T. S. Eliot called "Bovarism" – talking-to-hear-yourself-talk, to impress yourself and your listener with a depth of feeling and thought that doesn't refer to anything outside itself.

Virtually everything anyone says (and most of the things they do) in *Who's Who* is placed in invisible italics that communicate that it is being said for effect. The characters talk in a code that declares itself as code and asks the viewer to treat it as code, though the characters themselves, of course, may be ignorant of its "codeness" (Emma Bovary or Othello would, after all, be the last to perceive their own Bovarism). To hear Francis and Lord Crouchurst utter "Bad luck!" as a term of consolation (in a tone implying that losing your fortune is no different from being outscored in a football match), or Alan formulaically invoke keeping "open house," is to encounter words used not as bearers of truth and meaning, but as incantations in a magical ceremony.[5]

The viewer is, in the Brechtian sense of the term, *alienated* from what is being presented – placed at critical distance, the better to process it as the expression of an abstract system of relationships and understandings. Leigh goes against the grain of "realist" presentation, which attempts to make the viewer forget he is watching a movie, to induce a deliberate skepticism and awareness of the constructed nature of the work and the lives portrayed in it. The goal is to pull the viewer *out of the work*, to hold him at a certain emotional and intellectual distance from what is being presented, in order to reveal "the structurality of its structure" (in Derrida's phrase). There are a variety of alienation devices in *Who's Who* beyond the rhymed characters and events and repeated lines I have already mentioned. Characters constantly mouth phrases that call attention to themselves as "canned," clichéd, or "processed" in one way or another.

Sometimes the received nature of a character's utterances is obvious, as when April comments that "a picture is worth a thousand words" or that a doctor's signature "looks just like a doctor's signature." At other times, it may be a little less so. For example, in the three- or four-minute sequence during which we are introduced to Alan, he tells his office mate Kevin that the Queen Mother is "a great lady and a very gracious person," who "deeply grieved" when King George "passed away." He then goes on to call Petula Clark "a very courageous woman" who has "made a new life in a foreign land," for which he "greatly admire[s] her." A minute or so later he adds that he himself lives in "a garden apartment" in "a very nice situation," where he and his wife April "tend to be open house," and that night they intend to "spend a quiet evening in." And in the next scene in the film, Alan consoles April by telling her that another woman who is April's cat pedigree nemesis is "an evil, idle gossip" and "a frightened woman."

Richard Kane's slightly stilted delivery makes it clear what it going on. Alan is uttering Newspeak, though in a sense more insidious and subversive than Orwell's *1984* conveyed. No Big Brother forces Alan to talk this way; he does it to himself. The Queen Mother phrases are from a celebrity bio; the King George reference is from the obituary notice in the paper; the remarks about Petula Clark are from the Sunday supplement; the apartment description is from a house and garden magazine for the horsey set (Alan must have seen it in the doctor's office). And, last but not least, the comment about the pet breeder is from a television talk show – if it isn't something Alan's mother said to him when he was six to console him when the school bully picked on him. They are all bumper-sticker substitutes for thought and feeling – pious, approved, middle-brow sentiments – a cartload of processed, canned feelings packaged for public consumption that bear as little relation to actual life as what is broadcast on television news programs on any given night.

Even more than his close relation, Laurence, Alan is a modern-day Polonius, turning experience into a series of boilerplate platitudes, as if thinking and feeling were no different from making a soufflé: You combine preestablished ingredients according to a recipe, whip it all together with a little feeling, and out comes the guaranteed top-quality product. It is the inversion of everything Leigh has devoted his career to. The mystery and uniqueness of individual experience evaporates. Even Alan disappears; he is erased by his own rhetoric. He is a transparent, invisible man; when we look in his direction, we see right through to the Sunday supplements. If we listen for him, we only hear other people's words and feelings.

If Alan were the only missing person in the film, we might think these remarks were merely intended to satirize his upper-class pretensions (which they do). But he is not the only chameleon, only the most self-taught one. Virtually every character in *Who's Who* has the same relation to his or her experience that Alan does, cycling through empty routines (Samantha's "girl, girl, chap, chap"); shopworn imitations of cleverness (Samantha's *faux* witty response to Nigel's "Thank you for coming"); hollow catch phrases (Alan's "You don't know what it is to be young and free"); inane witticisms (Francis' "I was detained by a lady on the stairs"); and verbal pose-striking (the talking-for-effect at Nigel's party). It is all phrase making, bits, business, games, positionings, posturings, preenings.

Even while Alan is hopping from one cliché to another concerning Petula Clark, the Queen, and his own life, his office mate Kevin is indulging in another set of clichéd, coded responses – making a trite pun (involving "homosexuality" and "hemophilia"), slapping his own hand over a verbal indiscretion, and grimacing and groaning on cue in displays of formulaic male rallying. While Kevin and Alan prance their minuet, Leigh intercuts a shot of two other members of the office staff, Anthony and Giles, pausing outside their office door to indulge in an interaction that is as much in code as Kevin's and Alan's. They jauntily skip from male locker-room heartiness (discussions of their dates in terms of being a "breast" or "leg" man) to high-arts chaffing (is opera bashing "frank" or "Philistine"?). Meanwhile, in an inner office, Francis, the senior member of the brokerage firm for which they all work, is shown engaged on the phone rattling off another kind of male code connected with stocks and bonds. (His telegraphic references range from "bed and breakfasts" and "runs" to whether a call is from "A. A." or "A. H.") There is no escape from the codes, postures, and affectations, no matter where we look.

Not even off the job, at home, or at play. As the narrative shifts from the characters' public to their private lives, the formulas don't drop away but merely shift their ground. Giles, Nigel, Samantha, and Anthony are as mannered at the dinner party as they are in their work interactions. Alan and April are just as enslaved to approved attitudes at home ("Sherry, *cherie?*") as Alan and Kevin are at work. In this view of it, life becomes a kind of dumb show in which everyone is mimicking a set of preformulated attitudes and prefabricated poses. In this orgy of publicity, privacy disappears. Life becomes its outside. Experience becomes generic. Its mystery and wonder and interiority are erased.

It is shrewd of Leigh to have organized his narrative around scenes involving financial management, stock trading, animal breeding, autograph collecting, pet photography, and a dinner party. All are worlds of artificial, symbolic values, which is why you can be wiped out on the stock market over lunch by a rumor (or your fortune can be made by a hot tip), just as surely as you can be blackballed in the cat-pedigree world by a judge who decides that "Conrad's nose is too long," or ruined by giving a dinner party where the guest list or seating is wrong or the silverware laid out incorrectly.

The generality of the expressive situation should prove that Leigh's target is a state of imaginative derangement that has nothing to do with class or economics. The problem *Who's Who* examines is not really manners and mannerisms, how these characters talk or interact, but how they think and feel. In this nightmare vision of depersonalization, not just the characters' words and gestures but their ideas and emotions are received. They think with someone else's brain and feel with someone else's heart. In this world of surfaces, identity is skin-deep. Style is everything; content nothing. These characters are their clothes. It's not what you are that counts, but what you wear. The filmmaker most committed to deep definitions of selfhood has created a film of the shallowest possible selves.[6]

Yet, at the same time, it is important to recognize that the power of *Who's Who* (and the reason Leigh was attracted to the subject) is that the film is *not* a total contradiction or inversion of his own beliefs, but an exaggeration of them. In the passage quoted in the Stylistic Introduction, Madame Merle said that we are constituted by the surfaces of our lives. As she puts it, "every human being has his shell and you must take the shell into account." These are propositions I argued that Leigh would agree with and which all of his films affirm. In *Who's Who* he simply takes the concept of having a shell a little further than he usually does. That is to say, in effect, Leigh's target in *Who's Who* is not really someone else's understanding of life; it is his own. One might say that he is testing the point at which *having* a shell (which he believes is a fact of life) becomes *being* a shell (which horrifies him). In other words, Leigh is engaged in exploring the limits of his own view. To complete the parallel, I might add in passing that James was doing the same thing in *The Portrait of a Lady*. As much as James may have subscribed to Isabel's view of expression and perceived Merle's limitations (she is, after all, a kind of villain in the novel), Merle also represented an aspect of his own understanding of life, which is what makes her critique of Isabel so compelling.

The number and equality of treatment of the characters in *Who's Who* contribute to the feeling that no one is distinguishable from anyone else. This seventy-five-minute film has sixteen more or less equally important characters (more by far than any other of Leigh's works up to *Topsy Turvy*, including films almost twice as long), with the result that they pass before us in a near blur. In the early scenes, the upper-class figures in particular come and go so rapidly and indistinguishably (talking, gesturing, acting, and dressing so similarly), that they seem interchangeable. Everyone looks, talks, and acts like everyone else. Does that voice belong to Nigel or Giles? Which of the near-homonym names did that other character just mention? Which one is Nigel and which is Giles, anyway? (Or was it that we just saw or heard Kevin, who bears more than a passing resemblance to Giles?) Is that female face called Samya, Samantha, or Selina? Then again, does Samya go under the name of Sonya at a few points (as a few of my students are convinced is the case)? Is even Alan certifiably Alan, or is he Jack (as Francis appears to call him at one point)? The title of the film is not only a pun on the status seeking of the characters, it is a question that even a fairly attentive viewer finds himself asking at least a few times during a screening.

Leigh's camera angles and positioning add to the indistinguishability in several scenes. The two brief scenes in the hallway in which Anthony and Giles do their "hail-fellow-well-met, breast-man/leg-man routine" (at least I *think* it is Anthony and Giles) are photographed from the chest down. All a viewer sees and hears is standardized male "slap 'em on the arm" gestures and standardized "How's it going, old man?" tones. The breakup of Nigel's party is similarly photographed at one point from the characters' necks down. In both instances, we don't really miss the faces, and it is fair to say that they would add nothing, since the characters' facial expressions would undoubtedly be just as generic as their tones, gestures, and stances. These figures don't need faces.

To invoke Lévi-Strauss (an appropriate reference point in this triumph of poststructuralism), in this world nothing is "raw"; everything is "cooked." From the stock market to the world of cat breeding, styling, and photography, to the worship of celebrities, to the way you and your guests interact at a dinner party, nothing has any intrinsic value; everything takes its value from its place in the system. "Reality" is a meaningless concept; as Nabokov said, it should always be put in quotation marks. Nothing is merely itself; everything is what it is because of the system of conventions, rules, relationships, and references it is plugged into.[7] Form has replaced content.

Language has become completely decoupled from meaning. Where Alan and April can be said to hold "open house" and a financial reverse can be called "bad luck," anything can mean anything. It's all gestures, poses, indications of feeling. All of life has become a version of Beverly's "Is it for us?" Beaujolais remark. One character can express dismay that the forks are on the wrong side of the plates with the same degree of passion (in fact, somewhat more) with which another says she is down to her last twenty thousand pounds a year. What does it tell us about the relationship of expression to truth and feeling when the prime minister's secretary can write you that "Mrs. Thatcher was delighted to hear from you, and is delighted to send you a photograph . . . with her warmest wishes" and mean it, not deceitfully or hypocritically, but as a perfectly sincere and candid utterance?

In one of the most harrowing (and diabolically clever) touches, even five-year-old Serena (whose identity, even more than her name, more than half-rhymes with Samya and Samantha) is shown to have already been woven into the film's artificial systems of signification (both the systems the characters are aware of and the systems Leigh creates with his movie). In one of Leigh's slyest doublings, young Serena's greeting of Francis is paired with the vamp Samantha's greeting of boys at Nigel's dinner party. The younger and older girls identically cross their legs and captivatingly lounge backward on the sofa when a man is heard approaching the room. The point is that even little Serena has already learned the rules of "femininity," "seductiveness," "poise," and "allure." In this film, even a five-year-old has internalized the artificial system of signification. There is no such thing as childhood; no such state as innocence; no realm of nature unpolluted by culture.

It is not accidental that a number of the scenes in *Who's Who* focus on acts of seeing or being seen. Kevin and Alan voyeuristically look out of their office window at two other characters cavorting in a neighboring office. April poses her cats for a pet photographer. Alan costumes himself and poses for his guests. Samantha (and young Serena) pose to be seen by men. The problem Leigh is dramatizing is not only that appearance has become everything, it is that seeing someone (or being seen by them) has replaced interacting with them. Visionary relations replace social relations; experience becomes a mental phenomenon. The characters in *Who's Who* have turned life into a series of imagined relations that could not contrast more sharply with the physicality of Leigh's own understanding of experience. No filmmaker is less Hitchcockian or more critical of purely "visionary" relationships with experience (in both the optical and the imaginative sense). In their focus on surfaces and denial of depths, *Who's Who*'s characters have left their bodies behind and evaporated in a steam of thought.

As we have seen, one of the major problems Leigh focuses on throughout his oeuvre is the fallacy of abstract relationships to experience. In their different ways, Peter, Pat, the Thornleys, Keith, Beverly, and virtually everyone in *Who's Who* live in their heads, while the entire stylistic and narrative enterprise of Leigh's work is devoted to reinstating the claims of the body and the senses. The embodiment of Leigh's style, the physicality of the performances he elicits, are in and of themselves implicit critiques of the unreality of these characters' relations to experience.

In this respect, Leigh's work presents a particular challenge for critics who would explicate it. It is in the nature of critical explication that it abstracts meanings similarly to the way the flawed characters in these films do. For most critics, too, nothing is merely itself. Everything is symbolic of or related to something else in a chain of inter- and intratextual signification. But that intellectualism, that mentalistic transformation is precisely the relationship to experience (both lived and viewed experience) that Leigh is critiquing in these works.

The critic who views *Bleak Moments, The Kiss of Death, Nuts in May, Abigail's Party,* or any of Leigh's other films in terms of their abstract cultural meanings, translating events and interactions into symbolic or metaphoric significances, is part of the problem that is being anatomized in these works. Leigh's films are attempts to bring us to sensorily embodied and temporally aware ways of knowing that are alternatives to our inveterate symbolic and metaphoric ways of processing information – including those employed in criticism. One might say that Leigh's style is designed to resist critical generalizations and correct critical abstractions as much as to resist and correct characters' imaginative abstractions. He attempts to bring critics to their senses (and to sensorily and temporally informed modes of understanding) as much as his characters. To understand these works, we must learn to think without ideas. We must, in William James' phrases, "turn [our] face toward sensation" and "dive back into the flux," making the move from conceptions to perceptions.[8] We must force ourselves to navigate the second-by-second, beat-by-beat twists and turns of complexly unsystematic interactions, without the luxury of being able to take an abstract or symbolic shortcut around the details. In a word, we must learn actually to look and listen again, to stop thinking and begin caring.

The world of the characters in *Who's Who* has become as denatured and abstract as that of the stock exchange. Its sources of value are entirely imaginative. Identity and meaning are purely relational. You are not your body and mind and senses, but who you know, how you dress, where you are seated. All of the characters gleefully inscribe themselves into a "system" of connections and relationships. They exist only insofar as they can be versions of someone else. The film's insistent narrative circulation from character to character, class to class, and generation to generation is meant to drive home the point that virtually no one escapes (or even wants to escape) the relational system. The individual disappears. These texts have no authors. The system creates all of the meanings within it.

Everyone is imitating and attempting to impress someone else, as if authenticity and validation were only one step away, reality were just one level above them, at another doorstep just outside their own. *Who's Who* weaves an interlocking chain of players, each of whom attempts to fill his own emptiness by imitating someone else; but the irony is that the person they want to be, the identity they want to assume, is just as empty as they are.

There is no escape from the hollowness. Alan plays up to Anthony and Giles, junior stockbrokers; Anthony and Giles play up to Francis, senior stockbroker; Francis plays up to Lord and Lady Crouchurst, senior trust fund executors. Everybody at Nigel's dinner party plays at being somebody else, some imaginary sophisticated adult they wish they were. The horrific wit of Leigh's presentation is that when, partway into the film, we finally arrive at the vertiginous tip-top of the pyramid, when we are ushered into Lord and Lady Crouchurst's, we don't find an ideal that justifies all the imitation, but rather one more vacuum, only a more consummate abdication of individuality. Lord and Lady Crouchurst are themselves revealed to be playing only a slightly more elaborate version of the game everyone else lower down in the social pecking order is playing. In the first scene in which we see them, they are busily arranging a week's worth of lunches and dinners with other beautiful people, where all of the values are abstract and relational (wittily communicated in the tones with which various names and events are uttered). They have delegated their one potentially authentic, biological function, the raising of their daughter, to a nanny. Leigh's point is clear. In this circle of nullity, nothing is real. There is no there anywhere. *Who's Who* is a house of mirrors in which there are only reflections of reflections (in both the cognitive and the optical senses).

Most critics unfortunately seem to have missed the radicalism of the film. The otherwise insightful Paul Clements calls it "the least satisfactory of [Leigh's] work in dramatic terms," and Michael Coveney seconds the motion by arguing that, "having assembled all the various components and situations, Leigh fails to contrive a pulling together of the strands. There is no dramatic convergence."[9] Unpacked and expanded, these demurs translate into two related objections: first, that the film is static, lacking a decisive narrative action or a compelling problem to be solved; second, that the ending is flat and anticlimactic.

I would argue that what Leigh's detractors take to be deficiencies are integral to the vision of the film. As to the noneventfulness of the narrative, it is true that the film is really only a series of paralleled, repeated interactions and conversations; but, as I hope my previous discussion has demonstrated, far from being a shortcoming, the iterative, echoic quality of the narrative is an expression of the nature of these characters' lives. Leigh creates a world of endless, pervasive emulation, where looking and talking in imitation of the ways other characters look and talk is the point. Stasis, not action or movement, is the very definition of these existences.

The objection to the flatness of the ending betrays a comparable misunderstanding of Leigh's goal. Though we may crave catharsis, may want Nigel to rage, scream, or cry with despair in the film's final scene, Leigh deliberately denies us such release. If Nigel were to break down and wail, if he were to undergo a life-changing *anagnorisis*, not only would he not be who he is, but the promise of insight, transformation, or renewal would let the viewer off the emotional hook. As I noted in my discussion of *Nuts in May*, Leigh deliberately denies the viewer a cathartic release at the end of most of his films. He denies it at the end of *Bleak Moments*. He denies it at the end of *Abigail's Party*, when he could so easily work Laurence's death for high emotion but instead turns the scene into an absurd melee of mismatched tragicomic tones, crisscrossing arguments, and deliberately zany, irrelevant, or distracting bits of stage business (like Angie's "cramp"). He denies it here.

In the scene in his living room Nigel may well perceive some of the vacuity of his life as a result of the failure of his dinner party; but whatever his recognition may or may not be, Leigh keeps it in a decidedly minor key. Puccini's *La Bohème* is playing on the sound track, but the relation of the image to the music is one of disjunction. The scene emphatically does *not* resonate with operatic emotionality. Beyond the calculated mismatch of the emotional expressiveness of the music and the emotional inexpressiveness of the characters (an effect Leigh repeats in *Grown-Ups* in the scene in which *Swan Lake* plays in the background), Leigh prevents the viewer from paying too much attention to Nigel and his situation from accumulating very much emotional energy by having other things going on at the same time – talk, movements, and other characters coming into and moving out of the frame.[10] Leigh also refuses to provide a close-up of Nigel's face. (The slow zoom that ends the scene resembles that at the end of *Hard Labour* and is equally restrained in its emotionality.) *La Bohème* may be playing, but this world is the opposite of Puccini's lush evocation of grand emotional depths. If we are looking for emotional breakthroughs or breakouts from the systems in which the characters are inscribed, we shall have to look elsewhere than Nigel's eyes.

There are only four characters in *Who's Who* who even possibly escape from the systems that corrupt all the other human relationships in the film. The first is an office clerk named Sonya who seems entirely free of the airs and mannerisms of the other characters and expresses authentic, idiosyncratic feeling in several scenes (an event that is almost unprecedented in *Who's Who*). The second and third are the two characters visible through Kevin and Alan's window who cavort spontaneously and eccentrically in another office. And the fourth is the nanny at Lord Crouchurst's, who, despite the fact that she is treated as a functionary and denied a name by the other characters, shows just the sort of playful independence of spirit the Crouchursts themselves lack. But the sad fact of *Who's Who* is how little these four figures count for in the narrative. They are relegated to brief performances on its extreme margins. *Who's Who* is a sinking ship on which the only survivors are the servants, menials, and secretaries.

8

Inhabiting Otherness: *Grown-Ups*

One of the misguided criticisms of my work is that I patronize working-class characters. Now this is basically rubbish. Not true at all. What I actually do is put on the screen very accurate depictions of working-class people. And that is what you do not normally get on the screen. And because of that, when it's seen from the perspective of non-ordinary, non-middle-class characters it seems to be a statement about class tensions when it often isn't. It's just that that's who they are, basically. ... There's an enormous Anglophile population [in the United States], and they import all sorts of British television, but it's all the mythical British. As in *Masterpiece Theater*, it's not real.

– Mike Leigh

As we have seen, one of Leigh's basic narrative devices to test his characters and reveal their limitations is to pair them with antitypes. In *Grown-Ups*, Dick and Mandy are precisely the kind of students who give migraines to teachers like Ralph and Christine Butcher. And Gloria, in turn, exists to disrupt first Dick and Mandy's own small purchase on order and subsequently Ralph and Christine's. The meeting of matter and antimatter almost always generates farce, but what makes a Leigh film different from an Ealing picture is that the comedy is also serious. The comical outer events are vehicles for serious inner reassessments and revelations. The physical uproar leads to genuine emotional upheaval. Peter's awkward face-off with Sylvia, Trevor's clumsy interaction with Linda in her living room, Keith's flipped-out fight with Finger, Beverly's and Sharon's screaming meemies over Laurence's body, and Gloria's escapade in the Butchers' entrance hall represent transformative moments for the characters involved. Leigh's tickle may make a viewer laugh, but it can also bring him to tears of self-recognition.

The bizarre mix of tones is one of the hallmarks of Leigh's work. In

Grown-Ups' climactic scene, as Gloria first locks herself in the Butchers' bathroom and then clings to their stairway railing (with everyone around her yelling something different at the same time), even as we gasp for breath and tears of laughter stream down our cheeks, we also movingly feel Gloria's loneliness and desperation, Dick and Mandy's entirely understandable exasperation, and Ralph and Christine's states of emotional disconnection from each other and everyone else. The uncanny blending of farce and pathos brings us to an incredibly responsive emotional and intellectual state, precisely because we are not able to pigeonhole the experience as being one thing or another. In being forced out of our preestablished categories of response, in being emotionally boggled, our hearts and minds are strangely opened.[1]

Like most of Leigh's other works, *Grown-Ups* is organized in terms of parallel characters, events, and situations. The overarching comparison involves the film's two main couples. Not only are Ralph and Christine and Dick and Mandy both childless couples, living side by side in similar physical situations, but Leigh writes and edits the film so as to have successive scenes echo one another. In one brief sequence, for example, we watch first Dick and then Ralph interacting with their wives while lying down on the couch, Mandy putting the milk bottle out before going to bed followed by Christine doing the same thing, and finally, Dick and Mandy talking in bed followed by Ralph and Christine talking in bed.[2]

Leigh uses the parallels to set a kind of trap for the viewer at the start of the film. Dick and Mandy seem so rough, rude, and coarse, and Ralph and Christine so intelligent, articulate, well-educated, and polite (at least in comparison), that it is almost inevitable a viewer will conclude that the point of the juxtapositions is to reveal Dick and Mandy's faults and Ralph and Christine's virtues. Dick and Mandy bicker and argue so continuously and the Butchers interact in such a scrupulously polite and deferential way that it is almost inevitable that a viewer assumes that the arguments are evidence of the former couple's inferiority.[3]

Much as Leigh did with the implied comparison between the middle-class Keith and the lower-class campers in *Nuts in May* (and similarly to what he will do in terms of a subsequent comparison of "refined," middle-class Barbara with "tough," lower-class Mark in *Meantime*), he is encouraging the viewer to jump to a false conclusion. Ralph and Christine are gradually revealed to be in real trouble, while Dick and Mandy are shown to have by far the healthier and more loving relationship. Leigh turns our cultural stereotypes (against argumentation and in favor of agreement; against lower-class forms of expression and in favor of middle-class ones; against roughness and in favor of polish) against us. The result is that at some point partway through *Grown-Ups*, we are forced humbly to reevaluate everything we thought we understood.

About the disagreements in particular, we gradually realize that while Dick and Mandy express their differences the Butchers hide theirs. It takes a while for us to see what is really going on precisely because the Butchers have wrapped their discontent in so many layers of obliquity. We slowly realize that there is absolutely no real caring or communication between them, that polite forms and conventional formulas have completely replaced the genuine expression of feeling.

Ralph and Christine are in an ontological crisis as great as that of any of Leigh's earlier figures, and far from counting against them, Dick and Mandy's spats, chaffing, and arguments are in fact evidence of their ongoing emotional engagement with each other.[4] They care enough about and are open enough with each other to express their differences. Once that becomes clear, the viewer is chastened and half-ashamed that he has let his class prejudices color his judgments.

As I suggested in terms of the deliberate outrageousness of some of the shots in *Hard Labour* (like the hairy-back scene), there is a part of Leigh that clearly enjoys shocking, upsetting, or catching the viewer off guard in these ways. His work is quite calculatedly assaultive and provocative. In presenting these two couples Leigh deliberately encourages the viewer to jump to a false conclusion in order to trip him up or surprise him. He is deliberately playing a kind of trick on him.

But at the same time it is important to notice the difference between Leigh's tricks and those of a filmmaker like Hitchcock. Hitchcock's narrative surprises and reversals really teach us nothing; they merely manipulate our feelings, stoking up the drama, artificially creating suspense. The narrative misunderstandings and revelations Leigh orchestrates teach us important things. They alert us to certain forms of emotional prejudice to which we are susceptible. They show us how what passes for apparent harmony (like the behavior of the Butchers) can be a kind of emotional disconnection. They instruct us to process information in more careful, more sensitive ways. Leigh's devices move us to a more open, less judgmental relationship to what is on screen. Leigh is attacking emotional and intellectual clichés. He wants his characters to resist easy understanding, and to the extent that a viewer indulges in reductive, trite, or formulaic modes of knowledge, the film trips him up and shocks him out of them.

Dick and Mandy (*top*) and Ralph and Christine (*bottom*) – paradigms of radically opposed forms of human relationship and dramatic interaction (Photos courtesy the Kobal Collection: BBC)

One might say that Leigh's tricks (unlike Hitchcock's) are based, not on providing misleading information – not by telling us lies – but by showing us true things that we don't expect to be true. We misunderstand scenes not because they are deceptive, but because they are unconventional. It is not ultimately the director who misleads the viewer but the viewer who misleads himself. The reevaluations Leigh's work sponsors are attempts to move us to a place of truth: to force us to replace our abstract, shorthand, quick ways of knowing with slower, more attentive, more caring, longhand forms of knowing.

Once we have extricated ourselves from a mistaken interpretation of the relation of the two couples in *Grown-Ups* and have started to look and listen freshly, the real function of Leigh's comparisons and contrasts might be said to begin. They are a way of tuning up our eyes and ears, allowing us to hear vocal and emotional dog frequencies that we might otherwise not catch. As the film shuttles between scenes, events, and conversations featuring Ralph and Christine on the one side and Dick, Mandy, and Gloria on the other, we become sensitized to nuances of moods, tones, feelings, and forms of interaction that would not be apparent if we did not have the opportunity to see, feel, and think about everything twice, and to compare one instance with another.

The important point is that Leigh's parallels are not conventionally tendentious, ironic, or satiric. They don't merely contrast characters and situations, suggesting that one is right and the other wrong. Rather, the comparisons genuinely work in both directions to adjust our perception of each of the terms compared. They heighten and tune up our capacities of responsiveness. The goal is not to oppose Christine to Mandy or Gloria, or Ralph to Dick, but to help us to understand all five characters in a deeper way than we could if we didn't have the other as a cross-reference.

We hear particular tones and moods in Christine's voice because it is so different from Mandy's. We hear still other things in it because it is similar to Gloria's. The forced peppiness of both Gloria's and Christine's voices feels more like an act of will because we have the other to compare it with. We feel things about Ralph because he is similar to Dick in some ways (as a fairly passive, protesting, somewhat henpecked husband) while being different from him in others (in his emotional disengagement and spacey intellectualism). We feel things about Gloria that we wouldn't otherwise because we can compare her with Christine on the one hand and Mandy on the other.[5] Dick and Mandy, in turn, come off as entirely more admirable and interesting than they might otherwise seem because of the implied contrasts not only with Ralph and Christine but with their own houseguests, Sharon and Gloria.

Although Leigh often expects his viewer to make moral judgments (e.g., about Peter, Mr. Thornley, Keith, or Beverly), his conception of morality is really quite different from the one that informs most American films, in which morality is a primary characteristic, an inherent, internal quality that underpins and preexists behavior. In American film, moral essence precedes practical expressive existence. Characters are defined according to preexisting internal qualities, which they in effect merely act out. One might say that American characters are bad or good even when they are not doing anything. In Leigh's films there are no moral essences, only moral effects. Morality is not a state of mind, a quality of soul deeper than behavior, but a description of the specific effects of local behaviors at particular moments.

The difference between an essentialized and nonessentialized understanding of morality plays itself out in several different ways. In the first place, while American characters with their inherent moral qualities can be more or less "all good" or "all bad," Leigh's morally nonessentialized characters are almost always mixed in their qualities. In *Nuts in May*, Keith can be idealistic and noble in some respects yet narrow and intolerant in others; in *Meantime*, Barbara can be generous and kind yet aloof and patronizing at the same time.

The viewer's judgment of a character is made far more complex in the nonessentialized understanding of morality. It is neither as rapid nor as certain. It is changeable. And it requires extended contact with a character. Since there is neither a moral essence to be perceived nor an intentional heart to be plumbed, the only way to understand Leigh's figures is to live with them for a while, slowly inducing the structures of their personalities and emotions by watching how they play themselves out in time, while comparing them with other characters' behavior (and induced intellectual and emotional structures). Morality becomes a relative, tentative, mixed, shifting judgment about a figure's performances, not the revelation of an essential, inherent quality.

It would be hard to overstate the importance of what Leigh is doing in this regard. To assimilate the difference between an essentialized and nonessentialized view of expression is to change one's whole relationship to experience. One is forced to enter into a much more provisional and contingent relationship with experience than in the other sort of film. One is forced to engage oneself with sensory particulars. Truth takes on temporal qualities. Rather than diving down to make contact with static, clear intentional depths, one must surf turbulent, turbid performative surfaces. They are all there are. The nature of personal identity itself changes. No one is anything in general; everyone is his specific, moment-by-moment expressions. Consciousness does not exist (at least not as a determinative, defining predisposition); we are our mutable, local expressions. There is no "pure," ideal, mental self, only a congeries of impure, mediated expressions. There is nothing but surfaces.[6]

As I already suggested in my discussion of *Hard Labour*, one of the ways in which Leigh's characters can be understood is in terms of the relative rigidity, fluidity, or responsiveness of their interactions, ranging from those who are relatively "frozen" and "fixed" in their tones, styles, and interactions to those who are more "fluid" and "flowing." A function of the parallels in *Grown-Ups* is to bring out the extent to which the Butchers' relationships are more rigid and static than the interactions between Dick, Mandy, Gloria, and Sharon.

As an illustration of how the process of comparing different degrees of fluidity works in *Grown-Ups*, I shall cite three conversations. The first two involve the Butchers. In the first, Christine is in the kitchen, having just come home from work, and Ralph is supine on the sofa (a position that matches Dick's in many of the film's scenes). The following shouted exchange between the two rooms takes place:

RALPH: Is that you?
CHRISTINE: Hello.
RALPH: Tea's still warm, I think.
CHRISTINE: What tea?
RALPH: What?
CHRISTINE: What tea is still warm?
RALPH: The tea.
CHRISTINE: There isn't any tea.
RALPH: The tea I made.
CHRISTINE: Oh, you've made some tea, have you? Well, it must have gone for a walk in the garden.
RALPH: I shouldn't think it has. (*Pause.*) What's that? Scotch Mist?
CHRISTINE: No. It's a teapot. (*Pause.*) Without any tea in it.
RALPH: Mm. Mm. . . .

In the second conversation, Ralph and Christine are eating supper in their kitchen:

CHRISTINE: We're playing you on Wednesday.
RALPH: Oh, yeah?
CHRISTINE: Mmm.
RALPH: Mm. Mm. Hockey?
CHRISTINE: Netball.
RALPH: Mm. Mm. Saw Barbara at lunchtime.
CHRISTINE: I tried to phone her at lunchtime.
RALPH: She was having her lunch.
CHRISTINE: Mm. Mm. This was after lunch.
RALPH: Oh, well, she was probably taking a class.
CHRISTINE: *Within* the lunch hour, but *after* lunch. (*Pause.*) I've got to finalize the arrangements for the match. (*Long pause.*) Got any marking?
RALPH: Little, yeah. I'll do it later.
CHRISTINE: Mmm.
RALPH: What's after?
CHRISTINE: Pineapple rings.
RALPH: That all?
CHRISTINE: Cream.
RALPH: Um. Mmm. . . .

The third conversation involves Dick, Mandy, Sharon, and Gloria reminiscing about their school days (in an interaction that is structurally compared with a parallel moment in which Ralph and Christine talk about Dick and Mandy and segue into a discussion of the Loch Ness monster while *Swan Lake* plays on the stereo):

MANDY: I met our new neighbors yesterday.
GLORIA: What are they like, Mand?
MANDY: He was our old teacher at school.
GLORIA: No! – What's his name?
MANDY: Mr. Butcher.
SHARON: She won't remember him.
MANDY: No.
GLORIA: Butcher? What'd he teach?
MANDY: Religious Knowledge.
GLORIA: No. We had Flicky Fleet.
MANDY AND SHARON (*in unison*): We had him as well.
DICK: Flicky Fleet never taught RK.
MANDY, GLORIA, AND SHARON (*in unison*): He did!
GLORIA: I had him. He used to like me.
DICK: We had Motrum.
MANDY: Yeah, we had her, but we had Flicky an' all.

SHARON: Butcher took over from Flicky?
MANDY: Yeah, that's right.
SHARON: Mondays and Fridays.
DICK: Flicky Fleet took Geography.
MANDY: He didn't, Dick. He took RK.
SHARON: Oh, he won't remember.
DICK: Oh, I was always hopping off, anyway.
GLORIA: Yeah, I know you were.
GLORIA: I wonder if old Hugh's still Head Master?
SHARON: Piggy.
DICK: Dirty old bugger he was.
MANDY: He was an' all. He used to get us in his office.
SHARON: I had to sit on his knee.
MANDY: Used to throw things on the floor; make you pick 'em up.
GLORIA: He did that to me once.
MANDY: Was minnies then and all.
GLORIA: I never wore no minnies!
MANDY: Oh you didn't, but we did!
DICK: He was all right, old Piggy! . . .

Although the tones are a large part of the experience, and cannot be captured in the written lines, the differences between the two groups of characters should still be apparent. Dick, Mandy, Sharon, and Gloria may be sharp-tongued and blunt; they may contradict and argue with each other; but they are actually listening and responding. They pick up on each other's comments, feelings, tones and answer them, beat by beat. Their interaction flows and surges with exchanged energies. They feed off each other emotionally. Each successively picks up the ball and runs with it, juking and swerving in a new direction, constantly responding to the countermoves of the others.

Although the Butchers are unfailingly polite, they don't really communicate. They occupy and defend nonintersecting imaginative positions. As they stall and circle round the same points, endlessly repeating themselves, or asking the other to repeat himself, their conversation stands still. It is as if they were on different wavelengths (or different planets). Nothing one says really reaches the other. In fact, nothing even seems to be heard and understood by the other. Their conversation consists of isolated pronouncements that come from nowhere and go nowhere. The chilly factuality of their talk illustrates their emotional insulation and distance. They don't energize each other playfully or otherwise, rallying, chaffing, trading emotions, bouncing off each other's feelings the way the other group does; in fact, they hardly seem to be listening to or responding to each other, which is why they have to explain and reexplain absolutely everything to make it clear. Ralph and Christine are in a state of complete intellectual and emotional disconnection. They don't argue, of course, but one might say it is because they don't take each other seriously enough to argue. In the tea conversation, Christine is certain she is right; Ralph is certain he is. What is there to argue about? In the supper table conversation, they might as well be strangers who just met.

Dick, Mandy, Sharon, and Gloria are like beautifully responsive tennis players, finely attuned to each other's moves, appreciative of the spin the other is able to put on the ball, ready at each point to unleash their own lightning fast, perfectly timed countermoves, as is even more obvious in performance than in quotation. Ralph and Christine, in contrast, can't keep even the shortest volley going. They keep hitting the ball past each other, or not even getting it over the net into the other's court. Their countermoves are hesitant, desynchronized, and mistimed.

Ralph and Christine are characterized by verbal mannerisms and tonal routines that remain the same throughout the film. It is appropriate that their ways of speaking are so formulaic because the very problem they figure is an inability to adjust their performance in response to anything that is going on around them. Christine's way of talking consists of smarmy politeness laced with irony. ("Oh, you've made some tea, have you? It must have gone for a walk in the garden.") Her tone is relentlessly (and gratingly) upbeat. Ralph rules a universe apparently intelligible to him alone (which is why he is always complaining about everyone else's stupidity). His way of expressing himself consists of a set of crackpot theories, strictly personal associations, and self-referential allusions that pop up in scene after scene (as well as a comical verbal tic – a hum or grunt Leigh probably borrowed from Yasujiro Ozu's *Autumn Afternoon* or *Record of a Tenement Gentleman* – that Leigh wittily employs to summarize his state of disconnection and self-absorption). In a sense, Ralph and Christine are always and only talking to themselves: he, cocooned in his web of private references; she, playing little self-congratulatory verbal games with herself to reassure herself how kind and thoughtful she is.

The difference from Dick, Mandy, Sharon, and Gloria could not be more evident. As "low brow" as they may seem, they engage in genuinely exploratory voyages of discovery in every one of their conversations. Unlike those of the Butchers, their interactions are not confined to predictable formulas or limited to narrow ranges of moods or styles.

They can seemingly go almost anywhere – tonally, meditatively, intellectually – which is to say, within the limits of character, their identities and relationships can also.[7] Note how tonally fluxional and intellectually zigzaggy even the brief excerpt I quoted is. While the Butchers are locked into static positions, the other interchange is constantly shifting in its tones, moods, and attitudes. Dick, Mandy, Sharon, and Gloria can be sarcastic or dismissive at one moment, playful or wistful at another, and deliberately outrageous or comically provocative at another (as in Dick's final tip of the hat to good old Piggy). While the Butchers are emotionally frozen in place, the identities and relationships of the others emotionally stream and surge.

A final difference is that Ralph and Christine's conversation is focused and purposeful, while that of Dick, Mandy, Gloria, and Sharon is loose and meandering. That might seem to favor the schoolteacher couple, but not in Leigh's view. Ralph and Christine ask each other functional questions with practical answers; the others respond emotionally and go with the flow. Leigh is always in favor of looser, less tendentious, less programmatic interactions – unregimented, open-ended, free-flowing exchanges of energies that don't force a relationship to conform to an agenda or follow a schedule. The zigzag is the straightest, indeed the truest, path. As Emerson said, nature has no straight lines.[8]

After Renoir, Leigh is one of the masters of group scenes like the ones I have quoted. Leigh's vision of life is fundamentally social. Experience is not private and solitary. It is not something that takes place in your head (in the Hitchcock vein) and that you have alone. It is expressed and shared with others. Your identity is interactional. Leigh's great characters are never loners, visionaries, or outcasts; they bring themselves into their fullest and most exciting existence in their interactions with others. Like Renoir, Leigh regards group interactions as fundamental measuring sticks by which his characters may be assessed. One of the recurring issues in his oeuvre might be said to be the question of whether characters are able to interact as nimbly and responsively as Dick, Mandy, Sharon, and Gloria do here or whether their meetings are closer to resembling the Butchers' state of noninteraction.[9]

The great characters in Leigh's films are asked to do the same thing the actors he directs are: to become ensemble players, masters and mistresses of supple, fluid responsiveness. For Leigh, partnering is what both art and life are fundamentally about. In this respect, his aesthetic goes against the grain of American film acting, where the goal is not ensemble playing but "starring." Everything in the American system works to create star players. American viewers are attracted to star names; American directors tailor their scripts to feature stars; and the American publicity system rewards stars financially. Even most American critics are captive to the power of the star. When an actor such as Orson Welles, Jack Nicholson, Harvey Keitel, or Meryl Streep goes on a riff, steals a scene, chews the scenery, or serves up a big, fat emotion under glass, the pros and cons of the particular moment may be discussed, but the very notion of understanding experience in terms of stars or starring performances is almost never questioned.

Leigh regards "starring" (in life and in art) not as a triumph but a problem. In his dramatic universe the goal is not to solo but to partner; not to stand out but to fit in. Acting is interacting. Beverly shows what Leigh thinks of stars. Like a bad television talk-show host, she dominates every conversation, controls every beat, and fights to avoid being upstaged by anyone; but the work she is in clearly reveals Beverly's devotion to star-turns to be a moral nightmare. To star is to ignore others' needs. Peter in *Bleak Moments*, Mr. Thornley in *Hard Labour*, Keith in *Nuts in May*, June in *Home Sweet Home*, and Johnny in *Naked* cast themselves as the stars of the scenes in which they appear. They talk *at* but never really *with* anyone they meet. None of them can put his own emotional needs aside long enough to interact with anyone in a flexibly responsive way. (As Peter and Johnny demonstrate at the ends of their films, these figures run in terror from the prospect of giving up even a little control, sharing even a little emotional space with anyone else.) Leigh shows how horrific their starring is. Jack Nicholson's or Harvey Keitel's domination of screen space and upstaging of other actors is never critiqued by their own works in this way.

According to Leigh, our supreme creative achievements do not come by "starring" but by *interacting*. His greatest characters are asked to engage in delicate dances of interactional awareness and adjustment in which they complexly partner each other. Partnering can take many different forms – from the minor-key game playing of Sylvia with Norman and Hilda in *Bleak Moments* and the brief dance of affection that takes place between Naseem and Ann in *Hard Labour*, to the more intricate pas de deux performed in certain scenes in *Four Days in July*, *Ecstasy*, and *Meantime*, to the evening-length ballets of *High Hopes* and *Life Is Sweet*.[10]

The preceding should suggest that the much praised ensemble performances in Leigh's work are not just an accidental side effect of his rehearsal methods: They are at the heart of his vision of experience. For

Leigh (as for Renoir), we are essentially not individuals but members of a group. We share our identities with others and define ourselves in interaction with them. Identity is relational.

At the same time, it is important to add that, for Leigh (as for Renoir), the interactional nature of life does not in the least entail leveling, homogenizing, or eradicating individual differences. In fact, it maximizes them. To watch any of Leigh's works is to be plunged up to your eyeballs in expressive idiosyncrasy and bodily uniqueness. It is to be circulated through an almost dizzying variety of different ways of talking, moving, thinking, and feeling – each of which is honored. In every possible way, Leigh's casting, scripting, and photography communicate his supreme respect for personal differences. It is not unimportant that one of Beverly's shortcomings in *Abigail's Party* (like Melody and Dave in *Home Sweet Home*) is that she erases or ignores differences in thought and feeling (as when she assumes Sue feels the same way she does about divorce). Her smug knowingness prevents anyone from differing from her understanding of them (just as Laurence's does).

Respect for individual differences may not sound as unusual as it is, but in fact the overwhelming majority of films (and scripts) unconsciously tend to privilege a particular way of thinking, feeling, or speaking. In mass-market films, the preferred view is usually that of the middlebrow viewer the film is meant to appeal to and not confuse or offend, so that any character with the least degree of expressive individuality is treated as being eccentric or weird. In most art films, Kiarostami's being an exception that proves the rule, one can hear a particular screenwriter's "voice" emerging from every characters' mouth – Woody Allen's most interesting characters all sounding like little Woody Allens and Orson Welles' like versions of him. These films are a kind of one-man finger-puppet show. To the extent that a character has the "right" sound or set of feelings, we are meant to admire him or her. And if a character acts, thinks, or feels differently from the director's or screenwriter's ideal, we are meant to judge him negatively (or regard him as a kook).

The virtuosic visual and acoustic styles of many films are other ways of leveling individual differences (as when the spooky lighting in a thriller makes all the characters scary, or the Top 40 soundtrack in another makes everyone seem hip). Critics are fond of praising the "vision" of filmmakers who make highly stylized films, but the downside of this so-called vision is its blindness to other ways of feeling and being. The style swallows everything in its path or assimilates it to its purposes. The potential uniqueness of everything and everyone in the work is eliminated or attenuated.

The magisterial, omniscient, godlike view of characters and situations offered by the Hitchcock film is another form of leveling and homogenization. Hitchcock's style promotes one way of seeing everything and rejects all others. Characters in Hitchcock's works who can't "see" (in both the optical and imaginative sense of the term) things in his way are either punished by the plot (by being either murdered or stalked) or treated as being fatuous. There is only one "correct" point of view possible, the view figured by the style of the film.[11]

Leigh goes as far as possible in the other direction. He doesn't level, filter, or homogenize the view. He shows us that there can be many different attitudes, many different ways of understanding, many different points of view in any one moment, no one of which is necessarily better or truer than any other. In any gathering of people, there is always more than one way of encountering experience. His work is an exultant celebration of this diversity of views, tones, and feelings.

The scene I quoted in which Dick, Mandy, Gloria, and Sharon reminisce about their school days, or the one involving Gloria on the Butchers' stairway, illustrate the point. Leigh takes the viewer on a breathtaking journey through utterly distinct perspectives as the scripting, shooting, and editing moves from face to face, voice to voice, mind to mind. The characters may be flawed or inadequate in various ways, but each is allowed to be (and cherished for being) himself or herself to the ultimate: Gloria, the most Gloria; Mandy, the most Mandy; Dick, Christine, and the others, the most themselves anyone can be.

Whereas Hollywood generally wants the point of view of its scenes to be as "neutral," "objective," or "generic" as possible, because it subscribes to the possibility of general understandings on the part of the viewer and generic relations to experience on the part of its characters, none of the experiences in Leigh's work aspires to be general or universal. Leigh rejects the concept of a view from nowhere. He asserts the inestimable value of a distinctive, personal perspective – indeed, of many different and sometimes warring perspectives. Everything is always seen from a certain angle. We do not get things neutrally, but through a particular set of eyes and ears. And every set is unique.

While Hollywood movies are invariably organized around main characters who, because they are always intended to be imaginative surrogates for the average viewer, never differ radically from the average viewer's perspectives and feelings, Leigh's characters embody genuinely alien perspectives and forms of expression. Hollywood grants us easy, automatic identification with figures not very different from ourselves, while Leigh asks us to go out of ourselves and enter into truly strange and unusual points of view. While Hollywood implicitly flatters us by making identification so easy, Leigh humbles us and forces us to work by making it challenging.

Dick is genuinely different from most viewers, as are Mandy and Gloria. It takes effort to get our minds around them and our emotions into a place where we can appreciate them. The work we are required to perform in order to understand what we are watching is what frustrates many viewers of Leigh's work. The world is a world, not of ourselves writ large, our own emotional and intellectual structures flatteringly mirrored, but of genuine "others" with challengingly "other" points of view.[12]

In a Hitchcock scene, there is always an "ideal" point of view on everything, a "right" or "best" way of understanding (generally, the perspective that is as close as possible to the director's own coolness, detachment, and sardonicism). In many of his films, the ideal view is a godlike one through godlike eyes, a view from above, a view detached from and beyond any character's possible view. Such a view is inconceivable to Leigh. There can be no cosmic truth, no abstract, impersonal truth. All truth is local – true in one time, place, and situation; false in another. All truth is individual. Every understanding is anchored in a particular mind, body, voice. There is no perfect or ideal truth (let alone a godlike omniscient view); all truth is personal and partial.[13]

Watch the school days conversation or the stairway scene again. Which character's view is the best or right one? What is the ideal way to understand the scene? The questions answer themselves. The very point of these scenes is that there is *no* right, true, best view; there are only views – changing, subjective, limited, personal views – each different from the others (and loved for the difference). Leigh tells us that the ultimate achievement is to see the world through other eyes (and as many different sets of them as possible): not to aspire to an ideal impersonal perspective beyond fallible individuals, but to inhabit as many different perspectives as we can. That is, after all, what he himself does as an artist, and asks us to do as we watch his films.

As is always the case in his work, Leigh's style sets a standard of awareness that characters are judged in terms of their ability to live up to. In the case of *Grown-Ups*, the standard is the multiple-mindedness that Leigh's style itself attains. Much of the humor of the scene on the Butchers' stairway derives from the difference between the characters' personal mental entrapment in one limited way of seeing or another, and Leigh's photographic and editorial ability to see things in more than one way.

In this respect, Leigh is the real hero of *Grown-Ups*. His cinematic style is even more nimble than the most nimble interactions between his characters (like the conversation I quoted involving Dick, Mandy, Sharon, and Gloria). His scripting, shooting, and editing are the supreme illustrations of genuine openness to otherness – noticing, registering, and honoring alternative points of view. As I argued in terms of the scene between Ann and Naseem in *Hard Labour*, Leigh outdoes even the greatest of his actors' and characters' ensemble performances.

9

Manufactured Emotions:
Home Sweet Home

Very often, there are a lot of different things going on at a lot of different levels in my films. As far as I am concerned, these are worked out in terms of imagery and metaphor just like any other piece of art. . . . Sometimes I think it's very much on the edge in terms of the audience seeing the wheels going round. Of course, I'm always aspiring to [them] not seeing the wheels going round, and only being explicit through being implicit – saying to the audience, go away and let it carry on in your head.

– Mike Leigh

The horrors in horror movies are too external, too superficial, and too exceptional. *Home Sweet Home* shakes us in a way nothing by John Carpenter can because it depicts everyday, ordinary horrors like the horror of a self-centered, loveless life. While Hitchcock, Lynch, and the Coen brothers externalize their characters' problems, implicitly endorsing a psychology of victimization, Leigh tells us that we have no one to blame but ourselves. Our problems do not come from outside, but inside.

Leigh is a spiritual filmmaker in the sense that one of his central subjects is the way in which, in Blake's terms, characters "mind-forge" their own manacles and lock themselves in their own self-created imaginative "prisons." From *Bleak Moments'* Peter, *Hard Labour*'s Mr. and Mrs. Thornley, *Nuts in May*'s Candice-Marie and Keith, and *Abigail's Party*'s Laurence and Beverly, to Stan, June, and Hazel in *Home Sweet Home*, to later figures like Aubrey, Nicola, and Johnny, Leigh's damned inhabit hells of their own making.

At the same time, in nothing is Leigh more a product of the culture of Dickens, George Eliot, D. H. Lawrence, and F. R. Leavis than in his conviction that the condition of the individual's imagination has consequences for the larger society. The individual is part of a community of others whose destinies are inextricably intertwined. American film characteristically locates its drama in individual consciousness. It conceives of characters as atomistic – as being essentially independent; and understands experience in terms of private states of feeling and personal insights and visions (both of which are frequently unexpressed to others). Leigh is convinced of the opposite: that our most "private" imaginative and emotional states have public ramifications. Feelings and thoughts are always expressed in his work. Subjectivity is performed. Our imaginative aberrations matter because they play themselves out in our interactions with others.

Individual mental and emotional states have social consequences. Peter's fear of losing control profoundly affects Sylvia; Keith's imaginative derangement impinges on the lives of everyone around him; Beverly's concept of herself results in acts of cruelty to others. On the positive side, figures like Sylvia, Shirley, Mandy, and Wendy bring people together and enhance tolerance and mutual understanding as a result of their personal attributes. For this family filmmaker, everyone – whether they know it or not and whether they want to be or not – is part of an extended family.

Even Leigh's most apparently nihilistic or anarchic works (the farcical *Who's Who* and the apocalyptic *Naked* mark the tonal extremes) subscribe to the belief that the individual can never escape his or her involvement with others. Leigh's characters are woven into intricate systems of dependencies and responsibilities that make unavoidable claims on them (and that take their toll if individuals fail to recognize their involvements with each other). There are no loners, revolutionaries, or visionaries in Leigh's imaginative universe – or certainly no successful ones. There are no Byronic heroes. Even figures like Johnny and Sebastian in *Naked* play out their destinies in social and verbal interactions with others. If Hitchcock's characters are always fundamentally alone, locked into states of incommunicable vision and insight, Leigh's are never really alone even for an instant. They are always part of a group and they hold themselves in existence by interacting with others (even Brian, the otherwise solipsistic nightwatchman in *Naked*, exists only in his interactions with Johnny). Life is essentially ethical in the claims it makes on us.

Leigh's work has certain similarities with that of Samuel Beckett and Harold Pinter (the spirit of Pinter clearly informing the maintenance-man scene in *Meantime*, and that of Beckett influencing the scenes with

Brian and Archie in *Naked*), but the social side of Leigh's vision suggests a decisive difference between his work and that of Pinter and Beckett. Neither of the other two artists believes (as Leigh fervently does) that we bring ourselves into richest, fullest existence through our interactions with others.

Beckett, like his teacher Joyce, is thoroughly Romantic in his belief in the ultimate imaginative separation and insulation of his characters. What we are is in our hearts and heads; social interaction is frivolous or irrelevant to our deepest states of being. Pinter accepts the inevitability of social interaction but understands our relations with others as unavoidably predatory and draining. He does not believe that social interaction can be creative and stimulating in an entirely positive way. Leigh (like George Eliot and D. H. Lawrence) not only sees positive value in social interaction but absolutely requires that characters express themselves in practical interactions with others: To fail to engage ourselves socially is to abandon the most important part of our identities. We are absolutely required to express ourselves socially. Like Lawrence and Eliot, Leigh is fiercely critical of characters, like June here, Ralph Butcher in *Grown-Ups*, Nicola in *Life Is Sweet*, or Johnny in *Naked*, who shirk their social responsibilities. To attempt to withdraw from society into a private imaginative world (whether of monsters and UFOs, Marxist-feminist poses, Harlequin novels, or apocalyptic babbling) is to be relegated to the lowest circle of Leigh's hell.

Another similarity with D. H. Lawrence's work is that each of Leigh's films explores a network of intertwined imaginative issues on which the individual characters and scenes in the work might be said merely to be variations (what I previously referred to as the "echo-chamber" quality of Leigh's work). *Home Sweet Home* would be a slight and unimportant work if all it were doing was presenting the sexual escapades and personal shortcomings of a group of characters who live in the same housing development. The film is doing something much more complex: exploring a set of subtly interrelated emotional disturbances and imaginative disorders, which it parcels out into separate characters and scenes for the purposes of comparing, contrasting, and understanding them. The characters are sexually and romantically deluded in related ways. In their marriages, romantic fantasies, and sexual interactions, they are victims of fictional identities, which they arduously devote themselves to maintaining. To use the metaphor that Leigh employs in both *Hard Labour* and *Abigail's Party*, each of them is seized up in an emotional and intellectual "cramp," which manifests itself as a mechanical routine or pattern of thought and feeling.

June imagines her entire life in terms of Harlequin romance metaphors. She spends her time watching soap operas (when she isn't reading romance novels) and punctuates her talk with references to "suffering," "love," "attractiveness," and "desire" – concepts that, as she employs them, have as little connection to lived reality as they do when they surface in a Harlequin novel or a television show.

Hazel affirms her existence through flirting. If her flirtatiousness led to real sexual encounters it would not be as sad as it is, for then it would at least represent a genuine attempt to remedy her state of need and longing. But, as Leigh presents it, it is only something to break the tedium of vacuuming and add a little excitement to her afternoons.[1]

The men, being men, have other ways of locking themselves in padded imaginative cells. June's husband, Harold, burbles an endless stream of jokesy patter that insulates him from authentic contact or interaction with anyone. Stan, depending on how we interpret his character, withdraws into a self-absorbed state of selfishness, cynicism, or despair. (His emotional withdrawal is wittily metaphorized in terms of his bizarre identification with Frank Sinatra's "I Did It My Way," and visually in the image of him sitting alone listening to music with headphones on early in the film.) Gordon's perpetual drunken stupor is another way of being permanently AWOL from life.

The two social workers, Melody and Dave, function as sex-changed, comical doppelgängers for the main characters (as well as being variations on each other). Melody is an emotional body-double for Harold (and a distant cousin of Pat, Beverly, and Christine). She is so busy being upbeat that she is incapable of seeing how her perkiness erects an emotional wall between her and everyone she meets. Dave is a male version of June (and an anticipation of a character named Suzi in *High Hopes*). His revolutionary sentimentality is a variation on June's sexual sentimentality, it's just that his head is in a different romantic cloud (20,000 feet up in a fog of Marxist jargon). In Leigh's witty presentation of it, soap-opera Marxism is expressively indistinguishable from soap-opera eroticism – from its overheated jargon and its psychology of victimization, to its treatment of the world as a set of abstractly coded references with secret meanings comprehensible to only a wise few (a decoder ring view of life which resembles the kind of film criticism that treats the experience of a movie in the same way: as if everything meant something else and nothing were merely what it professes to be).

Two absolute commitments energize Leigh's work: a rejection of all idealized, abstracted, intellectualized understandings; and a belief in the centrality of social connection and involvement. The characters in *Home*

Sweet Home fail on both counts. Their understandings of themselves and their experiences are completely intellectual.[2] And they cut themselves off from involvement with and responsiveness to others. In Leigh's mind, it is really the same thing: To the extent that we filter experience through sentimental, idealized, mental states, we foreclose possibilities of true sensitivity and awareness.

Home Sweet Home is Leigh's loneliest film. Shrouded in their mentalistic mummy cloths, each and every one of the characters is profoundly isolated. They are cocooned in noncommunicating bubble universes, emotionally unable to give or share anything with anyone. No matter how many of them may be physically present in a scene or may *seem* to be interacting, they are locked in individual isolation booths. Even in putative "dialogue" passages, *Home Sweet Home* is a film of monologues. As Dave and Melody most egregiously illustrate, virtually every conversation in the film is a one-way street, with lots of talking *at*, but virtually no talking *with*. In Leigh's nightmare vision, these figures serve life sentences in solitary confinement, their conversations consisting of sequences of nonresponsive and nonintersecting pronouncements. (It is as if, after completing *Grown-Ups*, Leigh decided to set an entire film in the world of Ralph and Christine Butcher.) The isolation of the characters is obvious even in the largest gathering in the film: the scene during Tina's visit, in which Tina, Stan, Hazel, and Gordon eat dinner, sit together afterward in Stan's living room, take a walk, and return to Stan's house. Each of the figures is so trapped in his or her private sets of references and associations (e.g., Stan's fondness for Sinatra; Gordon's obsession with food and drink; Tina's state of withdrawal; Hazel's attempt to "mother" Tina), and locked into his or her fixed attitudes toward each other (e.g., Hazel's endless feuding with Gordon and flirting with Stan), that even a minute of real interaction is impossible.

Although characters may speak directly to each other, they don't really communicate. Leigh scripts many of the conversations in *Home Sweet Home* (including the interaction in Stan's house) to show that, rather than replying to each other, characters are actually only pursuing their own trains of thought. One character will say something, the next will "reply" by saying something unrelated, to which the first will then "reply" by continuing his or her own initial line of thought: Hazel asks Tina if she wears a bra; Stan says something about Frank Sinatra; Gordon talks about the time and wanting to be somewhere; Hazel mentions the bra again; Stan responds with more about Sinatra.

Even when characters are apparently responding to one another, they never really take one step outside their imaginative boxes. They are trapped in emotional and intellectual systems they cannot (and don't really want to) escape. Hazel will object to whatever Gordon says and admire whatever Stan says; June will take whatever Harold says as an insult and a slight. Everything is plugged into a preexisting system of feeling and relationship. However painful, the system is ultimately comforting. Everyone is straightjacketed in a self-imposed imaginative role, and straightjackets everyone else in an emotionally supporting role.

This is evident in the argument between Harold and June at the dinner table near the beginning of the film. Harold makes a joke about the pudding and June takes it as a criticism of her dinner menu; Harold asks whether she has recently seen her mother and June takes it as a slap at her dutifulness as a daughter. And so it goes. June plugs all of Harold's remarks into her personal set of associations, just as Harold plugs all of hers into his. It is a textbook dramatic lesson in the power of the subtext to inflect the meaning of the text – not on the stage but in life. Everything in the entire conversation takes its meaning from the private subtext. June, in particular, is so devoted to her idea of herself as unappreciated, misunderstood, and "suffering," that nothing Harold says or does can change it, in fact everything can only confirm it, and give her more proof of being misunderstood. Nothing can unseize her emotional cramp, for her deepest definition of herself is tied up in this fictional routine (which, needless to say, she doesn't even recognize as a routine).

The zero degree of emotional disconnection and unresponsiveness in the film is Stan's brief sexual encounter with a woman named Janice. (It is part of the macabre humor of Leigh's presentation that the woman remains nameless for most of the scene. Stan doesn't ask her name until *after* they have made love and she is about to leave, at which point Leigh also belatedly reveals that she has a limp.) Like Melody and Dave's respective meetings with Stan – or like every other interaction in *Home Sweet Home*, for that matter – Stan and Janice are so entombed in private imaginative worlds (Stan withdrawn within a cynical, skeptical silence, Janice immured behind a wall of formulaic nattering) that, even though they make love, they might as well be alone.

Home Sweet Home's structure is as tightly coiled as Ozu's. As in the work of the Japanese director, virtually every character, scene, and interaction is a version (or inversion) of another. Melody's patter matches and parallels Dave's. Janice's nonstop talk resembles both Melody's and Harold's. June's romanticism and sexual infidelity is apparently only a later stage of Hazel's teasing and flirtatiousness; and both women's sexual desperation and emotional neediness are domestications of Janice's. Stan's emotional disconnection is paralleled by Gordon's from Hazel, by Harold's from June, and by Tina's withdrawal from Stan. The walled-off emotional state of the adult characters is mirrored by the walled-off emotional state of the young people in the institution Tina is in. It is as if the film were a house of mirrors the characters were forced to wander in forever, endlessly meeting their doubles, never able to escape themselves. Or, given the obsessiveness of its dreamlike repetitions, perhaps the best way to describe the movie is as a nightmare from which they – and their creator – are unable to awake. Leigh's brain must simply have been saturated with visions of loneliness, disconnection, and entrapment during his creation of the work (which both formally and thematically stands as a companion piece to *Who's Who*).

Leigh uses the film's repetitions and variations not only to link but to suggest differences between characters and situations. When rhymes only half rhyme, they can tease out subtle dissimilarities between the terms involved. There are many traits that link the individuals in the film's four principal narrative groupings – the women (June, Hazel, and Janice); the men (Harold, Gordon, and Stan); the social workers (Dave and Melody); and the children (Tina and Kelly). But there are an equally large number of differences in the forms of loneliness, disconnection, or sexual frustration that subtly distinguish one person or group from another.

Another effect of Leigh's parallelisms is to generalize characters and events. For example, because we have already met Melody when we meet Dave, or insofar as Melody's and Dave's one-sided monologues reverberate in an echo chamber of other one-way speeches and relationships, we ask larger questions about failures of communication. We are moved ever so slightly beyond a merely personal understanding of characters and events to seeing them as representations of more general emotional and imaginative problems.

At the same time, as I suggested in my discussion of *Grown-Ups*, it is important to emphasize the nontendentiousness of Leigh's comparisons and contrasts. They almost never dictate specific interpretations. Even in his most fiercely satiric works – *Nuts in May, Abigail's Party, Who's Who*, and the present film – Leigh almost never uses repetitions to point up an easy irony, in the manner of Robert Altman. In fact, Leigh's repetitions tend to work in the opposite way. His parallels almost never force any *particular* conclusions on the viewer. While Altman uses echoes to close down perspectives and narrow interpretations, Leigh typically uses them to open up interpretive possibilities, to encourage a viewer to broaden his perspective, to reflect on what he is seeing from different angles. In *Home Sweet Home*, when the narrative moves from Stan to Gordon to Harold, or from Hazel to June to Janice to Tina, each of the individual figures and scenes becomes *more* complex, *more* interesting, and ultimately *more* mysterious because of his or her connection with the others. It would be much easier to condemn Stan's silence if we didn't have Harold's volubility as a counterexample of how talk is not necessarily better. It would be easier to be more critical of June and Hazel if they weren't paired with their respective spouses. It would be easier to dismiss Hazel if June didn't show us an even more disturbing version of the same problem. And so on.

As is always the case in Leigh's work, a viewer is taught how to understand scenes by attending to the differences between the characters' personal styles and Leigh's cinematic style.[3] June can stand as an illustration of the stereo effect. It would be hard to find two more different ways of imagining experience than hers and her creator's. While June's soap-opera understandings "idealize" love, Leigh scrupulously displays its unideal realities. While June strikes "romantic" poses, Leigh forces a viewer to take in, not only the physical shabbiness of her surroundings, but the emotional shabbiness of her actual relationships with men. While she sentimentalizes, Leigh's narrative is utterly unsentimental. That is why, although June's romanticism might pass muster in a Hollywood movie (where the idealized cinematic style would reinforce and repeat the character's personal imaginative style), it comes off as being completely fraudulent here (where Leigh's deidealized cinematic style contrasts with and undermines the character's idealized imaginative style). One might say that June is a character with a "Hollywood imagination" (a Joan Crawford/Bette Davis belief in the substitution of intentions in place of performances and the replacement of surfaces with depths) plunked down in an anti-Hollywood movie.

Leigh's scripting, shooting, and editing insistently bring into view aspects of experience that June attempts to wish away. Leigh, Su Eliot (who plays June), and Eric Richard (who plays Stan) find ways to represent just the sort of emotional complexities that June denies as a character. The scene in which Stan visits June at home, for example, is written and acted to be as far as possible from showing two lovers collapsing into each other's arms in a paroxysm of passion. Leigh presents us with a boorish, brutish man with a big nose and a heavy accent emotionally browbeating and manipulating a broad-hipped, middle-aged matron who wears thick glasses. Rather than being transported on the wings of passion, June is shown to be vulnerable and afraid, painfully torn between her need and her pride, unable to make up her mind whether or not she wants to go to bed with Stan. In the butterfly tonal flutterings of Eliot's brilliant performance and the mercurial shifts of beats in her interaction with Richard, the scene represents one of the most complex and moving moments in all of Leigh's work, precisely because June and Stan live through the sorts of emotional complications that Hollywood movies, Harlequin romances, and June's imagination omit from their accounts of life.

While June's vision of romance (like Hollywood's) is founded on the suppression of enormous chunks of lived experience, Leigh's entire cinematic enterprise is an effort to include the kinds of contradictory, mixed-up feelings that may coexist with genuine passion. While June devotes herself to an ideal of "pure" love, Leigh's style shows us the impurity of *all* experiences – loving and otherwise. While June wants life scrubbed as squeaky clean as the set of a soap opera, Leigh's scripting, blocking, photography, and editing are devoted to messing up the view. While June wants Hollywood simplicities, Leigh gives us the muddlement and mixed messages of life. In short, even as the characters in *Home Sweet Home* systematically engage in various forms of denial and forgetting, Leigh's style forces the return of the repressed. Leigh's is an art of inclusion, an art of not filtering things through a purifying idea or conception, an art of life-celebrating impurity.

In Leigh's vision of them, human relationships are never neat and tidy in the Hollywood way; real truth is always cluttered, messy, and multivalent. It is not accidental that the sound in many scenes of *Home Sweet Home* is "dirty" – with a radio playing underneath the dialogue. Even a simple conversation can't be conducted without distractions. Leigh deliberately keeps complicating, interrupting, and sidetracking things. For example, when Stan and Tina are about to have a moment together in the foster home, he has Kelly, another girl in the lounge, get into a brief argument with Tina, and a minute later has the cloddish Melody come striding in to interrupt them.

Emotional moments don't come simple and pure in Leigh's work. They won't swell and build. They won't inflate themselves. A potentially tender moment will be laced with comedy (as Norman's encounter with Sylvia is). A farcical scene (like Keith's fight with Finger) will be tinged with pain. A nostalgic reverie will be made more than a little stupid and absurd in the telling of it (like Angela's recollections of playing the piano). That's not an expression of cynicism or disillusionment on Leigh's part; it is simply his attempt to capture how things really are. It is in the nature of life to be compromised, conflicted, and impure.

Leigh declines to do the thing American films specialize in: creating juicy, unitary feelings. It can be done a dozen different ways: with a climactic narrative event, with mood music, with expressive lighting and photography, or with one of those scenery-masticating turns American actors of the Jack Nicholson, Meryl Streep, and Harvey Keitel ilk are experts at. The point is to provide clear, decisive, generic emotions that viewers can simply strap themselves into and blast off inside. The emotions in American films are deliberately kept simple so that they can be the feelings of anyone, anywhere, anytime – meaning that any viewer anywhere, anytime can instantly plug into them and identify with them. Leigh's scenes and performances aren't about creating big, generalized feelings but particular characters with particular emotional expressions anchored in a particular event, personality, or set of relationships. Nothing is pure or absolute or generic.

Leigh refuses to blend characters' imaginations and thoughts together with a unifying musical orchestration or to blend their emotions into a single big effect in the Hollywood way. Individual perspectives, feelings, and identities don't merge and blur. Personal differences are never erased. Nor in Leigh's view should they be. There are always at least as many different perspectives as there are people in a scene, even if the people are the closest of friends (as is the case in *Ecstasy* and *Four Days in July*) or in love (as with Dick and Mandy in *Grown-Ups* or later figures like Cyril and Shirley in *High Hopes* or Wendy and Andy in *Life Is Sweet*).

In fact, there is always one more personal perspective to be taken account of in Leigh's work than there are characters in a scene: the viewer's perspective, which invariably is different from that of any of the characters. That split almost never happens in a mainstream movie. In a Hollywood movie, the point of view of the main character is almost always the same as that of the viewer (though the viewer may be aware of a few facts or events the character isn't). If the character is attractive, good, and intelligent, his or her view is *the right view*, and is meant to be the view of a member of the audience. The points of view have to be similar, since the viewer is expected to see himself in the main character by plugging into, becoming, and experiencing the drama vicariously by participating in the feelings and thoughts of the character. That is the basis of identification.

Leigh's work isn't built around identification. In fact, it deliberately frustrates it. He doesn't want the viewer mindlessly to "become" his characters, as that would represent a suspension of critical judgment on the viewer's part. His point is not to collapse the space between viewer and character, but deliberately to hold the viewer somewhere a little outside of the character so that the viewer will bring one more point of view to what is already a feast of different perspectives. In other words, the goal is not the Hollywood one of getting us to suspend judgment, but the opposite: of forcing us to engage our intellects in order to make sense of strange and challenging material. Leigh doesn't want us to turn the characters into versions of ourselves, but to go out of ourselves and enter into perspectives *different* from our own.

All of which is why Leigh's work can leave mainstream viewers unsatisfied. They want their emotions purer than Leigh provides them. They want them bigger. They keep waiting for a moment when everything comes together, but Leigh won't give it to them. They want transformation and punishment, release and catharsis, but Leigh denies them those resolutions. They want scenes and groups of characters to be unified around one feeling, but Leigh gives them irreducible multivalence. They want imaginative merging and blending and communion. They want simple, big emotions. They want what June wants. (One might say that she is not only a Hollywood character but a Hollywood viewer.) But the emotional moments in Leigh's work are almost always muted. They are invariably impure and compromised – crossed with other, contradictory emotions. A moment can't swell, and the viewer can't expand within it, because something else is almost always going on.

At one of the most potentially romantic moments near the end of *Grown-Ups* – when Dick and Mandy are in bed making love and Dick finally agrees with Mandy's demand to have a baby (a demand that has accumulated a degree of importance by being repeated several times during the narrative) – Leigh has Mandy suddenly break the serious mood by comically protesting that Dick is leaning on a bruise and hurting her. Though a Hollywood-educated viewer might consequently call the scene unromantic, Leigh's point is not to deny romance but to tell the truth about it, to allow it to coexist with a range of other tones, other moods, other events. Sex, love, demands, impatience, nagging, babies, and bruises – comedy and gravity, irritation and tenderness, pain and laughter – can all be part of romance. Leigh's artistic goal is to find a form for romance that does not involve excluding all of the unromantic parts of life.

One might say that, in Leigh's work, one truth does not swallow another but is piled on top of it. A later point of view does not supersede a preceding one but sits alongside it. The multiplicity of truth is illustrated by the scene in *Nuts in May* in which, while Leigh shows Honkey and Finger and Ray telling jokes at the campsite, he intercuts shots showing how irritated and upset Keith and Candice-Marie are about the noise they are making. The point of the editorial juxtaposition is *not* to force the viewer to choose between Keith's exasperation and the others' innocent pleasure. Leigh does not want us to pick one as being right and the other as wrong. The point is that *both* emotions, *both* points of view are equally true to the moment.

Home Sweet Home introduces a new stylistic element into Leigh's work: there are far more close-ups during dialogue passages, as well as brief shots of characters silently thinking or feeling something than in any of Leigh's earlier films. The close-ups are used to reveal otherwise invisible feelings that contradict or qualify the characters' words and actions. The message is that even as our brains lie to us our emotions tell true.[4]

As the characters in *Home Sweet Home* attempt to simplify life, Leigh's scripting, editing, and photography complicate it. Near the end of the film, as June tells Harold that she doesn't need him, Leigh allows us to see in her eyes how profoundly needy she is. Even as she protests that she is all right, the twitchy tenseness of her neck and jaw tells us otherwise. While June and Harold attempt to pass reductive fictions on themselves (June playing the "strong, unappreciated woman" and Harold the "happy-go-lucky husband"), the brief pauses in their line deliveries and flickers of feeling visible in their faces reveal emotional truths that they would deny (and are probably not even aware of).

In scene after scene, the tight shots and reaction shots provide a stereoscopic view in which the viewer can read emotional realities at odds with what the characters themselves think they think, feel they feel, and believe they believe. For example, in the sequence in which Melody goes to Stan's house to persuade him to visit Tina, Melody undoubtedly believes that she is being the soul of kindness, and that she and Stan are having a genuinely caring chat. Yet Leigh shows a cascade of resentments, embarrassments, and hurt feelings flickering across both faces. Even as Melody and Stan attempt to cruise through the encounter on autopilot, Leigh's photography and editing document a demolition derby of emotional collisions.

The figures in *Home Sweet Home* have sold their souls to fictions. They have let synthetic thoughts and feelings substitute for real ones without even being aware of it. (In fact, they clearly prefer things this way.) In this invasion of the body snatchers, the characters' spirits have been taken over by alien forces. June, Harold, Hazel, Janice, Melody, and the others have lost their minds. Like horror-movie zombies, they think with someone else's brain. Indeed, they are so much the products of pop-culture understandings of life – from "True Love" to "I Did It My Way" – that they don't really exist as individuals. Like their emotions, thoughts, beliefs, and (in Harold's case) jokes, their identities are hand-me-down.[5]

As in *Abigail's Party* and *Who's Who*, Leigh rejects the notion that there is a "real" Hazel or June or Melody behind the artificial one. All of his work tells us that there is no free realm of consciousness separate from our compromised expressions. Consciousness does not precede expression, nor is it separable from it. Charles Foster Kane had childhood memories and desires separate from the cultural processing of his adult life, but in Leigh's work there is no free space of memory, desire, thought, or feeling outside of the compromised, contingent, mediated place in which we actually exist and express ourselves. There is no well of unpolluted emotion bottled up somewhere, waiting to express itself. There is no genie waiting to be set loose.

There is no "us" behind what we say and do separate from what we say and do. There is no Isabel Archer "nothing-expresses-me" identity apart from everything that does express us; no natural self behind the artificial self; nothing but the synthetic one. There is no June except the Harlequin-novel one; no Stan other than the emotionally withdrawn one; no Melody other than the fake-perky one. Most frighteningly of all (because of her youth), there is no bubbly, hopeful inner Tina waiting to bloom, given the right opportunities or attention. (That is the point of – and what is so frightening about – the scenes in which first Stan and then Hazel attempts to converse with her.)

It is important to recognize that even June's confession to Harold near the end of the film does not represent a break from the past – a deep, unconditioned, primordial recognition of her state of self-imposed enslavement. Leigh refuses to sentimentalize the moment. June is simply adding one more scene to the long-running "wounded woman" play in which she casts herself as star. Her confession is as bathetic as the rest of her life; not an escape from Harlequin feelings but a fulfillment of them.

Although these characters borrow their emotional styles from the mass media, Leigh departs from many contemporary artists in refusing to blame the media (or anything else in modern culture) for their condition. He declines to shift responsibility onto something or someone else. Here and in *Abigail's Party* and *Who's Who*, the characters' emotional problems are not attributable to causes outside themselves. Listening to Frank Sinatra did not make Stan the way he is, any more than being in a home made Tina the way she is. June's novel reading is different from that of Emma Bovary, and Leigh's analysis is different from Flaubert's in this respect. The problem, in Leigh's view, is not movies or television shows or pop culture, but the consumers of them. The mass media are not someone else doing something *to* us. They *are* us. They are a reflection of our own desires to escape ourselves and our experiences. Trash TV isn't brainwashing us but giving us what we want. We live our lives as soap operas not because we watch soap operas but for the same reason soap operas appeal to us: because we love to think of ourselves as engaged in grand, operatic emotional struggles. To blame Harlequin novels for vulgarizing our emotions is to reverse the causality. We read Harlequins because our emotions are already debased. They satisfy our preexisting desires for emotional clarity and simplicity.

The source of characters' problems is inside them. It is one of the major achievements of Leigh's films that a viewer feels his characters have insides. For all of the satiric thrust of his work, his figures are never turned into puppets, never treated as bundles of external mannerisms seen from the outside. Each is felt to be motivated by emotions and ways of understanding that are not farcical, but perfectly reasonable from their point of view. A viewer is made aware that (as Renoir put it) "everyone has his reasons." Each character is allowed to present a distinctive point of view that justifies his or her behavior.[6] It all makes sense to them.

This is the function of the scene in the backyard with Tina, for example. It exists to show that Stan is genuinely trying to connect with Tina to the limits of his ability (admittedly, not great). The scene in which June confesses her affair to Harold exists so she may justify her behavior not only to him but to us. The scenes between Hazel and Gordon allow us to feel Hazel's desperation and loneliness. These moments allow the characters to present their side of things, as it were.

It is as if Leigh set out, not only to choose the most repellent group of figures imaginable (that's relatively easy), but to find ways to allow them to justify their behavior (a great artistic challenge). The characters in *Home Sweet Home* are not only allowed to explain themselves (as June does to Harold) but also to give us such a deep view of their personalities (in the case of Stan and Hazel) that we can see that, by their own lights, they are being the best they are capable of being under the circumstances.

This leads to one of the most important points about Leigh's work. Notwithstanding the rebarbativeness of many of its characters and situations, it is fundamentally *empathetic*. *Nuts in May, Abigail's Party*, and this film communicate an uncanny sympathy for their main figures, however flawed and doomed they may be. Since we are forced to enter into the characters' perspectives on themselves, our relation to them cannot decline into dismissiveness, irony, or sarcasm. The inwardness of the view keeps us from judging them too externally and harshly. We feel their pain, their puzzlement, their frustrations, their weaknesses, their reasons for being what they are. Each of Leigh's characters has feelings a viewer has had at one time or another. In the scenes described above, we feel Stan's awkwardness and hesitation as he attempts and fails to "bond" with Tina. We feel June's shame and embarrassment over her need for Stan. We feel the emptiness of Hazel's and Harold's lives. Even figures as repellent as Stan or June, at least at moments, remind us of ourselves.

Furthermore, because Leigh's characters abundantly suffer for their sins and truly "get away" with nothing, we can't really hate them. Feeling sorry would be a more accurate description of our attitude – as long as it does not suggest superiority or patronizing. They find a way into our hearts, at least a little. As do all of Leigh's "awful" figures, June, Hazel, Stan, and the others suffer deeply for their deficiencies, torturing themselves as much as they torture anyone else. In fact, what makes the scenes in *Home Sweet Home* so affecting is less the pain characters inflict on others than the pain they inflict on themselves. June's scenes with Harold, for example, make clear not only that her suffering is self-inflicted but that she is hurting herself even more than she hurts him. In the scene in which she confesses to Harold her affair with Stan, our hearts go out to her even more than to her husband.

The final reason our hearts stay open is that, as is always the case in Leigh's work, the view keeps changing. At every point where judgment is on the verge of becoming too harsh, he will reveal a mitigating fact. Whenever a limited interpretation starts to emerge, he will disrupt it. Every time a pattern starts to stabilize, he will violate it. The viewer is forced to stay open.

Take Stan, the most despicable character in the film. Even in his case Leigh prevents us from locking into a negative view too rapidly or rigidly. At the start of the film, he actually seems superior to the other characters. He doesn't argue or complain like June or natter on like Harold. His quizzical detachment during his encounters with Hazel and Melody seems potentially admirable. He seems to take a somewhat ironic view of the other characters that aligns his perspective with ours. But just when we have been lulled into feeling that he is a potential ally (a point of view to plug into), Leigh shifts our understanding. There is the scene with Janice, where he seems utterly heartless; then there is the (deliberately delayed) revelation that he stood up Tina the same day; then there is the scene in which he goes over to June's (revealing that he is having an affair with more than one woman at a time), followed by his emotional abuse of her; then there are his romantic overtures to Hazel (who becomes the third woman in his life). As this flurry of scenes occurs, the viewer is forced to reassess everything he previously felt about Stan. He belatedly realizes that what he first thought was amusement (or bemusement) at the oddness of the others is actually something much more sinister and disturbing – a state of radical emotional disconnection from everyone around him.

At the same time Leigh shifts our understanding of Stan downward, he adjusts our understanding of Harold slightly upward. In the early scenes, Harold seems to be a lightweight with no inner life worth considering. With his idiotic banter, he might be a character in a sitcom. However, as we watch his interactions with June, he not only increasingly elicits our sympathy but, by the point at which June tells him of her infidelity, seems genuinely to be suffering and, arguably, to be one of the deepest characters in the movie. In short, we have to stay open and alert toward each of the characters in the film, continuously prepared to change our response as we go along.[7]

But it is slightly misleading to say that our understanding of these characters changes; a better way to put it would be to say that our understanding of them is never allowed to become as clear, final, and definitive as it is in a mainstream film. In my discussion of *The Kiss of Death*, I pointed out the semantic underdetermination of certain aspects of Leigh's presentation. Something similar is going on in terms of the presentation of the figures in *Home Sweet Home*. Sometimes it involves close-ups that won't quite "read" as definitely one thing or another, making it impossible to tell exactly what a character is feeling. There are plenty of tight shots of Stan's face during his interactions with Hazel, Melody, and Dave, but it is difficult to say exactly what they mean. (Is

Stan amused, exasperated, cynical, just not paying attention, or what?) At other times, the semantic underdetermination involves unglossed lines of dialogue or narrative events. Near the end of the film, Stan makes a comment about his mother's death and how hard it was to get the coffin down the narrow hall stairway, and we realize there is more to his life than we will ever understand. Similarly, a few minutes later, Stan gives Tina money, but if we attempt to figure out what precisely is going on it is hard to say. (Is he being genuinely kind? Trying to buy her affection? Attempting to bribe her to be silent about what she has seen?)

The presentation of Hazel in her early scenes is another example of Leigh's cultivated vagueness. It is extremely difficult for a viewer to tell what is going through her mind when she shows Stan her house in one scene or sits on the sofa with him in another. She may be trying to seduce him, of course; but she may only be somewhat clumsily flirting; in the first of their meetings, she may even be completely innocent. We may be the ones with the dirty minds. We don't know enough about her at the point these scenes occur to say; and, even later in the film when we do, we really can't go backward and clear up these early scenes retrospectively. Hollywood never leaves us in the dark in this way. We always know at least as much as the main character does. In Leigh, we know less.

My point is to suggest the extent to which characters and interactions remain mysterious even after the film is over – even in this work, which is far from featuring Leigh's most complex or elusive figures.[8] Leigh's characters and interactions won't quite come clear, which is not a flaw but a virtue. Figures, interactions, and events are as multivalent and unresolved as the most interesting ones in life.

As is true in his other work, Leigh's cinematic style in *Home Sweet Home* ultimately represents a way of knowing that critiques the personal styles of the characters. Each of them reduces everything and everyone in his path to a system of understanding – masculine or feminine, romantic or cynical, facetious or sentimental, as the case may be. Melody and Dave are only the capstones. They attempt to reduce all of life to their social worker/Marxist framework of knowledge, while Leigh's scripting, camera work, and editing create experiences that slip through all such prefabricated interpretive nets. While they generalize, he particularizes. While their personal styles eliminate mystery, he nurtures and honors it. While they understand the world as a collection of objects and power relations, he restores the spiritual inwardness and secrecy to experience and identity.

10

Challenging Easy Understandings: *Meantime*

At its simplest, things happen in the improvisations which I then structure, and that's the end product. But mostly that's not the case: Mostly what I do is to challenge what's happened and thus arrive at a more interesting dramatic essence.

– Mike Leigh

Many writers on film have a mistaken notion of art. They think it presents experiences packed tight with compressed meaningfulness, just sitting there waiting to be unpacked by the diligent critic. In the standard critical demonstrations, the greatness of *Citizen Kane, Vertigo,* or *2001* is that virtually every lighting effect, camera angle, or prop is freighted with interlocking significance. Criticism is the act of translating those stylistic details into an intricate series of significations. The critic exhumes the sermons the artist has artfully hidden under his stones. In this view, both creation and interpretation are acts of mastery – Faustian enterprises in which the artist operates from a position of ultimate knowingness that the critic and viewer aspire to equal.[1]

Of course, there are films that are organized in this way and yield to this kind of critical scrutiny – Hitchcock's work leaps to mind as an extended example, but that doesn't change the fact that it is a game-playing, puzzle-solving notion of art, that could probably only have come to the fore in a field as immature as film study. If we look at truly great works of art we find something quite different. They are more likely to be humble and tentative than displays of intellectual power and knowledge. They are more likely to be acts of exploration than presentations of compressed, prepackaged meaningfulness. Encountering them is more likely to feel like living through an unusually complex and demanding experience than like learning something.

To watch *Uncle Vanya* is not to move through a world of hidden meanings waiting to be decoded but to be exposed to psychological uncertainties and emotional complexities that are impossible to get to the bottom of. To stand in front of Rembrandt's portraits is always to be at least somewhat in the dark, uncertain about what you are seeing and what it means. His figures just slightly elude understanding – his own as well as ours. They won't snap into focus morally, psychologically, or semantically, not just the first time, but the hundredth time we look into their elusive eyes. To navigate Shakespeare's suspended, sliding clauses with their multivalent, unresolved metaphoric associations is not to be put in a position to excavate meanings hidden just under the surface, but to undergo a series of experiences too shifting and slippery to be pinned down as "meanings" or "knowledge." What is normally denoted by words like *knowledge, meaning,* and *significance* – something clear, definite, static, atemporal, and abstract – is the very opposite of these artistic experiences.

Meantime shows what it feels like for a film to be a genuine act of exploration for its creator, its actors, and its viewers. It is clear that Leigh and his actors went into the film not quite knowing where they would come out. The film takes the viewer on the same voyage of discovery that they underwent in the process of making it. The difference in the way it was made is why the characters and scenes don't offer a set of static, abstract meanings to be decoded but a sequence of flowing, shifting events to be lived through.

Its general subject is the relationship of two families headed by sisters. As Leigh often does, he organizes the film around a series of contrasts based on class and temperament. The premise is that the sisters' personalities are as different as possible and they have married into social and financial milieus at the opposite ends of the spectrum. Barbara is childless, financially and socially successful, lives with her businessman husband in a nice house in a suburban neighborhood, has a refined voice and mannerisms, a cool demeanor, and a fairly intellectual temperament. Mavis is irascible, blunt, outspoken, somewhat inarticulate, loud, coarse, and poor, and lives in public housing with a layabout husband and two twenty-something sons (who are themselves set up to be opposites: Mark is clever, cynical, sharp-tongued, and devious; Colin is quiet, innocent, meek, and mentally slower).[2] While the one couple is polite, deferential, and subdued in its interactions, the other family bickers and squabbles more or less continuously. The general situation was clearly chosen to allow for the possibility of a number of dramatic comparisons dear to Leigh's heart (involving contrasts between "refined" and "coarse" sisters, "bright" and "dull" brothers, and the manners and modes of expression of the upper-middle- and lower-class family members in general).[3]

But, beyond outlining a dramatic situation with many potential contrasts, clashes, and differences in points of view, it is clear that Leigh began, not with a set of points to be made, but a series of questions to be explored. For the one family, how might you act, talk, and feel if you were unemployed and on the dole? For the other, how might you act, talk, and feel if you were highly successful? For the socially and financially flourishing family, how might you interact with the less successful relatives? For the other family, how might you treat relatives who are much better off? How might financial marginality affect a father's relationship with his wife and grown sons, particularly given the coarseness of all involved? How might you act if you were in your early twenties and had nothing to look forward to in the way of financial improvement of your situation? What is it like to be a skinhead, a punk, a drifter? The questions are really endless for an actor or director, since new ones keep coming up as you go through a scene encounter by encounter and beat by beat. (If you were the father on the dole, would you let your son mouth off to you like that? What might you say in reply? What would your tone of voice or gestures be? How might the son respond? What would be your response to that?)

What makes the experience challenging for a viewer is that Leigh doesn't confine the question asking to himself and his cast. He wants the viewer to become an explorer also. Most other films make points and provide insights; Leigh requires viewers to move through situations without them. While other films simplify characters' personalities and interactions to facilitate understanding, Leigh's scenes and characters resist thumbnail glosses and delay judgments by presenting sensorily "thick" and cognitively "unanalyzed" experiences. Experiences don't come with handles to pick them up (in the form of a lighting effect, a musical orchestration, or a narrative puzzle to be solved). And their meaning keeps changing; the viewer is forced to keep revising his interpretations of events and characters, adjusting his understanding in the light of each new development. Instead of rushing to conclusions, the viewer must simply stay open. Knowing must give way to wondering and surmising.

Meantime's opening scene provides an illustration of the different way of moving through experience Leigh's work requires. Beginnings of films generally offer a series of glosses to help explain the general situation of the characters. Think of the opening minutes of *Citizen Kane*: The film uses every stylistic device possible (from expressionistic lighting, camera angles and movements to symbolic sets and tendentious musical orchestrations) to guide our interpretation of the experience. Meanings relating to bleakness, lugubriousness, loneliness, isolation, and decay are packed into every shot. The effect is abstract and intellectual; semantically clear, rich, and rewarding.

The opening of *Meantime* gives the viewer something much closer to the feeling of "raw" experience. Events are presented to some extent whole, undigested and unglossed. Following a few brief outdoor shots,[4] we watch two women and four men interact in the living room and kitchen of a home for four or five minutes. They obviously know each other well and have a number of unresolved emotional issues (which take the form of more or less continuous frictions, disagreements, and awkwardnesses); but Leigh lets the scene develop without making the least effort to establish either the participants' names, their relationships, or the cause of their frictions. Are they in the same family? Are they related at all? What is their problem?

Although subsequent scenes allow us to work out the names and biological relationships (we eventually figure out that we are seeing the members of the two families I described), more important questions remain unanswered for a long time, if not for the entire film: Why does the better-off couple (Barbara and John) seem to be on edge? Are they upset about something? What is it? Why is the worse-off sister (Mavis) so sullen and sour? Why is she so hard on one of her sons (Colin)? Why is the other sister (Barbara) so nice to him? Is the father of the two sons (Frank) rude to the father of the other family (John) at one point – or is that a misinterpretation of his tone of voice? Why does the relationship between the sisters seem so tense – or is that another misunderstanding on our part? Why does the one son (Mark) seem so smug, sassy, and insolent, especially when interacting with the man who is not his father? Why does the other son (Colin) seem so confused or withdrawn?

Not only does Leigh not provide answers to these questions, but the pace of the opening scene is so rapid that a viewer doesn't really have time to formulate them as questions. One personal interaction (mainly arguments and misunderstandings) gives way to another so rapidly that it is hard to keep up with them. Leigh declines to provide a road map to navigate by. Watching the scene is a little like being dropped into the middle of a tense dinner with people we don't know. We find ourselves in uncomfortable proximity to six prickly, complex people with lots of emotional baggage, attempting to make sense of what is going on, suspending judgment as long as we can, uncertainly drawing conclusions and changing our minds as we go along.

Unlike those in a mystery or thriller, these uncertainties are not attributable to a missing piece of information, which means they cannot be cleared up by having an answer provided by a subsequent scene. The questions I have posed (and many others) will never really be answered definitively; they stay a little fuzzy all the way through the film. They are as unresolvable as the uncertainties about what things mean in everyday life.

As an illustration, consider two of the events connected with the two brothers in the opening scene. First, Colin acts strangely during most of the scene. Second, at one point, instead of sitting in a chair like everyone else, Mark sits on top of the console television. Shortly after they leave, their host and hostess, John and Barbara, discuss the two boys as they get ready for bed. John expresses irritation at Mark's "rudeness," to which Barbara replies that the sitting on the TV wasn't meant to be insolent but a joke. They then go on to disagree about whether the other boy, Colin, is "retarded" (John) or simply hasn't been "taught how to act" (Barbara).

Note what Leigh is doing: First, he presents two unglossed sets of events – Colin and Mark behaving oddly – without an explanation of why either acts the way he does. Then he has two other characters offer contradictory "explanations" of the behavior. Since John and Barbara (who presumably know infinitely more than we do about the boys) cannot agree about the meaning of what we have just seen, rather than clearing anything up, the events now seem even *less clear* than they already were. The married couple's disagreement actually only adds another mystery to the film – namely, what is going on between Barbara and John that they should be arguing like this about such things as they get ready for bed? At the point when other films are busy "establishing" social, psychological, and moral truths about their characters, Leigh not only declines to "establish" anything; he multiplies the uncertainties. (Even after we have seen the entire film, we are no closer to knowing why Mark sat on the television set or Colin is so spacey.)

Characters and events just will not yield simple meanings. There is a later scene involving Mark similar to the moment of sitting on the television. He and a few of his friends are in a bar and he offers a young Black man a drink. When the man accepts, Mark first insults him by using a racial epithet, then apologizes (though his smirk and tone of voice make it unclear whether the apology is sincere). Is Mark a racist?

Is he taunting the man? Is he being mean or playful? Is calling someone racist names Mark's idea of a joke? Is his apology serious or mocking? Even more important, is the man a stranger or does Mark know him, and is this some sort of game they play? Would that make Mark's behavior less insulting or more? None of these questions is answered. We can't say what is really going on.

We can't say what is "really" going on because the notion of "really-ness" doesn't apply. Parsings of experience into jokes or rudenesses, sincere or insincere acts, racist or playful expressions are predicated on a thinner sense of life than Leigh provides. Mainstream work subscribes to a notion of essential truth – a truth waiting to be revealed just under the surface that clarifies fluxional surface expressions by anchoring them in simple motivational depths or secret meanings. In such a film (Hitchcock as usual providing the clearest illustration), the truth may be temporarily hidden from view, but it is somewhere to be found. There is a deep, resolving truth to be ferreted out (and the plots of the films almost always consist of the pursuit and discovery of it). If you had x-ray vision; if you were a fly on the ceiling in the right room; if you could overhear certain characters' thoughts; if you could see hidden events – you could discover it: "Ah, *that* is what he meant when he said this; *that* is what she was feeling."

Leigh doesn't subscribe to such a conception of truth. He gives us experiences that are not only unanalyzed but fundamentally unanalyzable into simplifying essences. In contrast to almost all of our previous filmgoing experience, we must negotiate complex expressive surfaces without being able to stabilize our interpretations by consulting basic motives and goals. The *Vertigo* form of meaning is predicated on a belief in the existence of clarifying, semantic depths. Experiences can be glossed in terms of abstract essences. Leigh simply doesn't believe in such an essentialized conception of experience. He won't let us dive beneath the flowing movements of history to ground ourselves in the essences of epistemology because he does not believe in essences. Existence not only precedes, but supersedes essence.

Character will not be reduced to an essence because characters are not organized around unifying central intentions. The scenes with the punk Coxy (brilliantly played by Gary Oldman) illustrate the complexity of identity in this world. In some scenes Coxy seems hostile and dangerous, in others childlike and innocent; in some serious, in others playful; in some he seems threatening, cruel, and unkind; in others, a genuine friend to Colin. The sequence in which Coxy and Colin go to Hayley's apartment demonstrates how rapidly the changes can succeed each other. There are at least three different Coxys even on the brief walk: As Coxy and Colin cross the courtyard, Coxy dances around and seems playful and madcap; then he seems nasty and mean-spirited as he taunts a Black man with racist jibes; then (to our surprise) he seems cowed and frightened when the man talks back to him. The changes continue after Coxy and Colin enter Hayley's apartment. Leigh first shows Coxy clowning around on Hayley's sofa in a playful way. The playfulness then gives way to behavior that seems downright cruel, as Coxy starts to tease and verbally torment Hayley. Then, when Hayley retreats into her bedroom, Coxy seems genuinely contrite and apologetic. Which is the real Coxy? Lest, trained by years of Hollywood movies (which privilege "deep" views and understandings), we be inclined to say the last – the contrite and sincere one – Leigh makes sure that the scene doesn't pause overly long on the "good" Coxy. The changes continue. A moment later Coxy locks Colin in Hayley's closet.

The complexity is more than the fact that Coxy keeps changing. Similar to the undecidability of the question of Mark's "rudeness" or "playfulness" when he sits on the television set or baits someone in a bar, *even at any one moment* it is extremely difficult to know what Coxy is feeling and intending. When he bounces on Hayley's sofa is he clowning around or being threatening? When he is apparently behaving offensively to her a moment later, is he being deliberately insulting, clumsily attempting to be cute, or even perhaps flirting with her? When he locks Colin in the closet a couple minutes after that, is it a joke, an act of sadism, an attempt to deflect attention from his feelings of guilt about his treatment of Hayley, an attempt to show Hayley how clever he is, or what? Gary Oldman's performance is pitched at the precise point where different, even opposite things can all be true. Coxy can be nasty, flirtatious, playful, self-centered, perverse, funny, dangerous, and innocently, clumsily boyish *at the same time*. There is no simpler, "real" inner Coxy hidden underneath the complex, changeable, unresolved outer Coxy.

Hayley's "real" thoughts and feelings are just as difficult to pin down. It is virtually impossible to know what she is thinking or feeling in her relations with Coxy, Mark, and Colin at any moment. Is she in love with Coxy? With Colin? With Mark? Does she even *like* any of them, or is she merely tolerating them? If these were multiple-choice questions, the only right answers would have to be something like "all of the above." Or consider Mark as yet one more illustration of what this degree of genuine irresolution looks like: Mark's relationship with Colin shows how a character can be both loving *and* critical, harsh *and* tender, competitive *and* protective, threatening *and* caring at one and the same moment.

All this should suggest the injustice a psychological approach does to Leigh's work. Psychological understanding (at least in the form it takes in most film production and criticism) is premised on the assumption that outer complexities (of behavior and expression) are traceable back to inner simplicities (of feeling and motivation). According to a psychological understanding of life, our identities are organized around unifying, nameable, governing intentions, emotions, and thoughts. A character either is or is not "in love," is or is not "mean-spirited," is or is not "fearful," is or is not "envious." This way of thinking is almost irresistible insofar as our minds, with cognitive parsimony, almost automatically tend to divide experience into either-or categories. We try to master experiential flux and multivalence by referring them back to underpinning constants. Leigh reveals the fallacy of motivational essentialism. He provides experiences that overflow conceptual containers.

The loose, nonpurposive nature of the scenes in *Meantime* reinforces the effect. Mark, Colin, Hayley, and Coxy repeatedly meet in a laundromat, a bar, and Hayley's apartment, but their interactions are given no particular emotional purpose or narrative goal. Leigh captures the eccentricity, mutability, and openness of identities and relationships that are not limitingly defined in terms of a game plan.

The point is not to mystify us but to expose us to genuine mysteries – complexities of feeling and relationship that won't be reduced to shorthand understandings. As a final illustration, consider the climactic interaction between Mark, Colin, and Barbara – surely one of the great extended sequences in all of Leigh's work.[5] Leigh presents a flow of verbal and visual experiences that absolutely resist being resolved into simple, underpinning intentions:

- What are Barbara's motives in inviting Colin to work for her? Is it an attempt to assert her superiority to her sister? Is she patronizing Colin? Is she expressing frustrated maternal impulses? Is she genuinely, generously trying to help Colin?
- What are Mark's motives in going to Barbara's house? Are his intentions basically good or bad? Is he envious of Colin being offered a job? Is he resentful that Barbara favors Colin over him? Is he acting as a spoiler to ruin Colin's opportunity? Is he honestly trying to help Colin to free himself from Barbara's smothering do-goodism?

- What is Colin thinking and feeling as he sits in Barbara's living room? Is he afraid Mark will take his job? Is he insulted that Mark is there (as if he needed a baby-sitter), or encouraged by his support? Why does he leave? Is it a result of something Mark says, something Barbara says, or his own decision? Is it an assertion of independence or a mere act of escape?

The point is not only that we *don't know* which of these possibilities are correct, but that in a very real sense we *can't choose* among them. In other words, while we can *verbally* distinguish states of "envy," "pride," "patronization," "kindness," "smothering," and "love," and *abstractly* discriminate between "good" and "bad" intentions or "positive" and "negative" feelings, in these scenes (as in life) these apparently contradictory states and feelings are hopelessly entangled.[6]

How are we supposed to understand Mark's speech about "principles"? Viewed in one way, especially given his reprehensible treatment of Barbara, any talk about how he has principles and Barbara, John, and his parents do not is hogwash. Viewed from another perspective, he seems at least half-right. In his strange, perverted way, Mark is motivated by some sense of ethical responsibility and does have Colin's welfare at heart. The moment shimmers at a place beyond categorization, unreachable by concepts like "candor" or "hypocrisy." Mark's speech is an act of manipulation, but that doesn't preclude its also being sincere and heartfelt.

Or consider Barbara's treatment of Colin near the end of the scene (when she becomes quite short with him). Is her irritation selfish or altruistic? That is to say, is she disappointed because Mark has frustrated her plan to "adopt" Colin as a surrogate child, or because he has spoiled her chance to help him be independent of Mark? Leigh shows us how inapplicable such an either-or is. If Mark is principled *and* unprincipled at the same time, Barbara is at one and the same moment both selfish *and* unselfish, both trying to help Colin *and* pursuing her own personal ends. To attempt to reduce either to anything simpler is to do violence to what Leigh presents.

As I argued in terms of the climactic scenes in *Nuts in May* and *Grown-Ups*, if we ask which perspective is the "correct" or "best" one, which character is "right," or who we are supposed to "believe" or "identify with," we get nowhere. That would be to assume that Leigh endorses the sort of superpersonal, absolute truth that exists in most mainstream films. In *Casablanca, Citizen Kane*, or *Psycho*, it is possible to attain a final, cumulative, "correct" view that subsumes and includes the partial views of the individual characters. There is an absolute, impersonal truth to be arrived at, and in fact arriving at it might be said to be the purpose of the narrative for the viewer. (The main character almost always finally attains that "ideal" view in most works – in Hitchcock's films, for example.) But, even when no character attains it (as is the case in *Citizen Kane*), the viewer does. As the ending of *Kane* grandiloquently illustrates, no matter how fragmented the temporal presentation and how halting the progress, the ultimate possibility of a general, comprehensive understanding is never really in question. Though the moral of *Kane* is sometimes said to be the opposite, it is clear that it tells us that there *is* a truth beyond individual biases.

Leigh simply doesn't believe in truth in general. In his work, there is no getting beyond truth's perspectival nature. In Emily Dickinson's term, all truth is "slant"; none is straight. The individual views of Mark, Barbara, Colin, and Haley do not cumulate in a general view, any more than those of Peter, Norman, Sylvia, and Hilda do, because a general, impersonal understanding is an unreality.

Barbara's understanding of what she is doing, Mark is doing, and Colin is doing is fundamentally different from Mark's or Colin's understanding of it and her. All three perspectives are equally right – and equally limited. All three are equally correct – and equally biased and partial. Each person has his own truth, based on who he is, what he has lived through, and what he brings to the particular moment. The film itself is the closest we can get to an understanding of the whole truth – an understanding that is irreducibly perspectival.

Even considering his characters individually, Leigh won't filter their personalities and interactions to purify their effect and function. Everyone's motives, goals, intentions are mixed and impure. American movies tend to see their characters in terms of moral and emotional absolutes: This one is good and that one bad; this one an idealist, that one a cynic; this one a hero, that one a villain. In Leigh, no one is simply right or wrong – no one is simply anything. Everyone is many different, contradictory things.

Sylvia is funny and loving (and deserves love and affection), but she is also intimidating to men, unpredictable, perverse, and self-defeating. Peter is a prig, but a sincere, well-meaning one. Trevor is innocent, liberating, and free, but also self-centered, irresponsible, and immature. Barbara is kind but also deeply flawed. Mark is cynical, negative, and cruel, but can also be thoughtful, intelligent, and right about some things. We want black and white, but Leigh gives us gray. We want a hero to cheer for and identify with, and a villain to dislike; but Leigh gives us prickly, strange, mixed (and mixed-up) figures.

Leigh and his actors won't "cheat" to make a point. He won't exaggerate the characters' qualities to make things easier on the viewer. Turn on almost any American film and you'll find a main character you can admire, a "good" figure (who is able to be so good because his problems are outside himself), whose consciousness the viewer can flatteringly "become." No character, no motive, no emotion is that simple or pure in Leigh's work. Heroism is imperfect (which is why the concept doesn't really apply). Virtue is flawed. Good intentions are expressed in troubling or mixed-up ways. Wendy, in *Life Is Sweet*, is as good a character as Leigh ever creates, but she is also a bit of a nag and a ditz. American film viewers feel frustrated by this state of affairs. Everyone seems stupid or inadequate in some way. Is Leigh mocking all of his characters? Is he cynical or despairing? Surely, we are not meant to "admire" Mark, Colin, Barbara? And the answer is no, we are not. But the imperfection of these figures is not a flaw or miscalculation on Leigh's part. Nor an expression of cynicism. It is his deeply humane appreciation of his characters' humanity. It represents his understanding that, in Lenny Bruce's phrase, truth is not what should be, but what is. In fact, if anyone deserves to be accused of despair or cynicism, it is the Hollywood filmmakers who feel that they have to idealize characters to make them valuable. Leigh respects and honors figures who are like the ones we meet in life, who are like us, with flaws, shortcomings, and every other kind of compromise. For Leigh, reality doesn't have to be prettified or simplified to merit our interest; what is, is good enough.

It would have been easy to make things simpler for a viewer by pushing Colin's, Barbara's, or Mark's performances just a hair further in one direction or another: Barbara could have been written and acted to have been just slightly more snobbish, patronizing, and affected: Mark just a little more envious, scheming, and mean; and, depending on the interpretation that was intended, Colin just a little more or less dependent on or resentful of Mark. A single wounded glance, a word, a tone of voice would have sufficed to work the trick for each of them; but thank God, they resist the temptation.

From the actors' perspective, one might say that Marion Bailey (who plays Barbara), Phil Daniels (who plays Mark), and Tim Roth (who plays Colin) don't play for clarity – for simple hardness, sweetness, badness, victimization, or any other simple reading – but for truth. They don't play for easy understanding – making Mark an envious malcontent, Barbara a snob or bounder, or Colin a victim of either of the others' machinations – in the Hollywood way. Rather, they do what the very greatest actors always do to the characters they play· They attempt to redeem and justify them. They fight to free them from clichés. They refuse to sell them out. They defend their character's point of view; they labor to make it tenable, to show that it is valid and complex, not stupid and craven. They protect their characters by loving them, by respecting them – the same way we defend our own positions in life; the same way you might defend a lover from others' reductive interpretations of his or her behavior.

Needless to say, Leigh and his actors don't achieve this degree of complexity by being vague. We aren't uncertain about Colin, Mark, and Barbara because the actors are ciphers (as in the states of pantomimic blankness Hollywood films employ), because the characters express *no* definite feelings, or because their scenes are emotionally uneventful, but because they express *so* much *so* vividly – so *many* emotions, simultaneously and successively. Mark is envious *and* concerned, loving *and* rallying, sarcastic *and* sincere. Barbara is patronizing *and* caring, more than a little bit a do-gooder *and* yet deeply concerned about Colin.[7] Colin is dependent *and* independent, strong in some ways *and* weak in others. The difficulty of Leigh's work isn't emptiness but fullness.

Even beyond the unclassifiability of the individual feelings in the scene in Barbara's living room, the beats keep shifting. Mark, Colin, and Barbara cycle through an extraordinary variety of emotions. Barbara is brisk, confident, and composed at the start of the scene but deeply wounded and shaken by its end. She is initially maternal and kind to Colin (treating him tenderly when they first meet), but badgering, snide, and cutting later on. Mark's rallying is fairly innocuous when he first arrives (joking about Colin being hit by a train), turns increasingly nasty and personal after Colin shows up (as he first taunts Barbara about putting on airs, then humiliates her about her childlessness and makes ugly insinuations about a rift with her husband), but mellows out at the end of the scene after Colin leaves (in his conversation with Barbara in the upstairs bedroom). Even Colin, though almost completely silent throughout, goes through a series of subtle changes and adjustments of relationship vis-à-vis Mark and Barbara. The cascade of glances, pauses, words, and gestures won't stop moving long enough for a viewer to take an intellectual snapshot.[8] Life lived at this pace resists static understanding.

Yet, as we have seen in previous films, the characters themselves are not necessarily able to keep up with the implications of Leigh's style. Even as the scene in Barbara's living room coruscates with flickering shifts of feeling, mood, and tone, Barbara herself attempts to stand still emotionally. She fights to maintain her poise and cool against the onslaught of Mark's needling. She tries to remain arch and ironic, above it all. In the work of another artist, her coolness might be a virtue, but at this point in a study of Leigh's work it should be apparent that he is opposed to coolness and poise – at least when they are achieved through acts of will. Barbara's relentless cheeriness throughout the film is evidence of a problem. Her poise is an act of denial. Like her distant relatives, Pat, Gloria, Beverly, and Valerie, Barbara holds herself together with will power (which is why, in the logic of Leigh's work, she will eventually break down).[9]

As if to tune up the viewer's eyes and ears before Barbara's climactic encounter with Mark, Leigh inserts an instructional scene just a few minutes earlier. As I pointed out previously, one of Leigh's favorite ways of indicating a character's limitations is to pair him or her with a kind of negative mirror-image: Pat meets Peter (two posers); Keith meets Finger (two self-centered, rigid types); Christine meets Gloria (two fake perky cheerleaders). When Barbara visits her sister's apartment to invite Colin to work for her, Leigh uses the moment to present a face-off between Barbara and her antitype, an unnamed maintenance man who happens to be in the apartment. (The man is played by Peter Wight, who goes on to play Brian, the night watchman, in *Naked*.)

In the most explicitly Pinteresque moment in all of Leigh's work, Barbara and the maintenance man verbally spar on the subject of money. Leigh orchestrates a hilariously "absurd" demonstration of how neither can get out of his or her respective imaginative box.[10] Barbara is trapped in an idealized, economics-course, Yuppie-ish conception of the importance of money; the maintenance man is imprisoned in a hippie-dippy, flower-child, Marxism-lite opposition to it. The completely nutty argument goes round and round, with neither character understanding a syllable the other utters. Contributing to the wonderful wackiness of the moment is the stratospheric disconnection of their verbal joust from the actual poverty of the apartment in which they are conducting the discussion. All the high finance never comes within a million miles of the problems of this high-rise.

Even more disturbing than the content of Barbara and the maintenance man's conversation, is its tone – smug, narrow, defensive, intolerant of differences of opinion. There is no surer sign of personal limitation for Leigh than for characters to confine themselves in imaginative straight-jackets this way – mentally and emotionally hog-tied in fixed, prefabricated notions of who they are, what their lives are about, and what they believe and know. The reason the young people in *Meantime* – even the most obnoxious, like the street punks – are more interesting than the adults is that, whatever their personal limitations and immaturity, they are at least a little less sure of who they are. Their responses to life may be eccentric, but at least they are not predictable. We can almost always anticipate what Mavis, Frank, Barbara or John is going to say or feel about something; the same could never be said of Colin, Mark, and Coxy.

Mark is another in the long line of Leigh's Boudu figures. His encounter with Barbara (and indeed the overall narrative pairing of his family with hers throughout the film) is a classic Leigh matchup of order, poise, and control on the one side (Barbara and John and their invite-the-boss-to-dinner suburban lifestyle), against subversion, disturbance, and emotional unpredictability on the other (wild-card Mark and Colin and their shout-at-each-other, disorganized scrape-the-bottom-of-the-barrel existence). As we have seen over and over again, Leigh, the resister of easy readings, easy relationships, and easy understandings, the disturber of cinematic complacencies, not surprisingly, takes the side of his Boudu-like disturbers of the peace.

Or perhaps the more apt artistic allusion would be to *Othello*. As Iago was for Shakespeare, Mark is to Leigh. Both are their creators' ways of unsettling received understandings and interrogating unexamined codes of social interaction. And as unappealing as both figures may seem to be on moral grounds, both are clearly stand-ins for their creators. Iago and Mark do what all great artists do: critique conventions, shake things up, and generate fresh responses. By "challenging" easy answers (as Leigh says he does in the epigraph to this chapter), they make creativity possible. (*Naked*'s Johnny is a later incarnation of the same principle, though a far less interesting, less complex manifestation of it.)[11]

As a character, Mark does the same thing Leigh does as a filmmaker: He tests fault lines; he exposes unexamined assumptions; he punctures pretensions; he puts what is static into motion; he forces the return of the repressed; he reveals the strangeness and artificiality of social rituals we previously took for granted. In this particular instance, he takes

Barbara apart like a puzzle, piece by piece, revealing and undermining each of the fictions around which she has organized her life.

The danger in this way of putting it, however, is that it makes *Meantime* sound more schematic than it actually is. That is the danger of most acts of critical interpretation. Critical descriptions invariably translate a work of art into a set of static structures. The narrative is pared down to a series of confrontations and climaxes. Interactions between characters are translated into abstract systems of relationship. Characters are described in terms of generic narrative functions. The work of art becomes its outline. The entire field of Cultural Studies is premised on a belief in the validity of this act of translating a work into ideological and sociological generalizations in this way.

Such an approach is actually suited to many films (like those of Hitchcock, Kubrick, Lynch, De Palma, or Stone, for example) which *are* fairly abstract and schematic in their understanding of experience. But it does violence to Leigh. His films are not abstract but sensorily tangible. His characters are not generic placeholders, but particular, complex individuals. His meanings are not static, but slippery and evolutionary. His scenes do not present schematic oppositions and contrasts, but eccentric, unclassifiable, particular expressive performances.

Take away the nuance, the mystery, the in-betweenness of the characters and situations and *Meantime* would become "a coming-of-age drama in which two troubled sons work out independent identities and break away from the emptiness of their parents' and relatives' lives." The greatness of the film, of course, is that it avoids such trite oppositions and easy emotional conflicts and resolutions. Mark (and every other character and situation in *Meantime*) is less abstract, less simple, less clear than that. He is more mixed, more multivalent and changeable, less generic and representative than Cultural Studies can deal with.

Leigh's films are not reducible to their plots or a set of abstract relationships between characters – any more than Tarkovsky's or Cassavetes' are. The thing we call plot is just a shorthand way of remembering an experience that is different from and far more complex than the actual events that are presented. Character as a coherent, predictable bundle of attributes doesn't even exist in these films. Leigh's characters and their interactions are far less resolved and more fluxional than their abstract values. The oscillations of feeling, tonal irresolutions, emotional in-betweennesses, and interpretive uncertainties are falsified when they are translated into the clarity of ideological or sociological abstractions.

To reduce *Meantime* to its events, and its characters to their symbolic functions is to ignore the actual experience of the work. The ending of the film can stand for all. It is indisputable that Colin leaves Barbara's, but what matters is *how* he leaves. Rather than making a scene and storming out "to assert his independence" (as a plot summary might have it and as a symbolic understanding of Colin might explain it), Colin undemonstratively and mysteriously shuffles out the door in a way that denies the viewer emotional clarification. When Colin subsequently shows up unannounced at Hayley's apartment, Leigh's decision to have Hayley *not* let him in (and the fairly chilly and exasperated tone of voice with which Tilly Vosburgh delivers her line) prevents a future relationship from even being hinted at that would sentimentally suggest a possible romantic resolution. Then, when Colin finally comes home, note how his return is staged to *deny* the viewer a Big Emotional Payoff in the Hollywood way. Rather than defiantly confronting his parents and his brother with the fact that he has had his head shaved, Colin is too embarrassed and ashamed to let anyone see it. Even the viewer doesn't have knowledge of it for a long time. (And when Mark finally discovers the fact and asks Colin about it, he even says he regrets having had it done.) There are no grand statements or rhetorical flourishes. Nothing is really resolved or clarified about Colin (or Mark).[12] Though we have lived life-times of experiences, we aren't very far from where we started in terms of clarifications.

These vaguenesses and graynesses are the heart and soul of Leigh's work and the very thing that makes for the greatness of his characters and events. This is knowledge pitted against the forms of knowledge that constitute almost all criticism. Leigh's scenes and characters resist all summary forms of knowledge. They hold us in a complicated, in-between temporally alive place – the place of truth.

11

Holding Experience Loosely: *High Hopes*

Hard Labour and *Meantime* were criticized by some on the far left for not showing
the barricades being manned, the revolution being made, for not fighting back. But
I'm not really concerned with coming up with simplistic answers. I'm concerned
with formulating questions and with stimulating the audience's sense of how things
should be.

– Mike Leigh

Leigh's sensibility is fundamentally comic, so it shouldn't be surprising
that playing, joking, and clowning around are among the most important expressive events in his work, or that many of his most interesting
characters, including Cyril and Shirley, the main figures in *High Hopes*,
relate playfully to their own experience. It is central to Leigh's conception of them that virtually everything they say and do has a faintly comic
tinge to it. Leigh establishes this at the very start, in a series of scenes in
which even the most unpropitious subjects are unexpectedly transformed
into brief comic bits or one-liners – from terrorism (Cyril's sardonic
"machine-gun the royal family" political views) to cacti (Shirley's hilarious routine about the names of her plants). The fact that the respective
audiences for these particular witticisms are the humorless Mrs. Bender
and the hopelessly obtuse Wayne makes the additional point that the
play exists for its own sake. Neither Wayne nor Mrs. Bender "gets the
joke," but that doesn't stop Cyril and Shirley from inflicting it on them.

Fortunately, their cleverness is not lost on each other. It is a sign of
the depth of their intimacy and evidence of how attuned they are to each
other's moods and pacings that Cyril and Shirley are not only each
other's best audience but also each other's best comic straight man and
sidekick. In the course of *High Hopes*, they improvise a series of comic

duets as nuttily inventive and nonchalantly responsive as anything Mike Nichols and Elaine May ever did.

Early in the film, while Wayne is bedding down in the neighboring room, they launch into the first of their dramatic collaborations, turning themselves into two old codgers complaining about the younger generation's noise:

> *Cyril and Shirley snuggle up in bed. Musical strains from Wayne's radio through the wall.*
> SHIRLEY: (*Laughing*) 'Ark at 'im.
> CYRIL: (*Mock aged parent*) You turn that radio off!
> SHIRLEY: (*Mock aged parent*) Wayne! I'll give you a smack!
> CYRIL: (*Mock aged parent*) What d'you think this is, a bleedin' disco? (*Both laugh.*)[1]

If that were the only example, it wouldn't be as important as it is, but Cyril and Shirley improvise similar comic routines throughout *High Hopes*. While some are brief (like the "E. T. go home" bit with Wayne at the bus station or Cyril's take-off of Rupert at the pub), others are quite extended (like the scene in which Cyril introduces Wayne to Shirley or the "died with his boots on" bedroom scene).

As I have already pointed out, one of Leigh's favorite narrative devices is to pair figures who have a large sense of play with ones who have little or none: Sylvia meets Peter; Trevor meets Sandra; Finger meets Keith; Mark meets Barbara. In terms of the general narrative trajectory of *High Hopes*, Cyril and Shirley's path first crosses Wayne's, then Mrs. Bender's, then Rupert and Laetitia's, and finally Valerie and Martin's.

One of the most frequently voiced objections to the supporting characters in Leigh's later work, and to Leigh's depictions of Rupert and Laetitia and Valerie and Martin in particular, is that they are "unrealistically" presented; however, I would argue that such a judgment is based on a simplistic conception of artistic "realism," because it assumes that every character must be presented with the same degree of complexity, detail, and verisimilitude. As Shakespeare's plays demonstrate, a work of art can achieve very complex effects by pairing "round" and "flat" characters, more complex figures with simpler ones, serious characters with comic ones, highly rhetorical with plain-speaking ones, exaggerated with understated ones. In *A Midsummer Night's Dream*, Shakespeare uses at least four mimetic styles in one work to tease out different feelings about love.

Although slightly less common than in drama, different styles of representation are employed in many films. Nicholas Ray's *Rebel without a Cause* is only the most obvious example of how a director can organize his work around a deliberate stylistic mismatch. Jim Backus plays his character literally as a cartoon: he *is* Mr. Magoo; while James Dean turns in the least cartoonish performance imaginable, playing his role with the most inward and anguished of Method inflections. In general, the expressive styles of the Brando, Clift, and Dean characters almost never mesh with the styles of any of the other characters in their films. Capra's work also relies heavily on differences in acting styles between Cary Grant, Gary Cooper, James Stewart, Barbara Stanwyck, and Jean Arthur, and the figures who oppose them.[2] The mimetic differences in these works are essential to their effect, beautifully expressing the emotional and intellectual differences between various characters, the inability of one character to speak the imaginative language of the other, the incapacity of one character to understand the other, to appreciate or enter into another's point of view.

In *High Hopes*, there is no question that Rupert and Laetitia and Valerie and Martin are simpler and less nuanced than Cyril and Shirley, but Leigh uses the stylistic mismatch for expressive effect. The "flatness" of the first two couples communicates their flat-mindedness, while Cyril and Shirley's expressive depth communicates their imaginative depth. Cyril and Shirley seem all the more complex because the others function as stylistic foils. (Leigh does the same thing in *Life Is Sweet*, with the stylistic contrast between Aubrey and Andy.)

Leigh was perfectly aware of what he was doing stylistically with the contrast between Cyril and Shirley and both Rupert and Laetitia and Valerie and Martin in *High Hopes*, telling the interviewer for the *New York Times*, shortly after the film's release: "One needs a different kind of language to depict different characters. I've used that combination of naturalism and caricature quite consistently."[3]

In particular, what Cyril and Shirley demonstrate when they play together that the other two couples lack, is the ability to enlarge their identities through theatricality. They show that they are no one thing. They show how many different tones, moods, and feelings can be held in suspension in one individual, how many different people exist, at least potentially, in each of us.

Leigh forces the viewer to compare the three couples by parelleling their scenes. For example, immediately prior to Cyril and Shirley's "died with his boots on" bedroom scene, Leigh inserts scenes showing first Rupert and Laetitia and then Valerie and Martin going to bed or in bed. Bedroom scenes in general are important dramatic moments in Leigh's work. They show how two people interact with each other when no one else is looking and they are presumably at their most open and relaxed. Bedroom chat establishes a baseline of comfortable intimacy against which more public and sometimes more stressful interactions can be measured. That is why all of Leigh's films at least briefly include similar private moments.[4]

A cursory glance at the bedroom scene between Valerie and Martin that immediately precedes Cyril and Shirley's bedroom scene might give the impression that the two couples are similar, since both Shirley and Valerie are engaged in games of sexual role playing with their spouses, but the difference is that Valerie and Martin's interaction takes all of the play out of play. The sexual role-playing game Valerie proposes ("You're Michael Douglas . . . I'm a Virgin") is entirely different from Cyril and Shirley's inventively flowing, multivoiced, multifaceted performance. While Cyril and Shirley creatively improvise new identities, Valerie's fantasy is derivative, involving imitating roles played by bad actors in worse movies. There's nothing personal or original about the game. While Cyril and Shirley's role playing fluidly shifts to mirror the second-by-second flow of their feelings, representing subtle shifts in their imaginative relationship, Valerie's "You be this and I'll be that" fantasy locks her and Martin into fixed, monotonic, mechanical roles that reflect their canned, received, off-the-peg understandings of personal identity. Cyril and Shirley's performance is profoundly collaborative and tenderly sensitive to each other's feelings; Valerie and Martin's is rigid and competitive ("*You* start. . . . *You* start! . . . *You* get on top. . . . No, I don't want to get on top"), with no real openness or responsiveness to the other person. (It is no surprise that the roles Valerie and Martin assume in their public lives are just as received and mechanical as the ones in the bedroom: Valerie plays the social climber and Martin the rake, with a robotic rigidity and lack of originality that would embarrass even an actor as uninspired as Michael Douglas.)

Rupert and Laetitia are also shown engaged in a role-playing sexual game. It involves Rupert chasing a screaming Laetitia with a toy named Mr. Sausage and, as that description suggests, is as unimaginative as (and even more infantile than) Valerie and Martin's sexual role playing. Leigh provides a more extensive view of Rupert and Laetitia's imaginative and emotional limitations in a bedroom scene that immediately precedes those of Valerie and Martin and Cyril and Shirley. Like Cyril and Shirley, Rupert and Laetitia have also just come back from a night out and are preparing to go to bed. They engage in a conversation that has absolutely none of the play Cyril and Shirley's displays. There is no fun, no flexibility, no inventiveness, no good-natured teasing or joking, no mutually responsive and stimulating exchange of emotions and energies. Rupert and Laetitia's so-called interaction consists of mismatched, nonintersecting pronouncements. They don't really listen, let alone respond to each other. Their "conversation" is closer to being a series of alternating monologues. Like a nightmare version of a singles' bar interaction with a stranger, their comments (the nature of which is summarized by Rupert's "Two steaks, same day, totally different . . ." and Laetitia's "I thank God every day I've been blessed with such beautiful skin . . .") leave no room for a response or reply. Rupert and Laetitia take their own pulses, so wrapped up in their own private worlds of self-referential memories and observations that they might as well be talking to themselves (and perhaps are). There is no communication here, just the staking out and defending of independent positions. Rupert and Laetitia are as rigid and mechanical in their relation to experience, and as emotionally estranged from each other as Mr. and Mrs. Thornley, Mr. and Mrs. Stone, Ralph and Christine Butcher, or Harold and June (which is why their mode of interaction reminds us of these earlier characters).

As I have pointed out, there is almost always an implied dramatic metaphor in Leigh's work. One way to think of many of his scenes is as contrasting characters who "script" their lives and relationships (here, Rupert and Laetitia and Valerie and Martin) with characters who show themselves capable of being dramatic "improvisers" (in this instance Cyril and Shirley). The first group limits their own and others' identities to predefined roles and modes of interaction, while the second stays genuinely open and responsive to each other and anything else that comes along.

The dramatic metaphor surfaces in *High Hopes* during Mrs. Bender's birthday gathering, where Valerie attempts to script and direct the "surprise" party to the point where the surprise, the party, and the interest disappear. Like Keith earlier, Valerie functions as a dictatorial actor-writer-director who refuses to tolerate the least deviation from her script and storyboard. For her, as for some film directors, actors are clearly cattle. She has decided how they should play their roles and has blocked out their positions and movements in advance. Rather than letting the people she has brought together bring their unique expressive gifts to a scene, so that they may exhibit feelings and attitudes different from her own, she robs them of their uniqueness by forcing them to play their parts according to her conception of them.

Needless to say, there is no filmmaker more opposed to this Hitchcockian notion of creation. For Leigh, both as a human being and a dramatist, sticking too closely to a script defeats the possibility of discovery, just as defining yourself or anyone else in terms of a generic role denies the individual his or her individuality. As the omnivorousness of his entire stylistic project indicates, the Hitchcockian director imposes his own point of view, his own way of seeing and feeling, on everything and everyone, leveling individual differences, erasing alternative understandings, generalizing viewpoints, and homogenizing experience. Leigh is committed to the opposite vision of experience: to the utter uniqueness of each individual's forms of thought, feeling, and expression. He is committed to open-ended explorations of selfhood and relationship in which the actor, the director, and the character hold themselves open at every stage of the dramatic process. For Leigh, creation is not about imposing your view on others, but about exposing yourself to alien ways of feeling and being.

As different as they may be from one another socially and economically, Rupert and Laetitia and Valerie and Martin are imaginatively indistinguishable.[5] All four typecast everyone they meet, like a bad Hollywood director, treating people as if they were functionally interchangeable. For Martin, the typecasting involves the assumption that women are whores and men entitled to sexual favors, which is why he feels free to proposition Shirley, emotionally abuse his girlfriend, and prey sexually on every woman he meets. "They're all the bleedin' same," he says at one point, and in his categorical understanding of experience, all women are.

Valerie is motivated by another kind of generalized understanding of experience. As her attempt to "become" Laetitia by mimicking her way of dressing and talking demonstrates, for Valerie you *are* your clothes and mannerisms. The unfathomable mystery of identity gives way to an externally defined, generic sense of selfhood.[6]

To Rupert and Laetitia, the typecasting of identity and experience involves treating anyone below their own social class as being indistinguishable from a tradesman. Rupert's "What made this country great was a place for everyone and everyone in his place" is the quintessential Central Casting maxim.

What is lost is not only genuine openness and responsiveness to experience, but an appreciation of imaginative "otherness." Both couples see absolutely everything and everyone in terms of their own personal perspectives. Like Peter, Mr. Thornley, Keith, Beverly, or June in earlier works (and like a Hitchcockian director), they transform everyone into a version of themselves. They trim experience to fit into their own tiny emotional and intellectual categories, inverting Leigh's own value system. Alien points of view are not only not recognized but cease to be imaginable. Differences disappear. Individuals are denied individuality. Valerie can't even conceive that Cyril and Shirley might want to behave differently at the birthday party than how she thinks they should behave. Rupert and Laetitia can't even imagine Mrs. Bender having ideas, feelings, and values different from their own. That is what makes for the bizarre irrelevance of Laetitia's "chat" with her about the value of her property, as well as why she is oblivious to the insulting double entendre of the "Have you your original features?" question that she asks Mrs. Bender. For Laetitia, as for the Mad Hatter, words mean only what *she* wants them to mean.

As I have noted, aesthetic issues invariably have ethical dimensions in Leigh's work: Peter's "monologues" in *Bleak Moments* (e.g., in the scenes in which he cross-examines Norman or lectures Sylvia), Keith's "scripting" and "directing" in *Nuts in May* (e.g., in the sing-along with Ray), and Beverly's desire to "star" in *Abigail's Party* all have moral consequences. To insist on "scripting," "directing," and "starring" in these ways not only makes for bad art: It is cruel. Martin's treatment of Valerie, Shirley, and his girlfriend; Valerie's treatment of Mrs. Bender, Shirley, and Cyril at the birthday party; and Rupert and Laetitia's treatment of Mrs. Bender, Shirley, and Cyril in their home not only show them to be bad "directors," they show them to be bad people.

In line with the justice structure of his work, Leigh never lets false stances succeed. Characters are punished or forced to recognize the limitations of their designs for living. In *High Hopes* the punishment for both couples is to be plunged into comical chaos. Life resists being scripted and stage-managed in the ways Valerie attempts to do, and people defy being leveled and controlled in the ways Laetitia attempts to do. Despite all of Valerie's planning (or rather because of it), Mrs. Bender's birthday party degenerates into confusion. Precisely because of their obsession with order, Rupert and Laetitia's house is turned into a madhouse. Experience overflows the intellectual and emotional containers each of the couples attempts to confine it to. Leigh's point is that to attempt to tailor experience to fit into our small personal perspectives (rather than opening ourselves to its diversity) is to doom ourselves to failure and confusion.[7]

Cyril and Shirley represent an entirely different approach to experience and interaction. They leave generic understandings of experience and Central Casting notions of identity behind. If Valerie and Martin and Rupert and Laetitia are metaphorized as control-freak actor-writer-directors who attempt to force life to conform to their narrow notions of it, Cyril and Shirley are imagined to be improvisers. They hold themselves emotionally and intellectually open and responsive to everyone who crosses their path – from Wayne to Mrs. Bender to Suzi. (Cyril and Shirley's imaginative and social responsiveness to Wayne's predicament is clearly meant to contrast with Rupert and Laetitia's treatment of Mrs. Bender.)

Rather than treating identity as something prepackaged and acquirable (the way Valerie thinks she can acquire Laetitia's identity if she wears the right clothes or Martin thinks he will be "cool" if he drives the right car), Cyril and Shirley understand selfhood to be a capacity; not something you have or achieve, but a streaming state of sensitivity and responsiveness.

Above all, Cyril and Shirley share Leigh's supreme respect for different ways of being, feeling, and knowing. They genuinely appreciate that the play of different tones, styles, and voices – both in their relationship with each other and their relationships with others – comprises life's excitement and interest. They may be surprised by Wayne's provincialism, dismayed by Mrs. Bender's conservatism, and offended by Rupert's rudeness, but they are under no illusions that they can ignore or dismiss these different points of view. Cyril and Shirley not only tolerate these differences, they positively *appreciate* them. Though they may not endorse these alien ways of thinking and feeling, they can still be entertained by, amused by, and provoked into new thoughts and feelings by them.

As their parodies and vocal impersonations suggest, like their creator, Cyril and Shirley function *empathetically*. They put themselves in others' shoes. To watch their interactions with Wayne is to see them sympathizing with his feelings of lostness or his Blimpy-induced stomachache (no matter how weird and comical they find him and his habits). To watch Cyril "doing" Rupert or Shirley "doing" Wayne or Martin is to see them imaginatively *entering into* Rupert's narrowness, Wayne's innocence, and Martin's machismo (even while not losing sight of their limitations).

Cyril and Shirley deeply and sympathetically inhabit the "otherness" of everyone they meet. Rather than treating the whole world as versions of themselves, as Rupert and Laetitia do, they go out of themselves to become *them*.

In this respect, they function the same way Leigh himself does as an artist. Rather than standing outside and judging, they go inside to understand. Getting inside others' hearts and heads, seeing things not from his own, but from others' points of view, is Leigh's supreme dramatic gift – and precisely what Rupert and Laetitia and Valerie and Martin are unable to do. (In fact, watching Shirley "do" Martin or Wayne, or Cyril "do" Rupert is as close as we can get to seeing Leigh's own zesty appreciation of different ways of being, feeling, and thinking in his own life.)[8]

The most important illustration of Cyril and Shirley's receptivity to different ways of being, feeling, and thinking is their openness to each other's differences of opinion and point of view. It is central to Leigh's imagination of Cyril and Shirley's relationship that they *don't* necessarily agree or see things the same way. Their relationship is woven out of *differences*. The differences may be comical (as when they give Wayne contradictory directions on how to get to the cab stand, in a scene that is probably indebted to the comical disagreement about which way is east and which is west in Ozu's *Late Spring*), semicomical (as when they briefly spar over whether they should go to Valerie's party), or deadly serious (as in their feelings about having a child), but they are honored, respected, and dealt with – not denied, suppressed, or erased.

Notice the contrast Leigh sets up with the other two couples. Valerie's forced chipperness and patronizing knowingness[9] is a denial of otherness, glossing over and ignoring the gap that separates her from everyone around her. In the case of Rupert and Laetitia, when Rupert has different opinions than Laetitia (as in their brief discussion of the opera), they vie for domination, with her ultimately winning the argument and converting him to her point of view. A monotonic universe dictates zero-sum games: When there are two views of anything, one must be right and the other must be wrong. One person must win and the other lose. The other two couples can't even tolerate, let alone make something of their differences, which is why they lead to awkward silences or the breaking off of relations altogether (as in the scene of Valerie's collapse).

Cyril and Shirley live in a more multivalent world – a place where different ways of understanding and points of view can coexist. When they disagree about directions to the cab stand, whether they should attend Valerie's party, or visit Mrs. Bender, they don't attempt to argue each other into submission, but enter into the other's perspective, which is why their differences ultimately lead to discovery. In the process of comparing their differences (and not always joking ones) and staying open to each other's points of view, Cyril and Shirley learn and grow.

That is ultimately what the "died with his boots on" bedtime scene – one of the greatest brief sequences in all of Leigh's work – illustrates. Cyril and Shirley's dramatic collaboration is stunningly complex and mobile. (It would hardly be an exaggeration to say that there are more emotional shifts and tonal adjustments in this five-minute sequence than in many entire movies.) Note not only how the two lovers turn the moment into a dramatic skit but how rapidly and supplely they respond to each other's leads – sometimes following the other, at other times taking things in a whole new direction. Tonally and emotionally, the sequence is one of the most nimbly inventive interactions in all of Leigh's work.

To mark how far we have come imaginatively since *Bleak Moments*, one only has to compare the litheness of Cyril's and Shirley's play with the angularity of Pat's and Hilda's or the clumsiness of Sylvia's and Norman's. Or, in terms of the relationship of lovers, note how much quicker and more supple the changes in this sequence are from Ann and Naseem's improvisation in *Hard Labour* (employing the concept not to describe the trivial improvisations of actors making up their lines, but the profound improvisations of characters adjusting their relationship). The scenes in the earlier works are recognizably from the same hand that created the interaction between Cyril and Shirley, but in this film it is a hand (and eye and ear) far more delicate, quick, and aware. As often happens in a dramatic career, Leigh's characters grow in their sensitivities and the complexity of their identities as he grows in his ability to depict them. His possibilities of expression create their possibilities of selfhood and awareness, which in this case are breathtaking in their range and fluidity. (The stage play *Ecstasy* is the turning point in this regard.)

Shirley begins by wittily casting Cyril and herself as characters in a Western. (" 'E died with his boots on!'") Cyril picks up on her reference and mock-chastises himself for getting so drunk. ("He was too pissed to take them off.") Shirley sidesteps the self-criticism to assume a nurturing stance. ("Do you want me to 'elp yer?") Cyril responds with gratitude. ("Oh, yeah.") Responding to Cyril's concession and taking a beat to mark a playfully dramatic shift of tone, Shirley turns jokingly extortive.

("What'll you gimme first?") Cyril plays desperate. ("Anything.") Given the degree of Cyril's feigned abjectness, Shirley decides to push her advantage with a humorously threatening warning. ("Anything . . . I might 'old you to that.") In response, Cyril plays at being so needy that he will agree to anything. First, he downright grovels. ("You name it!") Then expresses exaggerated gratitude. ("This is bloody good of you.") Given the completeness of Cyril's capitulation, Shirley, having triumphed, now relents from her threat and playfully transforms herself from mate in one sense to mate in another. ("Don't mention it, old chap.")

Once the power struggle is over and they are in a comfortably non-combative emotional place, Shirley morphs into a mommy singing a children's ditty. Cyril is her little boy. ("Unzip a banana.") Mum then gives way to mock-critical outsider clucking over Cyril's infantilism. ("His mum never showed 'im 'ow to undo 'is laces.") As if to assert his masculinity in response, Cyril switches his tone to generic tough guy. ("Give it a good tug.") But Shirley rejects a partnership with Jimmy Cagney and chooses to turn the interaction in a tender direction. ("Oh, I was going to ease it off.") But, as if not wanting to get too far imaginatively from Cyril, her next line comically reestablishes solidarity with his macho-man stance by inflecting the event in a playfully sexual direction. ("I'll tell you what. If I can't ease it off, I'll give it a good tug.") The tug itself is played for comedy, as Shirley takes a pratfall backward and she and Cyril share a good laugh. The comedy then gives way to the playful sexuality of Shirley's next question. ("Did you come?"), before she then morphs back into mum again, playing a game of "This little piggy went to market" on Cyril's toes.

That's less than half of the scene, which continues on beyond this point, but it should be sufficient to indicate not only the emotional fluidity of the interaction, but the differences in the two characters' "voices." The interest is the *concordia discours*. Shirley is flirtatious, romantic, and warm; Cyril full of sexual swagger and bravado. She is maternal, giving, and vulnerable; he is cool and laid-back. While sex is linked with nurturing and motherhood for her; for him, it connotes lust and eroticism. While she thinks of future consequences like children; he focuses on immediate pleasures. The *differences* are not treated as something to be resolved or ignored or glossed over but as a play of counter-charged energies that allow the characters to make something larger than either could alone, something valuable for both them and us.

The reason we know that Leigh is not asking us to take sides for or against Cyril and Shirley's different ways of expressing themselves (or, thank goodness, editorializing about a "failure of communication") is that their voices harmonize so beautifully, playing off each other so stimulatingly, creating something greater than either could achieve alone. Cyril and Shirley function like dancers who demonstrate that a great pas de deux is made, not by mirroring the other's movements, but out of sexual and emotional differences. The ideal partnering is one that trusts the other enough to allow each to move somewhat independently of (and, if need be, at odds with) the other. The greatest drama doesn't come out of merging, compromising, or blending individual points of view, but from honoring and bringing differences into play. To shift the metaphor to the art that Rupert and Laetitia are themselves incapable of appreciating, the effect is like an operatic duet in which two singers perform separate but intertwining melodies – vocally merging, separating, and merging again. They remain in sensitive relation to each other, even as they assert their differences from one another. The responsiveness of the interaction is what makes the duet so great.

How different are Rupert and Laetitia's disharmonies in their bedroom scene! Their voices have a formulaic weariness, as if they were not even listening but only going through the motions of pretending to converse. (The nagging, narcissistic, tedious insistence of Laetitia's remarks summarizes the tonal effect: "No, darling, how many times? . . . Is my neck looking a little saggy? Do you see any lines? Darling! . . . I thank God every day I've been blessed with such beautiful skin: you really are a very lucky boy. You take me for granted.") Rupert and Laetitia's voices, identities, moods, and positions are the opposite of responsive. They are frozen in place, a fact trivially expressed by the stasis of Laetitia's physical position and her reference to the coldness of Rupert's hands but profoundly captured by the iciness of her tones and the fixity of her and Rupert's imaginative positions.[10]

Cyril and Shirley's contrasting capacity to make something creative and entertaining out of their emotional and intellectual differences is illustrated in scene after scene of *High Hopes*, starting with the very beginning of the film when Cyril brings Wayne upstairs to see if Shirley can help him with directions. Their slightly different responses to the same basic situation create a delicately comic interaction. Shirley is kinder and more caring (she invites Wayne in, asks him to sit down, offers him tea); Cyril is more factual and intellectual (he hits the street-index book). She is more personal and hospitable (attempting to put Wayne at ease by humorously introducing him to her cacti); Cyril is more cynical, self-referential, and abstractly ideological (making a series of sardonic political and economic allusions). Which response is right?

Fun-house mirror images, doubles, and distortions – Laetitia and Rupert (*top*);
Valerie and Martin (*middle*); Shirley, Cyril, and Mrs. Bender (*bottom*) – "At
least Cyril and Shirley create something loving . . . and will be in a position to
feel and give things – to each other, to a possible child, or even to Mrs. Bender.
The other couples, in contrast, are consumers." – Mike Leigh

Which point of view is the best? There is no right or wrong. (This is not an American movie.) The point is *not* to choose between Shirley's ways of responding and Cyril's, but to understand that the play of differences is what makes for interest in both art and life.

If there were any doubt about the extent to which Leigh is not criticizing but *endorsing* Cyril and Shirley's expressive differences, the scene at Highgate cemetery immediately following the "died with his boots on" scene should make his position clear. Leigh orchestrates a series of comical jibes, needlings, and misunderstandings as Cyril and Shirley pursue different trains of thought in front of Karl Marx's grave. Shirley's sassy comment on Marx's "bigness" (intended as a joke about the size of the monument) is misunderstood by Cyril (probably deliberately) to refer to Marx's being an intellectual "giant." Her touching observation about the death of Marx's grandson, which injects a loving, personal note into the conversation, is deliberately twisted by him into a sardonic observation about the sad state of public health in the nineteenth century. In general (though, strictly speaking, the scene is nothing in general and everything in its second-by-second shifting particulars), while Cyril waxes intellectual about Marx's ideas, Shirley focuses on the life of the body and the senses. As he flies off into a stratosphere of ideological abstractions, she brings the moment down to earth with her comments about plants and flowers. While he is faintly cynical and despairing, she is ebulliently upbeat and life-affirming.

Just as in the "died with his boots on" scene, the flowing responsiveness of their performance – the give-and-take, the trading of perspectives – is the opposite of Rupert and Laetitia's noncommunicating noninteractions. In this scene, as in the various bedroom scenes, Cyril and Shirley do not stake out and defend fixed positions but hold themselves emotionally open to each other – exchanging energies, nimbly trading control of the beats, pursuing each other's metaphors, picking up on each other's words, puckishly twisting them, offering new paths for exploration, taking turns following and leading. As in any vitally alive relationship, they genuinely listen, respond to, and take direction from each other – as well as occasionally resist taking direction. Like Vaudeville troupers (or an old married couple) they nimbly adapt, josh, and tweak the other's perspective, moving slightly independently of it while staying in relationship to it. They never lose sight of the real goal, which is not to "star" (as "bad actors" like Valerie and Laetitia – or Beverly and Keith earlier – attempt to), but to keep the relationship going, the connection alive, as interestingly as possible. This flowing, moving exchange of energies is Leigh's model for all creative interaction – in life and art.

In the largest sense, Cyril and Shirley's difference from the other two couples comes down to the issue of how each "takes" experience. While Rupert and Laetitia and Valerie and Martin take things hard, Cyril and Shirley take them a little easy. Where the other two couples' relationship to experience is tense and tight, Cyril and Shirley's is loose. Their attitude to each other and everyone they meet is a little bit relaxed and laid-back (which is why Leigh imagines them as being "hippies"). They hold their experiences and relationships with others somewhat lightly – in Shirley's case, one might say even delicately.

Unlike the other couples in *High Hopes*, Cyril and Shirley don't pressure people to conform to particular expectations or interactions in order to follow predictable paths. They are willing to take them more or less as they are (which of course doesn't mean they have to like everything they get). Like certain other key figures in Leigh's earlier work – Sylvia, Trevor, Dick, Ray, and Colin come to mind – they have a slightly detached, ironic, or amused attitude toward their experiences, including even their fairly painful encounters with Rupert and Martin. One might say that they have a fundamentally comic relation to experience (as long as it is understood that that is not the same thing as not taking it seriously). They allow for a little "play" in their relation to it, a little flexibility and provisionality in how they take it.

In this respect, Cyril and Shirley might be said to be the embodiment of Leigh's own cinematic style here and elsewhere, whose lightly comic tone avoids rigid positions and hard judgments, and allows for a similarly relaxed and shifting relation to experience. What they do in their lives, he does in his work: allowing the possibility of feeling more than one way at the same time about things, and allowing yourself to change your mind and your feelings as you go along. Like them, he is in favor of letting dramatic moments play out in unpredictable, unconstrained, zigzaggy ways. Like them, he knows that to make interactions too focused and purposeful is to take the life – and the fun – out of them.

Cyril and Shirley can help us understand Leigh's own angle of vision as a filmmaker. When Cyril is doing his parody of Rupert and Shirley is making jokes about Martin or Wayne, they are doing the same thing Leigh did when he imagined Rupert and Martin and Wayne. He and they are finding ways to enjoy things that might otherwise threaten them. He and they are leaving moral judgments behind, suspending harsher views, and allowing themselves to be entertained by life's oddity and strangeness. While figures like Peter and Keith judge, Leigh smiles.[11]

The dramatic potential of a fundamentally "light" or playful relation to experience is something Leigh could have learned from the work of

Yasujiro Ozu. Both Leigh's and Ozu's styles embody essentially comical or "loose" relationships to their own material that overlap with the comical, playful, or "loose" attitudes of their own most interesting characters. They hold experience lightly. It would, in fact, not be too much to argue that this Mozartian tone is Ozu's supreme gift to cinema (even though any notice of it has been almost completely omitted from the tone-deaf writing of commentators like David Bordwell).[12] Like Leigh in *Bleak Moments, The Kiss of Death, Nuts in May,* and this film, Ozu also frequently organizes his narratives around contrasts between characters who have a large sense of play and those with little or none. (*Record of a Tenement Gentleman, Autumn Afternoon, Early Spring, Early Summer, Equinox Flower, Ohayo,* and *The Brothers and Sisters of the Toda Family* illustrate this kind of narrative organization.) The wonderfully "loose" and lightly facetious relationship between Noriko and Aya in Ozu's *Early Summer* is a likely specific influence on many of Leigh's most relaxed pairings, including Trevor and Ronnie and Cyril and Shirley.

Valerie and Martin and Rupert and Laetitia (like Pat, Peter, Linda, Keith, and Beverly earlier) have an entirely more strenuous, more moralistic, and more limited relationship to experience. They attempt to force unitary meanings on life. They pressure events and interactions to go in a particular direction, which is why everything they say and do is conducted with a certain tension. They can't simply allow things to happen; they can't "go with the flow" as Cyril and Shirley do. They won't follow someone else's lead. They won't entertain alternative perspectives. They can't hold more than one thought in mind or allow themselves to feel more than one feeling at the same time. They can't get outside of themselves imaginatively in order to be able to laugh at themselves or the situations they are in.[13]

Valerie and Martin and Rupert and Laetitia (along with Aubrey and Nicola in the film that follows this one) represent the continuation of an expressive genealogy in Leigh's work that runs from Peter, Pat, Mrs. Stone, and Mr. Thornley to Keith, Beverly, Laurence, and Barbara. They show us how, in being narrowly committed to our own personal narratives, we can screen out authentic contact with others. In clinging onto our own preestablished views, we can prevent ourselves from learning anything. A further lesson they illustrate is how our rigidity is traceable to feelings of uncertainty. We wrap ourselves up in our own views out of a desire for security.

The difference between the two sets of characters is ultimately related to how tightly or loosely we define ourselves, how trapped we are in a narrow conception of who we are. Valerie and Laetitia define themselves in the same limiting way they define everyone and everything else. They can't leave their narrow definitions of themselves behind, which is why they remain the same throughout the film. They are always, boringly and predictably, "themselves." In contrast, we can never quite predict Cyril's or Shirley's next remark or feeling. As their shape-shifting, voice-changing skits demonstrate, they allow a certain degree of "play" in their identities. They avoid being trapped in a limiting sense of character, a monotonic, univocal, predictable conception of selfhood.

At their best, like improvising actors, Cyril and Shirley break away from the limitations of having a fixed "identity." Rather than having a self, they have selves. This is not an entirely easy state to be in. Who they are is always to some extent unformulated, and their feelings unresolved. Rupert and Laetitia and Valerie and Martin always know who they are, and what they feel at every moment, because they remain in the same tonal and stylistic ruts no matter what happens to them. The point of Cyril and Shirley's dramatic improvisations is to show how they haven't closed up shop on their beliefs and emotions. They are, to some extent, open-ended and undefined.

With Cyril and Shirley, Leigh has met the challenge I defined at the end of my chapter on *Hard Labour*. He has created characters whose identities flow as freely as those of actors in a real dramatic improvisation. Cyril and Shirley's shifting, mercurial, improvised relations (which are loosely related to those of Mark and Colin in *Meantime*) communicate his sense that the energies of dramatic creation (the unpredictability, the enlargement of one's identity through creative role playing, the flexibility and fluidity of one's sense of oneself) can be lived.

There is a final important aspect of the scenes between Cyril and Shirley that I have left out of my account up to this point. Namely, that the verbal and social interaction is repeatedly interrupted by freighted pauses and silent close-ups in which Cyril and Shirley reflect on their experience. The first scene I quoted, the one in which Cyril and Shirley pretend to be old codgers upset by the younger generation's noise, is typical of many others in the film insofar as it consists of two fairly different texts: an outer social and verbal interaction in which Cyril and Shirley improvise a comic bit and share a laugh; and an inner meditative text that begins at the point where my previous description ended. In that second text, Shirley and Cyril simply think (Shirley about her desire to have a child, and Cyril about his relationship with Shirley and his disinclination to have children). Cyril's good-natured comical rant – "What d'you think this is, a bleedin' disco?" gives way to a sudden, surprising shift of mood, as Shirley first laughingly tells him to "Shut up. Don't laugh!" and then falls silent with a long, long pause that leads to a thought of having a child of her own, a pause which is then followed by an uncomfortable silence on Cyril's part:

SHIRLEY: Shut up. Don't laugh!
CYRIL: 'E'd get on your wick though, wouldn't 'e?
(*Shirley sighs. Pause . . .*)
SHIRLEY: I 'ope I don't have a kid that's a bit thick.
(*Pause. Cyril looks away.*)

The pauses turn the moment tonally inside-out. The scene shifts from silliness to seriousness in a pulse beat. Shirley goes from mocking Wayne to implicitly expressing sympathy for him; and Cyril and Shirley together go from animatedly sharing a joke to lapsing into unspoken private reveries, as they silently skirt one of the most delicate issues in their relationship.

An even more striking illustration of a meditative shift in the film occurs in the "died with his boots on" scene. There are several brief pauses early in Cyril and Shirley's interaction, and a longer one just following the point at which my account ended. After Shirley plays her game of "this little piggy" on Cyril's toes (incidentally almost breaking up the actor, Philip Davis, who has to bite on his scarf to keep from interrupting her lines with a laugh), she falls completely silent. The photography switches from long and medium shots to close-ups; Shirley's tone, mood, and manner change completely; and the scene suddenly deepens beyond anything we might have predicted based on its game-playing beginning. The beat shifts from being playful, romantic, or flirtatious to something much more serious.

We are clearly meant to read the moment as Shirley lapsing into a reverie about motherhood and Cyril's objections to having a child. Leigh provides a certain amount of psychological justification for the shift by allowing us to conclude that the erotic baby talk Shirley has been spouting ("Unzip a banana. . . . His mother never showed him to undo his laces. . . . This little piggy . . .") has reminded her of her desire to have a child; but however "motivated," the important point is the emphatic quality of the move inward. This meditative moment is clearly one of the main reasons for the scene's existence.

The rest of the scene presents an almost entirely inward voyage of consciousness. Cyril and Shirley continue to converse, but it is clear that all of the real events are taking place under the surface, beneath the words, in silent trains of thought. The drama has migrated out of the words and actions and into the minds of the characters. The meditative turns in the rest of the scene take several different forms – ranging from Shirley's associative shift from the "this little piggy" routine to thoughts of motherhood and the ensuing pause in which she uncertainly deliberates on whether she dares to bring up the subject of getting pregnant, to Cyril's turning on himself with his "You think I'm being selfish, don't you?" and then turning back the other way by saying he doesn't care what Shirley thinks. Cyril and Shirley pursue independent reflective paths, respond to each other's unspoken thoughts, turn on their own premises, criticize themselves, and react to their own statements.

Meditative moves of this sort are almost unprecedented in Leigh's work prior to *Ecstasy*, and even in the works that Leigh created between that play and this film, they were extremely rare. I noted a few instances of their occurrence in my discussion of *Home Sweet Home*. Some of Colin's and Haley's scenes in *Meantime* figure less extended experiments with a similar imaginative turn. *Four Days in July* also has a few scenes similar to those here in terms of characters' meditative capacities. Characters in earlier works (Pat, Norman, Keith, Finger, Beverly, Hazel, or Stan, for example) simply could not get outside of themselves enough to pivot on their own premises like this. To have a mind capable of reflecting on itself in this way is what it means to be fully alive in Leigh's late work. (Dawn and Jean in *Ecstasy* are arguably the first figures in Leigh's oeuvre with this degree of imaginative depth.)

Leigh's early films have intermittent close-ups and pregnant pauses, but they function quite differently. Compare the close-ups involving Norman, Pat, and Sylvia in the "guitar party" scene in *Bleak Moments* with those in the scene in which Cyril and Shirley host Suzi near the end of this film, for example. In the late works, close-ups are used to cultivate consciousness; in the early films they aren't. Furthermore, although the "breakdowns" at the ends of the pre-*Ecstasy* works may resemble the meditative moments here, they aren't really the same thing at all, since they are not only confined to the ends of the films (while being the warp and woof of experience in *Ecstasy*, *High Hopes*, and *Life Is Sweet*), but are merely negative in function (whereas Dawn, Colin, Cyril, and Nicola experience deep insights about themselves in the course of their works).[14] There is nothing more Ozu-like about Leigh's post-*Meantime* films than the way these acts of inward turning, far more than events, are the engines that drive them.

The dramatic climax of *High Hopes* consists of two back-to-back meditative scenes in which Cyril and Shirley come to fundamentally new understandings of themselves and their need for each other. In the first, which immediately follows the visit to Marx's grave, the two have a conversation in their living room with a friend named Suzi, whose narrative function is to be a parody of Cyril's revolutionary aspirations. As a consequence of a brief misunderstanding, Leigh orchestrates a triple recognition moment played out in a series of silent, emotionally freighted close-ups of the three figures' faces: Suzi feels hurt and foolish because Cyril has criticized the sincerity of her commitment to social justice; Shirley feels embarrassed at having inadvertently contributed to the insult, and empty about not being able to act on her desire to have a baby, of which Suzi has just reminded her by telling a story about another couple's inability to have children; and Cyril not only feels stupid and cruel since he has hurt Suzi's feelings but futile since he has just been forced to realize that, when it comes to being a revolutionary, he is not all that different from Suzi.[15] The drama is played out almost entirely inwardly, communicated almost entirely through looks and pauses.

The second meditative moment immediately follows the first, and involves shots of Cyril and Shirley in one bedroom and Suzi in another, as all three characters continue their respective inward journeys. Leigh first presents Suzi in a brief close-up (apparently still feeling hurt and reflecting on the impotence of her avowed revolutionary stance), then devotes the rest of the sequence to a bedtime conversation between Cyril and Shirley. They reflect on the meaning of their lives and relationship: Shirley talking about her desire to have a baby and her love for Cyril; Cyril wondering out loud about whether he has been fooling himself about who he really is. But, as in the "died with his boots on" scene, the words are only the outward and visible sign of an inward and spiritual journey. To adapt a phrase of Emerson's, "the real action of the scene is in the pauses." What Cyril and Shirley are thinking is far more important than what they say. The scene's power is precisely its inwardness – its turn out of action and into thought and feeling.[16]

The sea change in Leigh's work can be measured by the difference between this scene and the superficially similar scenes in *Grown-Ups* in which Dick and Mandy first argue about and subsequently decide to have a baby. The bedroom scenes in the earlier film are about discussing an event. They are about the various forms of expression two characters employ to express their different points of view. They are about the outside of life, the surface – the words, tones of voice, gestures, and facial expressions characters use to express themselves. There is no real inwardness; Dick and Mandy don't have minds or insides (which is why there is no need for close-ups in the editing or emotionally freighted pauses in the dialogue).

In contrast, the scene in *High Hopes* is almost all inside. It is not about how you talk, but how you feel. It is not so much about persuading someone else as about consulting one's own feelings. Cyril and Shirley's scene, in fact, results in no particular action or change in their behavior. (Though some viewers tend to misremember the scene, they do *not* agree to have a child.) It is not about outer but inner events. All that happens is that Cyril and Shirley *recognize* their need for each other and *feel* a little differently.[17]

Just as we know that Leigh endorses Cyril's and Shirley's comic styles because of their resemblance to his own cinematic style, we know that he endorses their meditative pauses and contemplative turns because he inserts his own meditative pauses and contemplative turns in *High Hopes*. The film is punctuated by moments in which Leigh holds a shot a beat or two beyond the normal length (generally either a close-up of a character's face – as at the end of the "died with his boots on" scene – or a shot of a briefly "empty" frame after the main characters have exited it). The goal is briefly to "pause" his narrative and allow the viewer a moment to reflect on what he has seen. It is another lesson probably learned from Ozu who himself frequently "rings a gong" and momentarily pushes the pause button at the end of scene.[18]

It would be only a small exaggeration to say that all of *High Hopes* exists in order to create these meditative moments, to make time and space within the pressure of the narrative for acts of reflection. Leigh opens up meditative spaces in the midst of the most ordinary parts of life, even in the unlikeliest places – as when Cyril stands wrapped in thought next to a steaming tea kettle early in the film. These moments matter to Leigh because they represent a break from the routines of life, an imaginative pause in which a character gets in touch with subterranean streams of feeling. In Cyril and Shirley's pauses, opportunities for intimacy and insight are born. In inwardness, discovery becomes possible.

If there is any lingering doubt about it, the concluding sequence of scenes, which culminates with Mrs. Bender's lapsing back into confused memories of her childhood and Cyril and Shirley taking her up on the roof to look down at the city from above, decisively affirms the importance of a meditative movement off to one side of the world of words and actions.

Cyril and Shirley are the only characters in *High Hopes* with the maturity to allow these silent moments of imaginative inwardness into their lives. While Valerie and Martin, and Rupert and Laetitia are completely defined by external, public, received roles, Cyril and Shirley dive beneath them (or, in the spatial imagery of the rooftop scene, rise above them). While the incessant hustle and bustle of the others drowns out the still, small voice of real feeling, Cyril and Shirley's silences are acts of listening for it and reestablishing contact with it.

Valerie and Martin and Laetitia and Rupert never get far enough outside of their narrow little routines to reflect on themselves in this way. Their fundamental problem is that they are unable to forget who they are. They are too sure they already know what they need to know to open themselves up to anything new. Leigh's sympathies are always with characters who are willing to admit that they *don't* know who they are – something cocksure figures like Sandra, Beverly, Keith, Samantha, Rupert, and Laetitia can never do. As Cyril demonstrates, it's in *not* being sure of ourselves, in admitting we *don't* know what our lives are about, that we can start to learn something. That might help to explain Leigh's attraction throughout his work to gentle, confused, uncertain, quiet, inarticulate, nominally "undramatic" figures like Sylvia, Hilda, Trevor, Colin, and Ray, and his revulsion from strong, powerful, bustling, verbal, more strikingly "dramatic" figures like Beverly, Keith, June, Rupert, Laetitia, Jeremy/Sebastian. (Johnny in *Naked* interestingly illustrates both imaginative possibilities: He is hateful when bombastic and theatrical but affecting when quiet and reflective – as in the bathroom scene with Louise.)

Study Martin's relationship with his girlfriend for an illustration of what the unexamined life looks like. While Cyril and Shirley keep checking their actions against their feelings, Martin's sex life (like Valerie's social life) is all dicey arrangements and empty chat. It is all outsides (clothing, manners, appearances); a series of social and sexual routines (based in received, unexamined business values); power games (dominant, blustering, threatening); and received roles (the man in charge; the woman submissive, apologetic, and begging). Genuine personal feeling never enters into it. His face would not be able to sustain the scrutiny of a single silence or a protracted close-up. Valerie, Rupert, Laetitia, and Martin move, move, move, and talk, talk, talk, but their noisy, busy chatter is the problem. They would undergo a crisis if they stopped talking and moving for even a minute (and Valerie does undergo a breakdown when her frantic activities are arrested), because feelings that their lives are devoted to denying might suddenly surface.

Karl Marx is a ghostly presence at the end of *Meantime* (in Dave, the social worker) and throughout *High Hopes* (in Cyril's disillusionment with the social and economic system). There is no question that Leigh sympathizes with many of Cyril's beliefs, including much of his Marxism. Many scenes in *High Hopes* are informed by understandings of race, class, and economics identical to Cyril's. The fearful Pakistani clerk in the drugstore (and Mrs. Bender's attitude toward her), the secretary who slights Cyril because he is only a messenger, the lampooning depiction of Rupert and Laetitia, and the economic conditions Cyril and Shirley endure (in comparison with those of a "capitalist" like Martin) are ways in which Cyril's creator expresses political and economic views with which Cyril would agree.

But where the artist and his character part ways is in their relative ranking of the importance of the personal and the political realms. One might say that, although Leigh agrees with Cyril about the unjust distribution of wealth and power in contemporary England, he disagrees with him about the ultimate importance of economics as an explanatory device. Leigh locates the problems the characters in *High Hopes* face and their solutions in the realm of their feelings and thoughts. The personal takes precedence over the political. Capitalism may well foster "false consciousness" of various sorts, but the problems of consciousness that Cyril and Shirley grapple with have little to do with economics or ideology.

If we don't see this from the presentation of Cyril and Shirley's basic situation, we should see it from the scene with Suzi in their living room. It demonstrates Leigh's belief that the personal can never be factored out of political or economic analysis. While Suzi focuses on politics, Leigh's script, camera work, and editing focus on Suzi. While she talks about ideology, Leigh calls attention to her family history, her facial expressions, her gestures, her emotional state. The scene makes it clear that Suzi's social analysis is a product of her personality and personal history (and not the other way around).[19]

Marxism (whether professed by Cyril or Suzi) represents a fundamentally different understanding of experience than the one Leigh offers. Marx believed that the most important aspects of life would yield to a totalizing, impersonal, and systematic analysis. The entire experience of

High Hopes is Leigh's reply to a Marxist understanding of life. Leigh's narrative is personalized – focusing attention not on institutions but individuals. It is particularized – understanding life not in terms of generalities and abstractions, but as a matter of one particular thing after another. And, rather than being systematic and comprehensively meaningful, Leigh's narrative is a little random and "open" in its structure.

In shot after shot, scene after scene, Leigh celebrates precisely what Marx left out of his analysis: the unique, the personal, the eccentric, the nonsystematic, the haphazard, and the accidental.[20] While Marxist analysis is devoted to thoroughgoing, pervasive meaningfulness, Leigh offers experiences that are semantically and ideologically a little underdetermined. While Marxism (like Freudianism) is a "tight" and "closed" explanatory system – one that aspires to include everything in its understandings and to make it supremely meaningful – Leigh's characters, interactions, and meanings run a little "wild." We see this from the way Wayne unpredictably moves in and out of Cyril and Shirley's lives (and the film itself);[21] from the way characters like Wayne and Mrs. Bender emphatically resist being treated as sociological types or representatives; and, above all, from the unsystematic, ideologically undetermined nature of Cyril and Shirley's relationship. But the greatest difference from the Marxist position is that, in scene after scene, moment after moment, *High Hopes* asks us to acknowledge the absolutely overwhelming importance of butterfly flutters of feeling and thought, of private inward turnings and meditative moments of mind that will never be made part of an ideological system of understanding or control. In this sense, the entire film might be said to be Leigh's meditation on the limitations of political understandings of experience.

12

Circulation Is the Law of Life:
Life Is Sweet

I do not make films which are prescriptive, and I do not make films which are conclusive. You do not walk out of my films with a clear feeling about what is right and wrong. They're ambivalent. You walk away with work to do. My films are sort of an investigation. They ask questions. They're reflecting.

– Mike Leigh

Leigh's work is energized by a productive doubleness. On the one hand, the characters are imagined to be as different as possible from each other and are allowed to figure utterly unique forms of thought and feeling. Yet they are simultaneously imagined to be members of a group, shaping their performances in relation to and in response to others. This doubleness is played out in Leigh's rehearsal process. One of the reasons he works with actors individually at first, and insists that they not discuss their characters with each other, is that he wants to avoid homogenizing their voices or blending their perspectives. He is absolutely committed to maximizing expressive, emotional, and performative differences. The uniqueness of the individual is virtually an article of faith.

Yet, at the same time, his characters are always imagined to be connected with others. Which is why the second stage of the rehearsal process goes in precisely the opposite direction to the first stage, involving joint improvisations (not unlike the ones Cyril and Shirley engage in) that put a premium on nimble, fluid, present-minded responsiveness.

The lesson of Leigh's work is that characters can be utterly, uniquely themselves and also have relational identities in which what they are is not their decision alone but a product of their interactions with others. Their identities are shared with others. This double pull has been a productive tension in all of Leigh's work. He insists that his best characters be original, unique, and creative; but he also requires that they function as members of a group: expressing themselves with others, *negotiating* complex social environments every minute of their lives. In this light, it is not surprising that so much of Leigh's work focuses on families (or surrogate families like the group of young people in *Who's Who*), since the family is the place where the assertion of individuality most powerfully intersects with the demands of belonging to a group. We are never more ourselves, or more someone else's, than at home.

It is central to Leigh's vision of identity that characters must *perform* their imaginations in interaction with others. None of Leigh's figures is allowed merely to think or feel his or her identity (in Isabel's "nothing expresses me" vein); the character must socially and verbally *express* what he or she is (as Madame Merle does).

That ability to *enact* their identities freely and creatively is what distinguishes Cyril and Shirley in *High Hopes*, and Wendy, Aubrey, and Natalie here, from the other characters in their films. Leigh is a believer in the religion of doing. His greatest characters triumph, not by rising above social contexts and forms of expression (in the visionary/romantic/idealistic mode), but by plunging into and mastering them. We must express ourselves *in the world*. That is what Wendy, above all, does throughout *Life Is Sweet* – with everyone from customers in Bunnikins, to friends like Aubrey and delicate negotiations with individual family members. Not to convert imaginative impulses into practical performances is to doom ourselves. As Leigh suggested to an interviewer, that is the fundamental difference between Nicola and Natalie:

> In . . . *Life Is Sweet* the character that tends to be neglected the most is Natalie, the plumber. In her quiet way, she's as much a nonconformist as Nicola. The difference is that the nature of her nonconformity doesn't preclude getting on with living and working and in some way fulfilling herself, within limited parameters. . . . She is out there, rolling up her sleeves, getting on with it.[1]

Leigh's commitment to the practical, social expression of imaginative impulses is built into the style of *Life Is Sweet*. The scripting, photography, and miking cooperate to hold the characters in relationship with each other. Leigh's work is closer to Jean Renoir's than to most American film in this respect. The American style employs close-ups and mood-music orchestrations to separate the characters and go inside them, in order to suggest the existence of socially unexpressed states of awareness and feeling; Leigh's characters assert their existence interpersonally – by talking, moving, and physically interacting. His figures' identities are never private, their dramas are never internal, even when they think they are (as Nicola does in this film). Leigh's scripting, photography, and sound design never allow them to be.[2]

As we have seen, the Hollywood notion of starring is alien to Leigh's view of life, which is why there are surprisingly few scenes in his work featuring a figure who dominates a scene in the way Jack Nicholson, Meryl Streep, or Harvey Keitel routinely does. (You can count on one hand the number of scenes in which characters appear alone in Leigh's work.) Rather than being organized around one or two central figures, his narratives almost invariably involve the relationship of three, four, five, or more characters. Life is not about power and preeminence but negotiation. There are no solo flights. No one is allowed to control the beats. (And if someone attempts to, as Keith does in *Nuts in May* or Beverly does in *Abigail's Party*, they are meant to be judged adversely.) No one is exempt from being corrected by, replied to, or upstaged by somebody else, and if they think they are, they are in grave emotional trouble.

This is not an abstract article of faith with Leigh. It is enacted in the very cinematic style of his work – in every shot and scene. The opening scenes of *Life Is Sweet* demonstrate the complexity of the effect: Nicola, Natalie, Wendy, Andy (and Aubrey, who joins the group a few scenes into the film) are endowed with utterly distinct gestures, points of view, body types, facial expressions, and voices. Each is accorded a sufficient number of lines of dialogue and enough screen time to weigh in with his or her individuality. None is a bit player, is perfunctorily presented, or exists merely to contrast with or be reactive to the others. Each is an utterly unique and important individual. Yet at the same time Leigh's scripting, shooting, and editing communicate each figure's ineluctable connectedness. The script presents a series of arguments that keep all four family members continuously "in" the scene verbally, even as the shooting and editing scrupulously keep moving from face to face and the sound design keeps all four voices in play. The message is double: They are individuals with radically different styles and points of view, yet members of a group too, and as such answerable to everyone else in the group.

In order to pull off the double vision, Leigh has to be extremely careful about how he scripts, stages, shoots, and edits his scenes. In opposition to Hollywood filmmaking practice, he must prevent the viewer from identifying with any one figure, or the narrative from privileging the dramatic situation of one figure over any other. It is absolutely essential that no one character be allowed to dominate, or one character's point of view be treated as being more important (or more definitive or final) than any other's. The situations of each of the characters are scrupulously respected – narratively, visually, acoustically, and socially. None is dismissed or downplayed.[3]

Circulation is the law of life. While American film is almost always centripetal, moving from the group to the individual, circling in ever more tightly on the consciousness of a central figure or figures, Leigh's work is centrifugal, distributing its narrative across a series of different characters. Knowledge does not involve digging ever deeper into one perspective, but moving nimbly across different points of view.

In this respect, *Life Is Sweet* resembles Ozu's work in more than the multigenerational nature of its narrative. For example, both the narrative organization and the visual style of *Tokyo Story* force the viewer to hold three, four, or five different personal perspectives in view at any one moment – from those of the old couple, to those of the various children and in-laws they are visiting, to those of the two grandchildren. None is stinted or shortchanged. Notice, for example, in the early scenes of *Tokyo Story*, how Ozu honors even the two young boys' feelings of displacement and disgruntlement at how their grandparents' visit disrupts their routines. A few minutes later, in the scene involving the cancellation of the Sunday outing, the boys' feelings of frustration and disappointment are given at least as much screen time and accorded as much attention as the feelings of their elders.

A further overlap with Ozu's mode of presentation is that truth is temporal for Leigh. In *Life Is Sweet*, we learn things in bits and pieces, with continuous slight adjustments of view and revisions of understanding. Leigh not only forces the viewer to keep circulating through different characters' perspectives in any one scene, but also from scene to scene keeps changing the viewer's understanding of any one character.

One way Leigh keeps both the spatial and temporal adjustments going is by circulating his characters through different narrative situations. We see Wendy and Andy talking and acting in one way with their children (in their role as parents); slightly differently when they are with Aubrey (as adult friends); slightly differently from that when they are together in bed (as husband and wife); and slightly differently from that at work and play – as when Wendy leads a children's dance class or functions as a salesclerk in a children's clothing store, or Andy interacts with a mate named Patsy or performs his duties as a chef in a large industrial kitchen. We similarly see Nicola and Natalie in a range of different situations engaged in different kinds of interactions: Nicola interacting with her parents, her sister, and her boyfriend; and Natalie with her parents, at work, and in a pub with her mates in the evening. It is not simply a matter of presenting the same character against different backgrounds. Wendy and Andy, Nicola and Natalie are really quite different people in each of these roles. We see entirely different sides of them, just as we do when we meet people in different situations in life.

This approach not only differs from Hollywood films, but from most of Leigh's own previous work. Generally speaking, though a viewer learned new things about Pat and Peter, Trevor and Linda, Keith, and Beverly, and adjusted his understanding as he went along, all the various aspects of a character eventually added up to one central understanding. In *Life Is Sweet* many of the scenes present entirely different aspects of the figures. Wendy may seem ditzy or nagging in the scenes at home, but is a cheerful, helpful salesclerk at the children's clothing store where she works. At home Andy seems a dotty, comical putterer and procrastinator, but on the job he is a disciplined, efficient supervisor. (Though that view is itself almost immediately adjusted: Leigh no sooner shows him the master of all he surveys, than he has Andy retreat into his office and kick back to read a magazine.) Although Nicola never leaves the house, Leigh makes sure that we get different views of her too. In two scenes in which her boyfriend pays a visit, sides of her personality completely invisible in the family scenes emerge (including a smile of pleasure and delight on a face that scowled in every other scene). Rather than being cumulative, with one small detail after another gradually adding up to a unitary picture, *Life Is Sweet* offers a series of tacking movements for which there can be no simple, unifying understanding. One must simply accept that Andy, Wendy, Natalie, and (surprise of surprises) even the robotic Nicola are capable of being different people in different situations. There is a lot to them, a lot of different "thems."[4]

Leigh's complication of the characters goes beyond showing them playing different roles in different situations. As Cyril and Shirley's interactions demonstrated, some of the characters in Leigh's post-*Ecstasy* work are endowed with an extraordinary degree of self-awareness, which allows them, as it were, mentally to turn on a dime. They are able to reflect on what they are doing and adjust their words and actions in response to their own internal streams of thought and feeling. *High*

Hopes and *Life Is Sweet* are Leigh's crowning masterworks in this respect. Wendy and Andy scrutinize their own situations, laugh at themselves, make jokes about their faults and foibles, and, in general, self-critically reflect on their own experiences throughout *Life Is Sweet*.[5] As he did in *High Hopes*, Leigh repeatedly opens meditative trapdoors that let a viewer glimpse extraordinarily complex and mobile states of consciousness that complicate the main characters.

Consider how Andy is presented. In the opening scenes he is a more or less stock sitcom father: a bumbling, comically incompetent head of a household, henpecked by his wife and daughters, who never gets around to household repairs and is conned into buying a dilapidated hot-snacks caravan by his flaky friend, Patsy. But just when we are about to conclude that there is not much to him, Leigh unexpectedly deepens the view. Andy is cleaning up the caravan and is being roundly criticized by Wendy for getting snookered when Leigh inserts the following exchange:

> WENDY: I mean, look at all of this – it's rubbish. . . . Well, I'm sorry, Andy, I can't get any enthusiasm for it.
> ANDY: I know you can't – it's obvious. To be honest with you, I'd appreciate it if you could. I could do with a bit of moral support.

Andy's pained tone of voice and expression of discouragement hit us like a ton of bricks. He is no longer a figure in a Ned Seagoon movie – no longer just an outside. He has feelings, and they have been hurt. As if to make sure we don't miss the change, a minute or two later Natalie comes out of the house and Andy has a brief exchange with her in which he again alludes to his hurt feelings (though, given the fact that he is talking to his daughter, he does it more obliquely, his tone less wounded and more jocular):

> WENDY: Yeah, 'e's got to save up now . . . pay for this 'eap o' whatsit.
> NATALIE: Well, so long as 'e's 'appy.
> ANDY: That's right, Nat! Thanks a lot – much appreciated!

Andy's depths of feeling and self-reflectiveness change everything in our understanding of him. This is an Andy who can look at himself, reflect on his own actions, and have doubts about what he has done, an Andy who is vulnerable, uncertain, and in quest of reassurance.

It is typical of the fluxionality of Leigh's work that these adjustments in our view of Andy are themselves almost immediately readjusted by subsequent bits of dialogue. Leigh cuts against the potential sentimentality of Andy's implicit pleas for sympathy by including lighter, semicomical exchanges immediately following both of the moments I have quoted. After the first passage:

> WENDY: 'Ave you ever seen those 'ot-dog fellas? They're all like that. (*She squashes her nose with her finger.*)
> ANDY: (*Laughing*) Don't know what you're talking about. . . .

And after the second:

> WENDY: Tell you what, Andy, I 'ope it don't rain tonight. You'll need your snorkel 'ere in the morning.
> ANDY: (*To Nicola*) I think she likes it – don't you?
> NATALIE: Yeah – she's over the moon.

The point is that we should not lock ourselves into a "hurt" interpretation of Andy any more than we should lock ourselves into a "clownish" interpretation of him. We have to keep moving emotionally – and personally. The meditative moment (compelling and important as it is) is not allowed to stop the tonal motion.

Andy's expressions of doubt and insecurity mark a turning point in Leigh's presentation. While the scenes prior to this held us pretty much on the surface of the lives of the characters and treated each of them fairly comically, from this point on (approximately a half-hour into the film) Leigh gives each of their insides. He takes the viewer on a journey into the interior of each of them by providing glimpses of their thoughts and feelings. From this scene on, *Life Is Sweet* will alternate between "inner" and "outer" views of the five main characters.

Immediately following the caravan scene, Leigh presents three parallel "going to bed" scenes – featuring Wendy and Andy in one bedroom, Nicola in a second, and Natalie in a third. The first (which involves Wendy and Andy chatting about their respective days prior to falling asleep and performs a narrative function quite similar to Cyril and Shirley's bedtime scenes in *High Hopes*) allows the two parents to give vent to thoughts and feelings too private and painful to be verbalized in the scenes with their children.

Andy is further deepened. He expresses his frustration with his job, encouraging us to realize that his purchase of the caravan was not a frivolous indulgence, but is connected with a dream of working for himself one day. ("Do you want me to carry on doing my brain at that bloody place for the rest of my life? . . . It's a risk – I admit that, but it's a risk worth taking, isn't it?") He has dreams and aspirations. He is endowed with an inner life.

The same thing is done with Wendy. A comical expression of her exasperation with Nicola surprisingly segues into a meditation on the discouragements of motherhood:

> Oh, I tell you what, Andy . . . she gets me in a right state, that girl. I 'eard myself shouting at 'er this mornin' and I thought "This isn't me. . . ." I don't recognize myself. You know? It's 'orrible. . . . Oh, I used to think . . . oh, it'd be so nice to go to discos together and . . . bring their boyfriends 'ome. Oh, well – there you go!

Our view of Wendy is completely altered. Everything we have seen up to this point needs to be reinterpreted. We had no idea she was capable of getting outside herself in this way – that she was either this introspective or this self-critical.

What makes these moments so wonderful is not anything in particular that is said, but the power of mind they reveal. Like Cyril and Shirley earlier, Wendy and Andy demonstrate an exhilarating ability to turn on themselves, to swerve away from their own earlier tones, to reflect on the meaning of their lives and relationships. Lying in bed, they can thrill us with their capacities of imaginative movement.

Wendy and Andy's scene is followed by intercut shots of the daughters in their respective bedrooms in which we are given similar, transformative, "deep" views of their thoughts and feelings. In one sequence, Leigh shows Nicola bingeing and purging on junk food and, as with Wendy and Andy, a character who was previously all outside suddenly is given an inside.

The timing of Leigh's presentation is one of the most remarkable aspects of his work, and the timing of the disclosure of Nicola's bulimia is critical. The scene comes precisely at the point where we are about to write Nicola off. Five minutes more and she would have become a cartoon stick-figure of teenage whining and discontent. We suddenly realize that she has a serious medical problem and is in emotional turmoil.[6]

The third bedroom scene, which shows Natalie in bed reading a magazine and subsequently overhearing the sound of Nicola's vomiting through the wall, is slightly less revisionary, but provides a brief glimpse into her soul. The expression on Natalie's face (which is italicized by the Ozu-like pause Leigh inserts at the end of the sequence) establishes that, notwithstanding her banter about feeding Nicola to a crocodile and her verbal sparring with her, she cares deeply about Nicola and is concerned about her problem.

These scenes provide "deep" views of characters' thoughts and feelings, but, as is always the case in Leigh's work, what is in the depths only makes itself felt insofar as it is expressed on the surface. The viewer does not encounter Wendy's or Andy's thoughts and feelings as "pure" states of consciousness, but as "impure" expressions. Leigh does not give us key-lighted closeups and mood music, but particular, eccentric voices, faces, and gestures. Thought cannot be separated from a thinker – a specific individual with a unique background in a particular situation. Character refracts everything we are. Wendy is still her feisty, inarticulate, stammering, critical, laughy self even when she is meditating on motherhood. Her reverie expresses her state of exasperation with Nicola as much as her disappointment with herself. Consciousness is mediated. Feelings cannot be separated from the compromised, polluted, confused utterances that express them. Our inner life is refracted by the mixed motives and mixed-up mentality of our personalities.

That in fact is what makes even Leigh's most attractive figures, Wendy and Andy in this case, difficult for many American viewers to like (and impossible for them to identify with). Leigh's characters are too particularized to plug into. Even their genuinely admirable ideals and sentiments are expressed in fundamentally flawed and compromised ways.

Hollywood characters are more generic and their expressions of thought and feeling purer and more absolute than this. Hollywood forms of expression are almost entirely liberated from the muddlements and cross-purposes Wendy and Andy display. When thoughts, feelings, and visions are rendered in terms of abstract verbal statements, key-lighted close-ups, or mood-music orchestrations, they are not only freed from social and linguistic constraints but from the psychological and emotional entailments of Leigh's work.

That is in fact a large part of the appeal of Hollywood film. When a girl watching *Titanic* identifies with the Kate Winslet character (and dreams about boys who are versions of Leonardo DiCaprio), the appeal of the film is that the emotions on screen (which she experiences and imagines to exist in others) are *not* flawed and contingent in the Leigh way. The love, the self-sacrifice, the longing, the heroism, the suffering of the stars in *Titanic* is absolute, pure, and uncompromised. It is extremely flattering to think of ourselves in this way. Who wouldn't want to imagine themselves to be this purely noble, glamorous, or heroic? The only problem, of course, is that it's a lie. Life isn't like this. What Wendy and Andy remind us of is that actual emotional expressions are never pure in this way. They are mediated, muddled, mixed up with other contradictory or compromising emotions. Real love is never as self-sacrificing and unconditional as Hollywood love. It is mixed with unloving feelings like selfishness and pettiness and impatience and the desire for appreciation. Real suffering and loss are not characterized by self-sacrifice and acceptance, but are laced with anger and resentment and self-justification. Real virtue is often critical and intolerant of others' deficiencies. And we lapse from virtue as often as we adhere to it. We lie to ourselves constantly with self-satisfied stories about how much harder *we* work, how much more *we* deserve success than others do. One might say that the very appeal of Hollywood film is proof of our emotional imperfections. We only fall for Hollywood movies because we are addicted to glamorizing our emotional states, to deluding ourselves, to telling ourselves comforting stories about ourselves. Their repressions are proof of our insecurity and need for flattery. Their purity is evidence of our impurity.

Leigh returns us to the real world, where intentions, feelings, and ideas are compromised, mixed, and impure. Wendy's reverie about her dreams of ideal motherhood is crossed with tones of resentment about how difficult Nicola is to deal with. Andy's sincere, noble dream of working for himself is a little fatuous and immature. Needless to say, that doesn't mean that Leigh is cynical or disillusioned. The genius of his work is how it captures the flawed poetry of everyday life. The beauty of the scenes between Wendy and Andy, here and throughout *Life Is Sweet* (like the beauty of the scenes between Cyril and Shirley in *High Hopes*) – both as dramatic creations and as human interactions – lies in how Leigh finds a way for love to be expressed in clumsy, compromised, mediated performances, without it being any the less love. (Cassavetes was a master of similar tonal effects, and was similarly misunderstood.)

In the bedroom scene in particular, Leigh choreographs a delicate comic operetta in which the mistakes, misunderstandings, mistimings, miscues, and disharmonies are the *beauty* of Wendy and Andy's duet. (It comes as no surprise that Leigh is an admirer of the work of Gilbert and Sullivan.) It was once said of Balanchine that only a supreme master of gracefulness could choreograph awkwardness so convincingly, and the point applies here. Leigh's scripting and Alison Steadman's and Jim Broadbent's acting brilliantly capture the clumsy, touching beauty of Wendy and Andy's interaction.[7] Though there is not space to go through the entire scene beat by beat, a glance at its first two or three minutes will suffice to summarize the effect. If we look at it from an ideal point of view, it can be viewed as a chorus of disharmonies: comical misunderstandings and tonal mismatches, attempts to twist each other's words and wriggle out of accusations. But if we look at it from a more realistic view and accept the necessary imperfection of all human expression and relationship in Leigh's work, it can be viewed as a beautiful, loving duet, sung by two fallible people wonderfully muddling through.

The scene starts off with Wendy scolding Andy about being conned by Patsy. ("Oh, Andy! . . .")[8] In the pattern the rest of the scene continues, Andy doesn't ignore or reject her comments, or merely dig in his heels defending his decision, but genuinely *responds* to what she has said. Wendy has couched her objection in terms of feelings of being personally betrayed and let down by him, so he responds by appealing to her on a personal note in return. Seeing her discouraged, he shares his own, even greater, state of discouragement about his current job (". . . d'you want me to carry on doing my brain in at that bloody place for the rest of my life?"). His tone of voice softens Wendy enough so that her irritation gives way to a far more conciliatory tone. ("No, of course I don't.") Now that her tone has become less hurt, and in general less emotional and more logical, Andy responds by changing his tone. He takes a slightly less personal tack and becomes brisk, practical, businesslike, and optimistically upbeat. ("Right! . . . if it works out, I'll jack in the day job.") However, Wendy's next remark shows that she can't quite follow him in this tonal direction; in assuming such rapid assent to his plans, Andy has gone much further than she is willing to go. Her response picks up his perspective but yanks him up short with a reality check and a plaintive tone. ("Andy, you can't jack in your day job without you got something definite to go to. . . .") If he is going to be brisk and businesslike, she is going to offer a cold splash of financial reality. Andy responds to her tough-minded practicality, not by arguing with it, but by taking an even more down-to-earth view of things. He switches from talking about frustrations and dreams to considerations of cold cash. ("On a Bank Holiday weekend, I could make . . . what? Two, two and a half thousand quid?") But though the subject is money, Andy's tone is not entirely practical. More than his mere financial logic, his boyish enthusiasm is what reaches Wendy, and we hear a more affectionate, protective tone in her next response – in fact, the most sympathetic tone she has used so far. ("Oh, Andy! You're just a big softy, you are!") Andy has brought out her maternal impulse; rather than being critical, she feels sorry for him, and, beyond that, the teams have changed. It is not Wendy against Andy any more, but Wendy and Andy together against Patsy. In response to Wendy's tonal softening,

Andy's tone also softens. Confessing his own doubts and uncertainties for the first time, as if in concession to her concession, Andy endorses her feeling of being on the same side with him by inviting her to share his dream and admitting his own uncertainties. ("Well, who's to say? All right, it's a risk – I admit that, but it's a risk worth taking, innit?")

The comical suppleness of the scripting and acting dramatizes a genuine "conversation" in the root sense of the word: a series of subtle "turnings" as Wendy and Andy keep moving from thought to thought, tone to tone, mood to mood, simultaneously expressing their own points of view and responding to the other's, in their comically stumbling, mismatched, mistimed way. If there were any doubt about the seriousness of their love, it would be removed by this seriocomic demonstration of their willingness to express, work through, and caringly deal with their differences in this way (rather than avoiding them or pretending they don't exist). This degree of subtle responsiveness to someone else's needs and feelings is the very definition of love.

One of the most remarkable aspects of Wendy and Andy's interaction is the way each is felt to be operating out of his or her personal center of interests and reference points, and to some extent to be pursuing his or her individual train of thought. Underneath the surface fluctuations, virtually everything Andy says is, in one way or other, an expression of his boyish impetuousness, ambition, and somewhat dreamy impracticality; whereas everything Wendy says is a reflection of her fundamental conservatism, caution, practicality, and concern for Andy's long-term welfare. Everything is anchored in a particular point of view.

The remainder of Wendy and Andy's chat illustrates the independence of their conversational trajectories even more clearly than what preceded it. At the point where I left off, Wendy responds to Andy's more humble tone ("All right, it's a risk – I admit that") by making a further conciliatory overture by pointing out that, even if the van doesn't pan out as a commercial investment it can be used as a camper, and alluding to how they could then have "a little bunk-up" in it. It is a major concession to him, and also an illustration of the practicality of Wendy's perspective. Andy picks up on her loving tone but, in line with his male range of references, turns her mention of going to bed in an explicitly sexual direction (as he will with most of her subsequent comments).

Leigh captures Wendy's independent train of thought by having her not pursue the sexual side of the "bunk-up" reference but instead be reminded of Aubrey bouncing around on his bed earlier that day. She does a comical takeoff on his voice and mannerisms (". . . Orthopedic . . . you know? . . ."). Andy picks up on Wendy's reference to Aubrey

Wendy and Andy – a model of sensitivity and responsiveness all of Leigh's work has been building toward

but continues his own sexual train of thought, turning the mention of Aubrey in a direction Wendy could not have intended, by warning her about Aubrey coming up behind her "with a cucumber." Wendy, un-fazed by Andy's sexual allusion, independently pursues her own personal train of associations, expressing how sorry she feels for Aubrey. Andy briefly adopts her point of view and agrees, but in line with his own interests turns the reference in a sexual direction one more time. And just as sex made Shirley think of motherhood in *High Hopes*, so Andy's sexual overtures and Wendy's answering sexual thoughts are followed by her motherly concern about whether Nicola has gone to bed yet, which is itself followed by the reverie I already quoted in which Wendy reflects on being a mother.

My point is that Leigh's scripting brilliantly communicates not only Wendy and Andy's subtle responsiveness to each other but the tempera-mental and personal differences that separate them. Wendy's remarks generally refer to family and friends, and are practical, nurturing, and caring in nature, while Andy's are more focused on his job and are more erotic, joking, playful (and less realistic). Each character's comments seem to emanate from a distinguishable emotional substructure that underpins his or her individual remarks, structures of personality that separate them no matter how carefully they listen to or respond to each other.

One sees the same quality throughout Leigh's work. Characters' expressions – however apparently meandering or flowing, however responsive to the particular dramatic moment or the conversational vagaries of a specific interaction – seem to emanate from a preexisting set of emotional structures and forms of understanding. There are no transcendental thoughts and no absolute emotions. There are no truths free from personality. Everything is a reflection of an individual point of view. Everything Wendy and Andy say says them. The Wendyness and Andyness of these truths can never be factored out. There is no unmediated, uncontaminated, uncompromised truth. The gel of character colors everything we say, do, and are.

While mainstream film, television, journalism, and politics aspire toward a condition of expressive homogenization in which everyone can rally round a common, shared truth, in which individual differences are erased or neutralized, Leigh celebrates uniqueness. He creates partnerships in which the partners don't blend or merge, but each brings something different to the table. The result is the most stimulating sort of relationship: one in which the individuals are both dependent and independent.

Another aspect of Leigh's scripting is the impression it conveys that characters can hold more than one view of something at the same time. When Wendy talks with Andy in bed about the caravan, she is both critical *and* supportive. When she interacts with Nicola in other scenes, she can seem both harsh *and* caring. When Wendy and Andy visit Aubrey's restaurant or apartment in several scenes, they can seem amused by his plans, critical of them, skeptical about them, genuinely supportive, and impressed by his efforts – *all at the same time*. That is the ultimate importance of the bedroom scene also: to show us that Wendy and Andy can feel many different (and even apparently contradictory) emotions at once, that they can hold more than one thought in mind at a time.

The ultimate measure of a Leigh character, or viewer, is his or her ability to remain as open to the multivalence of experience as Leigh is in his presentation of it. In this respect, Wendy and Andy are surrogates for Leigh and his ideal viewers. They are fluid, flexible responders who refuse to limit themselves to any one feeling, tone, mood, or interpretation of their experiences. Their multiple-mindedness about their own lives parallels Leigh's refusal throughout his oeuvre to filter his presentation of his characters and their interactions, to force them to make a single point or conform to a single tone. There is a certain degree of tonal and emotional sprawl or clutter in Leigh's scenes precisely because, in his view, experience is, in fact, a little loose and messy. The point is *not* to tighten and clean things up, *not* to sort out, or clarifyingly resolve the multiplicity of life. To narrow your relation to experience to any one thought, feeling, or tone is to tell a lie about it. Viewers of *Life Is Sweet*, like characters in it, are implicitly judged in terms of their capacity to remain as open in their understanding of experience as Leigh is in his presentation of it. We must stay as receptive to the multivalence of experience as Leigh's scenes do. We must stay as loose as Wendy and Andy are, and at all costs avoid the moralistic judgments that a figure like Nicola takes refuge in.

The discrepancy between Leigh's cinematic style and his characters' personal styles was the subject of most of the earlier films, but with the works of the late seventies, many of Leigh's main characters (from Dawn, Jean, Mick, and Len in *Ecstasy,* Eugene and Collette in *Four Days in July,* Mark and Colin in *Meantime,* Cyril and Shirley in *High Hopes,* to Wendy and Andy) are endowed with a degree of multiple-mindedness that resembles his in creating them and structuring their scenes. Their play of mind matches his.[9]

Wendy and Andy demonstrate capacities of imaginative movement even in scenes which might seem to be merely transitional or expository like the one in which Wendy debates what to wear to Aubrey's restaurant on its opening night. As Wendy models blouses for Andy and Natalie, the clothing triggers a series of random memories associated with it.

The scene is remarkable for at least two reasons: In the first place, it radically "opens up" *Life Is Sweet,* suggesting the existence of a world beyond the boundaries of the frame, and worlds of experience and awareness in the characters' minds that only fleetingly find their way into the narrative.[10] The fact that these moments don't bear fruit in terms of the plot is not a flaw in Leigh's narrative presentation (as if he had background material he couldn't quite fit into his film), but the source of their power. Wendy, Andy, and Natalie demonstrate their ability to move independently not only of each other but of the plot of the movie they are in. They have thoughts, feelings, and experiences that are not defined by the narrative. They can lever themselves outside of their present circumstances and put the film's events on hold to make a joke, reflect on their own actions, or refer to something beyond the narrative moment.[11]

The second point these scenes illustrate is what in *High Hopes* I called the "looseness" of Leigh's most interesting characters' interactions and relation to their own experience. Leigh knows that it is only in living life somewhat "loosely" that there can be real interaction. Real communication, a real meeting of minds can happen only in the open place beyond judgments of right or wrong, where we hold our own experiences and those of others lightly and nonjudgmentally, where we allow for multiple interpretations of the same event. When they are functioning at their best (as they beautifully are in the series of bedroom anecdotes and recollections), Wendy, Andy, and Natalie leave moral judgments behind and play with their experiences – joking, teasing, and enjoying the oddness and difference of their experiences in the same way Leigh did in creating these differences in their film. Their jocular bemusement at the weirdness of people and events, like Leigh's own when he makes these movies, tolerates a lot of different ways of being, makes room for a wide range of possible feelings and beliefs.

That is the beauty of the many apparently "pointless" scenes in which Wendy, Andy, and Natalie rally, chafe, and tease each other, tell tall tales, or engage in rambling, half-facetious conversations: the bedroom scene I already looked at; the scene in which Wendy jokes about getting a Rotweiler to eat Nicola (and Natalie trumps her mother's idea by proposing a pet crocodile); the scenes in which Wendy teases Andy about his uncompleted handyman projects; or Andy teases Wendy about Aubrey's sexual designs on her; the scenes in which Wendy and Andy tease Aubrey.

These moments wonderfully capture the essentially relaxed and playful relationship Wendy, Andy, and Natalie have not only with each other, but with their own experiences. They can turn even fears, anxieties, and sadness (whether minor like slipping on a spoon or major like having a daughter like Nicola) into a potential source of play and entertainment. They can briefly step imaginatively outside of their lives in order to keep themselves and their experiences in perspective. (What else is storytelling, joking, teasing?)

It is just this capacity of imaginative movement, the ability to entertain alternative understandings of their experiences that Aubrey and Nicola lack. While Wendy, Andy, and Natalie hold experience lightly, Aubrey and Nicola take things hard. They force tendentious meanings onto every event and interaction. Contrast Andy's tones when he reflects on buying the caravan with Aubrey's when he describes the restaurant to Wendy and Andy: Where Andy is loose, easy, and relaxed, Aubrey is tight – overly intense, locked into his own perspective, and narrow in his focus. Contrast Wendy's tones with Nicola's in any of the living-room interactions: Where Wendy is invariably playful, amused, and facetious, Nicola is relentlessly judgmental, overly earnest, and witheringly moralistic. In a word, like Peter or Keith, Aubrey and Nicola take themselves seriously (too seriously, which is of course the source of their comedy). To hold life so tightly is to deny it any play, to squeeze all of the potential entertainment out of it. All of which is to suggest why it is a trivial reading of the film to treat either character as merely providing comic relief. Nicola and Aubrey exist to contrast with the vision of selfhood represented by Wendy and Andy.

My students occasionally report that Aubrey's problem is that he is attempting to do something beyond his abilities, but Leigh goes to some lengths to show that he knows more than enough about cooking and running a restaurant to do what he sets out to. Leigh includes several scenes that show he is extremely knowledgeable about food and its preparation – arguably, more knowledgeable than Andy. The issue is not what Aubrey knows or doesn't know, but *how* he knows it. As with so many of Leigh's earlier figures, Aubrey's problem is who he *is*.[12]

Aubrey is a comic anthology of the ontological problems Leigh's previous work explores. Like a male version of Valerie, he thinks selfhood is something you simply can decide on and adopt – a ready-to-wear stylistic zipper-suit. Like a blend of Beverly, Laurence, and Alan, those earlier *faux* connoisseurs of the high life, he thinks if he employs "jaunty" mannerisms (tossing his pineapple from hand to hand and beating out tunes on his legs), throws around American slang ("no sweat," "megaconfident," "great team"), drives a sports car (red, of course), and wears sunglasses, a San Francisco Giants jacket, and a baseball cap at a sufficiently rakish angle, he *is* cool, sexy, and hip. Aubrey treats his identity the way the young people in *Who's Who* treated theirs: as if you could forge a self by gathering together the right collection of mannerisms. (His identity is cobbled together the way he cobbles his restaurant together, with bits and pieces of this and that.) Any other way to be yourself is a mystery to him. His sense of selfhood is shallower than skin-deep: It doesn't even extend to his ample epidermis. It stops at his silk jacket. In other words, it is entirely mental.

The ontological shallowness of Aubrey's conception of identity corresponds with the semantic shallowness of his sense of what a restaurant is. Ambiance, atmosphere, and appearance are everything. The name (French, needless to say) on the menu is more important than the taste on the plate. Of course, the plates themselves are black, because "It's all a matter of what picture you wanna' paint." (When it comes to confusing appearance with reality, Aubrey's parents might have been set decorator and costume mistress Beverly and art-collector Laurence.) In a classic Leigh confusion, he reverses the relation of depths and surfaces, confusing social appearances with emotional realities.

The decorations in the *Regret Rien* present a parable about the difference between superficial and deep meaning – in life and art. Like Salvador Dali or Alfred Hitchcock (or the critic or viewer who gratefully decodes the meanings they offer), Aubrey thinks that you can create significance simply by putting something in a frame and spotlighting it. Hitchcock tacks a few stuffed birds on the walls of Norman Bates' office and "morbidity" appears; Aubrey hangs up a bird cage to indicate "the Sparrow," a cat to indicate "the street," a gas mask to indicate "the war," an accordion to indicate "the music of Paree," and he thinks he's created those meanings. It's the semantic equivalent of a heat-and-eat meal: instant, effortless, and ultimately insubstantial. It takes no time or commitment on the part of the artist to create, and no energy or involvement on the part of the viewer to consume (which is why it results in no growth or nourishment).

Aubrey has not learned the lesson the film he is in teaches – that meaning (the meaning of a life, a family, a place, a relationship with another human being) can only be created with time, effort, care, sensitivity, and beat-by-beat responsiveness. Meaning must be *made*, it cannot simply be *indicated* (which is why the meanings in Leigh's work are so different from and take so much more effort to comprehend than the metaphors and symbols in Hitchcock, Lynch, the Coens, Stone, and similar artists). As all of Leigh's work is devoted to demonstrating, meaning cannot merely be willed; it must be worked into being. It cannot simply be declared; it must be earned. It isn't made abstractly and quickly, but slowly and arduously.

The entire stylistic enterprise of Leigh's work contrasts with that of American film in this regard. While the transcendental or visionary truth of Sternberg, Welles, or Hitchcock is instantaneous (like Aubrey's cat and accordion set decorations, you simply "see" the meaning and it exists), the practical, social truths of Leigh's works are a product of complex, careful, loving human interaction. They take time to make in the first place, and they keep changing from second to second. They take work for a viewer to apprehend and effort to keep up with. Knowledge is slow and arduous. It's not something you suddenly "get" (as in visionary film), but something that is gradually and progressively achieved. Leigh's meanings are not fixed and static, like Hitchcock's and Aubrey's birds, but in motion, in flight, continuously being lost and recaptured every second.

Like Aubrey's notion of set decoration, the insistently metaphoric methods of most American films elevate the truth of *ideas* over the truth of *experiences*. Meanings are rendered in a kind of intellectual shorthand in which "this means that" in a strictly intellectual way. A sled means a lost childhood; a cavernous living room means loneliness; ominous music and shadowy lighting mean spiritual emptiness and nostalgia. Leigh is committed to a more spatially involved and temporally extended sense of truth. Truth is not the product of a viewer's or a character's mental relation to a series of sounds and images (the heart of the metaphoric-symbolic method), but is the result of the viewer's and character's complex, gradual process of interacting with a series of people and events extended across space and time. Leigh's characters do not interact in terms of glances, and his viewers cannot take in his meanings at a glance. His meanings must be lived through and lived into.

Aubrey's off-the-peg sense of selfhood and just-add-water understanding of meaning seem all the shallower insofar as they are juxtaposed to the complexities of identity and involvement that Wendy and Andy display.[13] The difference is comically summed up in the contrast between the semantic shallowness of Aubrey's "Marry me, Wendy. . . . I love you" and Wendy and Andy's illustration of what real love and marriage involve. What Wendy and Andy are (both as characters in a movie and people living a life) is achieved gradually and tentatively, in the time and space of interactions as complex as the ones I have described. Their individual identities and relationship with each other are not brought into existence instantly, effortlessly, and unilaterally by means of a prop (a pineapple), a costume (a sports jacket), or a pickup line ("You know, you look fantastic"), but are lived through and worked into existence one beat at a time.

Yet as different as they may be from Aubrey, Wendy and Andy show themselves capable of doing the same thing Leigh's style does: imaginatively entering into and sympathizing with his and other alien points of view (even ones as odd as the lady with the stuffed dog and the ration stamps). Aubrey, in contrast, is trapped in his own view of everything. As the comical misunderstandings in his interactions with Wendy illustrate, he doesn't really listen to, respond to, or understand any point of view beyond his own (a point Leigh makes wittily by having Timothy Spall insert a "delay" before most of his responses, as if he were perpetually out of synch with the world).

There is no play in Aubrey's understanding of himself or others.

While Wendy, Andy, and Natalie's relationship to each other and everyone they meet freely flows and changes from moment to moment, holding many emotions and thoughts in suspension, Aubrey is locked into static forms of selfhood and formulaic ways of interacting. Like Peter, Sylvia's boss, Keith, or Beverly, Aubrey reduces interactions with others to mechanical "routines." Leigh comically summarizes the shallowness of Aubrey's conception of conversation in terms of his singles' bar approach to interaction, in which he apparently employs the same pickup lines with every woman he meets: "You know you've got beautiful hands, legs, hair, blah, blah, blah." As is always the case in Leigh's work, since Aubrey is playing a role that is inherently false, and playing it badly and mechanically, there is no depth to his performance. In his world, where surfaces are everything, everything is on the surface.

Leigh makes it clear that, notwithstanding the fact that he is a source of amusement to others, Aubrey himself has absolutely no sense of humor. To be able to laugh at himself or respond to Wendy and Andy's good-natured joshing, he would have to be capable of seeing the limitations of his own ways of understanding. He would have to step outside of himself and see things from another point of view, at least for a moment.

As was the case with Keith, Beverly, Christine, Barbara, and other similar figures, Aubrey's performance is unsustainable. He falls apart when his restaurant fails. As befits his generally comic function, Aubrey's "breakdown" is shallow – more comic than pathetic – but it is telling that the film won't let the viewer off with mere laughter. As he so often does, Leigh tonally walks the line between seriousness and comedy. As Aubrey writhes on the floor in a drunken stupor, he is ridiculous, but (like the figures I have compared him with) is held just this side of caricature. We feel his pain (however self-inflicted) and consequently feel at least a little sorry for him. He reaches us emotionally. As absurd as he is, we can't quite laugh him off.

Almost everything I have said about Aubrey applies to Nicola, who functions as his doppelgänger. As much as Aubrey, Nicola is trapped in a single point of view and way of taking everything, contravening everything the style of *Life Is Sweet* itself teaches us about how to understand life. She too has an off-the-shelf identity, the only apparent difference being that whereas Aubrey gets his notion of who he is from MTV, she takes hers from *The Female Eunuch*. Her identity is as much the product of a recipe as his – in her case, a mix of "save the world" Marxist poses and ecological slogans, spiced with unspecified feminist resentments.

In his typically witty yet understated way, Leigh establishes a contrast between Nicola and her sister that brings out the fundamental fraudulence of Nicola's identity: While Nicola's definition of originality involves playing a stereotypical, received role, Natalie genuinely creates a unique identity at odds with gender stereotypes and finds a way to express her sense of herself in the world. In other words, the nonrevolutionary is the genuine "revolutionary," while the avowed "revolutionary" is the real slave to fashion.

The general problem with both Aubrey's and Nicola's identities is that they are based on *ideas* of who they want to be (or think they are) rather than expressing who they are through *events* and *interactions* (as Wendy, Andy, and Natalie, however imperfectly, do). As Keith and Beverly demonstrated most vividly, Leigh is deeply opposed to *mental* relations to experience.[14] The physicalization of the presentation of his intellectual characters (Aubrey and Nicola in this instance) is a way of critiquing their conceptual relations to experience by emphasizing corporeal realities that they would gloss over. In other words, Nicola's and Aubrey's bodies tell truths about them that their words and ideas attempt to ignore.

Although Nicola and Aubrey function as narrative "twins," Leigh establishes Nicola's greater importance, not only by making her a member of the family (Wendy can't leave her behind, or Leigh's narrative forget her, as they do Aubrey), but by giving her an inside. The bulimia moment in the bedroom and the two scenes with her boyfriend force the viewer to enter into Nicola's point of view and take her much more seriously than we would otherwise.

As befits her greater narrative importance, Nicola's unraveling is longer and more serious than Aubrey's. She is broken down in a series of steps, as first her unnamed boyfriend (played by David Thewlis, who will star in *Naked*) and then her mother disrupt her sense of who she is. Leigh arranges the scenes back-to-back so as to create, in effect, one long assault on Nicola's sense of herself in a gradually rising dramatic crescendo. The fallacies and contradictions of her belief system are revealed as it is dismantled step by step.[15]

Although there are superficial resemblances to Mark's encounter with Barbara, the conversation between Nicola and Wendy is closer to resembling Shirley's final bedroom conversation with Cyril, insofar as it figures the possibility of one character intervening to break another's patterns in a nonadversarial way. Wendy's interaction with Nicola is stunningly kind, sensitive, and responsive. There is no space to go through it detail by detail, but suffice it to say that the brilliance of the scene (both as a dramatic creation and as the representation of a human interaction) is Wendy's (which is to say, Alison Steadman's) extraordinary capacity of tonal, emotional, and intellectual responsiveness. Wendy listens to Nicola and actually responds to each of her fears, anxieties, and misunderstandings, attempting to lever her out of each of her stuck places, one after the other (though I would note that the response is tonal and emotional more than semantic and intellectual). Just as Shirley did with Cyril, Nicola's frozenness is thawed simply by having someone actually respond to (rather than merely reject or jeer at) her rigidities and misunderstandings. One might say that Wendy's emotional openness and imaginative sympathy, her ability to enter into Nicola's point of view, is itself a reply to Nicola's narrowness and fixity. In other words, what matters is not anything that Wendy says in particular, but the continuous patience, care, and sensitivity with which she says it. Wendy's ability to flow imaginatively and emotionally is what makes Nicola's imaginative and emotional melting possible.[16]

Whereas Aubrey and Nicola imagine that human relationships can be quick and easy, this scene is testimony to Leigh's belief in the time and effort any important human interaction requires. While Aubrey and Nicola believe that you can become something by striking a pose and embracing an abstract system of beliefs, this scene demonstrates the care and work and constant attention it really takes to be (or to mean) anything.

Wendy's interaction with Nicola is difficult, slow, and challenging. Leigh's acknowledgment of the pain Wendy and Nicola have to undergo to forge a relationship is what keeps the scene from sentimentality. This mother–daughter meeting of the minds never softens into soulful glances or mood-music orchestrations. Nicola clings to her old ways of knowing and feeling as if her very life and definition of herself depended on them (as, in her view, they do). She fights the understandings that Wendy offers, tooth and nail – resisting, arguing, denying every point, viciously retaliating and counterattacking every step of the way. For Wendy to face such opposition and not either give up or harden into her own state of countervailing resistance and argumentation is proof of how deeply she cares about Nicola. The only thing that can meet this degree of resistance and keep going is love.

It would be only a slight overstatement to say that all of Leigh's work has been building toward the ideals of performance that Shirley and

Wendy represent. The possibilities of imaginative flexibility, relaxed intimacy, and emotional responsiveness that are only intermittently realized by Sylvia and Norman in *Bleak Moments*, Ann and Naseem in *Hard Labour*, Dick and Mandy in *Grown-Ups*, Colin and Mark in *Meantime*, Carol, Dawn, Len, and Mick in *Ecstasy*, and Eugene and Collette in *Four Days in July* come to fruition in the interactions between Shirley and Cyril in *High Hopes* and Wendy and Andy in this film.[17]

In fact, the last couple could almost be the preceding one twenty years later in their relationship – Cyril's teasing Shirley about wanting to snoop around Valerie's house giving way to Wendy's razzing Andy about his unfinished home-improvement projects, and Shirley's jokes about Wayne looking like E. T. being succeeded by Andy's jokes about Aubrey and Patsy. Cyril's "everyone in his place" takeoff of Rupert transmutes into Wendy's "Orthopedic, five 'undred quid, you know" parody of Aubrey; and the responsive suppleness of Cyril and Shirley's "died with his boots on" bedroom improvisation is matched by Wendy and Andy's bedtime interaction.

From Sylvia's interactions with Norman and Mark's with Colin, to those involving Wendy, Andy, and Natalie, one of Leigh's favorite ways of imagining the relationships of his most interesting characters with each other is to think of them as actors improvising a scene together. Both *High Hopes* and *Life Is Sweet* employ an implicit dramatic metaphor: the notion that a man and a woman in a loving relationship can function like actors playing off each other's leads, supporting each other's performances, giving each other energy, stimulating each other with new associations, challenging each other to move in new directions.

That is to say, all of Leigh's work explores the possibility of actually *living* as freely, flexibly, and playfully as actors improvising together. The early films are anthologies of failures, documenting the chasm that loomed between Leigh's imagination of life's possibilities and his characters' actual expressive performances. It is only in the works from *Ecstasy* and *Grown-Ups* on that he dares to imagine characters who are as imaginatively multiple-minded and fluid in their interactions, as sensitive and responsive as he himself is as a dramatist and filmmaker. As a family, Wendy, Andy, and Natalie *live* the imaginative possibilities that Leigh's cinematic style embodies.

Wendy, Leigh's greatest imaginative creation, fully deserves to be called an artist of life, an artist of the ordinary. As Shirley and Cyril were in *High Hopes*, she is clearly an alter ego for her creator, the head of a kind of dramatic repertory company, who not only choreographs a dance class that resembles a drama workshop in the first scene of the film, but choreographs family life in every scene.

Wendy shows us what, in Leigh's view, it is to be an artist. It is not (in the "actors are cattle" mode) to get individuals to figure *her* vision of them, to turn them into clones of herself, but (in the Cassavetes, Renoir, or Ozu vein) to encourage each of them to express him or herself distinctively and personally. Like Leigh as a director, Wendy allows each figure she interacts with to make his or her own unique expressive contribution. Like Leigh in a workshop situation, she is not only willing to work with what she has, but celebrates the differences. Like Leigh, she "directs" not by dictating, but by doing something as simple as listening to what they want to give.

Wendy's supreme achievement as head of her family, like Leigh's as the head of his dramatic repertory company, is her powers of circulation, her ability to enter into and honor different points of view. She connects with each of the figures around her, not by staying where *she* is, but by going out of herself to meet them where *they* are. Her art is the art of putting herself imaginatively in the shoes of others – even others as odd and different from herself as Aubrey, Donald and Tracy, Nicola, or an old woman with a stuffed dog.

Wendy's achievement is the same as that of Leigh as an artist. Beyond everything else, his is an art of empathy. He does not stand outside and judge (like Altman), but goes inside to understand (like Renoir, Ozu, and Cassavetes). His art involves seeing and presenting each character, not from *his* vantage point, but from the character's own unique, self-justifying (and frequently self-deluding) perspective. Leigh's entire oeuvre stands as evidence that this, for him, is what it is to be an artist. It might even be said to be the reason Leigh became a dramatist and filmmaker – not to impose his own point of view on others, but to leave himself behind, to circulate among alien points of view, in order genuinely to appreciate and understand different forms of being.

Leigh's work takes a viewer on the same adventure. It allows him or her to inhabit a variety of emotions, imaginations, and ways of thinking and feeling, temporarily becoming others in the true otherness of their being. For Leigh, as for Wendy, such ventures outside oneself, such exercises of sympathetic imagination, are the definition of love.

13

Desperate Lives: *Naked*

"They give birth outside a grave, the light gleams an instant, then it's night once more."

– Samuel Beckett, *Waiting for Godot*

From its opening scene, *Naked* is the most volatile, visionary, and kinetic work in Leigh's oeuvre. It begins with a lurching tracking shot along a grim Manchester night alley, where we see in a blur the film's protagonist, Johnny, raping a woman he obviously knows under a street lamp. In the scene that follows, Johnny steals a car, and Leigh has the camera go along on the night ride down almost empty highways to London. The camera work is much more visceral than Leigh's normal style, but it is perfectly apt for what ensues in *Naked* – a more darkly violent film than any of his previous work. Centering around solitary, marginal characters, *Naked* is utterly removed from the messy, conflicted, sometimes caring family relations and domestic life upon which most of Leigh's work focuses.

Naked centers around Johnny, the most eloquent character yet to appear in a Leigh film, and follows his aimless meandering for forty-eight hours around London. Johnny is a working-class drifter and Dostoevskian-style intellectual – a social outsider like Cyril, the motorcycle messenger hero of *High Hopes*, but intellectually sharper and lacking the moral and psychological comfort of a political ideology or the sweetness visible beneath Cyril's quiet anger and class resentment. In fact, Johnny is a man whose capacity for anger and cruelty are the strongest elements in his personality. Women bear the brunt of his physical and emotional rage, and are casually manhandled, insulted, and rejected by him. Not that he is any more understanding and caring with men, but with them his anger is merely verbal and the rage never expressed physically. In fact, in two hostile encounters with men on his nighttime peregrinations, Johnny is unable or unwilling to defend himself and is severely beaten.

Johnny is given a ferocious, mercurial performance by David Thewlis, who succeeds in imbuing him with emotional complexity, largeness of mind, intellectual curiosity, and charismatic presence. Add to this his elegance of movement, wit, and perverse charm, and his capacity to attract women becomes, on one level, understandable.

Wispy-bearded, tall, thin, dressed in black, looking much older than his twenty-seven years, Johnny is given to endlessly articulate riffs on subjects ranging from the significance of supermarket barcodes, the architecture of modern office buildings ("post-modern gas chambers"), the "guts" and "viscera" of London, to the nature of time and God. His soliloquies and harangues can be simultaneously absurd, compulsive, irrational, perceptive, and truly poetic and visionary.[1]

Johnny is a portrait of a despairing, frenetic man who, though genuinely reflective, has devoted most of his intellectual resources and imagination to relentlessly dazzling verbal exhibitions and corrosive put-downs. He is a man whose talk centers much more on the nature of the cosmos and God than on his own feelings, desires, or autobiography. He says almost nothing about his own life, referring only once to his barmaid mother in a perverse, black comic line about her being dead but "still a good fuck."

Johnny is a master of wordplay and puns like "Thanks for the mammeries" and "Homerphobic." In one scene, after being kissed, he nastily sings, to the tune of Handel's *Hallelujah*, the "Halitosis!" chorus. He compulsively ridicules ("takes a piss") the other characters with a barrage of barbed remarks and questions. For example, when he sees his ex-girlfriend Louise's (Lesley Sharp) room for the first time, he remarks, with cruel irony: "Oh! It's de-lovely! I see you've got a ceiling at the top with a floor on the lower level, and a wall at either side. And only a single bed. Sad, really. . . ." Louise, clearly, still loves him, so his put-downs have no other justification than malice for malice's sake.

Johnny is a waste – a self-aware, intellectually arrogant, and at times dangerous figure. He is a man who is always outside, with infinite places to go but nowhere he can feel emotionally at home enough to stay. All the women he encounters after he flees Manchester for London, though distinctively different, share a painful neediness. They almost all crave affection and love. Johnny may be seductive, but it would seem to require little insight and instinct for self-protection on the part of these women to be wary of this aggressive, sharp-tongued, tense, unwashed man. Most of the women he meets, however, turn a blind eye to the threatening and broken aspects of Johnny and hungrily embrace him. In a sense, the women are active collaborators in their own pain and rejection. Among them is Louise, who is sturdy, weary, working-class, and Manchester-born, and toward whom Johnny has strong feelings but little sexual interest. There is also her unemployed, masochistic, punk-outfitted, oddly beautiful, drugged roommate, Sophie (Katrin Cartlidge), who not long after she meets Johnny has sex with him. Leigh depicts the sex between them as alternately quietly passionate and tender, then visceral, hard, and hurtful. The sex provides a mixture of pleasure and pain, though it is Sophie who absorbs all the physical maltreatment. However, despite Johnny's aggressively grabbing Sophie's face and banging her head on the arm of a sofa, she is devastated when he leaves the flat. Of course, her response doesn't justify his behavior, but it tells us two people are involved and that the woman is a collaborator in her own victimization.

In a Hollywood film, the sex would have been deodorized and have had less immediacy, less sense of two banged-up people hungrily scrambling for each other and for some momentary pleasure from a life where little of it has existed. Hollywood would probably either construct the sex scene as an elaborately prurient and glamorized set of rituals and games or shoot it from the perspective of a frightened, brutalized heroine, whose feelings would be underlined with dramatic close-ups and reaction shots. If the film was shot for sexual glamour, it would use a number of different camera angles, or it might construct a dreamy montage (all entangled body parts and rumpled white sheets), topping it off with some romantic superimpositions. In *Naked*, the sex scene is brief and the style unadorned, characterized by straight-on, middle-distance shooting of Johnny and Sophie. The scene evokes neither sexual titillation nor sentimentalization of Sophie as a pitiful victim. Johnny also encounters an older woman (Deborah MaClaren) – Jane Austen-reading, tattooed with a skull and crossbones, bleary-eyed, and alcoholic. She despondently opens herself up to him sexually, and he kisses her tenderly in return. In his usual manner, however, he then uses force, painfully jolting her head and pulling her hair. Obviously, that doesn't put her off, for she undresses and wants him to "fuckin' bite me." Suddenly he stops and looks at her with distaste, as she pathetically tries to make herself more attractive while mouthing loving words and striking what she thinks is a sexy pose. Turned off and ever willing to put people down, Johnny humiliates her, telling the woman that she looks like his mother. He goes on to refuse sex with her, and while she sleeps he tops it off by stealing her books.

Finally, there is a cardigan-wearing, silent, translucent-skinned, mournful waitress (Gina McKee) who takes Johnny to the neat flat she sublets, where he bathes, relaxes, and wants to linger. (She has sublet the flat from two cultivated gay men, and Leigh, as usual, carefully details the flat's decor: an ornate mantelpiece, well-stocked bookcases, and Greek classical and other ornaments.) In this case, however, after some desultory conversation about dogs and clocks, she suddenly starts to cry and just as abruptly angrily tells him to "bug off," tossing him out into the cold. Her behavior is left unexplained, but one senses that she herself is too wounded and alienated to make any human connection, and she clearly knows Johnny isn't the man to salve that pain. Leigh, as always, avoids the predictable. Johnny curses her out, but doesn't hit her. He just tries to change her mind by arousing guilt, informing her he has nowhere to go and it's a bitterly cold night outside. His shift in tactics, however, gets him nowhere. She remains tormented and implacable.

In *Naked* every character is emotionally isolated, bruised, or aimless; the film is permeated with a vision of hopelessness. This atmosphere pervades the relationships between men and women – the men being harsh, violent, or terrified of commitment, the women emotionally starved, solitary and often setting themselves up as victims. Yet, though Johnny engages in aggressively sexist behavior, the film's point of view is not misogynistic. *Naked* does not endorse the actions of its male characters. Some critics of this film, which has aroused particular revulsion in some feminist viewers, find it impossible to imagine that a character like Johnny could be both simultaneously sexist and seductive, and that so many of the women characters could be masochistic. From this critical perspective, any director who is capable of depicting a character given to racist or sexist actions as a complex, tortured human being – someone who can muddy the audience's sympathies – must by definition be racist and sexist.[2]

All this critical finger pointing and labeling results from the critics' need to simplify the complexity of Johnny's character. They crave mainstream films like *Thelma and Louise* or such small independent, feminist works like *Ballad of Little Jo* – films where the men who are sexists elicit no sympathy, and where the audience and the critics know just whom to root for and identify with. These films revolve around strong, defiant heroines encountering a number of hideous, stereotyped male foils whose behavior ranges from the intensely obtuse and crass to the murderous. In a sense, what these critics and viewers are calling for is a variation on socialist realism – feminist realism – the world shaped in accord with right-thinking political constructs, freeing reality of its contradictions, ambiguities, and ironies.

Obviously, that is not where Leigh's directorial method and vision lie. When his films work best, his characters' feelings and actions deny the audience easy sympathy or antipathy. In fact, though most of the women characters in *Naked* are mistreated by men, they also have a powerful need for them. Leigh also will not allow them to be reified into pure sex objects or victims, and a couple of the women characters, though never sadistic, are also capable of being sexually aggressive. In fact, the only relatively strong and empathetic character in the film, as is so often the case in Leigh's work, is a woman, Louise. Though Louise clearly also needs men, and gives no hint or suggestion that she is a feminist or even sees the world from a feminist vantage point, her earthy solidity is the only bedrock in a film built on the most transient and painful relationships.

The misogyny, at least on Johnny's part, is one among a number of personal qualities that are an expression of the self-loathing underlying his behavior and the lives of most of the other characters. Of course, to say that Johnny hates himself does and should not explain away his sexist behavior or make his actions any more acceptable. It is just that Johnny is too intricate and contradictory a figure, a man of too many parts and emotional nuances, to be subsumed under or reduced to a single category like a "misogynist" or a "sexist."

Much of the film takes place during a couple of agonizing days on the streets of London. After Sophie begins to clamor for his love, Johnny flees Louise's flat and heads for Soho. On the barren streets he meets a stunted, homeless Glaswegian couple, the head-tossing Archie and his less voluble girlfriend, Maggie (Ewen Bremmer and Susan Vidler), who hurl an almost incomprehensible form of expletive-filled English ("fuckin" used as verb, adjective, and noun). In this sequence, Johnny is almost paternal and gentle (especially toward Maggie), behaving in an amiably detached manner toward this graceless, raging pair. He treats the wailing, sub-Strindbergian couple as if they were members of some comic species (he calls Archie a "petulant dwarf").

He has a very different sort of encounter with a fellow autodidact – a solitary, voyeur (he spends his evenings sadly peering through a window at the same alcoholic, tattooed woman whom Johnny rejected). Brian (Peter Wight), a philosophical watchman, guards a vacant, ultramodern office building, a product of the speculative buildings of the Thatcher era. Brian is a much wearier and more controlled and conventional figure than Johnny. Though he is not immune to the occasional cliché – "Waste not, want not" – he is the only other intellectually and spiritually oriented character in the film and engages in a real exchange of ideas with Johnny. Brian reads the *TLS* and the Bible, and knowingly works at a job, in Johnny's words, "a monkey could do." His only escape from this quietly desperate and oppressive life is the dream of a solitary future in a crumbling cottage on the Irish coast.

Johnny sharply debunks Brian's fantasies about the future by asserting that God "is a nasty bastard" who "despises you," that greed and pain are the human condition, and that it is a hopeless world where man has no future and will ultimately cease to exist. Johnny's vision is apocalyptic, though not much more intellectually sophisticated than sophomoric philosophizing about the fate of the cosmos. In the context of the film's generally inarticulate characters, however, Johnny's talk seems more learned, original, vivid, and sparkling than it is. (All of it was augmented by Thewlis immersing himself in Leibnitz, Spinoza, Schopenhauer, and Stephen Hawking's *A Brief History of Time* in order to get a feeling for the kind of reading and references that might have shaped Johnny's gloomy vision.)

However, it is not the intellectual content of Johnny's talk, but the profound, natural linking of the ideas to his personality and consciousness that make them resonant. The ideas are deeply felt by both Johnny and Leigh, and provide the film with a metaphysical dimension – a vision of the universe's bleakness and meaninglessness – that Leigh has never mined before, but that he sees as expressing his "own deepest feelings."[3] Still, for all Johnny's rhetorical and allusive deluge, the final word shared between them is Brian's, who solemnly warns Johnny, "Don't waste your life" – a cautionary sentiment that Johnny is too far gone to heed.

Leigh has constructed a gallery of truthful characters. The one glaring exception, striking a thoroughly false note, is the character called both Jeremy and Sebastian (Greg Cruttwell), Louise and Sandra's landlord, who looks like a young Dirk Bogarde and indeed could be taken as homage to the Bogarde of Losey's *The Servant*. With his champagne-sipping and Porsche-owning contempt, this upper-class poseur has the same lineage as his much more comic, less demonic counterparts in *High Hopes*, the Boothe-Braines.

Jeremy serves as a totally vicious alter ego for Johnny – his scenes usually intercut with Johnny's (e.g., the film cuts from Johnny having sex with Sophie to Jeremy's sex scene with the waitress Giselle). He is a sneering misogynist and sadist who tries to humiliate, hurt, and emotionally batter all the women he encounters. The pain he inflicts is more ominous and single-minded than anything Johnny indulges in. He draws blood from the women during his acts of lovemaking, which are essentially turned into acts of rape. Jeremy lacks any redeeming charm or vulnerability. He is a man whose nihilistic behavior – he hates children, sees human beings as pathetic, doesn't mind AIDS because "the world could do with a bit of pruning" – goes over the top, he is a caricature of an upper-class, drawling, decadent psychopath. Jeremy is a man who feels he can't be touched, seeing himself as guarded by money and class privilege; he is often shot from a low angle, evoking his power over the women he tramples. His characteristic response to the pain and anger he causes women is a complacent smirk and a smothered laugh. As in *High Hopes*, Leigh again demonstrates that his hatred for the upper class and the self-interested, avaricious, money culture can turn his genius for giving a layered, empathetic life to his characters into unrelieved caricature. In this case, he does so with a figure who represents the pathological underside of respectable Thatcherism.

Jeremy serves to make the more complex, less predictable Johnny look a great deal more sympathetic. For though Johnny generally behaves maliciously and cruelly toward women, he is sometimes still capable of acting with some care and self-control. There is a stirring, tender scene that captures Louise and a bloodied, exhausted Johnny singing wistfully about returning home to "rainy Manchester." One feels the genuine friendship and warmth that exists between the two underneath his baiting (he contemptuously calls her "career girl") and general callousness toward her. Also, his behavior toward female characters like Maggie and the cafe waitress, though not brimming with warmth and affection, is relatively restrained – even, for a time, pleasant.

Johnny the man who feels he deserves nothing and should be punished coexists with the man who is belligerently eloquent, intellectually disdainful, and sadistic. In one scene, he hitches a ride with a silent, sullen poster man whom he helps to put up posters advertising a performance entitled *Therapy?* featuring a large mouth with gritted teeth, which the man then pastes over with a small sign saying "Canceled." The image leads Johnny to one of his nonstop monologues on the nature of walls ("a potent motif for civilization") and the word *canceled*, lacing

Louise and Johnny in the bathroom scene – the smallest, briefest island of calm and tenderness in a sea of confusion

it with a sharp put-down of the man for "promulgatin' vacuities." Predictably, the man becomes enraged and assaults Johnny, abandoning him to curse impotently and, twitching and coughing, to crawl around in the empty road. To top off the evening, Johnny is later gratuitously attacked by a gang of teenagers, who leave him looking like a black lump on the sidewalk. Though Johnny may not literally abuse himself, he behaves like a man who is constantly asking for a beating.

It is not that Johnny's self-hatred makes him more sympathetic to us, or that Leigh tries to vindicate his heartless, solipsistic behavior. Through the film, however, one does sense Leigh's identification with Johnny's vulnerability, imagination, verve, and existential despair. These qualities make the character less a monster and more a lost soul. Leigh's tendency to fuse realism and stylization, his distilled or heightened form of realism, where he caricatures, satirizes, or just makes his characters more expressive and expansive than they would normally be, also grants us a bit of distance from Johnny. The audience can simultaneously respond viscerally to the character and view him with some aesthetic distance as a larger-than-life figure. At the moments Johnny turns into a less extreme variation of Raskolnikov in Dostoyevsky's *Crime and Punishment*, or a more articulate and sexual and less pathological version of

Martin Scorsese's Travis Bickle, Leigh allows the audience sufficient detachment to permit themselves to be at the same time fascinated and repelled by Johnny.

Like almost all Leigh's films, *Naked* contains a great deal of comedy and occasionally evokes a sense of the absurd (the behavior of the Glaswegian couple); but the humor never provides genuine relief from the film's overarching sense of damnation. The lost Sophie speaks out of the side of her mouth, and in her dazed manner can at times be truly witty. When Johnny, undressing her, fumbles with the laces on her leather vest, she says, "We tried the stairs, now try the elevator," and points to the zipper. And when he mockingly asks, "Would you describe yourself as a happy little person?" she wryly responds, "Yeah . . . I'm the life and soul." Her wit, however, affords her little self-protection or sense of self-worth. Toward the film's conclusion she sadly stumbles away in tears to face new bouts of humiliation.

Louise is not in a much better situation than Sophie. Although she has sufficient strength and will to stand up to Jeremy's sexual threats (she threatens him with castration), her life is little but boredom and despair. She is balanced and caring but acutely conscious that she is facing a dreary life, with so few options (she hates her office job) that even an impossible future with Johnny is something to long for.

Finally there is Sandra (Claire Skinner, who played the calm, wry Natalie in *Life Is Sweet*), the pretty, very middle-class, normal nurse who owns the house in which Louise and Sophie rent rooms. She returns to the house from her trip to Zimbabwe at the film's end, and is appalled by the disorder. Sandra is efficient and professional in tending to Johnny's sprains and bruises, but, agitated, speaks in strangled, unfinished sentences; her need for order clearly springs from a feeling that the world, including her own, is out of control. That feeling is reinforced by an injured and debilitated Johnny, who nonetheless retains enough of the old Johnny to mimic her, and even halfheartedly come on to her. The scene, however, does not carry even a hint of Johnny threatening Sandra. After the two beatings, he's become somewhat passive and lacks the energy to behave manically or sadistically. Like all the other characters in *Naked*, Sandra can't keep more than the surface intact – life just won't quite hold together. In her characteristic stammering mode of speech she says, "when . . . how . . . will . . . the world . . . ever . . . ," with Johnny completing her sentence and affirming his vision – "end."

In a Leigh film the physical setting is almost always subordinate to the interactions and reactions of his characters. The prime emphasis is generally placed on the facial expressions and body movements of the characters. For example, when Johnny sits in a Soho doorway, Leigh's camera shoots the street in documentary style. Leigh is, however, no Loach, and it is never as important for him to evoke the social reality and fabric of London (the squares, cafes, bistros, peep shows, prostitutes, and porno shops of Soho) as it is to illuminate the plight of his characters. Even in Loach films that center on individual figures, *Kes* or *Raining Stones*, the focus is as much or more on the documentary texture of social reality and institutions – schools, pubs, dance halls – than on the plight of his central figures. In *Naked*, on the other hand, the camera's prime focus remains on Johnny's expressive face – his feelings, thoughts, and soliloquies – while, both aesthetically and socially, the London cityscape usually remains unexplored in the background of the shot.

Naked feels formally bolder, more conscious of design – light and shadow, color and image – than Leigh's other works. Aided by the imaginative cinematography of Dick Pope, Leigh uses shadow, light, and silhouetting in striking ways. There are some early scenes in Louise's flat that are shot in silhouette with a blue light and a carefully conceived wall-color scheme. There is also a scene between Brian and Johnny talking inside the vacant office building shot in a dark space in silhouette, while whatever light existing in the room derives from the all-white shades in the background right behind them. The stunning use of light and silhouette in this scene provides some aesthetic relief for the audience, as Johnny engages in one of his inordinately long monologues. There is even one long, theatrically lit and visually arresting take where a haunted-looking, backlit Johnny stands in full shot amid the desolation and darkness of the East End wasteland (the great empty space is used to accentuate the sense of alienation), with another homeless man seen dimly in the background against a hollow shell of a building. For a moment, Johnny becomes more than an abrasive, anguished drifter; he becomes a figure out of Beckett or Giacometti – the embodiment of man alone in an empty universe.

The creation of resonant images and symbols of this sort has normally not been Leigh's prime directorial mode, but though Johnny may be a larger-than-life character on a picaresque journey of sorts, he is no portentous symbolic figure or social type. His behavior is too naturalistic. Leigh doesn't provide the audience with a simple rubric to get a handle on Johnny: Social victim, sociopath, product of a dysfunctional family, existential antihero are all within the realm of probable interpretations, but none exhausts the possibilities. Leigh's Johnny cannot be mistaken for a character like the one Harvey Keitel plays in Abel Ferrara's *The Bad Lieutenant* – a man who indulges in one elongated nihilistic rant against God, morality, and life itself. Johnny's talk is not only more eloquent, but it contains much dark humor and a great deal of fluctuating mood and tone. Johnny elicits a mixture of audience sympathy and revulsion that Ferrara's one-dimensional antiheroes are incapable of evoking. When Johnny rejects his last life raft – Louise's offer to go back to Manchester with him – stealing her money while fleeing to nowhere, hopping and wincing painfully down the middle of the street as the camera tracks away from him, we instinctively feel it is right that such a destructive and ravaged figure does not receive a last-minute reprieve. The film, however, also suggests throughout that there is something humanly valuable, even a strain of compassion and idealism, that could be salvaged in Johnny. Leigh, without ever sentimentalizing him, leaves the audience with a profound feeling of loss at the end. There is even a faint hope against hope on the audience's part that all may not be over for Johnny.

There is no question that *Naked*'s dark, metaphysical vision is shaped by the general pessimism and sense of malaise and social decline that dominates post–Thatcher England. Leigh is a politically aware director, who believes that life in present-day English society is gradually becoming more inequitable and oppressive. However, though he clearly views his characters' emptiness as being related to their inhabiting a society where many people are on the dole and homeless, and where being born working-class still constricts life's possibilities, none of this sufficiently explains, for example, Sophie's plight. The film never suggests that the advent of a measure of social justice and equality could transform the lives of characters like Sophie or Brian. Leigh avoids reducing Johnny's behavior to a set of political and social variables or treating it as merely a manifestation of a social problem. It is Johnny the individual, not Johnny the homeless social victim or member of a displaced working-class intelligentsia, who is terrified of making personal commitments and incapable of using his powerful intelligence and literate wit in a productive way. The responsibility for his self-destructive behavior is not reductively arrogated to Thatcher, to capitalist greed and exploitation, or even to the inequities of the English class system.[4]

Naked's emphasis is an existential one. It is a film about a variety of isolated, emotionally hobbled characters trying to live with themselves and other people in a meaningless universe. Their pain is determined less by their economic situation than by their psychological and spiritual states of being. For Leigh, despair of this nature is not a middle-class luxury but something that touches us all.

Epilogue: The Feel of Life

We are in the business of not only making people believe and care and all those things, but *laugh*. We are in the business of being funny, basically, of being comedians, and that's not to be underestimated.

– Mike Leigh

Over the past thirty years or so, American artists and viewers have scaled down their expectations for the art of film. It is as if, as a result of the pervasive cultural hypocrisies, deceits, and betrayals of the seventies, eighties, and nineties, artists and intellectuals have lost faith in art as a form of truth. Engagement, seriousness, and sincerity have been revealed to be a mug's game so often that it appears that the only honest stance that remains is to stand outside the established systems of understanding, critical of all and believing in none. The ironic mode has, ironically enough, become the last refuge of the caring heart.

The result is the triumph of what Paul Ricoeur called "the hermeneutics of suspicion." Skepticism (or the sterile formalism of academic criticism) fills the void left by faith. In a world where truth-telling is despaired of, one's powers of debunking, revealing, and exposing become the measure of one's virtue. Art and criticism become essentially negative in their functions. Art is viewed as existing solely to help us see through the limiting systems around us, and art that doesn't make that its main function is viewed as being complicitous with those systems.

The best we can ask of our films and filmmakers is to be "smart," "sassy," and "wised-up" (to the tricks, games, and overall fraudulence of the system) in the approved Pauline Kael way. The search for truth gives way to play with cinematic forms and jokesy pop-culture allusions. The results are the stylistic back-flips and video-store in-jokes of *Pulp*

Fiction, the empty narrative tricks and ingenuities of *Fargo*, the stylistic slickness of *L.A. Confidential*, the world-weary sardonicism of Altman's work, and the critical praise heaped on these and similar works. It's all about not being trapped by codes. If all art can do is to reflect on oppressive cultural rules and conventions, then the purpose of art is to negotiate them deftly, to deconstruct them devastatingly, to play with them puckishly, and throughout it all, to avoid taking any of them seriously.[1]

The debased pop version is our culture of irony. The knowing wink, nod, and smirk are everywhere. From Letterman to MTV to life, the point is to be wised-up, with-it, bouncy, weightless. Hipness, coolness, and detachment are the supreme virtues. Art and life are reduced to "styles," "surfaces," "spin," "looks." This stance appeals to teenage boys above all because it requires no emotional knowledge or commitment. It's all up in your head as a set of clever ideas and knowing allusions. It's easy. It's safe. It threatens nothing and asks nothing of the viewer. It is a kind of cynicism or despair, of course, but don't worry; everything is stupid anyway. It's all just a big joke, lark, goof, game. Don't you have a sense of humor? Art doesn't really matter. Only a fool would take any of it seriously or get upset about it.

Leigh embraces a different vision. His films refuse to conform to the culture of reduced aspirations. They are not "stylish" or "clever." They do not play narrative games or take a viewer on an emotional roller-coaster ride. They are deadly serious (which doesn't preclude them from being delightfully hilarious at the same time). They explore real emotional and intellectual problems. They reflect deeply on the world we live in. They ask questions about who we are and offer insights into the ways we hurt ourselves and others: What does it feel like to be this person? Why can't that individual give or receive love? Why is this one so unhappy? Why does that one treat others so badly? Why can't this one even see that he has a problem? What is it about this situation that causes pain? Could anything relieve it?

While archness, coolness, and detachment are the name of the game in the culture of irony, Leigh's films defeat distancing strategies. They assault and batter us. Their perceptual and narrative shocks deny the viewer intellectual leverage over the experiences they present. They implicate him; they snare him into caring (even as he may resist). In a culture devoted to knowingness, they dare to ask questions to which they don't know the answers. They conduct explorations without knowing in advance where they will come out.

This is filmmaking not as a stylistic chess game but as about life-and-death issues. In this conception of it, art is a way of understanding our most complex experiences. Although art has perennially taken a back seat to science as a way of knowing in twentieth-century culture, an artist working in Leigh's way is doing something at least as important as a biologist, chemist, physician, or physicist. Any difference between the scientist and the artist weighs, in fact, in the artist's favor, in that the artist is grappling with a realm far more complex and elusive than the physical world – the world of human thought and feeling.

However, even for the few critics who are committed to the truth-value of artistic expression, Leigh's work might be said to camouflage its complexity. Most of the great twentieth-century modernists (from Eliot, Pound, and Joyce; to Beckett, Faulkner, and Stevens; to Pinter, Pynchon, and Gaddis) have convinced us that "advanced" art must be abstruse. Within the realm of film, serious "artistic" expression is thought to involve various kinds of stylistic defamiliarization, narrative dislocation, and semantic obliquity. Leigh's work does not justify its existence in such ways. The subject matter seems utterly prosaic – ordinary people doing ordinary things. The narrative presentation is simple and straight-forward – no flashbacks, no unreliable narrators, no violations of chronology. The style is unrhetorical in the extreme – no editorial razzle-dazzle, visual sublimities, or acoustic stylization.[2] Compared to the work of Akerman, Schroeder, Ruiz, or Fellini, Leigh's family dramas – his stories about mothers, fathers, lovers, and teenagers – just don't seem to qualify for the artistic cutting edge.

Leigh's work is difficult, but in a different way from the canonical modernist works. The demands made are less on our intellect and knowledge (in the mode of *The Waste Land*, *Ulysses*, and *The Cantos*), than on our capacities of sensitivity and awareness. In other words, no amount of literary or cultural knowledge will make Leigh's work easier. The only knowledge that can help us is knowledge of life and human emotions (which is unfortunately far less common among critics than the other sort of knowledge). But what makes the films doubly hard is that while Leigh requires us to draw on our knowledge of people and situations we have encountered outside of the movie theater (in a way that a filmmaker like Hitchcock never does), he asks us at the same time to abandon our customary forms of social and emotional understanding.

Leigh's characters frustrate conventional psychological and moral judgments; their situations deny normal, formulaic emotional responses. In *Nuts in May* and *Grown-Ups*, the lowbrows are ultimately shown to be "smarter" than the intellectuals. In *Meantime*, the filial "odd couple" is revealed to be emotionally more intimate than the happily married "normal" couple. Clichés are shredded; stereotypes and expectations violated. Our desire for clarity, resolution, and catharsis is denied. "Villains" do not necessarily recognize their faults. "Heroes" and "heroines" can be deeply flawed. Or to put it more accurately, there are no villains, heroes, or heroines. Virtue is partial and shaded and imperfect. The viewer must enter into a genuinely fresh and unformulated relationship with what is on screen. Since most of our conventional conceptual categories won't suffice, we must give up the comfort of conceptions and return to the rawness of perceptions – reading flickering facial expressions, listening for subtle shifts in tones of voice, responding to interactions with extraordinary sensitivity, adjusting our understanding as we go along.

Leigh's specialty is the presentation of fraudulent or self-deluded stances of various sorts, but it is important that he makes them *almost* indistinguishable from sanity. The point is to prevent the viewer from treating the characters as other than himself, to deny him the luxury of holding the experience at arm's length. Because we are almost always tricked into sympathy with characters before we notice their faults (and often maintain sympathy with them even after we see their faults), the films reach into our lives and get under our skin.

The absence of a strongly inflected visual style is an essential aspect of Leigh's project insofar as it means that the experiences his films provide are somewhat unglossed. Watching his films is less like *learning about* something (with stylistic signposts telling us what is important and what things mean) than *living through* unassimilated experiences, the way we do in life. Moving through Leigh's scenes is a lot like having things happen to us in life. We are taken on a voyage without a road map to guide us. We are denied shorthand or abstract ways of knowing. We are put on the qui vive, forced to figure things out step by step. The films don't simply refer to, summarize, or offer conclusions about experience. They offer experiences that test our powers of perception in the same way experiences in life do.

As far as the ordinariness of Leigh's characters and the prosaicness of their situations go, I would argue that what appears to be artistic conservatism is in fact the most radical aspect of Leigh's work. While most modernist artists typically set their works somewhere above and beyond the world of ordinary people and affairs, Leigh refuses to pull the forms of art and life apart. In his view, the imaginative issues the greatest works of art grapple with are the same as those ordinary people face every day of their lives: at work, on a date, dealing with a salesman, coping with strangers on vacation, hosting a party, interacting with a relative, working through issues in a romantic relationship, getting along with a difficult daughter. Furthermore, unlike most other works of art, his films are not governed by special rules and forms of expression different from those used by ordinary people in their everyday lives. Every scene in Hitchcock or Lynch tells us how their art represents a way of encountering life different from our ordinary, everyday consciousness; every scene in Leigh tells us that artistic expression is not somewhere beyond ordinary life but continuous with it. In contradiction to the Platonic view, art is not an expression of "purer" impulses and "otherworldly" insights, but is a condensation and intensification of the forces and structures of everyday interaction. As Frank Stella once noted, we are accustomed to having our paintings lifted off the floor, surrounded by air, up on the wall. Leigh's conception of art denies this idealizing margin. He sees the work not as being off to one side, representing a world more ideal and pure than the one we live in, but as continuous with life. The experience captured in his films is just as stimulatingly, complexly, challengingly messy, dirty, and compromised as life outside the movies.

Another way to put it is to say that Leigh imagines his best and most interesting characters to be artists of life, whose practical, worldly achievements are not fundamentally different from his own achievements as a filmmaker. Sylvia unsticks conversations and thaws frozen identities the same way Leigh does as a screenwriter and director. Trevor eludes others' attempts to organize his life in the same way Leigh's scenes frustrate a viewer's reductive understandings. Mark challenges understandings in the same way Leigh does. Couples like Cyril and Shirley and Wendy and Andy interact with each other as complexly, sensitively, and creatively in life as the greatest cinematic scripting, photography, and editing could ever indicate as an imaginative possibility in art. Sylvia and Norman, Trevor and Ronnie, Mark and Colin, Dawn, Mick, and Jean, Wendy and Andy, Cyril and Shirley use language as allusively, playfully, and deviously as poets and playwrights – with as much indirection, metaphoric displacement, and subtle suggestiveness – because, in Leigh's view, in terms of their imaginations, they are indistinguishable from poets and playwrights.

One would be hard-pressed to find works that imagine the everyday experiences of ordinary people as being of more astonishing interest and mysterious complexity.³ Leigh sees no fundamental difference between his artistic expressions and the everyday expressions of people in love affairs, arguments, and the rest of nonartistic life. He reminds us that only high-culture snobbery keeps us from recognizing that everyone we meet has these imaginative powers.

Leigh is generally thought of as a satirist or social commentator, but it is the argument of this entire book that that is a limited way to understand his work. To translate his films into a series of moral judgments and stances (as Dennis Potter did with *Abigail's Party*, for example) is to do it a profound injustice. In the deepest view, in fact, one might say that Leigh's work is pitched *against* moral judgments of the sort Potter translated it into. It is not accidental that the characters in Leigh's work who move through life striking Potter-like moral stances are the most profoundly limited ones.

Mr. Thornley, Keith, Ralph Butcher, Dave, Barbara, Rupert and Laetitia, Suzi, Nicola, Johnny, and Sebastian demonstrate the inadequacy of moral judgments to take in the feel and meaning of the life that is actually around them. Leigh's cinematic style is emphatically opposed to the intellectual and emotional styles of these characters. Where they narrow the perspective on an event, viewing everything and everyone in terms of their own point of view, Leigh circulates the viewer through a variety of views, no one of which is ultimate or final. Where they divide people into opposing camps of black and white, wrong and right, us and them, Leigh clearly relishes and respects different ways of being. While they dourly judge and categorize, Leigh's humor is a way of suspending judgment. His bemused tone is a form of toleration and enjoyment.

With characters like Peter, Mr. Thornley, Keith, and Barbara, Leigh shows us that moral judgments arise from states of fundamental insecurity, and that if we are comfortable with our identities and situations (as Sylvia, Trevor, Dick, Mandy, Shirley, Wendy, and he himself clearly are) we can *enjoy* the differences between ourselves and others rather than putting ourselves in opposition to them, or forcing a choice between us and them. Leigh's comic style is the embodiment of his ability to *appreciate* differences. Its scenic and narrative shagginess and bagginess and its circulation through different points of view are ways of resisting psychological and emotional narrowness of all sorts. Leigh replaces judgment with wonder at the range of human diversity. His work is less about judging than understanding.

It is important not to forget what it feels like to watch these films, or what it must have felt like for Leigh to make them. The sheer gleefulness of Leigh's presentation – the playfulness, the zaniness, the calculated outrageousness – simply leave moral categories behind. What must it have felt like to write, rehearse, and shoot the scenes in *Home Sweet Home* in which Melody and Dave deliver their crazed monologues? Or for Leigh as a screenwriter deliberately to suppress Janice's name and her limp until she says goodbye following the lovemaking scene with Stan? Or, in *Life Is Sweet*, to have selected Paula's egregiously unflattering costume and makeup and to have scripted and blocked the nutty body positions in the scene in which she plays the drums with Aubrey? What must it have felt like to rehearse and shoot the scene in *Hard Labour* in which Mr. Thornley struggles into his pajamas, or the one in which he gets his back rubbed down with liniment? (One can almost hear Leigh chortling off-camera at these deliberately outrageous moments.) What must it have felt like to script the scene in *Meantime* in which Barbara and the building supervisor have their weird, nonintersecting conversation? (Or, during postproduction, to lay in the off-the-wall music that underpins it?) Or to decide to end *Abigail's Party* with Laurence's heart attack and various characters' over-the-top responses to it (and then to add Angie's comical muscle spasm and the throbbing sound track into the mix)? Or to choreograph Gloria's wild scene on the stairs in *Grown-Ups?* Or to have egged on Jane Horrocks' twitchiness in *Life Is Sweet?* Or Mike Bradwell's in *Bleak Moments?* What must it have felt like to block and rehearse Pat and Peter's silent face-off in *Bleak Moments?* Or to create in the editing room the virtuosic twenty-nine-cut silent sequence in which Pat, Peter, Hilda, Sylvia, and Norman have their tea?

Moral judgments don't come anywhere near doing justice to the weird comedy of these moments. The inventiveness of Leigh's conceptions, the zestiness of the acting, the bite and punch of the editing, the extremity of the situations leave ethical glosses in the dust. These moments communicate not a feeling of scolding and finger wagging, but the exhilaration Leigh and his actors must have felt in creating them.[4]

Precisely because the unclassifiable strangeness of these moments defeats didactic forms of understanding, they give the viewer the feeling of participating in the same creative thrills that Leigh must have experienced making them. The viewer is moved to a place beyond ideas, beyond moralisms, almost beyond understanding – a place of exuberance, power, and energy. It's a wonderful place to get a work to, and one that offers a stunningly upbeat feeling about life. The outrageousness, iconoclasm, nuttiness, and eccentricity of Leigh's choices give us firsthand experience of what it feels like to leap out of the emotional and intellectual boxes, the tired, conventional forms of behavior and expression, in which the characters themselves are trapped.

Leigh is holding up a performative ideal to them and to us. In the very process of creating these films he shows what it feels like to leave behind received forms of understanding and canned modes of being – what it feels like to enter into endless fresh, unclassifiable, and creative transactions with life.

Notes

Biographical and Cultural Introduction

1 Leonard Quart, unpublished interview with Mike Leigh, September 23, 1996.
2 Michael Coveney, *The World According to Mike Leigh* (London: Harper-Collins, 1996), p. 39.
3 Ibid., p. 56.
4 Quart, unpublished interview.
5 Ibid.
6 "Mike Leigh's Original Features" (interview with Leigh by Graham Fuller), in Mike Leigh, *Naked and Other Screenplays* (London: Faber and Faber, 1995), p. xiv.
7 Paul Clements, *The Improvised Play: The Work of Mike Leigh* (London: Methuen, 1983), p. 8.
8 "Mike Leigh's Original Features," p. xiv.
9 Ibid., p. xix.
10 Ibid., pp. xvi–xvii.
11 Julian Barnes, *Letter from London* (New York: Vintage Books, 1995), p. 221.
12 PBS clearly felt that Leigh's low-budget, idiosyncratic films were unable to provide the kind of literate escape to which an audience looking at handsomely mounted, nostalgic, impersonal works like *Brideshead Revisited* was accustomed.
13 James Park, *Learning to Dream: The New British Cinema* (London: Faber and Faber, 1984), p. 100.
14 Lee Ellickson and Richard Porton, "I Find the Tragicomic Things in Life: An Interview with Mike Leigh," *Cineaste* 20, no. 3 (1994): 16.
15 Ray Carney would like to express his disagreement with the statements in this paragraph and the two that follow. For a positive appreciation of this aspect of Leigh's work, the reader is referred to Chapters 2, 3, 6, 7, 8, and 11, as well as the Epilogue.
16 "Mike Leigh's Original Features," p. xiii.

17 Ellickson and Porton, "I Find the Tragicomic Things in Life," p. 15.
18 Quart, unpublished interview.
19 "Mike Leigh's Original Features," p. xiii.
20 Mirra Bank, "Mike Leigh," *Films in Review* 48, no. 1/2 (January/February 1997): 31.
21 Clements, *The Improvised Play*, p. 35.
22 Ibid., p. 33.
23 Quart, unpublished interview.
24 For a contrasting view of Leigh's work as being fundamentally optimistic, hopeful, and life-affirming, the reader is referred to Ray Carney's Stylistic Introduction, Chapters 4, 8, 11, 12, and the Epilogue.

1. Stylistic Introduction: Living beyond Consciousness

1 Leigh has acknowledged the influence of Ozu and Renoir, and the technique of basing his films on differences of perspective may have been learned from them. It is also standard dramatic practice in the theater, where events are almost always less important than personal perspectives.

2 For example, Leigh's short, *Old Chums*, dramatizes the interaction of two characters whose points of view surge and change almost second by second (from the distance to intimacy, formality to ease, agreement to misunderstanding, thoughtfulness to indifference – and back again). I find it breathtakingly exciting but many American students to whom I have shown it see nothing beyond "a rambling, apparently pointless conversation."

3 Leigh's short, *Probation*, is his most succinct dramatization of the brick walls that separate individual minds. A young Black man interacts with a group of other figures who are so trapped in their own private emotional and intellectual boxes (based on stereotypes about Blackness) that they are unable even to "see" the man in front of them, let alone genuinely understand or communicate with him. For a filmmaker as committed as Leigh is to the interactional nature of experience, there could be no more serious failure than these states of imaginative insulation.

4 One might say that the reason studio films put so much emphasis on doing (and their characters are so busy a-doing), is that they have a very shallow sense of being. Apart from what they *do*, their characters *are* very little. If they stopped doing things, they would in effect cease to exist – to count narratively. To put it conversely, it is because characters in Hollywood films are not defined by the accumulated weight of lived experience that what they think or feel at any given moment assumes such inordinate importance. The least gust of thought defines one's course where there is no ballast of character.

5 In line with the location of the drama outside characters' consciousness, the characters themselves would not necessarily understand a viewer's descriptions of these films. Gloria would say the problem is Dick; but we see it is herself. The Butchers would say that their problems began with the family that moved in next door, but we see that they cause their own unhappiness.

Keith would say Finger makes trouble, but we see that Keith creates his own crisis.

6 Unless the character is insane, of course (for example, like Norman Bates in *Psycho*). Not to be capable of seeing yourself clearly is the very definition of insanity in Hollywood film, which only confirms how self-knowledge is taken for granted. In Leigh's work, where *everyone* is at least somewhat deranged in this sense, derangement cannot be defined in this way.

7 There is an extended discussion of this subject, as well as many other matters summarily treated here, in my "Two Forms of Cinematic Modernism: Notes Towards a Pragmatic Aesthetic," in *A Modern Mosaic: Essays on Modernism in the United States*, ed. Townsend Ludington (Chapel Hill: University of North Carolina Press, 2000), pp. 385–435; and a briefer consideration of the contemplative bias of cinematic presentation in my "A Polemical Introduction: The Road Not Taken," *Post Script: Essays in Film and the Humanities* 11, no. 2 (Winter 1992): 3–12. Both are available on my web site at: <http://people.bu.edu/rcarney>.

8 There is no space here to go into why idealized presentations should seem so "natural" to American viewers, but suffice it to say that American culture is still living out the legacy of Romanticism, both in its exalted modes and in its debased forms of melodramatic and sentimental expression. (The Hollywood aesthetic has important similarities with the late-eighteenth-century cult of sensibility, and the work of Mackenzie in particular. We live in a new age of sentimentality – a fact Leigh makes the subject of one of his films, *Home Sweet Home*.) Broadway plays, popular music, television shows, movies, and novels all bombard us with the message that seeing, thinking, and feeling *are* more important than social expression and interaction. The culture of visionary sublimity relentlessly conveys the message that vision is power – that unexpressed thoughts and emotions are enough – that you need *do* nothing in particular. You need only feel and see.

9 There is also the fact, of course, that most American actors are more interested in defending their personal images than portraying their characters' identities. In other words, they would rather sabotage their performances than look bad, which is why in role after role they present themselves in attractive, sweet, nice, cute, or cuddly ways. As I am not the first to notice, even the villains in American films are generally charming, dashing, witty, or playful – never truly ugly, grotesque, or pathetic. (And of course the existence of villains is itself a reflection of an idealizing simplification, since there are none in life.) Truth is relentlessly sentimentalized in these works – patterned to conform with the simplicity of our endocrine systems.

10 There are characters in Leigh's work who, in effect, attempt to live as if they were characters in American movies, as if one's identity could be generic and one's life were a matter of abstract ideas and unenacted feelings. But the difference from American film is that Leigh shows what trouble that causes. Figures like Keith, Beverly, Suzi, Nicola, and Aubrey are found wanting precisely because of their unwillingness or inability to translate inner states into outer expressions. Their conceptions are at an angle with

their expressions. Their willingness to let ideas and feelings take the place of expressive performance is their undoing.

11 Henry James, *The Portrait of a Lady*, chap. 19. I take Sargent's great double portrait "Mrs. Fiske Warren and her Daughter Rachel" to be a visual representation of the same difference. See my *American Vision: The Films of Frank Capra* (Hanover, NH: University Press of New England, 1996), pp. 1–27 and 55–65 for more on Sargent's relation to James, and their joint critique of American visionary stances.

12 It is surely not accidental that the transcendental understanding of selfhood came to the fore in the culture that crossed capitalist notions of individuals as more or less interchangeable position holders with democratic conceptions of equality. Americans are plastic men and women in a plastic culture.

13 Ellickson and Porton, "I Find the Tragicomic Things in Life," p. 13.

14 Leigh's brilliant *The Short and Curlies* (a short included on the Criterion laserdisc of *Naked*) is his most hilarious demonstration of the inexorability of character. Clive, Joy, Charlene, and Betty can never be anything other than what they are – but that is enough. The situation is not necessarily comic, however. The same is true of Beverly, Laurence, Angela, and Tony in *Abigail's Party*, and is the source of their doom. All of Leigh's work is pitched between the two visions, the comic and the tragic, of the consequences of selfhood.

2. Fictitious Selves: *Bleak Moments*

1 I have discussed differences between sociological and imaginative understandings of art in the 1996 preface to my *American Vision*, pp. xi–xxii; my "A Yellow Pages of Criticism" (review of *The Johns Hopkins Guide to Literary Theory and Criticism*), *Partisan Review* 62, no. 1 (Winter 1995): 138–143; my "Looking without Seeing," *Partisan Review* 58, no. 4 (Fall 1991): 717–723; my review of David James's *Allegories of Cinema* in *American Studies* (Lawrence: University of Kansas) 32, no. 1 (Spring 1991): 123–124; and my "A Polemical Introduction: The Road Not Taken," *Post Script* 11, no. 2 (Winter 1992): 3–12.

2 No filmmaker is more committed to the individuality of his characters or more critical of characters who themselves embrace generic identities. It is telling that even the two Leigh films which, more than any of his other work, feature "types," *Abigail's Party* and *Who's Who*, imagine their characters' expressions to be personally distinctive. Beverly's unpredictable shifts of tone in the first film and Samantha's idiosyncratic gestures and movements in the second repeatedly remind us of their untypological individuality. Furthermore, the stereotypical nature of the characters and expressions in both films is clearly presented, not as a fact of life (or art), but as a profound problem to be dealt with. Insofar as Laurence and Beverly in the first work or Nigel and Samantha in the second embody forms of group thought and speech, they are in deep emotional trouble.

   To put it in other terms, while the allegorical abstraction of *Thelma and Louise* practically begs for a generalized ideological or metaphoric reading (and in fact has nothing interesting to reveal to a more personal analysis), the expressive uniqueness and mercuriality of Leigh's characters resist it. Figures like Sylvia, Colin, and Wendy are *only* interesting in their expressive particularity.

3 For more on this subject, see the opening pages of my "When Mind Is a Verb: Thomas Eakins and the Work of Knowing," in *The Revival of Pragmatism*, ed. Morris Dickstein (Durham, NC: Duke University Press, 1998), pp. 377–403.

4 As is the case with the orphanage in *Home Sweet Home*, the single institution depicted in *Bleak Moments*, a sheltered workshop for the retarded, is clearly thought of as a group of individuals, not as a bureaucracy above and beyond and controlling the lives of the people in it.

5 Noël Simsolo, "Strictly Controlled Improvisation: An Interview with Mike Leigh," *Cinema* (Paris), 1972, pp. 23–28 (translated from the French by John Gianvito).

6 Leigh's debt to Ozu is deep and pervasive. Leigh's boss is clearly indebted to the boss in Ozu's *Early Summer*, and his narrative function almost identical – in Ozu, Satake's flat-mindedness contrasting with the imaginative nimbleness of the women with whom he interacts, specifically with the litheness of Aya's and Noriko's exchanges. (As another likely borrowing from Ozu, though a less important and probably unconscious one, there is also a scene in Ozu's *Early Spring* in which two men discuss the traffic outside their office building, as the boss does in a scene here.)

7 Pat is a type that clearly haunted Leigh's imagination. Her forced cheerfulness and subsequent breakdown anticipate many later figures – from Beverly in *Abigail's Party* and Gloria and Christine in *Grown-Ups* to Barbara in *Meantime* and Valerie in *High Hopes*. In each case, the smiling mask is peeled off to reveal the grimace beneath.

8 Another way Leigh cultivates the feeling that any particular view is partial is by suggesting that even the simplest visible actions and expressions are informed by a complex subtext of emotional and intellectual inclinations that extend beyond them. Since any one thing Pat, Sylvia, Peter, or Norman says or does only provides a glimpse of a larger invisible psychological subtext, the impression is that there is much more to their emotional lives than what is visible at any one moment.

9 Ellickson and Porton, "I Find the Tragicomic Things in Life," p. 12. Leigh displays an almost gleeful delight in surprising the viewer. The concatenated narrative outrages of *A Sense of History* (written by Jim Broadbent and directed by Leigh) are only the most extreme illustration of the point.

10 Peter Ansorge, "Making up the Well-Made Plays for Today," *Plays and Playing*, no. 4 (1975): 14.

11 Leigh includes breakdowns or other sorts of disillusioning collapse near the ends of many of his films: in scenes involving Mrs. Thornley in *Hard Labour*, Trevor in *The Kiss of Death*, Keith in *Nuts in May*, Beverly in *Abigail's Party*, Nigel in *Who's Who*, Gloria in *Grown-Ups*, June in *Home Sweet Home*, Barbara in *Meantime*, Valerie in *High Hopes*, and Nicola in *Life Is Sweet*, for example. It is one of the most common narrative events.

12 This inhabitation of an alien point of view – seeing things, at least in part, from the perspective of the character – is critical to the effect of Leigh's work. If a viewer is unwilling or unable to do it, the films lose much of their emotional power. The viewer must to some extent suspend his own personal perspective and sympathetically enter into Keith's, Gloria's, Dick's, Mandy's, Stan's, June's, or Mark's view of things in order to experience the states of cognitive dissonance that Leigh is interested in inducing.

13 Leigh is known for his playfulness in his life as much as in his art. There are many stories about how, even in fairly serious situations, he almost invariably assumes a semicomic stance, adopting the same half-playful attitude many of his most interesting characters do.

14 The tonal irresolution of Leigh's scenes is one of his greatest achievements. As examples in other works of similar degrees of tonal complexity I would cite the fight scene in *Nuts in May*, the heart-attack scene in *Abigail's Party*, the scene in *Grown-Ups* in which Gloria locks herself in the bathroom and sprawls on the stairs, the birthday party scene in *High Hopes*, and the sex scene in *Life Is Sweet*.

15 I would argue that this is precisely what overly moralistic readings of Leigh's films and characters forget. They ignore the tone of his depictions. Any discussion of Rupert and Laetitia or Aubrey and Nicola, for example, must come to grips with the essential playfulness of Leigh's presentation of them.

16 The scene with "the enthusiastic teacher" is one more step in Leigh's indictment of Peter. Leigh wants to make sure we understand that Peter's rejection of Sylvia in the preceding scene is symptomatic of Peter's way of going through life. (The schoolteacher unable to interact in other than a pedantic way will reappear in *Grown-Ups* in the character of Ralph Butcher.)

3. Personal Freezing and Stylistic Melting: *Hard Labour*

1 This, I take it, is the meaning of Leigh's "Camberwell conversion." While the whole emphasis at RADA was on mastering formal rules and conventions, Leigh's life-drawing class experience at Camberwell Art School showed him that art was fundamentally about seeing the world around him. Art was life seen freshly and truthfully. Formulas, recipes, received notions only block the view – in both art and life. Leigh's own struggle, as a student in art school, to break free of conventions in order to enter into a personal artistic relationship with what was around him interestingly becomes the drama enacted in most of the films. Virtually all of the characters, in their different ways, are (like the Royal Academy faculty and many of the students) trapped in conventional, "genre-based" ways of being, knowing, and feeling, which they are then invited to leave behind in order to enter into a fresh emotional and imaginative relationship to what is around them. (Though it is only a sidelight, it is surely not accidental that Peter in *Bleak Moments* is not only thought of as being a teacher but has a bit of the donnish quality of some of Leigh's own drama school instructors.)

2 Leigh's deidealizations have their intellectual roots in his formative years.

Sixties "bare-your-body-and-scream" theater was all around him as a drama student (all the more enticing to a young student in that such expressive outrages were frowned on by the RADA faculty). Paul Morrissey's early films, *Trash* and *Flesh* in particular, which brilliantly employ their characters' physicality as expressive devices, made a deep impression on Leigh just at the point he was starting out as a filmmaker. (*Flesh* coincidentally played at the same theater immediately after the closing of Leigh's stage production of *Bleak Moments*.) Morrissey's work and certain forms of avant-garde drama were more influential on the young Leigh than the entirely more conventional work of John Osborne or any of the other so-called Angry Young Men with whom his films are usually lumped.

3 I have more on cinematic abstraction, derealization, and "aboutness" in the 1996 preface to my *American Vision*, pp. xii–xiv; my "A Polemical Introduction," *Post Script*, pp. 3–12; my "Two Forms of Cinematic Modernism," *A Modern Mosaic*, pp. 385–96; and my chapters on *Love Streams*, *Faces*, *Minnie and Moskowitz*, and *A Woman under the Influence* in my *The Films of John Cassavetes: The Adventure of Insecurity*.

4 This is what makes Christine's politeness in *Grown-Ups* entirely different from Wendy's in *Life Is Sweet* or Shirley's in *High Hopes*. Christine's "kindness" is a fixed pose, *not* a genuine response to anyone else's perspective or emotions; Wendy's and Shirley's politeness is a form of empathy, a way of sympathetically opening themselves to everyone they meet. While Christine is frozen in place, they flow.

5 Since Mr. Thornley and Mrs. Stone are narrative doubles, it is not surprising that there is a similar scene between Mrs. Stone and her greengrocer later on, in which the grocer is flexible and responsive while Mrs. Stone is rigid and hostile. Like the tallyman with Mr. Thornley, the grocer offers Mrs. Stone the opportunity to break her patterns of response; like Mr. Thornley, she is unable to.

6 The subtlety of Leigh's presentation and the viewer's lack of general knowledge is such that even many of the points in the preceding paragraph are debatable. Perhaps the boss never did melt in the first place; maybe it was only our hope. Perhaps what I have characterized as Mr. Shore's snideness and condescension is an attempt at genuinely good-natured humor. Leigh trusts his viewer enough to allow such uncertainties to exist. He creates worlds where things are not black and white, but gray.

   I would note parenthetically that there are similarities between Pat and Sylvia's boss in *Bleak Moments* and Mr. Thornley's boss here (as well as with the building superintendent in *Meantime*): All seem equally fond of the sound of their own voices and ability to play with words. Given the similarity, it seems possible that they are based on an actual employer or supervisor from Leigh's work life.

7 Shakespeare's work, of course, is the greatest example in all of art of this exhilarating countermarching against his own previously attained positions. He breaks his own patterns, messing up his own clarities. The emerging coherence of each of the plays is repeatedly undermined by his own imaginative proliferations, extravagances, and revisions.

8   I would note, however, that Leigh avoids exaggerating her freedom. It is a freedom of consciousness only. Not only is Mrs. Thornley's body still enslaved to her husband, but the confessional scene shows that her mind is still enslaved to the church's views of her wifely duties (and her feelings of guilt for violations of them). Leigh makes sure we see that, when Mrs. Thornley comes home from confession, though *our* view of her may be changed, no one else's is, and nothing has materially changed in her life.

4. Existence without Essences: *The Kiss of Death*

1   One might reply that there are "problems" in Leigh's films that lend themselves to courses of action – in *Grown-Ups*, for example, what Dick and Mandy are going to do about Gloria and whether Dick will give in to Mandy's badgering about having a baby. But Leigh's narrative is not really organized around the presentation of these problems or the discovery of solutions to them. The two situations in *Grown-Ups* function less as problems to be solved than as issues to create conflicts between Dick, Mandy, Gloria, and Sharon. The same is true of Andy's "goal" of working for himself in *Life Is Sweet*. The viewer isn't thinking about it during most of the scenes. It doesn't focus our viewing experience or tell us what to pay attention to on a moment-by-moment basis. The interest of individual scenes is more local.

2   I would note that I am dealing with *The Kiss of Death* slightly out of chronological order because it allows me to keep Leigh's "hollow-man" trilogy (*Nuts in May*, *Abigail's Party*, and *Who's Who*) together in my discussion. The exact dating of the individual works is, in any case, complicated by the fact that many of them were mounted on different dates a year or more apart – once as a play and then as a film, with another work (either as play or film) frequently intervening between the two presentations of the first work.

3   The scene in which Trevor lies on his bed thinking is another illustration of suggesting the existence of a free imaginative space without weakly specifying it. Many of Leigh's other films present similarly indeterminate states of consciousness which open up the narrative in similar ways. Notice the function of Mrs. Thornley's poppy and smile in the ironing scene in *Hard Labour*, the presentation of the states of mind of the main characters in shots near the end of both *Hard Labour* and *Who's Who*, the scene in *High Hopes* in which Cyril stands in front of the steaming kettle, and the scene in *Life Is Sweet* in which Wendy is dusting.

Ozu is the great master of this effect of allowing moments of thinking to remain slightly unexplained. In fact, I would argue that the scene of Trevor up in his bedroom is almost certainly indebted to similar scenes involving Taeko in *The Flavor of Green Tea Over Rice* and Kiyoshi in *Floating Weeds*. The point is that, by avoiding specification of what is exactly going on, by leaving a lot of space for the characters to think without pinning down what they are thinking, both Leigh's and Ozu's work leaves space for the viewers to think also.

4 It would not have been hard for Leigh to have assigned Trevor and Ronnie clear intentions, goals, or purposes. Trevor could have told Ronnie or his mother in an early scene that he was lonely and wanted a girlfriend, or Ronnie could have told Trevor that he felt henpecked and wanted to break up with Sandra. Or the narrative could have shown Trevor and Ronnie doing things to make the same point: Ronnie could have had a series of fights with Sandra that would hint at their need to break up, or could have been more assertive about trying to get her into the sack – or whatever. Or Leigh could have indicated Trevor and Ronnie's feelings through some form of stylistic processing – a kick-lighting effect, a tendentious framing, a longing close-up, a sad and wistful musical strain on the soundtrack. (The jaunty, playful music – the first extended use of orchestration in Leigh's work – emphatically does *not* function to emotionally cue the viewer into particular interpretations of scenes or shots.)

   In any of these scenarios, the whole effect of the film would change. Once the "goal" or "problem" had been established, every successive scene would necessarily have been read by the viewer as furthering or retarding its achievement. *The Kiss of Death* would turn into one of those "yuppies-on-the-make" American movies. Leigh not only does none of these things to focus the viewing process, but inserts a number of scenes that exist precisely to show us that even the goals the characters say they have are not to be trusted. The scene in which Ronnie brings Sandra to Trevor's house, for example, demonstrates that Ronnie is not reducible to the goal he may seem to have at this point – to bed Sandra. In a similar vein, Trevor's subsequent refusal to kiss Linda shows that he too is not reducible to the simple goal of getting a girl into bed.

5 Leigh has acknowledged Renoir's influence, and a number of Boudu (or Falstaff) figures run throughout his work, starting with *Bleak Moments*, which might be said to have two: Hilda representing Boudu's unconventional bodily positions and Sylvia his puckish relation to social ceremonies wit. *Nuts in May*'s Honkey and Finger, *Grown-Ups*' Gloria, *Meantime*'s Mark, and *Naked*'s Johnny similarly function as Boudu figures.

   No doubt part of the appeal of the Boudu story to Leigh is the parallel with his own cinematic enterprise: He is a kind of a cinematic Boudu who shatters sentimental idealizations. He is the guest at the dinner party who upsets others because of his refusal to go along with derealizing conventions. (The resistance Leigh's "A-to-Z" speech encountered at the 1996 "Independent Spirit Awards" luncheon literalizes my metaphor.)

6 This paragraph describes Linda as she is up to the "kiss-of-death" scene, but, though it is so subtle as to be almost imperceptible (what a joy for a film, an actress, a director to dare such subtlety of presentation!), Linda seems to change slightly at that point. At the start of *The Kiss of Death* she seems as shallow and one-dimensional as Trevor. She is brash, unreflective, willful, opinionated, and knowing. But, as unpromising a case for development as she may seem to be, she is apparently deepened and complicated by her encounters with him. By defeating her attempts to regiment and control him, Trevor forces her out of her habitual patterns of response. She becomes

deeply interesting around the point of the "kiss-of-death" scene because, for the first time, she seems at least a little unsure of what she is doing or what she wants. Unlike Sandra, Linda becomes confused and upset. Sandra's narrative function, in fact, is to be a foil to Linda in this respect. Sandra's blockheaded clarity and consistency of purpose, her inability to be confused, make Linda seem all the more interesting.

7 I would emphasize once more that, as is always the case in Leigh's work, the "free" characters are still somewhat limited by their personalities. That is to say, the freedom of Leigh's characters is not an Isabel Archer–like state of absolute transcendental freedom. Characters' movements and possibilities are always constrained by what they are.

Yet, at the same time, it is equally important to emphasize that Leigh's "free" characters are considerably less defined by "deep" psychological and emotional traits than the characters in most Hollywood films. Figures like Sylvia, Mr. Shore, and Trevor (and Shirley and Wendy, much later in Leigh's work) are better understood as capacities of responsiveness than as bundles of fixed attributes. They are less a set of stances and attitudes than powers of movement. We can't really predict what Sylvia or Trevor will say or do next. There is a stimulating vagueness to their identities, and an open-endedness to their performances.

The situation is really quite different in most American films, where a figure's shifting expressions are felt to be underpinned by a psychologically and emotionally unchanging or essential "character." The viewer may come to understand Kane, Norman, Rick, or Hal slowly, and may change his mind about them in the course of their films, but what they are is, in effect, always already there, waiting to be understood. Their identities are not relational in the way Sylvia's and Trevor's are. One might say that the American character takes his or her identity from a deep, enduring self, while Leigh's best and most interesting figures make theirs up as they go along in interaction with others. The Leigh figures who are emotionally and socially predictable (figures like Peter, Mr. Thornley, or Sandra and Linda here) are in trouble.

8 This is one aspect of a reply to the reading of Leigh's work offered in Quart's Biographical and Cultural Introduction.

9 Coveney, *The World According to Mike Leigh*, p. 111.

10 It is a hazard of psychological descriptions that they implicitly clarify, unify, and stabilize experiences that are too complex to be contained by psychological terms. To call Trevor's state of mind "uncertainty" or "ambivalence" is to simplify and detemporalize the movements of mind Leigh presents by verbally reducing them to an underlying, unitary mental state ("ambivalence" or "uncertainty"). The degree of ambivalence and uncertainty Trevor and Linda display is betrayed by the clarity, stasis, and simplicity of such terms. The notion of uncertainty or ambivalence normally implies some constant, consistent purpose that one is uncertain or ambivalent about – as if Trevor and Linda were adhering to a game plan which they were merely having momentary doubts about. But the point of Trevor and Linda's tonal oscillations is that they *don't* have a game plan; they

don't know what they want or what they are doing from moment to moment. They are not hesitating in the process of pursuing a fixed path, undecided about which way to go or feel, but much more confused and less knowing than that.

11 My *Speaking the Language of Desire: The Films of Carl Dreyer* (New York: Cambridge University Press, 1989), pp. 225–250, my *The Films of John Cassavetes: The Adventure of Insecurity*, pp. 50–55, and my "Two Forms of Cinematic Modernism," in Townsend Ludington, ed., *A Modern Mosaic*, pp. 345–359, have more on the difference between temporal and atemporal understandings, as well as on the difference between sensorily embodied and intellectual relations to experience.

12 It is telling that Ozu's work is often misread by American critics (most recently in the work of David Bordwell) as being more like an American movie than it actually is. The whole "modernism" and "tradition" opposition that Ozu's work is discussed in terms of translates his "durational" understanding into a "deadline" one. This approach makes his work static where it is fundamentally dynamic. It views it as being about a crisis, the replacement of one static state ("tradition") by another ("modernity"), when it is actually a vision of life in terms of anti-apocalyptic avoidance of crisis states, choices, and ultimatums. It is a vision of continuous, generational change, renewal, and more change, without end.

13 As evidence of the process-orientation of his view, Leigh's original intention was to end the film by having Trevor and Ronnie actually "go on," driving down the road and meeting more girls.

5. Defeating Systems of Knowing: *Nuts in May*

1 Altman's work, in contrast, is an example of filmmaking about "them." If the difference from Leigh's direction is not clear, compare *Nuts in May* with *Health*. Altman's characters are "types." Leigh's are individuals. Altman is interested in culturally representative figures, and his target is cultural forms and forces. Leigh is interested in individual emotional and imaginative states. Altman's characters are much more general than Leigh's and at a certain imaginative distance from the ordinary lives of his viewers; it's a large part of Altman's appeal. His characters are safe to dislike. It would be a rare viewer who saw himself and his own personal beliefs, actions, expressions as being under attack. His characters always live in a galaxy far away.

2 In terms of director-figures in the earlier films, Sylvia is the imaginative alternative to Keith. Rather than attempting to impose her vision on others, she encourages them to be themselves, to bring what they alone can to an interaction.

3 It is evidence of Leigh's commitment to undermining false positions that several of the breakdown scenes are among the weakest in his work. I have in mind the breakdowns undergone by Christine in *Grown–Ups*, Barbara in *Meantime*, Valerie in *High Hopes*, and Monica in *Secrets and Lies*. Christine can stand for all. Her breakdown (which involves her plea to Ralph for

"sex, love, a family") comes across as flat and unmotivated (making us momentarily aware of Leigh the puppeteer pulling the strings). However, its very falsity is testimony to the insistence of Leigh's determination to bring his deluded characters to their knees, down to some sort of ground zero of reality where they must confront their own falsity.

4   *A Sense of History*, the short film Jim Broadbent wrote and stars in and Leigh directed, represents an even more extreme denial of catharsis. The viewer cries out for self-awareness from the horrific central figure; Leigh and Broadbent devilishly deny it. (As an indication of how much more sentimental Leigh's recent work is, I would note that the ending of *Secrets and Lies* goes in the other direction. It gives us what we want rather than what we need to hear, which is probably why the film was received so well.)

5   The distribution of the narrative across different points of view at an emotional crisis, this refusal to allow any one figure to "star," is one of Leigh's basic techniques. Like Ozu in this respect as well, he deliberately resists overfocusing his scenes around a single figure. We see the hilarious, madcap results in *Grown-Ups* when Gloria is sprawled on the Butchers' stairway. The editing and sound design keep the viewer circulating among six different personal perspectives. He similarly circulates the viewer through four emotional takes on Laurence's heart attack at the end of *Abigail's Party*. As an illustration of a related temporal form of emotional complication, in *Life Is Sweet*, Leigh has Andy comically slip on a spoon to interrupt the emotional climax of Wendy's argument with Nicola. Just as Leigh pulls the rug out from Andy at the height of his authority as a chef, he pulls the rug out from under the viewer at the very point he may want to recline into a simple, big feeling. The viewer is kept emotionally in motion.

6   Michael Coveney calls the film "fall-over funny" (*The World According to Mike Leigh*, p. 100), but the tone is, fortunately, far more complex than that. As an illustration, the tent-pitching scene originally ran more than eight minutes and was much funnier than it is in the final print. The thrust of my argument is that Leigh was right to cut the scene. It is important that Keith not be caricatured, a lesson from which many American comedy directors would benefit. Less is more. To be able simply to laugh at Keith would let the viewer off the hook. The sacrifice in comedy is a gain for complexity.

7   We are similarly forced to keep changing our feelings about Candice-Marie: while her tones initially seem quite critical and nagging (as when she goads Keith into asking Ray to turn down his radio or makes him apologize to him), after developing a friendship with Ray, she seems quite sensitive and compassionate; then, at the end of the film, she seems completely dotty.

8   Leigh's decision to have Ray leave the campsite just prior to the fight is part of his strategy of complicating things. If the final face-off had been between Keith and Ray (or if Ray had been present to take Finger's side), it would have been much easier for the viewer to ridicule and reject Keith.

9   In all candor, the degree of responsiveness that Leigh's tonal shifts demand is beyond many viewers. Most audiences with whom I have watched the film cannot change attitudes and feelings as fast as Leigh requires them to.

Rather than remaining genuinely open and responsive, most viewers tend to decide on an interpretation and stick with it. (Keith is boorish; Keith is arrogant; Keith is ridiculous; Keith is a satire of hippies; Keith is bullied by his wife; etc.) Though that works with most other movies, it does violence here. Leigh demands that the viewer stay supremely open. One might say that these viewers have the same emotional problem that many of these films dramatize: They prefer fixed ideas to genuine emotional and intellectual openness.

10 This process of violating expectations is one of Leigh's most important effects, and I would note that his method is not merely mechanically to undermine the favorable and revise the viewer's opinion downward. As we shall see, *Grown-Ups* improves our opinion of a group of characters as it goes along, and Leigh's filmed one-act play, *The Permissive Society*, deliberately makes the main character, a boy who brings a girl home on their first date, seem as unsympathetic as possible early in the work, only to attempt to explain and redeem his behavior at the end. Leigh's goal, of course, is not merely to get us to change our minds one way or the other, but to get us to think and feel freshly, with whatever result.

6. Losing Track of Who You Are: *Abigail's Party*

1 Dennis Potter, "Trampling the Mud from Wall to Wall," *The Sunday Times* (London), November 6, 1977, p. 35.

2 Coveney, *The World According to Mike Leigh*, pp. 118 and 120. Alan Bennett (who rates the film one of his all-time favorites) similarly describes Beverly as "a brutal hostess with shoulders like a lifeguard and a walk to match" (Coveney, p. 119).

3 Ian Buruma, "The Way They Live Now," *The New York Review of Books*, January 13, 1994, p. 9.

4 Coveney, pp. 117 and 120.

5 Ibid., pp. 117–118.

6 All of Leigh's work employs externals as signs of internal disturbance: *Nuts in May* uses Keith and Candice-Marie's obsessions about processed food to suggest that their identities are processed. Similarly, in *Hard Labour* and *High Hopes* (whose Veronica and Valerie might be Beverly's sisters), Leigh's target is not the women's mass-produced furniture, dresses, hairstyles, and table settings, but their mass-produced values. His focus on characters' insides is why Leigh's critiques are *not* class-bound. Plastic furniture covers may be a middle-class malady; shrink-wrapped identities are everywhere.

7 Leigh's complex appreciation of the issues at stake in the creation of character – in life and art – is traceable to his dramatic training and interests.

8 This should suggest the fallacy of Coveney's talk about Laurence's "suppressed racism." The concept of suppression implies the existence of depths that are just not here, as well as suggesting that Laurence's views on race are personal, when Leigh's very point of having them expressed in such formulaic ways is to show us that they are as received and clichéd as his views on automobiles.

This, in fact, is what makes *Abigail's Party*, *Who's Who*, and *Home Sweet Home* much greater (and more frightening) than works like *Citizen Kane* or *Velvet Goldmine*. Welles' and Haynes' characters are entirely more conventional: They are premised on a fairly sentimental Romantic notion that the personal self, soul, voice, and imagination can get lost in a system or be overwhelmed by it, but they don't dare to depict Leigh's world – one in which the personal self simply ceases to exist. Kane and Slate have tender, sensitive, sincere hearts and souls, buried under layer after layer of cultural packaging and cinematic processing. (Slate is emphatically *not* the tabula rasa his name connotes.) Laurence and Beverly have no personal hearts and souls – buried, suppressed, lost, or otherwise. Leigh is closer to Foucault than to Wordsworth. On a more positive note, I might add that, Haynes' *Safe* does what his *Velvet Goldmine* does not. And Mark Rappaport's work (I am thinking of *Local Color* and *The Scenic Route* as illustrations) in its own way moves beyond the myth of the lost self to a truly modern vision of the self having been so completely invaded by alien forces that there is nothing merely "personal" left that is separate from them.

    I have a more extended discussion of the fallacy of "surface–depth" understandings of experience in the 1996 preface to my *American Vision: The Films of Frank Capra*, pp. xii–xvii. For analogues in American film to what Leigh is doing, I would refer the reader to the work of two of the most important postwar American filmmakers: John Cassavetes and Tom Noonan. Like Beverly or Laurence here, Noonan's and Cassavetes' characters are located beyond the grade-school notions of truth and falsity, sincerity and insincerity that inform mainstream American film. When Mickey (in Noonan's *What Happened Was*) or Freddie and McCarthy (in Cassavetes' *Faces*) boast or tell a tall tale, like Shakespeare's Cleopatra and Othello, or Chekhov's Astrov, they are passing fictions on themselves as much as attempting to pass them on anyone listening to them.

9 That is the mistake Coveney makes in characterizing Angela's remarks here and elsewhere as connoting "warmth." Angela is playing a part as much as Beverly. It's just a different one: She is a get-along, go-along figure who agrees with everyone about everything all of the time. Functioning as a cross between a doormat and a rubber stamp, she does not figure agreeability but self-erasure. Her problem is not psychological but ontological – a much more serious state of affairs.

10 Leigh finds Beverly's breathless superlatives so revealing (and entertaining) that he will put them into the mouths of at least three subsequent characters: *Who's Who*'s Samantha, *Home Sweet Home*'s Melody (whose "super" is iterated as formulaically as Beverly's "fantastic" to imitate the tone of caring without a jot of feeling), and *Life Is Sweet*'s Aubrey. Aubrey follows in Beverly's imaginative footsteps not only in the hollowness of his enthusiasms and his fondness for her "yeah, great" interjection, but, more profoundly, in his conviction that how an experience (or a life) is packaged is more important than whether there is anything *in* the package.

11 The difference between an open and a closed identity, a character's dependence on scripts or freedom from them, is an issue that haunted Leigh's

imagination as a dramatist and director. It surfaces throughout his work: from Pat and Peter in *Bleak Moments* to Keith in *Nuts in May* to Aubrey and Nicola in *Life Is Sweet*. Each of these figures cuts himself off from the ebb and flow of experience to play a fixed, regimented role that depends on adhering to a "script."

12 In this respect, Laurence resembles Keith, who fancies himself most natural when his ideas are most processed.

13 Jean-Paul Sartre, *Being and Nothingness: An Essay on Phenomenological Ontology*, trans. Hazel Barnes (New York: The Philosophical Library, 1956), pp. 59–60.

14 As illustrations of the various forms "bad faith" can take, consider Peter and Pat in *Bleak Moments*; Veronica in *Hard Labour*; Keith and Candice-Marie in *Nuts in May*; Beverly and Laurence here; Samantha, Giles, Anthony, and Alan in *Who's Who*; June and Hazel in *Home Sweet Home*; Valerie and Laetitia in *High Hopes*; and Aubrey and Nicola in *Life Is Sweet*.

15 In life, of course, we actually judge others by their actions and only ourselves by our intentions. But, as I already argued in the Stylistic Introduction, it is in the nature of American film that we treat the main characters as versions of ourselves, which is to say we judge them, not as we judge others in life, but as we judge ourselves – by reference to internal states.

16 This bullying need for personal validation runs throughout Leigh's work: Peter bullies Norman; Keith bullies his neighbors; Beverly bullies Laurence (and her guests); June bullies Harold; and Johnny bullies Sophie – in attempts to convince themselves and others that they are cultured (Peter and Laurence), on the side of truth and virtue (Keith), suave and sexy (Beverly), long-suffering (June), or don't need love and affection (Johnny).

17 Leigh's work is devoted to the belief that what you "really" are can never be achieved through an act of will or thought. When figures like Wendy or Shirley are good, they just are. Leigh was a child of the sixties, and though I am sure he would deny it, there is a faith in "naturalness" and an opposition to achieved identity in his work that allies him with the decade's hippies. He distrusts all willed, mental stances, all intellectual positions. Our consciousnesses always betray us.

18 The novels of D. H. Lawrence explore similar emotional situations in which characters attempt to "will" themselves to be something they are not and cannot really be. The paintings of John Singer Sargent are a pictorial representation of a similar state of tension of the achieved identity. See my *American Vision: The Films of Frank Capra*, pp. 55–68.

19 For a crash course on Leigh's temporal control of his viewers' understanding, I would highly recommend viewing the short film *Afternoon* and the one-act play, *The Permissive Society*. In both cases, Leigh controls when we know what we know so as masterfully to ensure the maximum emotional effect of the very small things that do happen. Leigh's temporal control is one of the most remarkable aspects of his presentation.

20 Leigh's play, *Goose-Pimples*, provides another example of how the horrors of the final half-hour of a work can become much more shocking because

the humor of the preceding hour encouraged the audience to lower its guard.

7. We are the Hollow Men: *Who's Who*

1   See my "Looking without Seeing," *Partisan Review*, pp. 717–23, for an overview of some of the consequences of this understanding of art.

2   When it comes to parallelism, Leigh's touch ranges from the delicate to the heavy-handed. His cross-references can be almost subliminal in the subtlety of their wit, as in the various references to "peanuts" or the comparisons of individuals' abilities to handle objects in *Bleak Moments*. Less frequently, at other moments, like the scenes involving the priest and the nun in *Hard Labour*, Leigh's comparisons and contrasts can be as pointed, arch, ironic, snide, and crude as Altman's.

3   *Abigail's Party* uses repetition similarly. Insofar as almost all of Beverly's greetings and offerings to her guests are repeated, their "phraseness" is revealed. For the viewer, they shift from being felt as feelings to being perceived as words.

4   The figures in *Who's Who* have less in common with the characters you meet in mainstream movies than with the figures imagined by Stanley Elkin, Thomas Pynchon, and William Gaddis. The work of Mark Rappaport is the greatest cinematic illustration of this Foucauldian understanding of experience.

5   Leigh will continue this exploration with Dave, Melody, Hazel, Harold, and June in *Home Sweet Home*.

6   This should suggest some of the grounds for my disagreement with Leonard Quart's strictures against Leigh's "exaggerations" or "caricatures" in his Biographical and Cultural Introduction. It seems to me that it is a mistake to use the simplicity or flatness of some of Leigh's characters as a stick to beat him, as if every character had to be a nuanced, complex, "realistic" depiction. Leigh presents the poseurs, frauds, bounders, and Sloane Rangers in his films in deliberately iterative, foreshortened, or typological ways to suggest their lack of emotional depth or complexity in comparison with more "rounded" other figures in the same works. The cartoon flatness of *Who's Who*'s figures, *Home Sweet Home*'s Melody and Dave, *High Hopes'* Rupert and Laetitia, and *Naked*'s Jeremy not only indicates their ontological limitations but, by contrast, make the more "rounded" characters seem even deeper. (Shakespeare and Henry James do the same thing in their art.)

7   Leigh's training at RADA (where artistic expression was treated largely as a matter of mastering conventions) hovers as a formative influence in his work, though never more obviously than here. Nigel and Anthony are ghosts who continue to haunt Leigh from his student days.

8   William James, *Writings, 1902–1910* (New York: The Library of America, 1987), pp. 745–746 and 951. I have a more extended discussion of the limitations of various forms of critical abstraction (particularly as figured by "symbolic" and Cultural Studies approaches to film) in the 1996 preface to my *American Vision: The Films of Frank Capra*, pp. xii–xvii; in my "When

Mind is a Verb: Thomas Eakins and the Work of Doing," Morris Dickstein, ed., *The Revival of Pragmatism: New Essays on Social Thought, Law, and Culture*, pp. 377–379; and in my "Two Forms of Cinematic Modernism: Notes Towards a Pragmatic Aesthetic," Townsend Ludington, ed. *A Modern Mosaic: Essays on Modernism in the United States*, pp. 385–435.

9 Clements, *The Improvised Play*, p. 82; Coveney, *The World According to Mike Leigh*, p. 133.

10 The fact that characters get up to go to the bathroom in this scene seems not unimportant. Keith in *Nuts in May*, Mr. Thornley in *Hard Labour*, Melody in *Home Sweet Home*, and Sandra in *The Kiss of Death* are also shown at similar moments. The point of these excretory interruptions is not merely to shock or amuse the middlebrow viewer by including bodily functions normally excluded from film's denatured definitions of reality; it is to reassert fundamental claims of nature against what Leigh feels to be the predations of culture – to reestablish touch with reality in worlds of pervasive unreality.

The physicality of the performances, the emphasis on bodies and bodily functions, and the fights (as when Keith gets into the fight in *Nuts in May* or Johnny is beaten up and thrown out into the cold in *Naked*) are efforts on Leigh's part to force his viewers (and his characters, if they are capable of learning anything) to recognize realities that are not part of an artificial system. Leigh wants to spring us (and them) free from our mental traps by bringing us to our senses.

8. Inhabiting Otherness: *Grown-Ups*

1 Chekhov's distinctive blend of comedy and pathos is a possible influence, as is Cassavetes' *Husbands*, which not only similarly mixes tones but includes a confrontation between a husband and wife followed by a scene on a stairway resembling the one in *Grown-Ups*.

2 *High Hopes* works a triple variation on this last sequence by including successive scenes involving three different couples in bed.

3 Mandy nags Dick about a range of issues from unperformed household repairs to his drinking to her desire to have a baby. Dick responds with countersarcasm and retaliates obliquely by verbally heaping abuse on a friend of Mandy's named Sharon. Leigh will set up a similarly misleading domestic situation in *Life Is Sweet* (the only difference being that the friend who is criticized by the wife is a mate of the husband).

4 Leigh's attitude toward differences of opinion can easily confuse a viewer new to his work. Contrary to general cultural imperatives in favor of happy-face agreement and unanimity of thought and feeling, Leigh does not negatively judge his characters for arguing with each other. He does not have the customary middle-class dread of confrontation and argumentation. So unopposed is he to the give-and-take of honest argumentation that one of his favorite ways of creating drama is to have his characters express differences of opinion – even characters in the most loving and tender relationships. (The method might be called "drama by disagreement.")

To be able strongly to express different points of view is a sign of a healthy relationship, in Leigh's mind. Ralph and Christine (like Valerie and Rupert in *High Hopes*) cannot bear to disagree. Their disagreements lead to silence, anger, or breaking off relations, while Dick and Mandy's lead to interestingly inventive collaborations. In the process of comparing their differences (and not always joking ones) and staying open to each other's points of view, Dick and Mandy make something both dramatically interesting and humanly valuable.

The same thing confuses many viewers about the opening scenes of *Life Is Sweet*. They assume that the disagreements between Wendy, Andy, and their children are meant to be judged negatively, while the opposite is the case. What a viewer might regard merely as rudeness or unpleasantness, Leigh regards as passionate engagement and responsiveness. (The bickering Dick and Mandy might in fact be younger versions of the bickering Andy and Wendy before they had children.)

5   Gloria's ebullience is reminiscent of Pat in *Bleak Moments* and Beverly in *Abigail's Party* and anticipates Melody in *Home Sweet Home* and Barbara in *Meantime*. All four characters have mental identities and exist in similar states of tension, willing themselves to feel and be what they clearly are not.

6   See the chapters on John Cassavetes' *Opening Night* and *Love Streams* in my *The Films of John Cassavetes: The Adventure of Insecurity*, pp. 45–55 and the "Epilogue" of my 1994 Cassavetes book for more on nonessentialized presentation.

7   The greatest and most exhilarating example of this fluidity of interaction and identity in Leigh's oeuvre is the work that immediately preceded *Grown-Ups*, a 1979 play, *Ecstasy*. Leigh creates four characters, Len, Mick, Dawn, and Jean, who exceed even Dick, Mandy, Sharon, and Gloria (and, later, Wendy, Andy, and Natalie in *Life Is Sweet*) in their ability tonally to turn on a dime. In a matter of minutes, they can go from threatening each other to expressing tenderness; from getting upset to shrugging it off with a joke; from racism to warmth; from tough talk to waxing sentimental over a memory. What makes the group interactions of *Ecstasy* even more complex than those in *Grown-Ups* is that none of the four main characters are relegated to secondary or supporting roles, as Sharon and sometimes Gloria are here.

8   As I suggested in my discussions of *Bleak Moments* and *Nuts in May*, there is almost always a veiled parable about acting and directing in Leigh's work, and another way of describing the difference between the two styles of conversation would be to say that Dick, Mandy, Christine, and Sharon provide an exhilarating demonstration of the kind of performative responsiveness of which great acting consists, while Ralph and Christine illustrate what bad acting looks like. Needless to say, I am *not* criticizing the acting of Sam Kelly and Lindsay Duncan, who play Ralph and Christine. As in ballet or ice skating, it's only the most accomplished performer who can capture the impression of rigidity, awkwardness, and imbalance – and the most sensitive and alert director or choreographer who can direct it.

The preceding caveat is not merely academic. John Cassavetes and Tom

Noonan, two of the most important recent American directors, are examples of artists whose careers were adversely affected by the fact that their depictions of awkwardness, in *Husbands* and *What Happened Was* respectively, were taken by critics as evidence of their own artistic awkwardness. To be able to depict clumsiness and confusion on screen is a very different thing from being artistically clumsy and confused. So accustomed are we to the intellectual smoothness of ideal presentations that the roughness of an unidealized presentation seems like a mistake.

9   In *Who's Who*, for example, it is evidence of the fundamental inadequacy of the young people that not a single one of their interactions is conducted with even a fraction of the responsiveness of the scene I quoted with Dick, Mandy, Gloria, and Sharon. Both in the office and at the dinner party, the characters stake out and defend preestablished, static, nonintersecting positions. Leigh was extremely aware of the difference between the two ways of interacting. A film which I unfortunately don't have space to discuss, *Four Days in July*, parallels contrasted conversations between two groups of characters, and asks the viewer to compare the conversational responsiveness of one with the unresponsiveness of the other.

10   I would note, in passing, that there is a female bias in Leigh's work (as there is in the work of most heterosexual male artists). His greatest, most sensitive, most supple performers – Sylvia, Jean, Collette, Shirley, and Wendy come to mind – are almost always "ballerinas" rather than "danceurs."

11   In Hitchcock's work any figure who holds a less cynical or skeptical view of life, a more passionate, sincere, emotional, or engaged way of feeling or mode of interacting than the director has, is invariably punished or satirized by the narrative. The director's point of view (in Hitchcock's case, an icy, detached, clinical, and sardonic one) is the only "right" one, the only "safe" one.

12   Leigh's work is founded on the cultivation of "otherness." It documents alien ways of thinking, feeling, speaking, and being, and depends for its effects on the viewer's genuinely entering into alien perspectives. No filmmaker has a less homogenized view of life or expression. For more on this subject, see my *The Films of John Cassavetes: Pragmatism, Modernism, and the Movies* (New York: Cambridge University Press, 1994), pp. 33 and 286 n. 4; my "Two Forms of Cinematic Modernism: Notes Towards a Pragmatic Aesthetic," in *A Modern Mosaic: Essays on Modernism in the United States*, pp. 392–398; and the concluding paragraphs of my "A Yellow Pages of Criticism," *Partisan Review*, pp. 138–143.

The work of Robert Altman might be thought to be doing the same thing, but I would argue that it is not. Altman distributes his narratives away from a single central figure, but when he does it, it invariably represents a reduction of the individual figure's power. Points of view are multiplied, but to the diminishment of each's importance. The individual voice is lost in the roar of the crowd, and individuals are made victims of larger systems of meaning. When Leigh spins his narrative away from the control or domineering view of any one character, he empowers each of the characters by giving them distinctively vivid, free, independent, and nonsatirized consciousnesses. The conversation I quoted between Gloria, Mandy, Dick, and Susan makes the point as much as the scene with Gloria on the Butchers' stairs: No matter how many characters there may be, each set of emotions, thoughts, memories, fantasies, dreams, disappointments, and desires is respected and honored as unique and important. The difference between Leigh and Altman is summed up in the tonal difference between their work. While Leigh displays a comical bemusement at the oddities he creates and an easy, nonjudgmental acceptance of diversity, Altman is narrower, harsher, and much more critical in his stance. Though he is amused by their foibles and sees their limitations, Leigh still clearly loves many of his main characters – from Sylvia to Trevor to Dick and Mandy and the ones that follow. Love is an emotional relation to his material that is completely absent from Altman's work.

13 The fallacy of an impersonal view is dramatized in Leigh's works in terms of characters like Keith, Beverly, and Nicola who embrace abstract, superpersonal ways of thinking, feeling, and being (all of the "received" roles, tones, and identities manufactured and marketed by the culture), rather than trusting their own unique, personal, emotional, and intellectual points of view. They are the truly damned.

9. Manufactured Emotions: *Home Sweet Home*

1 This becomes clear by Hazel's second scene with Stan, in which, although she teases him, she doesn't act on her impulses. As was the case with Beverly, for this kind of woman imaginative game playing is an end in itself.

2 Peter, Keith, and Ralph are preliminary sketches for these figures. These characters' common problem is their "ideal" relation to experience. They let thoughts displace realities.

3 I would emphasize that this has nothing to do with Leigh consciously setting out to contrast his style of scripting, shooting, and editing with his characters' styles of thinking, feeling, and interacting. He is simply more sensitive and alert than they are, and whether he intends it or not, his capacities of seeing and caring invariably "place" their personal styles.

4 Although Leigh doesn't always use close-ups to make the point, film after film tells us the same thing. Even as Peter, Trevor, Keith, Christine, Barbara, Valerie, and Nicola attempt to pretend that all is well, their emotional confusions reveal the truth.

5 This state of radical inauthenticity clearly haunts Leigh's imagination – which is why it surfaces so frequently in his work – from Peter and Beverly, to Barbara in *Meantime*, Valerie in *High Hopes*, and Aubrey and Nicola in *Life Is Sweet*.

6 This is the deep difference between Leigh's work and Altman's. *Nashville*, *Three Women*, *The Player*, and *Ready to Wear* document Altman's (fairly corrosive) point of view about the characters but deny them opportunities to present justifying views of themselves. For all of their visual and narrative "openness," Altman's films are extremely "closed" and judgmental in terms of their intellectual perspectives.

7 Our views of June and Hazel also change in the course of the film, though more slightly – June going from prompting revulsion to eliciting a small degree of sympathy and compassion for her pain, and Hazel (who seems kind and thoughtful when we first meet her) going downward as the frivolousness of her flirting is revealed.

8 I would argue that Sylvia and Trevor are both far more complex and interpretively elusive than the figures here. *Meantime*, the film that immediately follows *Home Sweet Home*, will go still further in the direction of presenting unresolved identities and genuinely mysterious interactions.

10. Challenging Easy Understandings: *Meantime*

1 I have discussions of the limitations of the Faustian stance in the Epilogue to my *The Films of John Cassavetes: Pragmatism, Modernism, and the Movies*, pp. 271–281, my "Two Forms of Cinematic Modernism: Notes Towards a Pragmatic Aesthetic," *A Modern Mosaic*, pp. 386–96, and my "A Yellow Pages of Criticism," pp. 138–143.

2 Mark, the smart-aleck wisecracker, and Colin, the quiet, inarticulate, more inward figure, surface as imaginative alternatives at various points in Leigh's work. Colin is related to *Bleak Moments*' Norman and Hilda, *The Kiss of Death*'s Ronnie and Trevor, *Nuts in May*'s Ray, and *Ecstasy*'s Len; Mark is related to *Hard Labour*'s Mr. Thornley and *Grown-Ups*' Dick, and anticipates *Naked*'s Johnny and his demonic doppelgänger, Jeremy.

Over and beyond Leigh's interest in these two personality types, one must recognize that he creates contrasts simply for the pleasure and dramatic interest. Mark and Colin and their two families are examples of that, but so are the characters in *Ecstasy*, the guests at Beverly's cocktail party, and the two daughters in *Life Is Sweet*. (Nicola has a dry wit, is neat and tidy in her appearance, expressively restrained and precise, and is daddy's girl; Natalie is sloppy, emotional, undisciplined, over-the-top, and mommy's girl.) There is no necessity for any of the films to have these contrasting situations and characters beyond the fact that Leigh clearly relishes the spats and differences of opinion they create. While Hollywood gives us a middle-brow, middle-of-the-road, homogenized universe, Leigh's mind runs to extremes, variety, opposition, and contrast – if for no other reason than for the dramatic possibilities they can unleash.

3 The pairing of a childless couple and a couple with children (or in some films, a couple planning to have children) is another of Leigh's standard structural contrasts. He employs it in *Grown-Ups, Home Sweet Home, High Hopes*, and *Secrets and Lies*. In each work, a woman's childlessness functions as a shorthand indication of a larger emotional deficiency. It's not an observation about life, but a structural device. Leigh uses infertility – the trope of the frustrated childless woman – in the way Shakespeare uses Frenchness or rusticity, or a James Bond movie uses Russianness or Germanness, simply as a shorthand way of suggesting imaginative problems. (Other shorthand notations Leigh employs are women who are "house proud," as in *Secrets and Lies* and *Home Sweet Home*, in a bad marriage,

or who attempt to "mother" a needy outsider – as Christine does with Gloria and Barbara does with Colin.)

But what makes Leigh's work so much more complex than a James Bond movie is that, although his characters' problems may be initially indicated in such shorthand ways, only minutes into their works they become too complex to be collapsed back into the typology they were based on. In the present instance, Barbara is much more mercurial and multivalent, much more emotionally layered, than can be captured by the trope of the "unfulfilled childless woman attempting to mother her sister's boy." In other words, Leigh employs the sorts of simple typologies and black-and-white structural contrasts I have listed merely to leave them behind. They are not the meaning of the film itself but only the first step in creating it. As Richard Poirier once wittily described William Faulkner's similar structural ingenuities, the structure is not the work, but something the artist performs upon to make it – a kind of jungle gym for imaginative acrobatics that ultimately leave its rigidities behind by nimbly and supply playing off and against it.

4   Even these initial shots decline to "establish" meanings or to guide our interpretive process in the traditional way: In the first shot the camera pans to follow a red-clad jogger whom the viewer, naturally enough, assumes to be an important figure. The only problem with that hypothesis is that the jogger runs out of the frame after a few seconds and leaves behind a group of unidentified individuals whom, it develops, will become the real subjects of the movie. (His fugitiveness and our initial miscuing might be said to alert us to the fact that everything that follows must be caught "on the run" or not at all.)

5   "Real-time" temporal sequences are signature pieces in Leigh's work. I would note the similarity between the Barbara, Mark, and Colin scene and many of the other great sequences in Leigh's work: the sherry scene between Peter and Sylvia in her living room; the "kiss-of-death" scene between Trevor and Linda in her living room; the scene between Ann and Naseem in the cab stand; Wendy's conversation with Nicola in her bedroom; and Johnny's with Louise in the bathroom. What all of these moments have in common is that they present the second-by-second progress of an unformulated, uncharted relationship – something that clearly fascinated Leigh. Leigh's commitment to temporal presentation is a commitment to the "flow" of experience (and a rejection of all forms of "freezing").

6   My point is that the great scenes in *Meantime* defeat even the terms I am attempting to parse them with. Leigh creates experiences too complex to reduce to words and concepts. Language only betrays experiences this complex, changeable, and multivalent. As William James pointed out, language is inadequate for at least four different reasons: it *essentializes* (preferring pellucid depths to turbid surfaces); it *abstracts* (omitting the sensory side of experience); it *focuses* (organizing the sprawl of experience); and it *freezes* (stopping the flow of experience). That is, in fact, the reason works of art exist – to say what cannot be said in non-art speech. See my "A Yellow Pages of Criticism," pp. 138–143, and my "When Mind Is a Verb," pp. 377–379.

7 Although as an upwardly aspiring woman Barbara is loosely related to *Hard Labour*'s Veronica, *Abigail's Party*'s Beverly, and *High Hopes'* Valerie, the complexity of her presentation puts her in a class by herself. Veronica, Beverly, and Valerie are plain and simple frauds. Barbara is far too complex to be categorized in such a way.

8 My metaphor alludes to Bazin's writing on Eisenstein. Critics are fond of taking such interpretive "snapshots," which is why a moment like the one in which Coxy rolls around in the barrel is dwelt on out of proportion to its importance in the film. While scenes like the encounter between Barbara, Mark, and Colin won't stand still for appreciation and beggar our powers of verbal description, it is relatively easy to play metaphoric games with static images. In its quest for summarizable symbolic meaning, film criticism all too often lamentably ignores the fundamental temporality of the cinematic experience.

9 Unfortunately, Barbara's breakdown rings false. John comes home from work the evening of the Mark and Colin debacle and finds her in a drunken stupor, squatting in the corner of an upstairs room hugging a bottle. What's wrong with the moment is that Barbara becomes the very thing the entire movie so far had defended her against – a cliché: a woman with a lot of money, married to a highly successful husband, living in a nice house, whose frustration about her childless and loveless marriage is finally exposed. It is all just too simple and pat and static. Moreover, it tediously lectures the viewer about something that he understood much more complexly before it was spelled out. Barbara's breakdown is a trite, simple idea imposed from the outside on a character who up until this moment was too mercurial and complex to be held in such a reductive thought. The Barbara of the preceding film is too interesting for the kind of breakdown Leigh gives her. Leigh's narrative treats her as if she were the equivalent of Valerie, a shallow character, the shallowness of whose breakdown suits her. But the Barbara a viewer has come to know up to this point is not. Her encounter with Mark and Colin would have produced a much more interesting response than the one Leigh offers. The scene Leigh provides patronizes her.

It seems clear to me on the basis of his remarks to interviewers that Leigh himself does not understand how unfair and incorrect his treatment of Barbara is. He clearly has it in for a certain kind of female character and is apparently unable to appreciate that his own creation is more complex than his abstract conception of her was (with all due credit being given to Marion Bailey, who possibly made Barbara more interesting and complex than Leigh himself imagined her to be).

The problem with Barbara's and Christine's earlier similarly fraudulent breakdowns is that they do what Leigh successfully prevents from happening in his films' other scenes. The characters come out of character to have insights or undergo recognitions that just don't ring true. To be trapped in the boxes in which Christine and Barbara are is precisely *not* to be capable of stepping outside of oneself and falling apart in the way these two scenes imagine it.

10 Andrew Dixon's wonderfully weird scoring adds to the effect. (This is

Dixon's first collaboration with Leigh. They have worked as a team on all of Leigh's subsequent films.) I would note that, although nonsource orchestration (by Carl Davis) is employed in *The Kiss of Death*, and diegetic music is used extremely evocatively in *Abigail's Party*, music becomes of increasing expressive importance after Dixon joins Leigh's regular production team. It is worth repeating, though, that throughout his career Leigh's music functions quite differently from the music in a Hollywood film. Rather than simplifying the interpretive process by telling the viewer what to feel or how to understand a moment, it complicates it, as it does in the scene with the maintenance-man, by functioning, as it were, in emotional counterpoint to the action, playing against it, adding another layer of complexity to it.

11 The point of my reference to *Othello* is to suggest the inadequacy of moral judgments being applied to works of this complexity. Like Iago (and like many of the most interesting characters in art), Mark is far more interesting than a moralistic reading of his deficiencies would recognize. Reductive moral categories are entirely too simple to capture the complexity of his personality and narrative function. Leigh wants us to leave moral readings of experience to characters like Barbara, Peter, Keith, and Ralph.

12 It isn't just Mark and Colin who are held in an in-between place. Lest we want to demonize the parents after Colin returns home and they attack him for losing his job, Leigh has Frank sincerely offer to help him get his job back and Mavis sneaks into his room to offer him supper (though it is equally important to notice that neither of these offers is allowed to expand in its emotional resonance so much as to undo the preexisting toughness of the parents). In other words, even as Leigh countermarches against one sort of simple reading of Frank and Mavis (that they are heartless), he defends his film against the opposite simple reading (that they are loving). It is important, above all, for him to defend the end of *Meantime* against a conclusion whose sentimentality would undo everything that has been so thrillingly accomplished up to this point. Frank and Mavis are emphatically not "redeemed," nor does the family "come together" in the end. Life imagined with this degree of complexity resists being wrapped up with a ribbon and bow.

11. Holding Experience Loosely: *High Hopes*

1 I quote from the published screenplay, printed in *Naked and Other Screenplays*, which is of special interest because it contains Leigh's own stage directions and indications of tone.

2 The chapter on *Mr. Smith Goes to Washington* in my *American Vision: The Films of Frank Capra*, pp. 299–344, goes into detail about Capra's calculated use of different styles of acting in that film.

3 Susan Linfield, "For Mike Leigh, It's Rue Britannia," *The New York Times* (Sunday), February 19, 1989, p. 24.

4 Although these private moments generally occur in the bedroom, I include in the category other scenes in which characters interact in a relaxed manner. As examples of "bedroom scenes" that actually take place in bed, I

would cite the moments involving Hilda and Pat, Keith and Candice-Marie, Dick and Mandy, Ralph and Christine, Barbara and John, Eugene and Collette, Billy and Lorraine (two couples in *Four Days in July*), Wendy and Andy, and Nicola and her boyfriend. As examples of "bedroom scenes" in the expanded sense, I would cite scenes involving Hilda and Sylvia, Ann and Naseem, Trevor and Ronnie, Dawn and Mick, and Len and Jean (in *Ecstasy*).

5 That is the wit of Leigh's "doubling" of Valerie's and Laetitia's costumes. While the pairing of the two women seems merely ironic at a first glance (so that, when Valerie apes Laetitia's dress, we at first only register how different they are and how absurd Valerie's attempt to "be" Laetitia is), a deeper understanding of the film reveals that Valerie and Laetitia actually are almost identical imaginatively. Valerie is Laetitia and Laetitia is Valerie – even when they are not wearing the same hat. The class difference that separates them is a trivial distinction.

6 Like Beverly and Laurence in *Abigail's Party*, Alan in *Who's Who*, or Aubrey and Nicola in *Life Is Sweet*, Valerie thinks that you can become someone simply by having the right possessions, wearing the right clothes, or speaking in the right way. Leigh's work, obviously, is founded on a deeper view of identity.

7 Valerie undergoes a kind of nervous breakdown when her efforts are frustrated. As I suggested in the similar cases of figures like Peter, Mr. Thornley, and Nigel, the fact that Rupert and Laetitia don't break down only indicates that, in Leigh's view, they are in even worse shape than Valerie. They are incapable of even seeing their own futility.

8 Along with Wendy and Andy in the film that follows this one, Cyril and Shirley are the closest Leigh comes in his work to creating cinematic alter egos. The trivial aspect of this is that the plump, bearded Philip Davis (who looks so different from his earlier roles in *Who's Who* and *Grown-Ups*) even looks a bit like the bearded Leigh when he made the film. See the Frontispiece.

9 In this respect (and others), Valerie is related to Pat, Beverly, Gloria, Christine, and Barbara.

10 Some of Beverly's tones and phrases return with Rupert and Laetitia, as if writing Beverly's formulaic, telegraphic dialogue showed Leigh something he wanted to keep experimenting with. (Compare Beverly's "Come through" and "Hands, Tone" with Rupert's "Two steaks. Same day. Totally different" and "The dwarf" and Laetitia's "No, darling, how many times?" and "No cold hands.")

11 This is where I believe Quart goes wrong in reading Leigh's work more moralistically, and assuming that Leigh's attitude to Rupert and Laetitia in particular is one of anger. If that were so, and Leigh was using them to "get back" at Yuppies, it would be true that he had unresolved emotional issues he hadn't worked through. My feeling, however, is that to be able to play so lightly and wittily with characters is to prove that one is *not* angry with them, *not* threatened by them, *not* in an unresolved emotional state. Leigh's easy joking (which avoids meanness or cruelty) is proof that he is *not*

imaginatively in their thrall or guilty of being envious of them. His comedy – like Shakespeare's or Chekhov's – is evidence of a fundamentally healthy soul. Leigh sees the limitations of these characters so clearly because he is *not* threatened by them. That is why he can so wholeheartedly laugh at them. As is always the case, tone is everything.

12 The issue of how "easy" or "hard" you take experience, how loosely or tightly you hold it, is articulated in earlier works in the differences between Sylvia and Peter, Naseem and Mr. Thornley, Trevor and Sandra, Ray and Keith, Dick and Ralph, and Mandy and Christine. While the first individual in each pairing has a relaxed relationship to others and to his or her own experience, the second is in a state of tension. Peter, Mr. Thornley, Sandra, Keith, Ralph, Laurence, and Beverly pressure their experiences to bear particular meanings and their relationships to follow narrow trajectories. They "force" interactions to be focused, serious, and purposeful, squeezing the life, the fun, the discovery out of them.

13 One way of understanding the dramatic issue at the heart of *High Hopes* is to realize that in the early scenes Cyril is not nearly as flexible and relaxed in his relation to experience as Shirley (since he has prefabricated stances and canned attitudes in the form of his Marxist ideology and cynicism), and that the project of the narrative is to move him toward an increased openness and easiness of response. Cyril takes things too hard and must learn to take them a little more lightly. The narrative thrust involves moving him toward Shirley's easy openness – in effect, making him a little more like her in this respect.

14 The merely negative breakdowns in Leigh's post-*Meantime* films are confined to minor characters like Valerie and Aubrey (in *Life Is Sweet*). Valerie breaks down precisely because she is not capable of meditatively getting outside of her experiences and learning from them in the way Cyril and Shirley do. Her breakdown – like the comparable earlier breakdowns in Leigh's work (Pat's in *Bleak Moments*, Keith's in *Nuts in May*, or Gloria's in *Grown-Ups*) – figures merely a negative state – a collapse of illusions, not an epiphany.

15 Cyril and Suzi (like Mark in *Meantime*, Nicola in *Life Is Sweet*, Johnny in *Naked*, and Hannah and Annie, the two girlfriends in *Career Girls*) embody an issue that runs throughout Leigh's work: the question of how to translate unfocused personal energies into meaningful social expressions. These characters hold passionate convictions and have lots of energy but can't or won't find a place in the world to put them to practical use. As I have said before, Leigh reflects his cultural background in absolutely insisting that his characters *perform* their imaginations in socially engaged forms of expression. Cyril, Nicola, Hannah, and Annie figure the problem that faces any dramatist with Leigh's beliefs: how to *express* the imagination.

16 The play of mind Cyril and Shirley display here and throughout *High Hopes* points to a another difference between Leigh's and Altman's work. Altman's characters lack this ability meditatively to push the pause button on events, to take an imaginative step outside of themselves, or to move independently of the narrative and the claims of other characters, because they are denied

consciousnesses this rich and complex. While Leigh's characters have in-sides, Altman's are almost all outsides.

17 The move inward in Leigh's late work is not without its downside. With *High Hopes, Life Is Sweet, Secrets and Lies*, and *Career Girls*, Leigh allows states of consciousness to be socially, physically, and verbally unexpressed for the first time in his oeuvre. He relies on closeups and pushes the pause button in his editing in a way that brings his work a little closer to the sentimentality and slackness of Hollywood expression. At moments, the late work allows a state of feeling or awareness to be an end in itself. The strength of the works up through *Life Is Sweet* is that they *never* relax the requirement that characters translate their imaginative states into social interactions. Leigh's work was better when it was tougher on its characters – by requiring them to translate their thoughts and feelings into social expression.

18 As should be clear by now, Ozu is more than a ghostly presence throughout Leigh's work. A list of other borrowings from Ozu (beyond the ones I have already mentioned) are: Leigh's use of an empty frame to begin or end a scene; the shot of the children playing on an automobile at the end of *The Kiss of Death*, which resembles similar shots in both *Autumn Afternoon* and *Late Spring;* the similarity of the characters of Betty in *The Short and Curlies* and Shige in *Tokyo Story*, two talkative hairdressers with similar personalities who work in beauty parlors; and the comical, nostalgic bar scene involving Patsy and Andy in *Life Is Sweet*, which resembles any number of comical, nostalgic bar scenes in Ozu's work.

19 Leigh makes the same point in his presentation of Dave and Melody in *Home Sweet Home*. The personalism of his approach always instructs a viewer that ideology has its causal roots in personality, not the reverse.

20 These attributes also supremely describe Jean Renoir's work, which should suggest the important imaginative connection between the two filmmakers.

21 In Leigh's original conception, Cyril and Shirley took care of a second visitor in addition to Wayne, which would have opened up the narrative even more. However, the actor chosen for the role did not work out during rehearsals, and the part was cut.

12. Circulation is the Law of Life: *Life Is Sweet*

1 "Mike Leigh's Original Features," *Naked and Other Screenplays*, p. xxxi.

2 My point is that, even when Leigh's characters *want* to be loners, his scripting and editing won't let them be. Ralph Butcher has climbed into a tree house of his own private interests and references and pulled up the ladder after him; Stan is a social and sexual lone wolf; Keith and Beverly don't even realize that there is such a thing as others' needs and feelings. But the scripting and editing of their films show that they are connected with others even when they don't want to be and don't realize they are. As is always the case, the style is smarter than the characters. It teaches us to understand them better than they understand themselves. The discrepancy between their films' styles and their personal styles reveals what is wrong

with these characters. It shows that their failure to reach out to or allow themselves to be reached by others represents a misunderstanding of their own situation.

If a stylistic contrast is helpful, Hitchcock's cinematic style is very nearly the opposite of Leigh's: It *endorses* separation and undermines connections, so that in his films even characters who *think* they share others' values and *believe* they are interacting intimately with them, are in fact revealed to be alone. No matter how many Hitchcock characters are present in a scene together, each is locked in solitary confinement within his or her state of incommunicable consciousness.

3   I can imagine the argument being made that Nicola gives the lie to this generalization. Surely *her* viewpoint is not treated as having equal value to the viewpoints of Wendy, Andy, and Natalie. Surely *she* is depicted as being clearly flawed and inadequate. The reply is that the issue is not the moral, social, or psychological *desirability* of Nicola's point of view but its narrative *importance*. That is to say, even though Nicola's point of view is assuredly not as acceptable as those of the other characters, even though its limitations are satirized, it is of equal *importance*. It must be dealt with. It cannot be ignored. That is the point of Leigh's decision to depict a *family*. You can't simply ignore the members you don't like.

4   As an indication of how Leigh's work has changed in this respect, compare the narrative effect of the work scenes in *Bleak Moments* or *Grown-Ups* with those here. Though they slightly adjusted our views of Sylvia, Pat, and Peter in the one film, or of Dick, Mandy, Ralph, and Christine in the other, the characters were more or less the same at work as they were at home. Wendy and Andy are really quite different on the job and off. On the other hand, from his earliest films, as I have pointed out in previous chapters, Leigh has allowed his characters to show various aspects of their personalities in different scenes, so that Peter, Mrs. Stone, Mark, and all of the others can be different things at different moments.

Another change occurs in Leigh's work around this point in his career. In the 1980s, he became a father (of two sons), and his work gradually becomes more focused on the dynamics of family life. It shifts from stories about young people living their lives apart from their parents (*Bleak Moments, Who's Who, The Kiss of Death*) to ones dealing with families (*High Hopes, Life Is Sweet, Secrets and Lies*). It is not only that Leigh's films of the 1990s feature more parents with children, but that the point of view from which the story is told shifts from the perspective of the children to that of the parents. *Meantime* is much more interested in Mark and Colin than in their parents; *Life Is Sweet* is much more interested in Wendy and Andy than in their children. (Insofar as artists always to some extent are dealing with themselves, this change in point of view is a path almost every artist follows.)

5   What else is Andy's story of the "evil spoon" but a delightful display of his ability to step outside of his own accident and turn it into a humorous anecdote? As was the case with Rupert and Laetitia or Valerie and Martin in *High Hopes*, it is a measure of the relative inadequacy of Aubrey and

Nicola that they are unable imaginatively to pivot in place in this way. (Even Natalie, young as she is, shows glimmers of self-deprecating, self-critical, humorous self-awareness in some of her dialogue.)

6 As should be clear by now, the notion that a character not only causes her own problems but may be inflicting at least as much pain on herself as she inflicts on others is one of the basic dramatic premises of Leigh's work.

7 This scene is all the more exhilarating given the artistic background against which it is set. As a viewer watches Wendy and Andy's fluid, supple, mercurial, conversational give-and-take, it is impossible not to hear the contrasting, cacophonous echo of all the failed conversations that run throughout Leigh's previous work – all of the sticky, frozen, jumpy, painful, desynchronized, discordant interactions between Sylvia and Peter, Mr. Thornley and the tallyman, Mrs. Stone and the greengrocer, Trevor and Linda, Keith and Candice-Marie, Samantha and Anthony, Beverly and her guests, and Keith and Ray – to cite only the most obvious examples.

8 My account omits an interesting bit of deceit at the start of Wendy and Andy's interaction. Wendy expresses her dismay at Andy's purchase, but the seriousness of the moment is undercut by the viewer's comical awareness that Andy has misled her about the purchase price of the van in his immediately preceding line. (It cost far more than the two hundred quid Wendy apparently thinks it did.) The effect is to create a trademark Leigh moment that is both serious and comical at the same time – and that the viewer consequently doesn't quite know how to take. (Is he supposed to laugh at the "trick" Andy has played on Wendy, or be shocked at how Andy has misled her? Is he supposed to take Wendy's shocked tone seriously or comically?) It is one more example, on top of dozens of others, of how Leigh prevents the viewer from stabilizing an easy tonal relation to a moment.

9 As illustrations of what I am calling multiple-mindedness, I would cite two moments: the scene in which Wendy is told the news about Andy's accident on the telephone and laughs at its silliness even as she simultaneously expresses sympathy, and the scene involving Andy's return from the hospital in which it is made clear that Andy is both embarrassed and amused (he tells jokes) *and* in pain and in quest of sympathy (he winces and complains). What both scenes ultimately illustrate, even more than the characters' multiple-mindedness, is Leigh's multiple-mindedness toward his own material. He feels more than one way at once about it. The genius of his artistry is that, rather than suppressing his mixed feelings, he allows them to show.

10 As much as a Degas (or an early De Sica), Leigh's picture declares its partialness. *Life Is Sweet* is punctuated by moments in which the viewer is made aware that the characters have consciousnesses that extend outside of the film. Wendy's recollections of Donald and Tracey, the laugh she and Andy share about the angora sweater, her work at Bunnikins, her thoughtful pauses as she dusts Andy's graduation picture and some of her own dance memorabilia; Nicola's story about her job, her magazine reading and trip planning, her work and her interactions with her mates after work;

Andy's work as head of a kitchen and the experiences he has on the job, his dreams of working for himself – all represent thoughts and experiences that never quite make it into the narrative as events.

There are similar moments in Leigh's other work: for example, Mandy and Gloria's reminiscences about other events while they unpack the knick-knacks in *Grown-Ups*; the moment in *Home Sweet Home* in which Stan alludes to his mother's death and funeral; and Cynthia's refusal to talk about Hortense's father or her relationship with him in the disclosure scene in *Secrets and Lies*. This is a world complex enough to have secrets and private understandings that the viewer or other characters (like Natalie in the Donald and Tracy scene) don't have access to. These scenes open up their films in neorealistic ways. (Or they might be compared to the evocative moments in Ozu's work in which characters reminisce about the past or speculate about the future.) They indicate that there is a world outside the frame-space and more to the characters than will ever be fit into a narrative. As I already noted, Wayne opens up the narrative of *High Hopes* in a related way simply by walking in and out of it so freely and unpredictably.

11 In terms of the work of other directors, John Cassavetes' *Faces* is the most brilliant example of another film which includes characters who are granted capacities of imaginative movement that create the impression they are able to free themselves from the plot of the film they are in. They move somewhat independently of the narrative, or put it on hold. See my *The Films of John Cassavetes: Pragmatism, Modernism, and the Movies*, pp. 90–101.

12 Keith similarly knows a lot about healthy living, Beverly a lot about hostessing, and Barbara a lot about helping indigent relatives. But, as with Aubrey, their problems are not what they do or don't know, but who they are.

13 In one of Leigh's most understated but witty parallels, Aubrey's identity is compared with that of Nicola's boyfriend. Compare the two matched scenes in which the two figures pull up in their cars, walk to the front door, and ring the doorbell. Point by point, the performances are contrasted: Aubrey is playing at being what he is; the boyfriend just is. They may both be deeply flawed, but Aubrey is Sartre's waiter; the boyfriend's identity is authentic. (For the record, the boyfriend's part was originally considerably larger, and included a scene in which David Thewlis' character was introduced to Wendy and Andy which was cut.)

14 This is why it is important that, while Nicola is full of talk, talk, talk, about her convictions and her role playing, Natalie never once discusses her "revolutionary" stance (which is why many viewers leave *Life Is Sweet* without noticing the parallel with her sister). This is more than a question of artistic tact. To have Natalie discuss her job, her clothing, her definition of herself, her conception of gender, and the roles she plays would be to make them expressions of consciousness, when Leigh's very point is to suggest that the difference between her and Nicola is that Natalie is functioning from a deeper place than thoughts and ideas. As with the difference between the identities of Aubrey and Nicola's boyfriend, while Nicola is *trying* to be something (and therefore in a state of Sartrean "bad faith"), Natalie just *is* what she is. As always in Leigh's work, consciousness is never the source of

truth. In short, it is absolutely critical that his films successfully avoid the kinds of abstract, rational understandings that I or any other critic employ to interpret them. Lived truth is not the same as thought truth, and is in fact opposed to it in Leigh's work.

15 Leigh stages similar progressive assaults on characters in successive scenes with Keith in *Nuts in May*, Nigel in *Who's Who*, June in *Home Sweet Home*, and Barbara in *Meantime*. Leigh knows that plot is the weakest way to join scenes, and the logic of his sequences is never one of actions but of emotions. That is to say, even when the viewer may think that one scene leads to another simply to continue the trajectory of an event, it is almost always more helpful to think of the sequence as following the line of emotion.

16 The antecedents of Wendy's interaction with Nicola may be found as far back in Leigh's work as Sylvia's attempts to "loosen up" Peter and Norman in *Bleak Moments*, and the tallyman's interaction with Mr. Thornley and Naseem's interaction with Ann in *Hard Labour*.

17 With reference to Leigh's subsequent work, Louise and Johnny briefly achieve a similarly exhilarating ease of relationship in the bathroom scene in *Naked*, but only briefly. (See the illustration on page 234.) Unlike Nicola, Johnny ultimately defeats Louise's attempt at loving intervention. Under her influence he melts, but then almost immediately freezes up again.

13. Desperate Lives: *Naked*

1 There are moments when Leigh allows Johnny's talk to become too self-conscious and literary – too carefully honed. However, Johnny's talk is generally so permeated by colloquial language and profanity (e.g., "the present's peachy-fuckin' creamy"), that one almost always believes he's speaking in his own voice rather than some incongruously eloquent one grafted on to him by Leigh or Thewlis.

2 Leigh sees the sexist charge as "outrageous and offensive." He argues that there is no way he could make a film like *Naked* with these actresses, all of whom are "highly motivated feminists without their total commitment and collusion." In short, Leigh believes that none of the actresses would have actively collaborated in the project if they had thought the film to be male-chauvinist and misogynistic.

3 "Mike Leigh's Original Features," p. xl.

4 *Naked* never aims to be a social-problem film about homelessness like Antonia Bird's documentary-style, overwrought *Safe*.

Epilogue: The Feel of Life

1 The academy, never far behind the wider culture, follows suit by treating art as a tissue of "formal constructs and dynamic systems" (David Bordwell, *Ozu and the Poetics of Cinema* [Princeton, NJ: Princeton University Press, 1988], p. 2). I take the academic adulation of Hitchcock's contentless virtuosity in the fifties and sixties to be the precursor of more recent formalist approaches.

The bottomless skepticism that informs most ethnic, feminist, gay, and Cultural Studies approaches to film is another academic manifestation of this tendency. The mass-produced, assembly-line creations of Hollywood corporations may deserve such deprecatory and downright derisive treatment, but what these critics fail to realize is that real art does not yield to such a method. Art as a form of truth telling (in the Cassavetes, Kramer, Burnett, Loden, and Leigh modes) is left out. For more on the "hermeneutics of skepticism" in the academy, see my "A Yellow Pages of Criticism," pp. 138–143, and my "Looking without Seeing," pp. 717–723.

2   *Naked* is an exception. The film's visual and acoustic stylizations are evidence that Leigh was, for the first time in his career, attempting to express something he felt could not be done through mere dialogue and social interaction. The lighting and musical effects pick up an expressive burden that characters' interactions do not bear. Most of the street scenes as well as the long scene between Brian and Johnny in the office building are attempts to render states of imagination that have no social or verbal form of expression. The drama moves inward, out of the world and into the mind (of both the viewer and the character). The film is, in this respect, a "problem" film in Leigh's oeuvre. It figures, if not a loss of confidence in his entire previous expressive project, at least a serious change in direction, one that to this writer, at least, is quite troubling in its implications.

3   Shakespeare's work, of course, is the great example of imagining the expressions of ordinary people to be as complex as those of artists. Bottom, Coriolanus, Hamlet, Falstaff, Edgar, Lear's Fool, Iago, Desdemona, and Cleopatra use language as subtly and supply as their creator and are endowed with consciousnesses as complex, slippery, and multivalent as his.

4   The writing of Dickens and James, and the filmmaking of Welles and Wilder, come to mind as communicating a similar self-delighting exuberance. These energies are eternal delight.

Filmography

(All works written and directed by Mike Leigh)

Bleak Moments (1971)

Autumn Productions/Memorial Enterprises/BFI Production Board. Produced and edited by Les Blair, photography by Bahram Manoochehri, designed by Richard Rambaut, sound by Bob Withey, 111 mins.

Cast: Anne Raitt (Sylvia), Sarah Stephenson (Hilda), Eric Allan (Peter), Joolia Cappleman (Pat), Mike Bradwell (Norman), Liz Smith (Pat's mother), Christopher Martin (Sylvia's boss)

Video Availability: Water Bearer Films

Hard Labour (1973)

BBC TV. Produced by Tony Garnett, photography by Tony Pierce-Roberts, sound by Dick Manton, edited by Christopher Rowlands, designed by Paul Munting, costumes by Sally Nieper, 75 mins.

Cast: Liz Smith (Mrs. Thornley), Clifford Kershaw (Mr. Thornley), Polly Hemingway (Ann), Bernard Hill (Edward), Alison Steadman (Veronica), Vanessa Harris (Mrs. Stone), Cyril Varley (Mr. Stone), Linda Beckett (Julie), Ben Kingsley (Naseem), Louis Raynes (Mr. Philips)

Video Availability: Water Bearer Films

Nuts in May (1976)

BBC TV. Produced by David Rose, photography by Michael Williams, sound by John Gilbert, edited by Oliver White, designed by David Crozier, costumes by Gini Hardy, 80 mins.

Cast: Roger Sloman (Keith), Alison Steadman (Candice-Marie), Anthony O'Donnell (Ray), Sheila Kelley (Honkey), Stephen Bill (Finger)

Video Availability: Water Bearer Films

The Kiss of Death (1977)

BBC TV. Produced by David Rose, photography by Michael Williams and John Kenway, edited by Oliver White, designed by David Crozier, costumes by Al Barnett, music by Carl Davis, sound by John Gilbert, 80 mins.

Cast: David Threlfall (Trevor), Clifford Kershaw (Mr. Garside), John Wheatley (Ronnie), Angela Curran (Sandra), Kay Adshead (Linda)

Video Availability: Water Bearer Films

Abigail's Party (1977)

BBC TV Play for Today. Produced by Margaret Matheson, photography by Dave Mutton, edited by Ron Bowman, designed by Kenneth Sharp, costumes by Lindy Hemming, sound by Derek Miller-Timmins, 102 mins.

Cast: Alison Steadman (Beverly), Tim Stern (Laurence), Janine Duvitski (Angela), John Salthouse (Tony), Harriet Reynolds (Susan)

Video Availability: Water Bearer Films

Who's Who (1979)

BBC TV. Produced by Margaret Matheson, photography by John Else, edited by Chris Lovett, designed by Austen Spriggs, costumes by Robin Stubbs, sound by John Pritchard, 80 mins.

Cast: Simon Chandler (Nigel), Adam Norton (Giles), Richard Kane (Alan), Jeffrey Wickham (Francis), Souad Faress (Samya), Philip Davis (Kevin), Graham Seed (Anthony), Joolia Cappleman (April), Lavinia Bertram (Nanny), Francesca Martin (Selina), David Neville (Lord Crouchurst), Richenda Carey (Lady Crouchurst), Catherine Hall (Samantha)

Video Availability: Water Bearer Films

Grown-Ups (1980)

BBC TV. Produced by Louis Marks, photography by Remi Adefarasin, edited by Robin Sales, designed by Bryan Ellis, costumes by Christian Dyall, sound by John Pritchard, 90 mins.

Cast: Philip Davis (Dick), Lesley Manville (Mandy), Brenda Blethyn (Gloria), Janine Duvitski (Sharon), Lindsay Duncan (Christine), Sam Kelly (Ralph)

Video Availability: Water Bearer Films

Home Sweet Home (1982)

BBC TV. Produced by Louis Marks, photography by Remi Adefarasin, edited by Robin Sales, designed by Bryan Ellis, costumes by Michael Burdle, music by Carl Davis, sound by John Pritchard, 90 mins.

Cast: Timothy Spall (Gordon), Eric Richard (Stan), Tim Barker (Harold), Kay Stonham (Hazel), Su Elliott (June), Frances Barber (Melody), Sheila Kelley (Janice), Lorraine Brunning (Tina), Lloyd Peters (Dave)

Video Availability: Water Bearer Films

Meantime (1983)

Central Television/Mostpoint Ltd. for Channel 4. Produced by Graham Benson, photography by Roger Pratt, edited by Lesley Walker, designed by Diana Charnley, costumes by Lindy Hemming, music by Andrew Dickson, sound by Malcolm Hirst, 90 mins.

Cast: Marion Bailey (Barbara), Phil Daniels (Mark), Tim Roth (Colin), Pam Ferris (Mavis), Jeff Robert (Frank), Alfred Molina (John), Gary Oldman (Coxy), Tilly Vosburgh (Hayley), Peter Wight (estate-manager)

Video Availability: Fox Lorber Home Video

High Hopes (1988)

Film Four International/British Screen/Portman. Produced by Simon Channing-Williams and Victor Glynn, photography by Roger Pratt, edited by Jon Gregory, designed by Diana Charnley, costumes by Lindy Hemming, music by Andrew Dickson, sound by Billy McCarthy, 110 mins.

Cast: Philip Davis (Cyril), Ruth Sheen (Shirley), Edna Doré (Mrs. Bender), Heather Tobias (Valerie), Philip Jackson (Martin), Lesley Manville (Laetitia), David Bamber (Rupert), Jason Watkins (Wayne), Judith Scott (Suzi)

Video Availability: Academy Entertainment

Life Is Sweet (1990)

Thin Man/Film Four International/British Screen. Produced by Simon Channing-Williams, photography by Dick Pope, edited by Jon Gregory, designed by Alison Chitty, costumes by Lindy Hemming, music by Rachel Portman, sound by Malcolm Hirst, 102 mins.

Cast: Alison Steadman (Wendy), Jim Broadbent (Andy), Claire Skinner (Natalie), Jane Horrocks (Nicola), Timothy Spall (Aubrey), Stephen Rea (Patsy), David Thewlis (Nicola's boyfriend)

Video Availability: Republic Pictures Home Video (tape and disc)

Naked (1993)

Thin Man/Film Four International/British Screen. Produced by Simon Channing-Williams, photography by Dick Pope, edited by Jon Gregory, designed by Alison Chitty, costumes by Lindy Hemming, music by Andrew Dickson, sound by Ken Weston, 126 mins.

Cast: David Thewlis (Johnny), Lesley Sharp (Louise), Katrin Cartlidge (Sophie), Greg Cruttwell (Jeremy/Sebastian), Claire Skinner (Sandra), Peter Wight (Brian), Ewen Bremner (Archie), Susan Vidler (Maggie), Gina McKee (café waitress)

Video Availability: New Line Video (tape); Criterion Collection (disc)

Bibliography

Ansorge, Peter. "Making up the Well-Made Plays for Today." *Plays and Playing*, no. 4 (1975):12–16.

Armes, Roy. *A Critical History of British Cinema*. New York: Oxford University Press, 1978.

Auty, Martyn, and Roddick, Nick, eds. *British Cinema Now*. London: BFI, 1985.

Bank, Mirra. "Mike Leigh." *Films in Review* 48, no. 1/2 (January/February 1997): 29–34.

Barnes, Julian. *Letters from London*. New York: Vintage, 1995.

Bloch, Judy. "A Conversation with Mike Leigh and Alison Steadman." *The Pacific Film Archive Calendar* (Berkeley, CA), October 1991, pp. 1–5.

Buruma, Ian. "The Way They Live Now." *The New York Review of Books*, January 13, 1994, pp. 7–10.

Carney, Ray. *Speaking the Language of Desire: The Films of Carl Dreyer*. New York: Cambridge University Press, 1989.

"Looking without Seeing." Review of David James' *Allegories of Cinema*. *Partisan Review* 58, no. 4 (Fall 1991): 717–723.

Review of David James' *Allegories of Cinema* in *American Studies* (Lawrence: University of Kansas) 32, no. 1 (Spring 1991): 123–124.

"A Polemical Introduction: The Road Not Taken." *Post Script: Essays in Film and the Humanities* 11, no. 2 (Winter 1992): 3–12.

The Films of John Cassavetes: Pragmatism, Modernism, and the Movies. New York: Cambridge University Press, 1994.

"A Yellow Pages of Criticism." Review of *The Johns Hopkins Guide to Literary Theory and Criticism*. *Partisan Review* 62, no. 1 (Winter 1995): 138–143.

American Vision: The Films of Frank Capra. Hanover, NH: University Press of New England, 1996.

"When Mind Is a Verb: Thomas Eakins and the Doing of Thinking." In *The Revival of Pragmatism: New Essays on Social Thought, Law, and Culture*, ed. Morris Dickstein, pp. 377–403. Durham, NC: Duke University Press, 1998.

"Two Forms of Cinematic Modernism: Notes Towards a Pragmatic Aesthetic." In *A Modern Mosaic: Essays on Modernism in the United States*, ed. Townsend Ludington, pp. 385–435. Chapel Hill: University of North Carolina Press, 2000.

The Films of John Cassavetes: The Adventure of Insecurity (A Souvenir Program). Boston: Company C Publishing, 1999.

Cassavetes on Cassavetes. London and New York: Faber and Faber, 2001.

Clements, Paul. *The Improvised Play: The Work of Mike Leigh*. London: Methuen, 1983.

Coveney, Michael. *The World According to Mike Leigh*. London: Harper-Collins, 1996.

Ellickson, Lee, and Porton, Richard. "I Find the Tragicomic Things in Life: An Interview with Mike Leigh." *Cineaste* 20, no. 3 (1994): 10–17.

Foundras, Scott. "Director Leigh Discusses Craft." *Daily Trojan* (USC), October 2, 1996, pp. 7–8.

Gordon, Betty. "Mike Leigh." *Bomb*, no. 46 (Winter 1994): 30–33.

Hodgson, Clive. "An Interview with Mike Leigh." *London Magazine*, February 1979, pp. 68–76.

James, William. *Writings 1902–1910*. New York: Library of America, 1987.

Kennedy, Harlan. "Mike Leigh about His Stuff . . ." *Film Comment* 27, no. 5 (September–October 1991): 18–24.

Leigh, Mike. "Leigh's Way." *Stills*, no. 16 (February 1985): 14.

Naked and Other Screenplays. London: Faber and Faber, 1995.

Linfield, Susan. "For Mike Leigh, It's Rue Britannia." *New York Times* (Sunday), February 19, 1989, sec. 2, pp. 17 and 24.

Lister, David. "Where Losers Take All: Mike Leigh." *The Independent* (Sunday), January 12, 1982, p. 21.

Medhurst, Andy. "Mike Leigh Beyond Embarrassment." *Sight and Sound* 3, no. 11 (November 1993): 6–10.

Park, James. *Learning to Dream: The New British Cinema*. London: Faber and Faber, 1984.

Potter, Dennis. "Trampling the Mud from Wall to Wall." *The Sunday Times* (London), November 6, 1977.

Quart, Leonard. "The Religion of the Market: Thatcherite Politics and the British Film of the 1980s." In *Fires Were Started: British Cinema and Thatcherism*, ed. Lester Friedman. Minneapolis: University of Minnesota Press, 1993.

Unpublished interview with Timothy Spall, April 10, 1996.

Unpublished interview with Mike Leigh, September 23, 1996.

Riding, Alan. "An Original Who Plumbs the Ordinary." Interview with Mike Leigh. *The New York Times* (Sunday), September 22, 1996, sec. 2, pp. 1, 22–23.

Ruchti, Isabelle. "Interview with Mike Leigh." *Positif*, Spring 1990, pp. 18–22. (Translated from the French by John Gianvito.)

Sartre, Jean-Paul. *Being and Nothingness: An Essay on Phenomenological Ontology*. Translated by Hazel Barnes. New York: The Philosophical Library, 1956.

Simsolo, Noël. "Strictly Controlled Improvisation: An Interview with Mike Leigh." *Cinema* (Paris), 1972, pp. 23–28. (Translated from the French by John Gianvito.)

Smith, Gavin. "Worlds Apart: Mike Leigh on Video." *Film Comment* 30, no. 5 (September–October 1994): 80–82.

Taylor, John Russell. "Giggling beneath the Waves: The Uncosy World of Mike Leigh." *Sight and Sound* 52, no.1 (Winter 1982/83): 34–37.

Index